PENGUIN

GERMAN IDEAL

RÜDIGER BUBNER was born in 1941 at Lüdenscheid, Westphalia, in Germany. He studied philosophy and classics at the universities of Tübingen, Vienna, Heidelberg and Oxford, and became Professor of Philosophy at Frankfurt in 1973 and at Tübingen in 1979. He is currently Professor of Philosophy at the University of Heidelberg, and is a member of the Heidelberg Academy of Sciences. His areas of interest cover ancient philosophy, German idealism, hermeneutics, social philosophy and aesthetics. Professor Bubner's books include *Handlung, Sprache und Vernunft* (1976; second edition, 1982), *Geschichtsprozesse und Handlungsnormen* (1984) and *Welche Rationalität bekommt der Gesellschaft?* (1996), and in English he has written *Modern German Philosophy* (1981), *Essays in Hermeneutics and Critical Theory* (1988) and *Innovations of German Idealism*, which is forthcoming.

GERMAN IDEALIST
PHILOSOPHY

Edited and with Introductions by
RÜDIGER BUBNER

PENGUIN BOOKS

PENGUIN BOOKS

An imprint of Penguin Random House LLC
375 Hudson Street
New York, New York 10014
penguin.com

First published as *Deutscher Idealismus* by Philipp Reclam 1978
This translation published in Penguin Books 1997

Introduction and notes copyright © 1978 by Philipp Reclam
Translation of introduction and notes, 'Critique of Pure Reason',
'On the Nature of Philosophy as a Science' copyright © 1997 by Marcus Weigelt

The acknowledgements on pp. vii–viii constitute
an extension of this copyright page

ISBN 978-0-14-044660-9

Printed in the United States of America
9   10   12   14   15   13   11   8

Contents

Acknowledgements

Permission to reprint copyright extracts in this volume is acknowledged to the following sources.

Immanuel Kant: to Simon & Schuster, Inc. for *Critique of Practical Reason*, translated by Lewis White Beck, copyright © 1993 by Macmillan College Publishing Company, Inc.; to Cambridge University Press, H. B. Nisbet and H. S. Reiss for 'Idea for a Universal History with a Cosmopolitan Purpose' from *Kant: Political Writings*, edited by Hans Reiss, translated by H. B. Nisbet (1970).

J. G. Fichte: to Cambridge University Press for *Science of Knowledge*, edited and translated by Peter Heath and John Lachs (1982); to Cambridge University Press for 'On the Spirit and the Letter in Philosophy', from *German Aesthetic and Literary Criticism*, edited by David Simpson (1984); to Continuum Publishing Company for 'Some Lectures Concerning the Scholar's Vocation', translated by Daniel Breazeale, from *Philosophy of German Idealism*, edited by Ernst Behler (1987).

F. W. J. Schelling: to Cambridge University Press, Peter Heath and Errol E. Harris (translators) for 'Ideas for a Philosophy of Nature' from *Texts in German Philosophy* (1989).

G. W. F. Hegel: to State University of New York Press for *The Difference Between Fichte's and Schelling's System of Philosophy*, translated by Walter Cerf and H. S. Harris (1977); to Oxford University Press for *Phenomenology of Spirit*, translated by A. V. Miller (1977); to Cambridge University Press, H. B. Nisbet and Allen Wood for 'Elements of the Philosophy of Right' from *Cambridge Texts in the History of Political*

Thought, edited by A. W. Wood, translated by H. B. Nisbet (1991); to Cambridge University Press and H. B. Nisbet for *Lectures on the Philosophy of World History: Introduction, Reason in History*, translated by H. B. Nisbet (1980).

Introduction

A MODEL OF PHILOSOPHY

Anyone attempting to define philosophy would end up in an awkward situation. We bear the inherited weight of a long tradition, and we can no longer ignore our historical models. It is therefore perfectly justifiable to examine the most distinguished eras in the history of philosophy for insight into the tasks and possibilities of philosophy. The period delimited by the names of Kant and Hegel is most certainly one of these eras. Though we have grown accustomed to calling it 'German idealism', this label is not altogether well chosen and is only partly valid in the case of Kant.

There can be no doubt that throughout the long history of human thought, philosophy rarely climbed such heights as in the few decades around the year 1800. Probably only the flowering of ancient philosophy in the Athens of Plato and Aristotle would bear comparison. Any new student of philosophy who wishes to become aware of the potential of thought might well be referred to these two exemplary epochs. By studying them he or she will realize to what degree abstract speculation can be pursued without losing touch with reality. Reflective thought develops intricate paths of reasoning without losing its track and is capable of converting conceptual complexity into a systematic coherence. The modern reader is struck by a lively confidence of thought, a genuine sense of responsibility to the whole, and also an adventurous mental attitude. Given these premises, philosophy thought itself capable of attaining an all-embracing understanding of reality by means of reason. Since nowadays philosophy tends to be more humble in its aspirations and more limited in its competence, we attribute to the classical high points of our tradition the significance of models.

The belief in philosophy as the supreme science was handed down to German idealism from classical antiquity. It was clearly impossible, though, to base this kind of philosophical self-understanding on an unquestioned store of ancient ideas. The philosophical awakening at the turn of the nineteenth century was motivated precisely by the conviction that the old tasks in the quest for systematic knowledge had been left unexecuted. At the same time, there was a growing expectation that the strength of human reason had ripened sufficiently to fulfil these tasks definitively. Beginning with Kant, we observe, in the light of the independent development of the modern natural sciences, a growing awareness that the inherited claims of purely rational or metaphysical knowledge required a renewed justification. If metaphysics was not merely to repeat the words of a venerable tradition, but also, as the title of Kant's *Prolegomena* demanded, to be able in the foreseeable future 'to appear as a science', it would for the first time, by way of a fundamental self-critique of reason, have to be based on a secure foundation. The principle of philosophical self-grounding by way of critique was immediately taken up by Kant's successors and developed in a systematic way as an absolute principle. Fichte promised to deliver a *Foundation of the Entire Science of Knowledge* which would make the whole of human knowledge, the unity of all sciences, the theme of a supreme philosophical science and provide its definitive support. Schelling developed even more clearly the idea of a systematic coherence of all rational knowledge as the prerequisite for absolutely unshakeable philosophical knowledge. Finally, Hegel said that it was time for philosophy, which translates from the Greek as 'love of wisdom', to cast off this restraint and to become a fully valid science. The most perfected system of German idealism, Hegel's encyclopedic dialectic, saw itself, with some caution, as the final stage of a development, at which philosophy seemed most truly realized, because the old task of a comprehensive science had been definitively accomplished.

THE STARTING POINT

Metaphysics was the name traditionally given to the supreme theory of pure reason in which philosophy dealt with Being as a whole. Since the Greeks, it had usually been regarded as a theory concerning the true basic structures of all reality. Greek thought had as its aim a knowledge of what really exists, why it exists and the way it exists. Philosophy had the task of penetrating the veil of sensory appearances and, by virtue of reason, comprehending the truth of the underlying reality. Truth lies beyond the individual aspects of reality as exhibited to the scientific specialist. By pursuing a particular, restricted line of enquiry one is blind to the whole. The truth of all that exists can only be obtained by an unrestricted view of the whole. The truth of reality and a comprehensive orientation towards the whole go together.

Greek philosophy had turned to 'logos' as the medium for fulfilling basic claims to knowledge. The translation of 'logos' as 'rational discourse' is imperfect, because we have to associate two concepts where an original unity was intended. Logos means the rational way of revealing and declaring that which exists in itself and is real. Only in logos can truth properly be found. And there is nothing that would escape logos; for there is no reality inaccessible to rational speech. The faith in universal logos provides the methodological foundation for the science of reason which aims at truth in its entirety. This corresponds to the idea of a uniform constitution of nature, a nature that exists in itself and that guarantees the lasting characteristics of everything that exists. This is relevant as much for theoretical as for practical issues; thus, an insight into the constitution or order of things, nature in itself, furthers our understanding of the empirical world and of life.

Following the rise of Christianity, the basic metaphysical idea of nature in itself had to disappear. The Being of metaphysics was superseded by the idea of a personal god to be worshipped as the creator of the world. The Christian tradition took possession of the old doctrine of logos and turned it into the word of God. Both the concept of truth and that of the world were robbed of their original status and applied to a person who speaks and creates. A long and profound process of secularization, beginning already in medieval theology and characterizing the entire modern enlightenment, was required to lead the substance of faith away from its theological background. Its religious guise removed, it became readily accessible to human devices. What had originally been part of the realm of God became a human property. The self-consciousness of the subject took centre stage, and the totality of the world assumed the status of an object in relation to it. This relation of subject and object set the basic pattern for modern thought.

Reality, thus reduced to objecthood, was accessible to human consciousness with its categories and ordering principles. The subject took control over everything that exists. Science was established on this basis and it conquered one aspect of reality after another with its methodological rigour and its quantifying calculus. Scientific knowledge is tested by experience because experience is the point where subject and object meet. In contrast to sober-minded empiricism, as propagated for example by Bacon at the beginning of the development of modern science, the traditional all-encompassing idea of logos must have seemed like empty chatter, devoid of any real substance. Consequently, a nominalist theory of language became generally accepted. Language, according to this theory, is a system of outward signs to transmit mental data validated by experience.

Both the formation of self-consciousness and the idea of experience as the basis of science marked the beginning of a far-reaching development of philosophical thought. Broadly speaking, they determined the two schools of rationalism and empiricism. Despite the various attempts to reconcile the two, the beginning of the development of German idealism was on the whole still characterized by the opposition of the rationalist and empiricist approaches. German idealism set out to reconcile the old conception of metaphysics with a new-found certainty of self-consciousness and with the world of objects investigated by the empirical, methodologically organized natural sciences.

THE UNITY OF IDEALISM

The fact that idealism endorsed a theory of pure reason, even though the term 'metaphysics' had lost some credibility, is of importance, because it alone explains the fresh impetus that philosophy received from Kant. The same Kantian impetus later led philosophy almost inevitably beyond Kant's critical restrictions on thought. Secondary literature sometimes claims that Kant, by projecting the structures of the mind out on to the empirical world, had the ingenious idea of interpreting rationalism and empiricism as two aspects of a single system. It is claimed that his transcendental philosophy thereby succeeded in unifying the two main streams of modern thought. It must not be overlooked, however, that his celebrated transcendental turn only became possible when the return to the neglected task of a pure science of reason, metaphysics, induced reason to examine itself critically. Transcendental reflection would otherwise be ungrounded and remain mysterious.

Kant's preoccupation with the problematic state of metaphysics explains the crucial difference between his transcendental turn and mere reflection on the part of consciousness. Consciousness, by means of its own powers, is always capable of reflecting upon itself. Descartes' 'ego cogito' used this possibility of consciousness in order to arrest, at an ultimate point of indubitability, the sceptical doubt about the reality corresponding to our perception. Similarly, such a self-absorbed consciousness only finds a way out of its immanence and back towards a substantial reality via a complicated proof of the existence of God. Descartes' philosophy, operating within the two realms of consciousness and the objective world, could not do without this construction borrowed from theology. Kant did, of course, work from the premises of the philosophy of mind initiated by Descartes. Nevertheless, his transcendental turn does not simply repeat reflection on the part of consciousness. It springs from the idea that reason is in disagreement with itself and that, in so far as it is reason, it cannot endure this contradiction. Within the greater framework of Kant's transcendental considerations, the 'I think' was given a well specified position under the title of transcendental apperception. Thus Kant was more than a philosopher of self-consciousness.

The Neo-Kantianism of the nineteenth century, however, created a different image. Influenced by progress in the natural sciences, it fashioned Kant into a kind of philosopher of science. In view of the '*factum* of the sciences', transcendental philosophy was to find the formal and universal *a priori* conditions for scientific research, with Kant as the pioneer in providing a logical basis for the empirical sciences. This interpretation of Kantian philosophy is an attack on its idealist implications. To this day it is widely accepted and, in retrospect, we can see that it does make sense. Nevertheless, it is based on a simplification that must be unmasked. Kant's intention was not simply to provide, with the help of philosophy, a foundation for the soundly functioning sciences. In providing help to the sciences, philosophy also reinforced itself, because it used the scientific paradigm of knowledge as the criterion for self-evaluation. A critique of reason was the first step in definitively fulfilling the task of a science of reason, of metaphysics. Hence an autonomous concept of reason remained the ultimate goal of philosophy.

The movement of German idealism could not achieve true greatness until it managed to demonstrate the unity of all existence as a whole. It is important to assess accurately the first stages of the movement, so as to be able to illustrate subsequent developments as consequences, not just as innovations. Kant and his successors both made reference to an autonomous concept of reason. This was Kant's great influence in the eyes of his contemporaries: it was he who gave back to philosophy the duty and courage to rely entirely upon reason. It seems necessary to redeem this authentic aspect of Kant's thought, an aspect which is insufficiently recognized by the aforementioned interpretations. These interpretations emerged in a time of widespread mistrust of idealism, long after it had passed its prime, and they presented Kant's philosophy as a healthy, moderate position which had been blurred and perverted by its hypertrophic successors.

There is certainly a pronounced tension between Kant's critique and the idealist conceptions of his successors. The initiator of this new philosophy was soon mystified because although his prophets, like Fichte, spoke in his name, they were heading in a very different direction. Hegel's fully developed idealism grew by consciously entering into debate with Kant's critical position, claiming to provide the completion of an already existing tendency. Hegel's dialectic wanted to take the ultimate step with a resoluteness which Kant was seen to lack. The difference between Kant and his successors, as accentuated by subsequent interpretations, should in no way be denied. Nevertheless, it is not coincidental that idealism built upon Kant's revolution of thought: it was able to refer to the concept of autonomous reason with a greater justification.

THE IDEALISTIC ELEMENT

What is idealistic about German idealism? This label in no way signifies that blind enthusiasm for things unreal which common sense refers to disparagingly as bloodless idealism. The idealist soil nourished, for instance, Schelling's philosophy of nature, which, as opposed to the subjectivist reduction of reality, wanted to re-legitimize nature in an almost materialistic way, as existing of its own accord. Even Hegel's philosophy, although unconditionally confessing its idealism, is filled with a realism that can compete with Aristotle's renowned sense of reality. Hegel turned away from the fanciful ruminations of his contemporaries and focused his attention entirely upon the substance of reality. His idealism is based on the conviction that a merely invented philosophy, one that springs from the arbitrariness of the individual, cannot last. Philosophy must stand on solid ground. According to Hegel's famous words, philosophy is nothing except 'its time comprehended in thought'.

Idealism bears its name because ideas are the key to solving the task of conclusively aligning the metaphysical doctrine put forth by reason with what is evident in self-consciousness. According to the Platonic definition, ideas are of a purely mental nature and are yet full of substantial determination. Ideas cut through to reveal the actual content of a given thing. Although they need to be grasped intellectually, they convey the most basic statements about reality.

The gap between consciousness and the thing in itself, between subject and object, is bridged by the idea. Resorting to this model seemed to provide a systematic way to realize philosophy as the supreme science, particularly by taking reflection on the part of the self seriously. Ideas allow the construction of a world, once the self-certainty of consciousness is adequately understood. In this sense, the old claim of metaphysics was restored, but the old form of metaphysics was surpassed. This is what shaped the idealistic character of philosophy from Kant to Hegel.

By recognizing the faith that idealism had in the capacity of pure thought, it is possible to understand in what way the great German philosophy still serves as a model today. It would be too easy to think of a model as just that which is worthy of imitation. A model, rather, sets up standards to be recognized even if their demands are not easily met. The radicalness of relying entirely upon the power of ideas and of exercising to the utmost the possibilities of our reason illustrates a second characteristic of idealism that makes it so fascinating to study. One would have to look hard for a chapter in the history of philosophy which contains a comparable fervour of conceptual development and density of discussion. A remarkable intensity of intellectual exchange, of the productive proposal and development of shared intentions dominated the two short generations between Kant's major work, the *Critique of Pure Reason* of 1781, and Hegel's death in 1831.

Concepts were established, refuted and developed further in rapid succession. Before projects were ripe for execution, they were already abandoned and integrated into new and even more extensive edifices of thought. This dynamic process seems to have been based on an inner logic. Although the progress in philosophy that had been initiated by Kant's epistemological critique is associated with the names Reinhold, Fichte, Schelling, Hegel and others, it was nonetheless profoundly necessitated by the nature of the problem itself. German idealism must not be presented simply doxographically. It also needs to be understood as a history of reason, in which projects provoke critique and thereby inevitably insist on improvement.

Hegel understood the history of modern philosophy in this way, and this is not merely a case of latecomer's arrogance. Those things in Hegel's absolute system attributable to an overestimation of his own capacities were enumerated by the sequence of his critics from Feuerbach to Marx. Meanwhile, the criticism in Hegel's wake demonstrates retrospectively that it is legitimate to interpret the history of philosophy in the light of a necessary development of thought, rather than as a contingent sequence of authors and books. Despite turning away from idealist systems, the critics continued along the line of such a history of reason by appealing to the rational inevitability of the next step. The currents of post-Hegelian philosophy overlapped in their expectation of a historically pressing and rationally compelling transformation of absolute theory into a radical praxis that would leave nothing unchanged.

One essential prerequisite for taking philosophical lessons from idealism is recognizing the consequence of its inherent intellectual development, which continued well into the materialist and praxis-oriented criticisms of idealism in the nineteenth century. The strength of this philosophy is not so much expressed in one or another completed system, in harmoniously mastering all its contents, or in deducing all available knowledge from one particular principle. The point is not to make a dogmatic decision for or against Kant's critical philosophy, Fichte's science of knowledge, Schelling's philosophy of identity or Hegel's absolute dialectic. It is also not the point definitively to weigh up the rights and wrongs of the different positions. Nor is a philosophical interest in idealism limited to the attempt to represent it in a historically faithful way.

It is necessary to focus on the underlying driving force of the movement of idealism; it is not enough to be merely edified by its attractive but dated view of the world. That idealist philosophy can still be effective today stems from its conception of thought as working its way towards independence by acquiring the power to recognize its own limitations; in this process it broadens its horizon step by step. This is the aspect of the idealist tradition that still manages to inspire contemporary thought in so far as it is not frozen by an association to a given branch or school.

SUBSTANTIVE QUESTIONS

Which substantive insights do we owe to idealism? The goal of idealist or classical German philosophy across the breadth of its thematic spectrum was to conceive the unity of subject and object. Idealism thereby responded to the above-mentioned condition of modern philosophy. Nothing similar had ever been suggested by ancient cosmology. The secularization of Christian ideas left behind a subject that was both turned inward to its own mind and confronted with an alien world as the sphere of objects. Any effort to create unity within the subject–object relation, however, is doomed to fail, because the opposition inherent in this relation quietly remains intact. As long as subject is defined by object, or object by subject, neither of the two sides can encompass itself and the other simultaneously. A successful synthesis is therefore only possible in the name of reason, even though the claims of pure reason cannot be formulated independently of the given subject–object relation. With the help of reason itself, the unity of subject and object can be established because, rationally speaking, an opposition no longer exists.

This unity, of course, has many faces. It can be sought in the fields of epistemology, of practical and political philosophy, of aesthetics, of the philosophy of nature and of history. Despite the diversity of objects of investigation, to the philosophical eye each exhibits a physiognomy similar to the others. The systematic achievements of idealist philosophy resulted, therefore, from pursuing similar structures in the most distinct areas of research. Though each time new and different, an unchanging general principle can be discerned.

The process of recognition that takes place when confronting the various parts of idealist systems provides cohesion and completeness within them. After all, the ultimate guiding principle in all areas of research is that of philosophical contemplation itself. Philosophical reason comes back to itself as it proceeds through the variety of issues. Systematic breadth and completeness of the whole have the same origin.

This view invites the objection that a seamless coherence of the whole is bought at the price of levelling differences. It is objected that all issues are dealt with at such a level of abstraction that they look alike anyway, or that a comprehensive system of the world can only be conjured up from this indiscriminate grey-on-grey by skilful rhetoric. These objections were voiced early on against the idealist movement and they deserve to be taken seriously.

In the first instance, one must see the importance attributed by philosophy to the independent sciences after Kant's critique, and the energy that philosophers invested in assimilating the available knowledge. Given the sources on which he drew for his philosophy of nature, Schelling was clearly up with the times. Kant's and Fichte's philosophies of right reflect an intimacy with the doctrines of jurisprudence. Hegel was well versed in many fields, maybe more than anyone else in the history of philosophy since the universal genius of Leibniz. Thus, Hegel's encyclopedia rests on relatively solid scientific ground. The fact, however, that philosophical reflection on results in scientific research is determined by its epoch, as becomes clear from a distance, can hardly be used to reproach the idealists.

The frequently peddled idea that the idealists are jugglers of concepts who rely entirely upon their talents of abstraction and don't care very much about advances in other disciplines must be dismissed. On the contrary, in many areas their systematic projects are convincing because they are rich in empirical data and often closer to the philosophical moment than particular scientific disciplines, which labour under distorted methodological perspectives. The influence of Hegel's aesthetics on art scholarship shows, by example, how philosophical analysis can be a stimulus for other disciplines. Basically, the doubt about the competence of systematic philosophy in various fields of knowledge expresses a fundamental conflict between philosophy and science. It flared up most dramatically in the nineteenth century after the closing of the idealist epoch, and today the sciences seem to have come out on top. An awareness of this background enables one to evaluate the idealists' systematic achievements more impartially.

The substantiality of the philosophical statements that idealism dared to make about non-philosophical knowledge can best be measured by the endurance of its solutions to problems in contemporary debates. We are separated by almost two centuries from the beginning of idealism, and a century and a half has passed since its decline. Is not the philosophical situation quite a different one, and has not the progress in the sciences entirely exceeded the capacity of philosophical understanding? This question, however, goes beyond philosophy's attempt at self-clarification guided by the model of idealism, and it aims at convincing solutions. It is a well-known hermeneutic fact that each epoch selects from its heritage whatever will answer to its own needs. The history of idealism's reception highlights the different parts of its canon to which subsequent epochs were particularly sensitive. This relativity and selectivity should make us cautious. All definitive statements about which aspects of idealism, according to Croce's formula, have died and which are still alive have since become outmoded. This question, however, should not be disregarded.

The idea of an encyclopedic system as such, one that aims at total assimilation of all knowledge, probably has the least chance of ever being restored again. The explosive multiplication and growth of specified sciences over the last one hundred years makes it impossible for philosophy to assimilate them fully. This does not, however, affect areas of systematic philosophy that are based on the idea of the rationally determined unity of subject and object. In particular, the aim of explaining theory and praxis from one single root has proven to be indispensable. This is expressed in the efforts to substantiate rational ethics as well as in analyses which explain scientific activity as a product of particular interests. In any case, theories about our political and historical world cannot free themselves from an idealist heritage, because it was idealism that coined the central problems of their discipline. The humanities and social sciences could hardly be imagined without the foundation laid by classical philosophy. Even epistemology and philosophy of science, though affiliated to the natural sciences, have not been able to do without insight into the subjective constitution of the investigated object, despite what the positivist schools occasionally suggest. Dialectic continues to be a methodological tool in philosophical discussion. In overcoming nominalism, philosophy of language is reconsidering idealistic interpretations of language. Aesthetics still largely operates within the framework established by Kant and Schiller, Schelling and Hegel. We know of no other ideal for education aside from the one created and passed on to our educational institutions by idealism. Although this list continues and will certainly change in the course of time, it does mention a few important and problematic issues of contemporary philosophy in which the idealist intellectual heritage lives on.

PHILOSOPHY IN ITS TIME

Let us step back from these questions of substance and take a look at the great German philosophy as a historical phenomenon in its epoch. The impression of intellectual achievement is only intensified when one remembers the historical conditions under which idealism arose. The intellectual climate in Germany was altogether provincial and backward compared to western Europe. The collection of small German states lacked a centre comparable to Paris with its significance for the arts and sciences in France during the seventeenth and eighteenth centuries.

Kant had started more or less from scratch in the remoteness of Königsberg and he subjected his critique of reason to a lengthy preparation before presenting it to the public at a very mature age. There had, of course, been schools of philosophy in Germany. Kant did pick up the themes and terminologies of Christian Wolff (1679–1754) and Alexander Baumgarten (1714–1762). But in its substance, Kant's transcendental philosophy was something completely new and unheard-of. It was widely received as a Copernican revolution. The intellectual sparks set off by his philosophy ignited in many places and brought about sudden transformations in general thought. Although irresistible during the following decades, the actual influence of his philosophy started only sporadically: with Karl Leonhard Reinhold (1758–1823), a former Jesuit pupil and one-time freemason in Vienna, with Salomon Maimon (1754–1800), a Polish Jew with an erratic education, with Johann Gottlieb Fichte, son of poor parents and scholar at the Royal Saxon School, and finally with Schelling, Hölderlin and Hegel, the young Turks of the traditionalist and protestant theological seminary in Tübingen. There was no real national forum at that stage where philosophical ideas could be pursued. It was only formed, and quickly so, in the course of the development of idealism. Within a few years, a general philosophical debate was underway. It overcame long-standing divisions, established certain concepts as common knowledge, moved the hearts and minds of its participants with topics of recognized urgency; every independent mind was in a hurry to participate in this latest advance in the human spirit.

The political revolution in France gave particular encouragement to the intellectual revolution in Germany. It was clear to Fichte and the seminarists from Tübingen that, in the realm of thought, the changes they were bringing about were decisive for the whole of mankind. The long-term social and political effects of idealism, starting with the Young Hegelian critics and Marxism and extending into contemporary philosophy, have confirmed that self-assessment. At the same time, however, a motif developed that was to be revived after Hegel's death in the post-idealist epoch and that has since been passed on. The Germans, or so it is said, had their revolution only in their heads. This power of thought which remains only thought without being translated into action can easily coexist, it is said, with reactionary conditions in political reality.

Indeed, the times were not very favourably inclined to idealism. Fichte's affirmative writings, in which he welcomed and justified the French Revolution, had to be published anonymously in 1792/93, the title page reading: 'Heliopolis, in the last year of the old darkness'. A few years later, when Fichte had become established in a professorship in Jena, the absolute self propagated by his science of knowledge was suspected of amounting to atheism. This public scandal led to Fichte's temporary withdrawal from the academic world where he had been particularly influential among students. His admirers included the rebellious theology students from Tübingen, who could cherish their enthusiasm for freedom only under the shelter of a pact of friendship, as the seminary's governing body watched suspiciously for any sympathies stirred by the revolutionary events on the other side of the Rhine. This was the atmosphere within which the early sketches of Schelling and Hegel emerged. Hope for a fundamental change in existing conditions stood in blatant contrast to the historical reality of a fragmented Germany. This contrast remained typical.

More than a decade later, while he was writing his first major work, the *Phenomenology of Spirit*, Hegel welcomed the foreign occupier Napoleon as a reformer when he marched into Jena in 1806. By means of external force, Napoleon was, according to Hegel, paving the path of necessary progress in Germany. There was a mood of change during the wars of liberation, and this proved a more favourable time for idealism, but it was short-lived. The ideas of contemporary philosophy had a decisive influence on the foundation of Berlin's university in 1810, but the climate soon changed again. After the Karlsbad resolutions of 1819, and in order to secure publication of his book in 1821, Hegel had to give in to censorship and make changes to the liberal content of his philosophy of right. Consequently, the book was abused by critics as an ideological glorification of Prussian monarchy and Hegel himself was deemed the official court philosopher.

Hegel's death brought about a division in his school that was evidently also the result of external political factors. This intrusion of political affairs meant the inevitable end of philosophical self-confidence. The so-called Right-Hegelians made their peace with the powers of state and church, while the Left-Hegelians stood in constant opposition to these authorities. Historically speaking, the Left was a more influential group. It conceived philosophy as a critique of existing conditions and systematically denounced those that remained neutral in this debate as traitors to reason. Marx finally called for revolutionary changes in praxis and thereby left the sphere of pure theory behind once and for all. It became fully evident that the ways of politics and idealist thought did not harmonize, that, in fact, they ran in opposition to each other.

DECLINE AND RECEPTION

At that time, it was said that idealism had collapsed. The realization of the idealist intentions in Hegel's philosophy, which claimed to have fulfilled in an encyclopedic system the demands of true science by means of reason alone, suddenly seemed merely an illusion. Philosophers were disillusioned as to the potency of their discipline. Theories committed to historical praxis dismissed the World Spirit as the product of a professor of philosophy unable to adapt to practical and political reality. It became popular to scoff at idealism as the dangerous hubris of academic idols.

As well as this departure from a belief in the validity of idealist philosophy in favour of praxis, it was the powers of technical development and the wider influence of scientific progress that sowed the seeds of doubt about absolute speculation. In particular, the metaphorical idiom and the distance from empirical phenomena that characterized the idealist philosophy of nature now seemed to make problematic the scientific claims of philosophy. What it means to be scientific has since been determined by the natural sciences. Thought, if it is to have any chance of survival at all, must succumb to their positivist creed. The branch of philosophy that deliberately and carefully proceeds from scientific data is called philosophy of science. Philosophy of science arose, like the movements that recruited philosophy for praxis and life, around the middle of the nineteenth century in an unambiguous confrontation with idealism. This division is visible even today, and the two positions established back then still provide the essential arguments in the critique of idealism.

The end of idealist philosophy, however, seems to have been proclaimed too hastily. In retrospect, it becomes more obvious than at the point of controversy itself that the two main streams which replaced classical philosophy in the nineteenth century were fed by ideas that had grown in the very lap of idealism. On the one hand, the idea of praxis repeated the all-embracing claim of the Hegelian system and extended it beyond mere theory. A final barrier was to be overcome in order for the theorems of the systems to become serious action. In the step beyond idealist philosophy, then, the ideal of perfection lingered on as a motif.

On the other hand, reflection upon the knowledge that empirical sciences achieve independently of philosophy revalidated the premise that had marked the origin of the entire idealist movement in Kant's critique of reason. The more idealism strove towards its absolute shape, the less it was oriented to the sciences. The dispute, therefore, is about the appropriate emphasis of the critique of reason and speculative dialectic. In a certain respect, this is a dispute between Kant and Hegel that arises whenever philosophers, in opposition to the absolutist gesture of pure thought, turn their attention towards the particular sciences. Thus, the step beyond idealism can also be interpreted as a step back to its origins.

The inconspicuous resurgence of elements of idealism even after the end of its reign and even within arguments directed at its refutation demonstrates that the fertility of the ideas it generated has not yet been exhausted. In the history of philosophy, the period following idealism can rightfully be classified as the post-idealist epoch. In many respects, philosophical thought is still held captive by the spell of this impressive model.

Rüdiger Bubner
Translated by Marcus Weigelt

Biographical Notes

IMMANUEL KANT (1724–1804)

Born on 22 April 1724 in Königsberg, the son of a saddler, Johann Georg Kant. During his lifetime, Kant never left the vicinity of his home town. He first studied at the pious Collegium Friedericianum; from 1740 he studied philosophy, mathematics and theology at the local university. Until 1755 he worked as a private tutor in various families. He took his Masters degree in 1755 and was given a *venia legendi*. Kant stayed on for fifteen years as a university lecturer and turned down other offers until 1770 when he was given the professorship in logic and metaphysics at Königsberg that he had been after. From 1766 to 1772 he was the sub-librarian at the royal palace library. After many years of labour, during which he published very little, the *Critique of Pure Reason*, the work that was to revolutionize the entire philosophical world, appeared in 1781. This work was completed by the *Critique of Practical Reason* (1788) and the *Critique of Judgement* (1790). Together with numerous other works from this time, they made Kant the dominant philosophical figure as well as a celebrity. From 1792 to 1797 he was in conflict with the Prussian king concerning the question of authority in matters of religion. Consequently, he published the text *The Conflict of the Faculties* in 1798. He gave lecture courses until 1796. Kant died on 12 February 1804.

JOHANN GOTTLIEB FICHTE (1762–1814)

Born on 19 May 1762 in Rammenau, Lausitz, the son of a weaver. Through patronage Fichte was able to attend the Princes' School in Pforta, followed by university studies in theology in Leipzig until 1784. Then he served in various positions as a private tutor, the last in Zurich, where he got engaged. In 1791 he went to Königsberg in order to introduce himself to Kant, who was his main philosophical inspiration, with the manuscript of his *Critique of All Revelation*. Kant arranged its publication (1792) and he was attributed authorship. In 1794, Fichte's first major work, the *Foundation of the Entire Science of Knowledge* was published. In the same year, he was granted the professorship in philosophy at Jena (succeeding K. L. Reinhold). Fichte left Jena in 1799 because of the 'atheism debate' and went to Berlin, where he gave lectures (like the *Address to the German Nation* of 1807/8) virtually without interruption until he got a professorship at the newly founded university. Fichte died in Berlin on 29 January 1814.

FRIEDRICH WILHELM JOSEPH VON SCHELLING (1775–1854)

Born on 27 January 1775 in Leonberg, son of a clergyman. From 1790 Schelling was a student at the seminary in Tübingen, and was friends with Hegel and Hölderlin. He published his first philosophical work, *Of the Ego as the Principle of Philosophy*, in 1795. He worked as a private tutor and then, with Goethe's help, got a professorship at Jena in 1798, where he worked with Hegel from 1801 onwards. His first major work, *The System of Transcendental Idealism* (1800), founded his philosophy of identity, which definitively surpassed Fichte. In 1803 he married Karoline, A. W. Schlegel's first wife, who was a central figure of the Romantic circle in Jena. Schelling soon got a professorship at Würzburg, became a member of the Academy of the Sciences in Munich in 1806, and later its secretary. In 1809 he published the *Philosophical Investigations Concerning the Essence of Human*

Freedom. He lectured in Erlangen 1820–26, received a professorship in Munich in 1827, and was appointed to Hegel's chair in Berlin in 1841, where his first lecture course made a great impression (Engels and Kierkegaard were among the audience). Schelling died on 20 August 1854 in Bad Ragaz (Switzerland).

GEORG WILHELM FRIEDRICH HEGEL (1770–1831)

Born on 27 August 1770 in Stuttgart. Hegel studied theology and philosophy at the protestant seminary in Tübingen together with Schelling and Hölderlin. Years of private tutoring followed in Bern and Frankfurt. In 1801 he qualified as a lecturer at Jena, where he worked together with Schelling. In 1807 he went to Bamberg as editor of a newspaper. During that time his first major work, the *Phenomenology of Spirit,* was published. From 1806 to 1816 Hegel was headmaster of a secondary school in Nürnberg. He married Marie von Tucher. The *Science of Logic* was published in 1812–13. Hegel was appointed to the professorship he was after at Heidelberg in 1816, where he produced the *Encyclopedia of the Philosophical Sciences.* In 1818 he accepted an appointment at the recently founded university in Berlin, where he came to be hugely influential. In 1821 he published his *Elements of the Philosophy of Right.* After Hegel's death on 14 November 1831 his essential Berlin lectures were published by his pupils.

Bibliography

General Reading

Beck, Lewis White: *Early German Philosophy: Kant and his Predecessors.*
Cambridge, Mass.: Harvard University Press, 1969.

Beiser, Frederick C.: *The Fate of Reason. German Philosophy from Kant to
Fichte.* Cambridge, Mass.: Harvard University Press, 1987.

Bubner, Rüdiger: *Innovations of German Idealism.* Cambridge: Cambridge University Press, forthcoming.

Kelly, George A.: *Idealism, Politics and History. Sources of Hegelian Thought.*
Cambridge: Cambridge University Press, 1969.

Kant

Allison, Henry E.: *Kant's Transcendental Idealism. An Interpretation and
Defense.* New Haven: Yale University Press, 1983.

Beck, Lewis White: *A Commentary on Kant's Critique of Practical Reason.*
Chicago: Chicago University Press, 1960.

Bennett, Jonathan: *Kant's Analytic.* Cambridge: Cambridge University
Press, 1966.

——: *Kant's Dialectic.* Cambridge: Cambridge University Press, 1974.

Guyer, Paul: *Kant and the Claims of Knowledge.* Cambridge: Cambridge
University Press, 1987.

Guyer, Paul (ed.): *The Cambridge Companion to Kant.* Cambridge: Cambridge University Press, 1992.

Henrich, Dieter: *The Unity of Reason. Essays on Kant's Philosophy.* Cambridge, Mass.: Harvard University Press, 1994.

Neiman, Susan: *The Unity of Reason. Rereading Kant.* New York, Oxford:
Oxford University Press, 1994.

Paton, H. J.: *The Categorical Imperative. A Study in Kant's Moral Philosophy*. London: Hutchinson, 1947.

Strawson, Peter F.: *The Bounds of Sense. An Essay on Kant's Critique of Pure Reason*. London: Methuen, 1966.

Walker, Ralph C. S.: *Kant*. London: Routledge & Kegan Paul, 1978.

Fichte

Breazeale, Daniel and Rockmore, Tom (eds.): *Fichte – Historical Contexts / Contemporary Controversies*. Atlantic Highlands, New Jersey: Humanities Press, 1994.

Hartnack, Justus: 'Fichte: The First but Decisive Step of Absolute Idealism', in Hartnack, *From Radical Empiricism to Absolute Idealism*. Lewiston, N.Y.: Edwin Mellen Press, 1986, pp. 35–65.

Neuhouser, Frederick: *Fichte's Theory of Subjectivity*. Cambridge: Cambridge University Press, 1990.

Seidel, George J.: *Fichte's Wissenschaftslehre of 1794. A Commentary on Part I*. West Lafayette: Purdue University Press, 1993.

Schelling

Bowie, Andrew: *Schelling and Modern European Philosophy. An Introduction*. London: Routledge, 1993.

Brown, Robert F.: *The Later Philosophy of Schelling. The Influence of Boehme on the Works of 1809–1815*. Lewisburg, Pa.: Bucknell University Press, 1977. London: Associated University Presses, 1977.

Esposito, Joseph L.: *Schelling's Idealism and Philosophy of Nature*. London: Associated University Presses, 1977.

White, Alan: *Schelling. An Introduction to the System of Freedom*. New Haven: Yale University Press, 1983.

Hegel

Avineri, Shlomo: *Hegel's Theory of the Modern State*. Cambridge: Cambridge University Press, 1972.

Beiser, Frederick C. (ed.): *The Cambridge Companion to Hegel*. Cambridge: Cambridge University Press, 1993.

Forster, Michael N.: *Hegel and Skepticism*. Cambridge, Mass.: Harvard University Press, 1989.

Pinkard, Terry: *Hegel's Phenomenology. The Sociality of Reason*. Cambridge: Cambridge University Press, 1994.

Pippin, Robert: *Hegel's Idealism. The Satisfactions of Self-Consciousness*. Cambridge: Cambridge University Press, 1988.

Rosen, Michael: *Hegel's Dialectic and its Criticism*. Cambridge: Cambridge University Press, 1982.

Taylor, Charles: *Hegel*. Cambridge: Cambridge University Press, 1975.

KANT

Kant, in founding philosophy anew at the beginning of the idealist era, not only proceeded from a traditional theory of pure reason, but also observed its historical decline. Since Aristotle's day, the supreme science of reason had been called metaphysics. In the meantime, this old war horse of philosophy had fallen into disrepute, for nothing in it had yet been clarified and everything was still in dispute. In particular, the modern scientific model revealed the deeply dissatisfying state of the philosophical discipline of pure reason. The non-philosophical sciences, meanwhile, had demonstrated a way of actually acquiring knowledge. This state of affairs was, of course, intolerable. The concept of reason and the confusion in its discipline displayed a very immediate contradiction. Hence, some fundamental efforts had to be made in the name of reason itself in order to bring clarity to the situation. Philosophical theory needed new and secure grounds to rest on.

In order to establish such grounds, however, no other tool was available apart from reason itself, hence, reason had to try to come to terms with itself. In trying to do so, basic philosophical attitudes were changed and became very different from the dogmatic directness of the metaphysical tradition. The task of re-substantiating philosophy became part of a critical self-examination of reason, in which examiner, examinee, and the criterion for examination are one and the same. Here, reason became critical. The critique that Kant raised and that appears in the title of all three major works originally entailed a rigorous examination and a separation of the legitimate from the illegitimate. The ultimate aim of his critical method, never just an end in itself, was articulated in a shorter work: *Prolegomena to Any Future Metaphysics that Will be Able to Appear as a Science.* Here, Kant sought to elucidate the intentions of his initially ill-received *Critique of Pure Reason*.

The plan of his theory of reason was precisely this: to satisfy the scientific standards of physics and mathematics, and, by way of critique, to restore the hereditary privileges of reason. Kant, to be sure, did not succeed in elaborating a definitive new system on the basis of a critique of reason. Its impact was, on the contrary, based on that critical turn which took reason back to itself. Here the idea of pure reflection was realized for the first time. Later, Kant's successors carried it beyond the mere task of critique and expanded it systematically. In the idealist systems of post-Kantian philosophy, however, prophecy was not fulfilled as expected. Once reflection was deemed absolute, it led to the abandonment of critique, and a metaphysics which had radically been subjected to doubt was finally restored.

When speaking of transcendental reflection, Kant clearly contrasted it with the transcendent exuberance of metaphysical speculation. The transcendental question did not immediately apply to objects of knowledge, but to the conditions for the possibility of knowledge as such. Kant saw it as the task of his critique to investigate these. We have to understand that we can only talk of real knowledge with respect to the world of experience which is investigated by our empirical sciences. Any knowledge that is not based on experience and that is supposedly absolute terminates in illusion. We have, antecedently, ordered the world of possible objects of experience by means of the forms of intuition of space and time, as well as by means of the categories of reason which are the most general means of unifying manifold sensory data. Those antecedent or *a priori* accomplishments of subjectivity with respect to its objects are investigated in transcendental reflection. Transcendental reflection deals, therefore, with the conditions responsible for constituting the subject–object relation as such, a relation that grounds all knowledge. This is exactly what the famous question, 'What makes synthetic judgements *a priori* possible?', is fundamentally aimed at.

Transcendental reflection articulates the relation of subject and object. It takes objects to be appearances relative to a subject, and it therefore refrains from making claims about things in themselves, as they would exist independently of any relations to a subject that knows or perceives them. In the same way, an analysis of the accomplishments of reason is insufficient for gaining a concept of purely rational subjectivity, a subjectivity without any reference to a world of experience. In both cases we would otherwise regress towards metaphysics again, for it had just been demonstrated that subject and object can be meaningfully conceived of only in relation to each other. A pure reason that would lie beyond reason directed at empirical objects, and that would therefore have to be called transcendent, can no longer be grasped by a theoretical philosophy whose primary task is critique. Pure reason, however, is not thereby dismissed forever from philosophical service. In Kant's classification, it is transferred into the field of practical philosophy.

Rational praxis begins where theoretical knowledge reaches its limits. In the moral law, reason plays a role that is not empirically restricted and that is therefore unconditional. Kant, then, proceeded from the indisputable validity of the categorical imperative. In this formula, he interpreted the moral 'ought' of which everyone has an immediate sense as the expression of a purely rational characteristic of human beings. The authority of conscience shows that this moral obligation forms part of the experience of every individual prior to any instruction or rational argument. Kant's second major work, the *Critique of Practical Reason*, substantiated the philosophical interpretation of pure reason in so far as it is linked with the indisputable certainty of an obligation to moral action.

What the categorical imperative, interpreted this way, demands is this: 'Act such that the maxim of your will could at any time be the principle of a general jurisdiction.' While an action is demanded, only its form is prescribed, such that its content has to be supplied by varying, subjective maxims. Whichever specific shape the maxim guiding a particular action may take, it must at least meet the one essential standard of being able to become a universal law. What matters is the universalizability of private maxims. As a matter of principle, in one's actions one ought only to be guided by rules that could be equally valid for anyone else. In this case, one's concrete actions would follow the principle of reason, for reason has, by its nature, a universal validity.

Action according to the universal laws of reason, however, presupposes the freedom to determine one's will, independent of individually fluctuating interests and dominant environmental influences. Freedom is not a given; it has to be acquired as practical autonomy. Action from pure reason and the presupposition of freedom are mutually dependent. Freedom has to be presupposed for a possible rational praxis, and praxis has to be guided by reason in order for freedom to be real. Thus, freedom means both freedom from external determination and freedom to self-determination. Even the most basic observations, however, seem to indicate that every action is determined by outside causes. Scientific results, for example in psychology or sociology, further strengthen the idea of a universal determinism.

In order to solve this problem, we have to assume a dual nature of human beings. While capable of rational autonomy by dint of their free will, humans are also part of the empirical world, and therefore are subject to its laws. Assuming this dual nature, however, only makes sense if there is a possible transition from one realm to the other. The transition, presupposed in Kant's practical philosophy, from causal necessity to the freedom of an unconditionally determined will, is one of the most difficult aspects of his philosophy. It also has a particular importance, though, because his theoretical and practical philosophies are connected with each other such that the validity of unconditional or pure reason can only be guaranteed by the two together. The initial task of philosophical critique is fulfilled when this connection between theory and praxis is demonstrated.

The fundamental significance of the moral law to Kant's entire project explains the rigidity and the formalism with which he defended it. The content of the argument can best be explained against the background of his intention to fence off sophist ways of reasoning. Uncompromising duty always has eloquent opponents who try to weaken it and who look for exceptions to it. It would seem prudent to adapt moral demands to every situation and to individual capacities. Kant's imperative, however, tries to depart from such ifs and buts once and for all. The moral law would be destroyed at its very foundation if its unconditional validity were to be relativized. It is therefore intrinsically nonsensical to subordinate the categorical demand made by pure reason to the judgement of an individual or to the varying assessments of similar cases.

Kant's ethics have always been reproached for being distanced from reality. There are obvious reasons for the objections that are raised, but it must be said that it was also clear to Kant himself that the demand of reason in its categorical imperative stood high above the level of everyday life. None of us act only and unfalteringly from purely rational motives. To Kant, this did not seem to be an objection to the demand that we ought to act in such a way if we take ourselves seriously as rational beings. In the mode of obligation within which our true nature can alone be experienced, there is no room for concession. We would even run into a deep misconception of ourselves if we refused to accept the unconditional priority with which our rational determination confronts us when it restrains our own dominant interests.

This opens up a gulf, with the empirical reality of human praxis on the far side, and it is one that is difficult to bridge. The idea that it would have to be bridged was common to all of Kant's successors, who felt very strongly the need to change the world. Kant himself, no doubt, was interested in mediating the principles of morality with the process of history. This is demonstrated by those of his works that are not counted among the strictly transcendental investigations. The *Idea for a Universal History with a Cosmopolitan Purpose*, for example, expanded the rational demand made initially on the individual to fit the framework of human society. This essay, intended for a general audience, shows Kant as a representative of the Enlightenment, applying philosophical ideas to the fortunes of mankind and hoping to contribute to change for the better.

In view of the tension between the rational and the empirical, Kant's third major work, the *Critique of Judgement*, proposed a very different and highly ingenious solution to the problem. The faculty of judgement that has the general function of correctly relating a universal to a particular, exhibits a new dimension of transcendentally created meaning. After dealing with the laws of nature in the theoretical section and the moral demands in the practical section, we are now confronted with phenomena of inner order and expediency, such as teleological formations in organic life on the one hand, and works of art on the other. The analysis of their effects on the mind or consciousness exhibits a relation of reception and stimulation. Meaningful structures in animate nature or in art harmonize with our faculty of knowledge. The feeling of relief on encountering them is experienced as intellectual pleasure. Kant has thereby, and in a way that is still valid today, managed to determine some basic elements of aesthetic experience, emphasizing the close analogy between nature and art.

The doctrine of the faculty of judgement as the authority which mediates between empirical concretion and the transcendental sphere not only shed new light on the entire venture of critical philosophy, but also indicated the course for an uninterrupted philosophical development. Its aesthetic reflections inspired Friedrich Schiller's programme in popular education, his idea of an 'aesthetic education of man'. Kant's lasting impact is manifest in Fichte's letters about 'The Spirit and the Letter', the most important of which is reprinted below. And the teleological approach of the *Critique of Judgement* was picked up especially by Schelling in his philosophy of nature.

THE TEXTS

The Preface to the Second Edition of the *Critique of Pure Reason* names the requirements for a science that is to proceed on a 'secure course'. These requirements can be taken from the examples of already established disciplines. The security of logic depends on mere formality. Mathematics and the natural sciences, on the other hand, show that whatever reason can grasp of an object is something that reason itself must have put there already. Objects of knowledge are not merely given, they are constituted. The science of pure reason, as a branch of philosophy, has to make revolutionary progress in its basic approach, as has already occurred in the modern sciences. It must absorb the idea that the objects of rational knowledge depend on the possibilities of our faculty of knowledge. A particular *a posteriori* experience is preceded by a universal *a priori* conceptual accomplishment. An attempt at pure empirical observation, independent of this accomplishment, would be unable to tell us anything. Reality only becomes accessible on the basis of forms of order that are pre-designed by reason and that are therefore independent of experience. The well-known example of Hume's problem of causality may be of help in clarifying this task: how it can be possible that in empirical reality we make a causal connection between cause and effect, not on the basis of an experience, but prior to it and thereby constituting it. Here we have to assume concepts of causal order that originate in reason. It is important to emphasize, however, that these *a priori* concepts remain entirely connected with concrete experience. Without a corresponding perception, they would be empty and useless.

Consequently, transcendental philosophy investigates the *a priori* conditions for the possibility of experience, while any other objects, conceived of beyond this realm of experience, have to be dismissed in the critique as unknowable. The objects of experience constituted in this way are part of the realm of appearances, i.e., of the world as it appears to us and as it is accessible to us. We can have no theoretical knowledge about things in themselves beyond their particular appearances, which are manifest in human knowledge. With respect to praxis, however, aside from empirical behaviour in the world of appearances, there is the possibility of an unconditional determination of the will by means of reason. Here, reason is not subject to the same restrictions as it is in theoretical knowledge. The initially rejected transcendent use of reason is legitimized with respect to human action in a world defined according to the ends posited by reason itself. Thus, theoretical and practical philosophy complement each other. The negative result that the critique of knowledge reached is complemented by the positive aspect of opening up the efficacy of reason in praxis. Once reason had critically enlightened itself about its own limits and possibilities, it confronted the unreflective dogmatism of conventional metaphysical schools. The 'criticism of the organ' was a 'treatise on the method, not a system of the science itself'. The critique went beyond the dispute between schools, in so far as one of its purifying functions was preparing a future metaphysics that conformed to the recognized standards of a science.

The Preface to the *Critique of Pure Reason* had already mentioned the transition from theory to praxis. The first few paragraphs of the *Critique of Practical Reason* give an exposition of the elementary principles with which practical philosophy, as understood by Kant, should be equipped. To be highlighted first are those practical principles that our will, as the origin of all action guided by reason, is subject to. Subjective principles that are only valid for oneself are called maxims. On the other hand, objective principles that are valid for every rational being are called laws. The former were presupposed by Kant simply as a fact of life; people adopt widely differing behavioural patterns. The discipline of ethics, on the other hand, is interested in the practical laws in which subjectivity is disregarded and which deserve recognition only by virtue of reason. As opposed to knowledge concerning nature, the validity of laws has no *a priori* guarantee in the realm of praxis. On the contrary, here we only find imperatives to which we ought to adhere in so far as we understand ourselves as rational beings, but which human nature does not readily obey by itself as it vacillates between sensory impulses and rational determination. Only the 'holy will' of a god that acts solely from reason would be above the moral 'ought' and the obliging aspect of rational motivation. The hypothetical and the categorical imperative must also be distinguished. The hypothetical imperative is effective only when it assigns the means which a rational being must choose to a given end. The categorical imperative is valid unconditionally, regardless of the changing aims of different agents. Only the categorical imperative, because it is valid for any will determined by reason, exhibits practical laws. Since concrete determinations have an empirical basis and appeal to the emotions and the self-love of the agent, the categorical imperative must be purely formal. Concrete principles are always part of a theory of happiness, or, to translate this traditional idea of morality into more contemporary words, part of a theory of a 'prosperous life' (*eudaimonia*). Kant sharply contrasted his own moral philosophy with this kind of approach. Due to its comprehensive structure of argumentation, it drew a dividing line between itself and all other forms of ethics. It looked for a motivation of action that would be free from finite conditions and subjective contingency and that would at the same time have the universal validity of a law. A motivation which is valid for every concrete action and which is accepted by all agents can only spring from pure reason itself. That is to say, it demands recognition absolutely and unconditionally, i.e. categorically, but can only be articulated as an imperative because of the empirically conditioned circumstance of the agent.

Finally, the popular philosophical essay *Idea for a Universal History with a Cosmopolitan Purpose* sought to mediate between the empirical realm and a purely rational determination of action. Here, Kant focused on the whole of our species and the unity of its history. In this dimension, what had seemed irreconcilably contradictory to subjective consciousness suddenly appeared meaningful. One must be confident of a final intention of nature, of a plan of providence, which is difficult for subjective consciousness to decipher, and which will only be fulfilled in the course of a developing mankind. Despite the tension which is produced by the antagonism of society, i.e. the social disposition of human beings combined with a focus on the individual's particular interests, the idea of a rational community in the practical realm is not undermined. This tension is revealed, rather, as a cunning means by which all-encompassing nature promotes the collective development of all forces. In accordance with the spirit of the Enlightenment, culture is thereby understood as a natural constraint that forces us to act morally. Our main problem consists in establishing a civil society that, in accordance with the tradition of political philosophy and in disagreement with the later Hegel, Kant identified with the state. Another task arose, namely that of making justice among people compatible with the domination of some over others. Ultimately, Kant envisaged a society consolidated as a state within a framework of states externally related to one another, regulated in the same way as the relation of citizens to one another. According to Kant, within such a league of nations the constant external threat to society would be warded off. World citizenship, i.e. cosmopolitan existence, is the ultimate end, and it makes the intricate course of history both comprehensible and transparent to reason.

Rüdiger Bubner
Translated by Marcus Weigelt

Critique of Pure Reason

PREFACE TO THE SECOND EDITION (1787)

Whether the treatment of that class of knowledge with which reason is occupied follows the secure course of a science or not, can easily be determined from its result. If, after several preparations, it comes to a standstill as soon as it approaches its real goal, or is obliged, in order to reach it, to retrace its steps again and again, and set off down new paths; again, if it is impossible to produce agreement among those who are engaged in the same work, as to the manner in which their common objective should be accomplished, we may be convinced that such a study is far from having attained the secure course of a science, but is merely a groping in the dark. To find this course would be a great service to reason, though many of the original aims, which were established without sufficient thought, will have to be abandoned as vain.

That *Logic*, from the earliest times, has followed this secure course, may be seen in the fact that since Aristotle it has not had to retrace a single step, unless we choose to consider as improvements the removal of some unnecessary subtleties, or the clearer determination of its subject matter, both of which are to do with the elegance rather than the solidity of the science. It is remarkable also, that to the present day, it has not been able to advance even one step, so that, to all appearances, it may be considered as completed and perfect. If some moderns have thought to enlarge it by introducing *psychological* chapters on the different faculties of knowledge (faculty of imagination, wit), or *metaphysical* chapters either on the origin of knowledge or the different degrees of certainty according to the difference of objects (idealism, scepticism, etc.), or *anthropological* chapters on prejudices, their causes and remedies, this could only arise from their ignorance of the peculiar nature of this science. We do not enlarge but only disfigure the sciences if we allow their respective limits to be confounded; and the limits of logic are definitely fixed by the fact that it is a science which does nothing but fully exhibit and strictly prove the formal rules of all thought (whether it be *a priori* or empirical, whatever its origin or its object might be, and whatever the impediments, accidental or natural, might be which it has to encounter in the human mind).

That logic should in this respect have been so successful is due entirely to its limitations, whereby it has not only the right but also the duty to abstract from all objects of knowledge and their differences, so that the understanding has to deal with nothing beyond itself and its own form. It was far more difficult, of course, for reason to enter on the secure course of science, considering that it has to deal not with itself alone, but also with objects. Logic, therefore, as a propaedeutic, forms only the vestibule, as it were, of the sciences, though logic is presupposed for the critical assessment of knowledge, while the acquisition of knowledge must be achieved in the sciences themselves, properly and objectively so called.

If there is to be an element of reason in those sciences, something in them must be known *a priori*, and this knowledge may stand in a twofold relation to its object, either as merely *determining* it and its concept (which must be supplied from elsewhere), or as also *making it real*. The former is *theoretical*, the latter *practical* knowledge of reason. In both the *pure* part, namely that in which reason determines its object entirely *a priori* (whether it contains much or little), must be treated first, so as not to confound it with what comes from other sources; for it is bad economy to spend blindly whatever comes in, and not to be able to decide, when money is short, which part of the income can bear the expenditure, and where reductions must be made.

Mathematics and physics are the two theoretical sciences of reason which have to determine their objects *a priori*; the former quite purely, the latter partially so, and partially from other sources of knowledge besides reason.

Mathematics, from the earliest days of the history of human reason, has followed, thanks to those admirable people, the Greeks, the secure path of a science. But it must not be supposed that it was as easy for mathematics as it was for logic, in which reason is concerned with itself alone, to find, or rather to pave for itself that royal path. I believe, on the contrary, that there was a long period of tentative work (chiefly still by the Egyptians), and that change occurred as a *revolution*, brought about by the happy thought of a single man, whose experiment pointed unmistakably to the path that had to be followed, and opened and traced out the secure course of a science for all time. The history of this intellectual revolution, which was far more important than the discovery of the passage round the celebrated Cape of Good Hope, and the name of its fortunate author, have not been preserved. But the story preserved by Diogenes Laertius, who names the alleged author of even the most minute of ordinary geometrical demonstrations, even of those which, according to general opinion, do not require such a proof, shows, at all events, that the memory of the revolution, brought about by the very first traces of the discovery of a new method, must have seemed extremely important to mathematicians, and thus remained unforgotten. The first man who demonstrated the properties of the isosceles triangle (be he Thales or another) had his eyes opened, for he found that he did not have to investigate what he saw in the figure, or in the mere concept of that figure, and thereby learn its properties; but that he had to achieve his knowledge by construction, by means of what he himself, according to concepts *a priori*, had placed into that figure. In order to know anything with certainty *a priori*, he must not attribute to the figure anything beyond what necessarily follows from what he has himself placed into it, in accordance with his concept.

It took a much longer time before the natural sciences entered on the highway of science. No more than a century and a half has elapsed since the ingenious proposals of Bacon partly initiated that discovery – partly, as others were already on the right track – and gave it a new impetus – a discovery which, like the former, can only be explained by a rapid intellectual revolution. Here I shall consider natural science only in so far as it is founded on *empirical* principles.

When Galilei rolled balls of a pre-determined weight down an inclined plane; or when Torricelli made the air carry a weight which he had previously determined to be equal to that of a definite volume of water; or when, in later times, Stahl* changed metals into lime, and lime again into metals, by withdrawing something and restoring it, natural scientists were given a revelation. They comprehended that reason has insight only into that which it produces itself after a plan of its own, and that it must move forward, according to fixed laws, with the principles of its judgements, and compel nature to answer its questions, but not be kept, as it were, in nature's shackles; for otherwise, accidental observations, with no previously fixed plan, will never be made to yield a necessary law, which reason, however, seeks and requires. Reason, holding in one hand its principles, according to which concordant appearances can alone be admitted to count as laws of nature, and in the other hand the experiments which it has devised according to these principles, must approach nature in order to be taught by it. It must not, however, do so in the manner of a pupil, who agrees to everything the teacher says, but of an appointed judge, who compels the witnesses to answer the questions which he himself has phrased. Therefore, even the science of physics entirely owes the beneficial revolution in its character to the idea that reason ought to seek in nature (and must not import into it by means of fiction) whatever it must learn about nature, and about which it could not have knowledge by itself, and that it must do this in accordance with what it itself has originally placed into nature. It is thus that the study of nature has entered on the secure course of a science, after having for many centuries done nothing but random groping.

Metaphysics, a completely isolated and speculative science of reason, which is raised above all teachings of experience and rests on concepts only (not, like mathematics, on their application to intuition), in which reason therefore is meant to be its own pupil, has hitherto not had the good fortune to enter upon the secure path of a science, although it is older than all other sciences, and would survive even if all the rest were swallowed up in the abyss of an all-destroying barbarism. Reason in metaphysics, even if it tries, as it

---

* I am not closely following here the course of the history of the experimental method, the origins of which are not very well known.

professes, only to understand *a priori* those laws which are confirmed by our most common experience, is constantly being brought to a standstill, and we are obliged again and again to retrace our steps, as they do not lead us where we want to go. As to unanimity among its participants, there is so little of it in metaphysics that it has rather become an arena that would seem especially suited for those who wish to exercise themselves in mock fights, and where no combatant has as yet succeeded in gaining even an inch of ground that he could call his permanent possession. There cannot be any doubt, therefore, that the method of metaphysics has hitherto consisted in a mere random groping, and, what is worst of all, in groping among mere concepts.

What, then, is the reason that this secure scientific course has not yet been found? Is this, perhaps, impossible? Why, then, should nature have afflicted our reason with the restless aspiration to look for it, and have made it one of its most important concerns? What is more, how little should we be justified in trusting our reason if, with regard to one of the most important objects of which we desire knowledge, it not only abandons us, but lures us on with delusions, and in the end betrays us! Or, if hitherto we have only failed to meet with the right path, what indications are there to make us hope that, should we renew our search, we shall be more successful than others before us?

The examples of mathematics and natural science, which became what they now are by one sudden revolution, should be sufficiently remarkable to warrant reflection on what may have been the essential elements in the intellectual transformation by which they have so greatly benefited, and to warrant at least the experiment, so far as the analogy between them as elements of rational knowledge and metaphysics allows it, of imitating them. Hitherto it has been supposed that all our knowledge must conform to its objects. But all attempts to establish something about them *a priori* by means of concepts and thus to enlarge our knowledge, have on this supposition come to nothing. We should therefore attempt to tackle the tasks of metaphysics more successfully by assuming that objects must conform to our knowledge. This would better agree with the required possibility of a knowledge of objects *a priori*, one that would settle something about them prior to their being given to us. We are here in a similar situation as Copernicus was in at the beginning. Unable to proceed satisfactorily in the explanation of the movements of the heavenly bodies, on the supposition that the entire collection of stars turned round the spectator, he tried to see whether he might not have greater success by making the spectator revolve and leaving the stars at rest. A similar experiment may be tried in metaphysics with the *intuition* of objects. If the intuition had to conform to the constitution of objects, I do not see how we could know anything of it *a priori*; but if the object (as object of the senses) conformed to the constitution of our faculty of intuition, I could very well conceive such a possibility. As, however, I cannot rest in these intuitions if they are to become knowledge, but have to refer them, as representations, to something as their object, and must determine this object through them, I can assume either that the *concepts* by means of which I arrive at this determination conform to the object, and I would again be as perplexed about how I can know anything about it *a priori*; or else that the objects, or what is the same thing, the *experience* in which alone, as given objects, they are known, conform to those concepts. In the latter case, I recognize an easier solution because experience itself is a kind of knowledge that requires understanding; and this understanding has rules which I must therefore, even before objects are given to me, presuppose as existing within me *a priori*. These rules are expressed in concepts *a priori* to which all objects of experience must necessarily conform, and with which they must agree. With regard to objects, in so far as they are conceived only through reason and conceived indeed as necessary, and can never, at least not in the way in which they are conceived by reason, be given in experience, the attempts at conceiving them (for they must admit of being conceived) will subsequently furnish an excellent touchstone of what we are adopting as our new method of thought, namely that we know *a priori* of things only that which we ourselves put into them.*

* This method, borrowed from the natural scientists, consists in looking for the elements of pure reason in *that which can be confirmed or refuted by experiment*. Now it is impossible, in order to test the propositions of pure reason, particularly if they venture beyond all limits of possible experience, to make any experiment involving their *objects* (as in natural science); we can therefore only proceed with *concepts* and *principles* which

This experiment succeeds as hoped and promises to metaphysics, in its first part, which deals with concepts *a priori*, of which the corresponding objects may be given in experience, the secure course of a science. For by thus changing our point of view, the possibility of knowledge *a priori* can well be explained, and, what is more, the laws which *a priori* lie at the foundation of nature, as the sum total of the objects of experience, may be supplied with satisfactory proofs, neither of which was possible within the procedure hitherto adopted. But there arises from this deduction of our faculty of knowing *a priori*, as given in the first part of metaphysics, a somewhat startling result, apparently most detrimental to the objects of metaphysics that have to be treated in the second part, namely the impossibility of using it to transcend the limits of possible experience, which is precisely the most essential purpose of the science of metaphysics. But here we have exactly the experiment which, by disproving the opposite, establishes the truth of the first estimate of our *a priori* knowledge of reason, namely, that it is directed at appearances and must leave the thing in itself as real for itself but unknown to us. For that which necessarily impels us to go beyond the limits of experience and of all appearances, is the *unconditioned*, which reason requires rightfully and necessarily to be present, aside from everything conditioned, in all things in themselves, so that the series of conditions become complete. If, then, we find that under the supposition that our experience conforms to objects as things in themselves it is *impossible to conceive the unconditioned without contradiction*, while, under the supposition that our representation of things, as they are given to us, does not conform to them as things in themselves, but, on the contrary, that the objects conform to our mode of representation, *the contradiction vanishes*; and if we find, therefore, that the unconditioned cannot be encountered in things

---

we adopt *a priori*, by so contriving that the same objects may be considered on one side as objects of the senses and of understanding in experience, and on the other, as purely objects of thought, intended for reason alone, which strives to go beyond all the limits of experience. And if we find that, by looking on things from this twofold point of view, there is an agreement with the principle of pure reason, while by adopting one point of view only, there arises an inevitable conflict with reason, then the experiment decides in favour of the correctness of that distinction.

in so far as we know them (in so far as they are given to us), but only in things in so far as we do not know them, that is, in so far as they are things in themselves, then it becomes apparent that what we at first assumed only for the sake of experiment is well founded.* However, with speculative reason unable to make progress in the field of the supersensible, it is still open to us to investigate whether, in the practical knowledge of reason, data may not be found which would enable us to determine reason's transcendent concept of the unconditioned, so as to enable us, in accordance with the wish of metaphysics, to get beyond the limits of all possible experience, with our knowledge *a priori*, which is possible in practical matters only. Within such a procedure, speculative reason has always at least created a space for such an extension, even if it has had to leave it empty; none the less we are at liberty, indeed we are called upon, to fill it, if we are able, with practical data of reason.† The purpose of this critique of pure speculative reason consists in the attempt to change the old procedure of metaphysics, and bring about a complete revolution after the example set by geometers and investigators of nature. This critique is a treatise on the method, not a system of the science itself; but it marks out nevertheless the whole plan of this

* This experiment of pure reason bears great similarity to what in chemistry is sometimes called the experiment of *reduction*, or generally the *synthetic* process. The *analysis of the metaphysician* divided pure knowledge *a priori* into two very heterogeneous elements, namely, the knowledge of things as appearances, and the knowledge of things in themselves. *Dialectic* combines these two again, to bring them into *harmony* with reason's necessary idea of the *unconditioned*, and finds that this harmony can never be obtained except through the above distinction, which is therefore true.

† In the same manner the essential laws of the motion of the heavenly bodies established as fact what Copernicus had originally assumed as a hypothesis only, and proved at the same time the invisible force (the Newtonian attraction) which holds the universe together. This force would have remained for ever undiscovered, if Copernicus had not dared, by a paradoxical yet none the less truthful hypothesis, to locate the observed movements not in the heavenly bodies, but in the spectator. A change in point of view, analogous to this hypothesis and later expanded in the *Critique*, is put forward in this preface only as a hypothesis, so as to highlight the first attempts at such a change, which are always hypothetical. In the treatise itself, however, they are proved not hypothetically but apodeictically from the constitution of our representations of space and time and from the elementary concepts of understanding.

science, both with regard to its limits and with regard to its internal organization. For it is peculiar to pure speculative reason that it is able, indeed bound, to measure its own powers according to the different ways in which it chooses its objects for thought, and to enumerate exhaustively the different ways of choosing its problems; thus tracing a complete outline of a system of metaphysics. This is due to the fact that, with regard to the first point, nothing can be attributed to objects in knowledge *a priori*, except what the thinking subject takes from within itself; while, with regard to the second point, pure reason, so far as its principles of knowledge are concerned, forms a separate and independent unity, in which, as in an organic body, every member exists for the sake of the others, and the others exist for the sake of the one, so that no principle can be safely applied in *any one* relation, unless it has been carefully examined in *all* its relations to the whole employment of pure reason. Hence, too, metaphysics has this singular advantage, an advantage which cannot be shared by any other science in which reason has to deal with objects (for *Logic* deals only with the form of thought in general), that, if it has been set, by means of this critique, upon the secure course of a science, it can exhaustively grasp the entire field of knowledge pertaining to it, and can thus finish its work and leave it to posterity, as capital that can never be added to, because it has to deal only with principles and with the limits of their employment, as determined by these principles themselves. And this completeness becomes indeed an obligation if it is to be a fundamental science, of which we must be able to say, '*nil actum reputans, si quid superesset agendum.*'

But, it will be asked, what is this treasure that, once purified by criticism, and thereby furnished with a permanent condition, we mean to bequeath to posterity in our metaphysics? After a superficial view of this work, it may seem that its advantage is *negative* only, warning us against venturing beyond the limit of experience with speculative reason. Such, no doubt, is its primary use: but it becomes *positive* when we perceive that the principles with which speculative reason ventures beyond its limits lead inevitably, not to an *extension*, but, if carefully considered, to a *narrowing* of the employment of reason, because, by indefinitely extending the bounds of sensibility, to which they properly belong, they threaten to supplant entirely the pure (practical) employment of reason. Hence our critique, by limiting speculative reason to its proper sphere, is no doubt *negative*, but by thus removing an impediment which threatened to narrow, or even entirely to destroy, its practical employment, it is in reality *positive*, and of very important use, if only we are convinced that there is an absolutely necessary *practical* use of pure reason (the *moral* use), in which reason must inevitably transcend the limits of sensibility, and though not requiring for this purpose the assistance of speculative reason, must at all events be assured against its opposition, lest it be brought into conflict with itself. To deny that this service, which is rendered by critique, is a *positive* advantage, would be the same as to deny that the police confer upon us any positive advantage, their principal occupation being to prevent violence between citizens, in order that each may pursue his vocation in peace and security. That space and time are only forms of sensible intuition, and therefore only conditions of the existence of things as appearances, and that we have no concepts of understanding, and therefore nothing whereby we can arrive at the knowledge of things, except in so far as an intuition corresponding to these concepts can be given, and consequently that we cannot have knowledge of any object as thing in itself, but only in so far as it is an object of sensible intuition, that is, as an appearance; all this is proved in the analytical part of the critique. This proves no doubt that all speculative knowledge of reason is limited to mere objects of *experience*; but it should be carefully borne in mind that this leaves it perfectly open to us to *think* the same objects as things in themselves, though we cannot *know* them.*

---

* In order to *know* an object, I must be able to prove its possibility, either from its reality, as attested by experience, or *a priori*, by means of reason. But I can *think* whatever I please, provided only I do not contradict myself, that is, provided my conception is a possible thought, though I may be unable to answer for the existence of a corresponding object in the sum total of all possibilities. Before I can attribute to such a concept objective reality (real possibility, as distinguished from the former, which is purely logical), something more is required. This something more, however, need not be sought for in the sources of theoretical knowledge, for it may be found in those of practical knowledge also.

For otherwise we should arrive at the absurd conclusion that there would be appearance without something that appears. Let us suppose that the necessary distinction, established in our critique, between things as objects of experience and the same things in themselves, had not been made. In this case, the principle of causality, and with it the mechanism of nature as determined by it, would apply to all things in general as efficient causes. I should, then, not be able to say of one and the same being, for instance the human soul, that its will is free, and, at the same time, subject to the necessity of nature, that is, not free, without involving myself in a palpable contradiction: for the reason that I had taken the soul in both propositions *in one and the same sense*, namely, as a thing in general (as something in itself), as, without a preceding critique, I could not but take it. If, however, our criticism were true, in teaching us to take an object in *two senses*, namely, either as an appearance, or as a thing in itself, and if the deduction of our concepts of understanding was correct, and the principle of causality applies to things only if taken in the first sense, namely in so far as they are objects of experience, but not to things if taken in the second sense, we can, without any contradiction, think the same will, if appearance (in visible action), as necessarily conforming to the law of nature, and hence *not free*, and yet, on the other hand, if belonging to a thing in itself, as not subject to that law of nature, and therefore *free*. Now it is quite true that I may not know my soul, as a thing in itself, by means of speculative reason (still less through empirical observation), and consequently may not know freedom either, as the quality of a being to which I attribute effects in the sensible world, because, in order to do this, I should have to know such a being as existing, and yet as not determined in time (which, as I cannot provide my concept with any intuition, is impossible). This, however, does not prevent me from *thinking* freedom; that is, my representation of it contains at least no contradiction within itself, if only our critical distinction of the two modes of representation (the sensible and the intelligible), and the consequent limitation of the concepts of pure understanding, and of the principles based on them, has been properly made. If, then, morality necessarily presupposes freedom (in the strictest sense) as a property of our will, since it produces, as *a priori data* of it, practical principles which belong originally to our reason, a production which without freedom would be absolutely impossible, and if speculative reason had proved that such a freedom cannot even be thought, the former supposition, namely the moral one, would necessarily have to yield to another, the opposite of which involves a palpable contradiction, so that freedom, and with it morality (for its opposite contains no contradiction, unless freedom is presupposed), would have to make room for the *mechanism of nature*. As morality, however, requires nothing but that freedom should only not contradict itself, and that it should at least allow of being thought, without having to be further understood, and that thus thought freedom should have no reason to place an obstacle in the way of the natural mechanism of the same act (taken in a different sense), so the doctrine of morality maintains its position, and so does the doctrine of nature. This would have been impossible if our critique had not previously taught us our inevitable ignorance of things in themselves, and had not limited everything, which we are able to *know* theoretically, to mere appearances.

This precise discussion about the positive advantage of critical principles of pure reason, can be demonstrated with regard to the concept of *God* and the *simple nature* of our *soul*; but this is something I shall omit here for the sake of brevity. We have seen, therefore, that I am not allowed even to *assume*, for the sake of the necessary practical employment of my reason, *God, freedom, immortality*, unless I deprive speculative reason of its pretensions to transcendent insight. Reason, namely, in order to arrive at these, must employ principles which extend only to objects of possible experience and which, if in spite of this they applied also to what cannot be an object of experience, really always change this into an appearance, thus rendering all *practical extension* of pure reason impossible. Hence I had to suspend *knowledge*, in order to make room for *belief*. For the dogmatism of metaphysics, that is, the presumption that it is possible to achieve anything in metaphysics without a previous critique of pure reason, is the source of all that disbelief which opposes morality and which is always very dogmatic.

Though it may not be too difficult to bequeath to posterity a systematic metaphysics, carried out according to the critique of pure reason, such a gift is not to be considered as of little value. We need only consider how reason is improved through achieving the secure course of a science, in place of its groundless groping and uncritical rambling, or the better use that our inquiring youth can make of their time when not brought up in the ordinary dogmatism by which they are early encouraged to indulge in easy speculations about things of which they understand nothing, and of which they, as little as anybody else, will ever understand anything – seeking new thoughts and opinions but neglecting the acquisition of sound scientific knowledge. The greatest benefit, however, will be that such a work will enable us to put an end for ever to all objections to morality and religion, and this according to the *Socratic* manner, that is to say by the clearest proof of the ignorance of our opponents. Some kind of metaphysics has always existed and will always exist, but with it a naturally given dialectic of pure reason. It is therefore the first and most important task of philosophy to deprive metaphysics once and for all of its pernicious influence, by blocking off the source of its errors.

In spite of these important changes in the realm of the sciences and the *loss* of its imagined possessions which speculative reason must suffer, all general human interests, and all other advantages which the world has hitherto derived from the teachings of pure reason, remain just the same as before. The loss, if any, affects only the *monopoly of the Schools*, and by no means the *interests of humanity*. I ask the most adamant dogmatist whether the proof of the continued existence of our soul after death, derived from the simplicity of the substance, or that of the freedom of the will as opposed to the universal mechanism of nature, derived from the subtle but ineffectual distinction between subjective and objective practical necessity, or that of the existence of God, derived from the concept of a most real being (the contingency of the changeable and the necessity of a prime mover), have ever managed to spread from the Schools and enter the consciousness of the public or exercised the slightest influence on its convictions? If this has not happened; and if in fact it can never be expected to happen, due to the unfitness of commonsense understanding for such subtle speculation; and if, on the contrary, with regard to the first point, the hope of a *future life* has chiefly rested on that peculiar tendency of human nature never to be satisfied by what is merely temporal (this being insufficient for the tendencies of its overall purpose); if, with regard to the second, the consciousness of *freedom* was produced only by the clear demonstration of duties, in opposition to all the claims of inclination; and if, lastly, with regard to the third, the belief in a great and wise *Author of the world* has been supported entirely by the wonderful order, beauty and providence everywhere displayed in nature, then this possession remains not only undisturbed, but acquires even greater authority, because the Schools have now been taught not to claim for themselves any higher or fuller insight on a point which concerns universal human interests than what is equally within the reach of the great mass of men (who are most worthy of our respect), and so to confine themselves to the elaboration of these universally comprehensible, and, for moral purposes, quite sufficient proofs. The change, therefore, only affects the arrogant pretensions of the Schools, which would fain be considered as the only judges and keepers of such truths (as they are, no doubt, with regard to many other subjects), allowing the public to use them only while keeping the key to themselves – *quod mecum nescit, solus vult scire videri*. At the same time the more moderate claims of speculative philosophers are also taken care of. They still remain the exclusive keepers of a science which benefits the masses without their knowing it, that is to say the critique of reason. This critique can never become popular, nor does it need to, because, if on the one hand the public has no understanding of the fine-drawn arguments in support of useful truths, it is not troubled on the other hand by the equally subtle objections. It is different with the Schools, which, like anyone rising to this level of speculation, get involved with both the arguments in favour and the objections, and are bound, by means of a careful investigation of the rights of speculative reason, to prevent, once for all, the scandal which, sooner or later, is sure to be caused even among the masses, and which results from the quarrels in which metaphysicians (and, as such, ultimately also the clergy) become involved, if ignorant of our critique, and by which their doctrine becomes in the end entirely perverted. Thus, and thus alone, can one cut off at the very root *materialism, fatalism, atheism, free-thinking disbelief, fanaticism,* and *superstition,* which may become universally injurious, and finally *idealism* and *scepticism* also, which are more dangerous to the Schools, only passing with great difficulty into the public consciousness. If governments think it proper ever to interfere with the affairs of the learned, it would be far more consistent with their wise regard for science, as well as for society, to favour the freedom of such a criticism, by which alone the labours of reason can be established on a firm basis, than to support the ridiculous despotism of the Schools, which cry danger whenever their cobwebs are swept away, cobwebs of which the public has never taken the slightest notice, and the loss of which it can therefore never perceive.

The critique is not opposed to the *dogmatic procedure* of reason in its pure knowledge, as science (for it must always be dogmatic, that is, derive its proof from sure principles *a priori*), but to *dogmatism* only, that is, to the presumption that it is possible to make any progress with pure (philosophical) knowledge from concepts (from philosophical knowledge) such as reason has long been in the habit of employing, without first inquiring in what way, and by what right, it has come to possess them. Dogmatism is therefore the dogmatic procedure of pure reason, *without a preceding critique of its own powers;* and our opposition to this is not intended to defend that loquacious shallowness which arrogates to itself the name of popularity, much less that scepticism which makes short work of the whole of metaphysics. On the contrary, our critique is meant to form a necessary preparation in support of a thoroughly scientific system of metaphysics, which must necessarily be carried out dogmatically and strictly systematically, so as to satisfy all the demands, not so much of the public at large, as of the Schools. This is an indispensable demand for it has undertaken to carry out its work entirely *a priori*, and thus to carry it out to the complete satisfaction of speculative reason. In the execution of this plan, as traced out by the critique, that is, in a future system of metaphysics, we shall have to follow the strict method of the celebrated Wolff, the greatest of all dogmatic philosophers.

He was the first to give an example (and by his example initiated, in Germany, that spirit of thoroughness which is not yet extinct) of how the secure course of a science could be attained only through the lawful establishment of principles, the clear determination of concepts, the attempt at strictness of proof, and avoidance of taking bold leaps in our inferences. He was therefore most eminently qualified to give metaphysics the dignity of a science, if it had only occurred to him, by criticism of the organ, that is, of pure reason itself, to prepare his field in advance, an omission due not so much to himself as to the dogmatic mentality of his age, about which the philosophers of his own, as well as of all previous times, have no right to reproach one another. Those who reject both the method of Wolff and the procedure of the critique of pure reason, can have no other aim but to shake off the fetters of *science* altogether, and thus to change work into play, certainty into opinion, and philosophy into philodoxy.

With regard to this second edition, I have tried, as was but fair, to do all I could in order to remove, as far as possible, the difficulties and obscurities which – and I am not perhaps without fault here – have misled even the most acute thinkers in their assessment of my book. In the propositions themselves, and their proofs, likewise in the form and completeness of the whole plan, I have found nothing to alter, which is due partly to the extensive examination to which I had subjected them before submitting them to the public, and partly to the nature of the subject itself. For pure speculative reason is so constituted that it forms a true *organism*, in which everything is *organic*, the whole being there for the sake of every part, and every part for the sake of the whole, so that the smallest imperfection, whether a fault or a deficiency, must inevitably betray itself in use. I venture to hope that this system will maintain itself unchanged for the future also. It is not conceit which justifies me in this confidence, but the experimental evidence of achieving the same result, whether we proceed progressively from the smallest elements to the whole of pure reason, or retrogressively from the whole (for this also is given by the practical objects of reason) to every single part; the fact being that any attempt at altering even the smallest item at once produces contradictions, not only in the system, but in human reason in general. With regard to the *presentation*, however, much remains to be done; and for this purpose, I have endeavoured to introduce several improvements into this second edition. These improvements are intended to remove, first, misunderstandings with respect to the Aesthetic, especially concerning the concept of time; secondly, obscurities in the deduction of the concepts of reason; thirdly, a supposed want of sufficient evidence in the proofs of the principles of pure understanding; and finally, the false interpretation placed on the paralogisms with which we charged rational psychology. To this point (only to the end of the first chapter of the *Transcendental Dialectic*) do the changes of presentation* extend, and no further. Time was

---

* The only thing which might be called an addition, though in the method of proof only, is the new refutation of psychological *idealism*, and the strict (and as I believe the only possible) proof of the objective reality of outer intuition on p. B305. However innocent idealism may be considered with respect to the essential aims of metaphysics (though it is not so in reality), it remains a scandal to philosophy, and to human reason in general, that we should have to accept the existence of things outside us (from which we derive the whole material of knowledge for our own inner sense) on trust only, and have no satisfactory proof with which to counter any opponent who chooses to doubt it. Since there is some obscurity in the expressions used in the proof, from the third line to the sixth line, I beg to alter the passage as follows: '*But this permanent cannot be an intuition in me, for all grounds of determination of my existence which are to be met within me are representations; and as representations themselves require a permanent distinct from them, in relation to which their change, and so my existence in the time wherein they change, may be determined.*' It will probably be urged against this proof that, ultimately, I am immediately conscious only of that which is within me, that is, of my *representation* of external things, and that consequently it must still remain uncertain whether there be outside me anything corresponding to it, or not. But by inner *experience* I am conscious of *my existence* in time (consequently also of its determinability in time), and this is more than to be conscious of my representation only. It is identical with the *empirical consciousness of my existence*, which can itself be determined only by something connected with my existence, yet outside me. This consciousness of my existence in time is therefore connected as identical with the consciousness of a relation to something outside me; so that it is experience and not fiction, sense and not imagination, which inseparably connects the outer with my inner sense. The outer sense is by itself a relation of intuition to something real outside me; and its reality, as distinct from a purely imaginary character, rests entirely on its being inseparably connected with inner experience, as being the condition of its possibility. This is what happens here. If, to the *intellectual consciousness* of my existence, in the representation 'I am', which accompanies all my judgements and all acts of my understanding, I could at the same time connect a determination of my existence through *intellectual intuition*, then that

too short to do more, and besides, I did not, with regard to the rest, meet with any misapprehensions on the part of competent and impartial judges. These, even though I must not name them with the praise that is due to them, will easily perceive, in the proper place, that I have paid careful attention to their remarks.

These improvements, however, involve a small loss for the reader. It was inevitable, if the book was not to be made too voluminous, to leave out or abridge several passages which, though not essential to the completeness of the whole, are useful for other purposes, and may be missed by some readers. Only thus could I gain room for my new and more intelligible presentation of the subject, which, though it changes absolutely nothing with regard to propositions and even to their proofs, yet departs so considerably from the former, in the whole arrangement of the argument, that interpolations would not have been sufficient. This small loss, which every reader may easily redeem by consulting the first edition, will, I hope, be more

---

determination would not require the consciousness of a relation to something outside me. But although that intellectual consciousness does indeed come first, the inner intuition, in which alone my existence can be determined, is sensible and dependent on the condition of time. This determination, however, and therefore inner experience itself, depends upon something permanent which is not within me, consequently only upon something outside me, to which I must consider myself as standing in relation. Hence the reality of the outer sense is necessarily connected, in order to make experience possible at all, to the reality of the inner sense; that is, I am conscious with the same certainty, that there are things outside me which have a reference to my sense, as I am conscious that I exist in time. In order to ascertain to which given intuitions objects outside me really correspond (these intuitions belonging to the *outer sense*, and not to the faculty of imagination) we must in each single case apply the rules according to which experience in general (even inner experience) is distinguished from imagination, the proposition that there really is an outer experience being always taken for granted. It may be well to add here the remark that the representation of something *permanent* in existence is not the same as a *permanent representation*; for the latter is changeable and variable, as are all our representations, even those of matter, and may yet refer to something permanent, which must therefore be something external, and distinct from all my representations, the existence of which is necessarily included in the *determination* of my own existence, and constitutes with it but one experience, which could never take place internally, unless (in part) it were external also. How this should be possible admits here of as little explanation as something that is at rest in time, the co-existence of which with what is variable produces the concept of change.

than compensated for by the greater clarity of the present one.

I have observed with pleasure and thankfulness in various publications (containing either reviews or separate treatises), that the spirit of thoroughness is not yet dead in Germany, but has only been silenced for a short time by the clamour of a fashionable and pretentious licence of thought, and that the difficulties which beset the thorny path of my critique, which are to lead to a truly scientific and, as such, permanent and therefore most necessary study of pure reason, have not discouraged bold and clear heads from mastering my book. To these excellent men, who so happily combine thorough knowledge with a talent for lucid exposition (to which I can lay no claim), I leave the task of perfecting those things which are here defective in its presentation. There is no danger, in this case, of it being refuted, but there is of it not being understood. For my own part, I cannot henceforth enter into controversy, though I shall carefully attend to all suggestions, whether from friends or opponents, in order to use them in a future elaboration of the whole system, according to the plan traced out in this propaedeutic. As during these labours I have become somewhat advanced in years (this very month, I entered my sixty-fourth year), I must be careful how I use my time, if I am to carry out my plan of providing a metaphysics of nature, and a metaphysics of morals, which will confirm the truth of my critique both of speculative and of practical reason, and I must leave the elucidation of such obscurities as could at first be hardly avoided in such a work, and likewise the defence of the whole, to those excellent men who have made my teaching their own. At individual points every philosophical treatise may be open to objections (for it cannot be armed at all points, like a mathematical one), without the organic structure of the system, considered as a whole, being in the least endangered. Only a few people have that versatility of intellect to consider the whole of a system, when it is new; still fewer have an inclination for it, owing to a dislike of innovation. If we take single passages out of their context, and contrast them with each other, it is easy to pick out apparent contradictions, particularly in a work that progresses as free speech. In the eyes of those who rely on the judgement of others, such contradictions may shed on any work an unfavourable light; but they are easily removed by those who have grasped the idea of the whole. If a theory possesses stability in itself, then effect and counterforce, which at first seemed so threatening to it, serve only, in the course of time, to smooth out the uneven parts, and indeed, if men of insight, impartiality, and true popularity devote themselves to it, to achieve in a short time also the requisite elegance.

Königsberg, April 1787
Translated by Marcus Weigelt, based on Max Müller

Critique of Practical Reason

PART I
DOCTRINE OF THE ELEMENTS OF
PURE PRACTICAL REASON

BOOK I
ANALYTIC OF PURE PRACTICAL REASON

CHAPTER I
PRINCIPLES OF PURE PRACTICAL REASON

I. DEFINITION

Practical principles are propositions which contain a general determination of the will, having under it several practical rules. They are subjective, or maxims, when the condition is regarded by the subject as valid only for his own will. They are objective, or practical laws, when the condition is recognized as objective, i.e., as valid for the will of every rational being.

Remark

Assuming that *pure* reason can contain a practical ground sufficient to determine the will, then there are practical laws. Otherwise all practical principles are mere maxims. In the will of a rational being affected by feeling, there can be a conflict of maxims with the practical laws recognized by this being. For example, someone can take as his maxim not to tolerate any unavenged offense and yet see at the same time that this is only his own maxim and not a practical law and that, if it is taken as a rule for the will of every rational being, it would be inconsistent with itself.

In natural science the principles of what occurs (e.g., the principle of equivalence of action and reaction in the communication of motion) are at the same time laws of nature, for there the use of reason is theoretical and determined by the nature of the object. In practical philosophy, which has to do only with the grounds of determination of the will, the principles which a man makes for himself are not laws by which he is inexorably bound, because reason, in practice, has to do with a subject and especially with his faculty of desire, the special character of which may occasion variety in the rule. The practical rule is always a product of reason, because it prescribes action as a means to an effect which is its purpose. This rule, however, is an imperative for a being whose reason is not the sole determinant of the will. It is a rule characterized by an 'ought', which expresses the objective necessitation of the act and indicates that, if reason completely determined the will, the action would without exception take place according to the rule.

Imperatives, therefore, are valid objectively and are quite distinct from maxims, which are subjective principles. Imperatives determine either the conditions of causality of a rational being as an efficient cause only in respect to its effect and its sufficiency to bring this effect about, or they determine only the will, whether it be adequate to the effect or not. In the former case, imperatives would be hypothetical and would contain only precepts of skill; in the latter, on the contrary, they would be categorical and would alone be practical laws. Maxims are thus indeed principles, but they are not imperatives. Imperatives themselves, however, when they are conditional, i.e., when they determine the will not as such but only in respect to a desired effect, are hypothetical imperatives, which are practical precepts but not laws. Laws must completely determine the will as will, even before I ask whether I am capable of achieving a desired effect or what should be done to realize it. They must thus be categorical; otherwise they would not be laws, for they would lack the necessity which, in order to be practical, must be completely independent of pathological conditions, i.e., conditions only contingently related to the will.

Tell someone, for instance, that in his youth he should work and save in order not to want in his old age – that is a correct and important practical precept of the will. One easily sees, however, that the will is thereby directed to something else which he is assumed to desire; and, as to this desire, we must leave it up to the man himself if he foresees other resources than his own acquisitions, does not even hope to reach old age, or thinks that in case of need he can make do with little. Reason, from which alone a rule involving necessity can be derived, gives necessity to this precept, without which it would not be an imperative; but this necessity is dependent on only subjective conditions, and one cannot assume it in equal measure in all men. But for reason to give law it is required that reason need presuppose only itself, because the rule is objectively and universally valid only when it holds without any contingent subjective conditions which differentiate one rational being from another.

Now tell a man that he should never make a deceitful promise; this is a rule which concerns only his will regardless of whether any purposes he has can be achieved by it or not. Only the volition is to be completely determined a priori by this rule. If, now, it is found that this rule is practically right, it is a law, because it is a categorical imperative. Thus practical laws refer only to the will, irrespective of what is attained by its causality, and one can disregard this causality (as belonging to the sensuous world) in order to have the laws in their purity.

2. THEOREM I

All practical principles which presuppose an object (material) of the faculty of desire as the determining ground of the will are without exception empirical and can hand down no practical laws.

By the term 'material of the faculty of desire', I understand an object whose reality is desired. When the desire for this object precedes the practical rule and is the condition under which the latter becomes a principle, I say, first, that this principle is then always empirical. I say this because the determining ground of choice consists in the conception of an object and its relation to the subject, whereby the faculty of desire is determined to seek its realization. Such a relation to the subject is called pleasure in the reality of an object, and it must be presupposed as the condition of the possibility of the determination of choice. But we cannot know, a priori, from the idea of any object, whatever the nature of this idea, whether it will be associated with pleasure or displeasure or will be merely indifferent. Thus any such determining ground of choice must always be empirical, and the practical material principle which has it as a condition is likewise empirical.

Second, a principle which is based only on the subjective susceptibility to a pleasure or displeasure (which is never known except empirically and cannot be valid in the same form for all rational beings) cannot function as a law even to the subject possessing this susceptibility, because it lacks objective necessity, which must be known a priori. For this reason, such a principle can never furnish a practical law. It can, however, be counted as a maxim of a subject thus susceptible.

3. THEOREM II

All material practical principles are, as such, of one and the same kind and belong under the general principle of self-love or one's own happiness.

Pleasure from the representation of the existence of a thing, in so far as it is a determining ground of the desire for this thing, is based upon the susceptibility of the subject because it depends upon the actual existence of an object. Thus it belongs to sense (feeling) and not to the understanding, which expresses a relation of a representation to an object by concepts and not the relation of a representation to the subject by feelings. It is practical only in so far as the faculty of desire is determined by the sensation of agreeableness which the subject expects from the actual existence of the object. Now happiness is a rational being's consciousness of the agreeableness of life which without interruption accompanies his whole existence, and to make this the supreme ground for the determination of choice constitutes the principle of self-love. Thus all material principles, which place the determining ground of choice in the pleasure or displeasure to be received from the reality of any object whatsoever, are entirely of one kind. Without exception they belong under the principle of self-love or one's own happiness.

Corollary

All material practical rules place the ground of the determination of the will in the lower faculty of desire, and if there were no purely formal laws of the will adequate to determine it, we could not admit [the existence of] any higher faculty of desire.

Remark I

It is astonishing how otherwise acute men believe they can find a difference between the lower and the higher faculty of desire by noting whether the representations which are associated with pleasure have their origin in the senses or in the understanding. When one inquires into the determining grounds of desire and finds them in an expected agreeableness resulting from something or other, it is not a question of where the representation of this enjoyable object comes from, but merely of how much the object can be enjoyed. If a representation, even though it has its origin and status in the understanding, can determine choice only by presupposing a feeling of pleasure in the subject, then its becoming a determining ground of choice is wholly dependent on the nature of the inner sense, i.e., it depends on whether the latter can be agreeably affected by that representation. However dissimilar the representations of the objects, be they proper to understanding or even the reason instead of to the senses, the feeling of pleasure, by virtue of which they constitute the determining ground of the will (since it is the agreeableness and enjoyment which one expects from the object which impels the activity toward producing it) is always the same. This sameness lies not merely in the fact that all feelings of pleasure can be known only empirically, but even more in the fact that the feeling of pleasure always affects one and the same life-force which is manifested in the faculty of desire, and in this respect one determining ground can differ from any other only in degree. Otherwise how could one make a comparison with respect to magnitude between two determining grounds the ideas of which depend upon different faculties, in order to prefer the one which affects the faculty of desire to the greater extent? A man can return unread an instructive book which he cannot again obtain, in order not to miss the hunt; he can go away in the middle of a fine speech, in order not to be late for a meal; he can leave an intellectual conversation, which he otherwise enjoys, in order to take his place at the gambling table; he can even repulse a poor man whom it is usually a joy to aid, because he has only enough money in his pocket for a ticket to the theater. If the determination of the will rests on the feelings of agreeableness or disagreeableness which he expects from any cause, it is all the same to him through what kind of representation he is affected. The only thing he considers in making a choice is how great, how long-lasting, how easily obtained, and how often repeated this agreeableness is. As the man who wants money to spend does not care whether the gold in it was mined in the mountains or washed from the sand, provided it is accepted everywhere as having the same value, so also no man asks, when he is concerned only with the agreeableness of life, whether the representations are from sense or understanding; he asks only how much and how great is the pleasure which they will afford him over the longest time.

Only those who would like to deny to pure reason the power of determining the will without presupposing any feeling whatsoever could deviate so far from their own exposition as to describe as quite heterogeneous what they have previously brought under one and the same principle. Thus, for instance, a person can find satisfaction in the mere exercise of power, in the consciousness of spiritual strength in overcoming obstacles in the way of his designs, and in the cultivation of intellectual talents. We correctly call these the more refined joys and delights, because they are more in our power than others and do not wear out, but, rather, increase our capacity for even more of this kind of enjoyment; they delight and at the same time cultivate. But this is no reason to pass off such pleasures as a mode of determining the will different from that of the senses. For the possibility of these [refined] pleasures, too, presupposes, as the first condition of our delight, the existence in us of a corresponding feeling. So to assume this difference resembles the error of ignorant persons who wish to dabble in metaphysics and who imagine matter as so subtle, so supersubtle, that they almost get dizzy considering it, and then believe that they have conceived of a spiritual but still extended being. If, with Epicurus, we let virtue determine the will only because of the pleasure it promises, we cannot later blame him for holding that this pleasure is of the same sort as those of the coarsest senses. For we have no reason to charge him with relegating the representations by which this feeling is excited in us to the bodily senses only. So far as we can tell, he sought the source of many of them in the employment of the higher cognitive faculty. In accordance with the principles stated above, that did not and could not deter him, however, from holding that the pleasure which is given to us by these intellectual representations and which is the only means by which they can determine the will is of exactly the same kind as that coming from the senses.

Consistency is the highest obligation of a philosopher and yet the most rarely found. The ancient Greek schools afford more examples of it than we find in our syncretistic age, when a certain shallow and dishonest system of coalition between contradictory principles is devised because it is more acceptable to a public which is satisfied to know a little about everything and at bottom nothing, thus playing the jack-of-all-trades. The principle of one's own happiness, however much reason and understanding may be used in it, contains no other determinants for the will than those which belong to the lower faculty of desire. Either, then, no higher faculty of desire exists, or else pure reason alone must of itself be practical, i.e., it must be able to determine the will by the mere form of the practical rule without presupposing any feeling or consequently any representation of the pleasant or the unpleasant as the matter of the faculty of desire and as the empirical condition of its principles. Then only is reason a truly higher faculty of desire, but still only in so far as it determines the will by itself and not in the service of the inclinations. Subordinate to reason as the higher faculty of desire is the pathologically determinable faculty of desire, the latter being really and in kind different from the former, so that even the slightest admixture of its impulses impairs the strength and superiority of reason, just as taking anything empirical as the condition of a mathematical demonstration would degrade and destroy its force and value. Reason determines the will in a practical law directly, not through an intervening feeling of pleasure or displeasure, even if this pleasure is taken in the law itself. Only because, as pure reason, it can be practical is it possible for it to give law.

Remark II

To be happy is necessarily the desire of every rational but finite being, and thus it is an unavoidable determinant of his faculty of desire. Contentment with our existence is not, as it were, an inborn possession or bliss, which would presuppose a consciousness of our self-sufficiency; it is rather a problem imposed upon us by our own finite nature as a being of needs. These needs are directed to the material of the faculty of desire, i.e., to that which is related to a basic subjective feeling of pleasure or displeasure, determining what we require in order to be satisfied with our condition. But just because this material ground of determination [motive] can be known by the subject only empirically, it is impossible to regard this demand for happiness as a law, since the latter must contain exactly the same determining ground for the will of all rational beings and in all cases. Since, though, the concept of happiness always underlies the practical relation of objects to the faculty of desire, it is merely the general name for subjective grounds of determination [motives], and it determines nothing specific concerning what is to be done in a given practical problem; but in a practical problem this is what is alone important, for without some specific determination the problem cannot be solved. Where one places one's happiness is a question of the particular feeling of pleasure or displeasure in each person, and even of the differences in needs occasioned by changes of feeling in one and the same person. Thus a subjectively necessary law (as a law of nature) is objectively a very contingent practical principle which can and must be very different in different people. It therefore cannot yield any [practical] law, because in the desire for happiness it is not the form (accordance with law) but only the material which is decisive; it is a question only of whether I may expect pleasure from obedience to this law, and, if so, how much. Principles of self-love can indeed contain universal rules of skill (how to find means to some end), but these are only theoretical principles* as, for example, how someone who wants bread should construct a mill. But practical precepts based on them can never be universal, for what determines the faculty of desire is based on the feelings of pleasure and displeasure, which can never be assumed to be directed to the same objects by all people.

But suppose that finite rational beings were unanimous in the kind of objects their feelings of pleasure and pain had, and even in the means of obtaining the former and preventing the latter. Even then they could not set up the principle of self-love as a practical law, for the unanimity itself would be merely contingent. The determining ground would still be only subjectively valid and empirical, and it would not have the necessity which is conceived in every law, an objective necessity arising from a priori grounds, unless we hold this necessity to be not at all practical but only physical, maintaining that our action is as inevitably forced upon us by our inclination as yawning is by seeing others yawn. It would be better to maintain that there are no practical laws but merely counsels for the service of our desires than to elevate merely subjective principles to the rank of practical laws, which must have an objective and not just subjective necessity and which must be known a priori by reason instead of by experience, no matter how empirically universal. Even the rules of uniform phenomena are denominated natural laws (for example, mechanical laws) only if we really can understand them a priori or at least (as in the case of those of chemistry) suppose that they could be known in this way if our insight went deeper. Only in the case

---

* Propositions called 'practical' in mathematics or natural science should properly be called 'technical', for in these fields it is not a question of determining the will; they only indicate the manifold of a possible action which is adequate to bring about a certain effect, and are therefore just as theoretical as any proposition which asserts a connection between cause and effect. Whoever chooses the latter must also choose the former.

of subjective practical principles is it expressly made a condition that not objective but subjective conditions of choice must underlie them, and hence that they must be represented always as mere maxims and never as practical laws.

This remark may appear at first blush to be mere hairsplitting; actually, it defines the most important distinction which can be considered in practical investigations.

4. THEOREM III

If a rational being can think of his maxims as practical universal laws, he can do so only by considering them as principles which contain the determining grounds of the will because of their form and not because of their matter.

The material of a practical principle is the object of the will. This object either is the determining ground of the will or it is not. If it is, the rule of the will is subject to an empirical condition (to the relation of the determining representation to feelings of pleasure or displeasure), and therefore the rule is not a practical law. If all material of a law, i.e., every object of the will considered as a ground of its determination, is taken from it, nothing remains except the mere form of giving universal law. Therefore, a rational being either cannot think of his subjectively practical principles (maxims) as at the same time universal laws, or he must suppose that their mere form, through which they are fitted for being given as *universal* laws, is alone that which makes them a practical law.

Remark

What form in a maxim fits it for universal law-giving and what form does not do so can be distinguished without instruction by the most common understanding. I have, for example, made it my maxim to augment my property by every safe means. Now I have in my possession a deposit, the owner of which has died without leaving any record of it. Naturally, this case falls under my maxim. Now I want to know whether this maxim can hold as a universal practical law. I apply it, therefore, to the present case and ask if this maxim could take the form of a law, and consequently whether I could, by the maxim, make the law that every man is allowed to deny that a deposit has been made when no one can prove the contrary. I immediately realize that taking such a principle as a law would annihilate itself, because its result would be that no one would make a deposit. A practical law which I acknowledge as such must qualify for being universal law; this is an identical and therefore a self-evident proposition. Now, if I say that my will is subject to a practical law, I cannot put forward my inclination (in this case, my avarice) as fit to be a determining ground of a universal practical law. It is so far from being worthy of giving universal laws that in the form of universal law it must destroy itself.

It is therefore astonishing how intelligent men have thought of proclaiming as a universal practical law the desire for happiness, and therewith to make this desire the determining ground of the will merely because this desire is universal. Though elsewhere natural laws make everything harmonious, if one here attributed the universality of law to this maxim, there would be the extreme opposite of harmony, the most arrant conflict, and the complete annihilation of the maxim itself and its purpose. For the wills of all do not have one and the same object, but each person has his own (his own welfare), which, to be sure, can accidentally agree with the purposes of others who are pursuing their own, though this agreement is far from sufficing for a law because the occasional exceptions which one is permitted to make are endless and cannot be definitely comprehended in a universal rule. In this way a harmony may result resembling that depicted in a certain satirical poem as existing between a married couple bent on going to ruin, 'Oh, marvelous harmony, what he wants is what she wants'; or like the pledge which is said to have been given by Francis I to the Emperor Charles V, 'What my brother wants [Milan], that I want too.' Empirical grounds of decision are not fit for any external legislation, and they are just as little suited to an internal, for each man makes his own subject the foundation of his inclination, and in each person it is now one and now another inclination which has preponderance. To discover a law which would govern them all by bringing them into unison is absolutely impossible.

5. PROBLEM I

Granted that the mere legislative form of maxims is the sole sufficient determining ground of a will, find the character of the will which is determinable by it alone.

Since the mere form of a law can be thought only by reason and is consequently not an object of the senses and therefore does not belong among appearances, the conception of this form as the determining ground of the will is distinct from all determining grounds of events in nature according to the law of causality, for these grounds must themselves be appearances. Now, as no determining ground of the will except the universal legislative form [of its maxim] can serve as a law for it, such a will must be conceived as wholly independent of the natural law of appearances in their mutual relations, i.e., the law of causality. Such independence is called *freedom* in the strictest, i.e., transcendental, sense. Therefore, a will to which only the law-giving form of the maxim can serve as a law is a free will.

6. PROBLEM II

Granted that a will is free, find the law which alone is competent to determine it necessarily.

Since the material of the practical law, i.e., an object of the maxim, cannot be given except empirically, and since a free will must be independent of all empirical conditions (i.e., those belonging to the world of sense) and yet be determinable, a free will must find its ground of determination in the law, but independently of the material of the law. But besides the latter there is nothing in a law except the legislative form. Therefore, the legislative form, in so far as it is contained in the maxim, is the only thing which can constitute a determining ground of the [free] will.

Remark

Thus freedom and unconditional practical law reciprocally imply each other. I do not here ask whether they are actually different, instead of an unconditional law being merely the self-consciousness of pure practical reason, and thus identical with the positive concept of freedom. The question now is whether our *knowledge* of the unconditionally practical takes its inception from freedom or from the practical law. It cannot start from freedom, for this we can neither know immediately, since our first concept of it is negative, nor infer from experience, since experience reveals only the law of appearances and consequently the mechanism of nature, the direct opposite of freedom. It is therefore the moral law, of which we become immediately conscious as soon as we construct maxims for the will, which first presents itself to us; and, since reason exhibits it as a ground of determination which is completely independent of and not to be outweighed by any sensuous condition, it is the moral law which leads directly to the concept of freedom.

But how is the consciousness of that moral law possible? We can come to know pure practical laws in the same way we know pure theoretical principles, by attending to the necessity with which reason prescribes them to us and to the elimination from them of all empirical conditions, which reason directs. The concept of a pure will arises from the former, as the consciousness of a pure understanding from the latter. That this is the correct organization of our concepts, and that morality first reveals the concept of freedom to us while practical reason deeply perplexes the speculative with this concept which poses the most insoluble of problems, is shown by the following considerations. First, nothing in appearances is explained by the concept of freedom, but there the mechanism of nature must be the only clue. Second, there is the antinomy of pure reason which arises when reason aspires to the unconditioned in a causal series and which involves it in inconceivabilities on both sides, since at least mechanism has a use in the explanation of appearances, while no one would dare introduce freedom into science had not the moral law and, with it, practical reason come and forced this concept upon us.

Experience also confirms this order of concepts in us. Suppose that someone says his lust is irresistible when the desired object and opportunity are present. Ask him whether he would not control his passion if, in front of the house where he has this opportunity, a gallows were erected on which he would be hanged immediately after gratifying his lust. We do not have to guess very long what his answer would be. But ask him whether he thinks it would be possible for him to overcome his love of life, however great it may be, if his sovereign threatened him with the same sudden death unless he made a false deposition against an honorable man whom the ruler wished to destroy under a plausible pretext. Whether he would or not he perhaps will not venture to say; but that it would be possible for him he would certainly admit without hesitation. He judges, therefore, that he can do something because he knows that he ought, and he recognizes that he is free – a fact which, without the moral law, would have remained unknown to him.

7. FUNDAMENTAL LAW OF PURE PRACTICAL REASON

So act that the maxim of your will could always hold at the same time as the principle giving universal law.

Remark

Pure geometry has postulates as practical propositions, which, how-ever, contain nothing more than the presupposition that one *can* do something and that, when some result is needed, one *should* do it; these are the only propositions of pure geometry that deal with an existing thing. They are thus practical rules under a problematic condition of the will. Here, however, the rule says: One ought absolutely to act in a certain way. The practical rule is therefore unconditional and thus is thought of a priori as a categorically practical proposition. The practical rule, which is thus here a law, absolutely and directly determines the will objectively, for pure reason, practical in itself, is here directly law-giving. The will is thought of as independent of empirical conditions and consequently as pure will, determined by the mere form of law, and this ground of determination is regarded as the supreme condition of all maxims.

The thing is strange enough and has no parallel in the remainder of practical knowledge. For the a priori thought of the possibility of giving universal law, which is thus merely problematic, is unconditionally commanded as a law without borrowing anything from experience or from any external will. It is, however, not a prescription according to which an act should occur in order to make a desired effect possible, for such a rule is always physically conditioned; it is, on the contrary, a rule which determines the will a priori only with respect to the form of its maxims. Therefore, it is at least not impossible to conceive of a law that alone serves the purpose of the *subjective* form of principles and yet is a ground of determination by virtue of the *objective* form of a law in general. The consciousness of this fundamental law may be called a fact of reason, since one cannot ferret it out from antecedent data of reason, such as the consciousness of freedom (for this is not antecedently given), and since it forces itself upon us as a synthetic proposition a priori based on no pure or empirical intuition. It would be analytic if the freedom of the will were presupposed, but for this, as a positive concept, an intellectual intuition would be needed, and here we cannot assume it. In order to regard this law without any misinterpretation as given, one must note that it is not an empirical fact but the sole fact of pure reason, which by it proclaims itself as originating law (*sic volo, sic iubeo*) ['what I will I decree as law', Juvenal, Satire vi].

Corollary

Pure reason alone is practical of itself, and it gives (to man) a universal law, which we call the *moral law*.

Remark

The fact just mentioned is undeniable. One need only analyze the sentence which men pass upon the lawfulness of their actions to see in every case that their reason, incorruptible and self-constrained, in every action holds up the maxim of the will to the pure will, i.e., to itself regarded as a priori practical; and this it does regardless of what inclination may say to the contrary. Now this principle of morality, on account of the universality of its legislation which makes it the formal supreme determining ground of the will regardless of any subjective differences among men, is declared by reason to be a law for all rational beings in so far as they have a will, i.e., faculty of determining their causality through the representation of a rule, and consequently in so far as they are competent to determine their actions according to principles and thus to act according to practical a priori principles, which alone have the necessity which reason demands in a principle. It is thus not limited to human beings but extends to all finite beings having reason and will; indeed, it includes the Infinite Being as the supreme intelligence. In the former case, however, the law has the form of an imperative. For though we can suppose that men as rational beings have a pure will, since they are affected by wants and sensuous motives we cannot suppose them to have a holy will, a will incapable of any maxims which conflict with the moral law. The moral law for them, therefore, is an imperative, commanding categorically because it is unconditioned. The relation of such a will to this law is one of dependence under the name of 'obligation'. This term implies a constraint on an action, though this constraint is only that of reason and its objective law. Such an action is called [a] *duty*, because a pathologically affected (though not pathologically determined – and thus still free) choice involves a wish arising from subjective causes, and consequently such a choice often opposes pure objective grounds of determination. Such a will is therefore in need of the moral constraint of the resistance offered by practical reason, which may be called an inner but intellectual compulsion. In the supremely self-sufficing intelligence choice is correctly thought of as incapable of having any maxim that could not at the same time be objectively a law, and the concept of holiness, which is applied to it for this reason, elevates it not indeed above all practical laws but above all practically restrictive laws, and thus above obligation and duty. This holiness of will is, however, a practical Idea which must necessarily serve as a model which all finite rational beings must strive toward even though they cannot reach it. The pure moral law, which is itself for this reason called holy, constantly and rightly holds it before their eyes. The utmost that finite practical reason can accomplish is to make sure of the unending progress of its maxims toward this model and of the constancy of the finite rational being in making continuous progress. This is virtue, and as a naturally acquired faculty, it can never be perfect, because assurance in such a case never becomes apodictic certainty, and as a mere pretence it is very dangerous.

8. THEOREM IV

The *autonomy* of the will is the sole principle of all moral laws and of the duties conforming to them; *heteronomy* of choice, on the other hand, not only does not establish any obligation but is opposed to the principle of obligation and to the morality of the will.

The sole principle of morality consists in independence from all material of the law (i.e., a desired object) and in the accompanying determination of choice by the mere form of giving universal law which a maxim must be capable of having. That independence, however, is freedom in the negative sense, while this intrinsic legislation of pure and thus practical reason is freedom in the positive sense. Therefore, the moral law expresses nothing else than the autonomy of pure practical reason, i.e., freedom. This autonomy or freedom is itself the formal condition of all maxims, under which alone they can all agree with the supreme practical law. If, therefore, the material of volition, which cannot be other than an object of desire which is connected to the law, comes into the practical law *as a condition of its possibility*, there results heteronomy of choice, or dependence on natural laws in following some impulse or inclination; it is heteronomy because the will does not give itself the law but only directions for a reasonable obedience to pathological laws. The maxim, however, which for this reason can never contain in itself the form of prescribing universal law, not only produces no obligation but is itself opposed to the principle of pure practical reason and thus also to the moral disposition, even though the action which comes from it may conform to the law.

Remark I

Thus a practical precept which presupposes a material and therefore empirical condition must never be reckoned a practical law. For the law of pure will, which is free, puts the will in a sphere entirely different from the empirical, and the necessity which it expresses, not being a natural necessity, can consist only in the formal conditions of the possibility of a law in general. All the material of practical rules rests only on subjective conditions, which can afford the rules no universality for rational beings (except a merely conditioned one as in the case where I desire this or that, and then there is something which I must do in order to get it). Without exception, they all revolve about the principle of one's own happiness. *Now it is certainly undeniable that every volition must have an object and therefore a material;* but the material cannot be supposed, for this reason, to be the determining ground and condition of the maxim. If it were, the maxim could not be presented as giving universal law, because then the expectation of the existence of the object would be the determining cause of the choice, the dependence of the faculty of desire on the existence of some thing would have to be made basic to volition, and this dependence would have to be sought out in empirical conditions and therefore never could be a foundation of a necessary and universal rule. Thus the happiness of others may be the object of the will of a rational being, but if it were the determining ground of the maxim, not only would one have to presuppose that we find in the welfare of others a natural satisfaction but also one would have to find a want such as that which is occasioned in some men by a sympathetic disposition. This want, however, I cannot presuppose in every rational being, certainly not in God. The material of the maxim can indeed remain but cannot be its condition, for then it would not be fit for a law. The mere form of a law, which limits its material, must be a condition for adding this material to the will but not presuppose the material as the condition of the will. Let the material content be, for example, my own happiness. If I attribute this to everyone, as in fact I may attribute it to all finite beings, it can become an objective practical law only if I include within it the happiness of others. Therefore, the law that we should further the happiness of others arises not from the presupposition that this law is an object of everyone's choice but from the fact that the form of universality, which reason requires as condition for giving to the maxim of self-love the objective validity of law, is itself the determining ground of the will. Therefore not the object, i.e., the happiness of others, was the determining ground of the pure will but rather it was the lawful form alone. Through it I restricted my maxim, founded on inclination, by giving it the universality of a law, thus making it conformable to pure practical reason. From this limitation alone, and not from the addition of any external drive, the concept of obligation arises to extend the maxim of self-love also to the happiness of others.

Remark II

When one's own happiness is made the determining ground of the will, the result is the direct opposite of the principle of morality; and I have previously shown that, whenever the determining ground which is to serve as a law is located elsewhere than in the legislative form of the maxim, we have to reckon with this result. This conflict is not, however, merely logical, as is that between empirically conditioned rules which someone might nevertheless wish to erect into necessary principles of knowledge; it is rather a practical conflict, and, were the voice of reason with respect to the will not so distinct, so irrepressible, and so clearly audible to even the commonest man, it would drive morality to ruin. It can maintain itself only in the perplexing speculations of the schools which have temerity enough to close their ears to that heavenly voice in order to uphold a theory that costs no brainwork.

Suppose that an acquaintance whom you otherwise liked were to attempt to justify himself before you for having borne false witness by appealing to what he regarded as the holy duty of consulting his own happiness and, then, by recounting all the advantages he had gained thereby, pointing out the prudence he had shown in securing himself against detection, even by yourself, to whom alone he now reveals the secret only in order that he may be able at any time to deny it. And suppose that he then affirmed, in all seriousness, that he had thereby fulfilled a true human duty – you would either laugh in his face or shrink from him in disgust, even though you would not have the least grounds for objecting to such measures if someone regulated his principles solely with a view to his own advantage. Or suppose someone recommends to you as steward a man to whom you could blindly trust your affairs and, in order to inspire you with confidence, further extols him as a prudent man who has a masterly understanding of his own interest and is so indefatigably active that he misses no opportunity to further it; furthermore, lest you should be afraid of finding a vulgar selfishness in him, he praises the good taste with which he lives, not seeking his pleasure in making money or in coarse wantonness, but in the increase of his knowledge, in instructive conversation with a select circle, and even in relieving the needy. But, he adds, he is not particular as to the means (which, of course, derive their value only from the end), being as willing to use another's money and property as his own, provided only that he knows he can do so safely and without discovery. You would believe that the person making such a recommendation was either mocking you or had lost his mind. So distinct and sharp are the boundaries between morality and self-love that even the commonest eye cannot fail to distinguish whether a thing belongs to the one or the other. The few remarks which follow may appear superfluous where the truth is so obvious, but they serve at least to furnish somewhat greater distinctness to the judgement of common sense.

The principle of happiness can indeed give maxims, but never maxims which are competent to be laws of the will, even if universal happiness were made the object. For, since the knowledge of this rests on mere data of experience, as each judgement concerning it depends very much on the very changeable opinion of each person, it can give general but never universal rules; that is, the rules it gives will on the average be most often the right ones for this purpose, but they will not be rules which must hold always and necessarily. Consequently, no practical laws can be based on this principle. Since here an object of choice is made the basis of the rule and therefore must precede it, the rule cannot be founded upon or related to anything other than what one approves; and thus it refers to and is based on experience. Hence the variety of judgement must be infinite. This principle, therefore, does not prescribe the same practical rules to all rational beings, even though all the rules go under the same name – that of happiness. The moral law, however, is thought of as objectively necessary only because it holds good for everyone having reason and will.

The maxim of self-love (prudence) merely advises; the law of morality commands. Now there is a great difference between that which we are advised to do and that which we are obligated to do.

What is required in accordance with the principle of autonomy of choice is easily and without hesitation seen by the commonest intelligence; what is to be done under the presupposition of its heteronomy is hard to see and requires knowledge of the world. That is to say, what duty is, is plain of itself to everyone, but what is to bring true, lasting advantage to our whole existence is veiled in impenetrable obscurity, and much prudence is required to adapt the practical rule based upon it even tolerably to the ends of life by making suitable exceptions to it. But the moral law commands the most unhesitating obedience from everyone; consequently, the decision as to what is to be done in accordance with it must not be so difficult that even the commonest and most unpracticed understanding without any worldly prudence should go wrong in making it.

It is always in everyone's power to satisfy the commands of the categorical command of morality; this is but seldom possible with respect to the empirically conditioned precept of happiness, and it is far from being possible, even in respect to a single purpose, for everyone. The reason is that in the former it is only a question of the maxim, which must be genuine and pure, but in the latter it is also a question of capacity and physical ability to realize a desired object. A command that everyone should seek to make himself happy would be foolish, for no one commands another to do what he already invariably wishes to do. One must only prescribe to him the rules for achieving his goal, or, better, provide him the means, for he is not able to do all that he wants to do. But to command morality under the name of duty is very reasonable, for its precept will not, for one thing, be willingly obeyed by everyone when it is in conflict with his inclinations. Then, regarding the means of obeying this law, there is no need to teach them, for in this respect whatever he wills to do he also can do.

He who has lost at play may be vexed at himself and his imprudence; but when he is conscious of having cheated at play, even though he has won, he must despise himself as soon as he compares himself with the moral law. This must therefore be something other than the principle of one's own happiness. For to have to say to himself, 'I am a worthless man, though I've filled my purse', he must have a criterion of judgement different from that by which he approves of himself and says, 'I am a prudent man, for I've enriched my treasure.'

Finally, there is something else in the idea of our practical reason which accompanies transgression of a moral law, namely, its culpability. Becoming a partaker in happiness cannot be united with the concept of punishment as such. For even though he who punishes can do so with the benevolent intention of directing this punishment to this end, it must nevertheless be justified as punishment, i.e., as mere harm in itself, so that even the punished person, if it stopped there and he could see no glimpse of kindness behind the harshness, would yet have to admit that justice had been done and that his reward perfectly fitted his behavior. In every punishment as such there must first be justice, and this constitutes the essence of the concept. With it benevolence may, of course, be associated, but the person who deserves punishment has not the least reason to count on it. Punishment is physical harm which, even if not bound as a natural consequence to the morally bad, ought to be bound to it as a consequence according to principles of moral legislation. Now if every crime, without regard to the physical consequences to him who commits it, is punishable, i.e., involves a forfeiture of happiness at least in part, it is obviously absurd to say that the crime consists just in the fact that one has brought punishment upon himself and thus has injured his own happiness (which, according to the principle of self-love, must be the correct concept of all crime). In this way, the punishment would be the reason for calling anything a crime, and justice would consist in withholding all punishment and even hindering natural punishment, for there would be no longer any evil in an action if the harm which would otherwise follow upon it and because of which alone the action was called evil would now be averted. To look upon all punishment and reward as machinery in the hand of a higher power, which by this means sets rational beings in action toward their final purpose (happiness), so obviously reduces the will to a mechanism destructive of freedom that it need not detain us.

More refined, but equally untrue, is the pretence of those who assume a certain particular moral sense which, instead of reason, determines the moral law, and in accordance with which the consciousness of virtue is directly associated with satisfaction and enjoyment, while consciousness of vice is associated with mental restlessness and pain. Thus everything is reduced to the desire for one's own happiness. Without repeating what has already been said, I will only indicate the fallacy they fall into. In order to imagine the vicious person as tormented with mortification by the consciousness of his transgressions, they must presuppose that he is, in the core of his character, at least to a certain degree morally good, just as they have to think of the person who is gladdened by the consciousness of doing dutiful acts as already virtuous. Therefore, the concept of morality and duty must precede all reference to this satisfaction and cannot be derived from it. One must already value the importance of what we call duty, the respect for the moral law, and the immediate worth which a person obtains in his own eyes through obedience to it, in order to feel satisfaction in the consciousness of his conformity to law or the bitter remorse which accompanies his awareness that he has transgressed it. Therefore, this satisfaction or spiritual unrest cannot be felt prior to the knowledge of obligation, nor can it be made the basis of the latter. One must be at least halfway honest even to be able to have an idea of these feelings. For the rest, as the human will by virtue of its freedom is directly determined by the moral law, I am far from denying that frequent practice in accordance with this determining ground can itself finally cause a subjective feeling of satisfaction. Indeed, it is a duty to establish and cultivate this feeling, which alone deserves to be called the moral feeling. But the concept of duty cannot be derived from it, for we would have to presuppose a feeling for law as such and regard as an object of sensation what can only be thought by reason. If this did not end up in the flattest contradiction, it would destroy every concept of duty and fill its place with a merely mechanical play of refined inclinations, sometimes contending with the coarser.

Translated by Lewis White Beck

Idea for a Universal History with a Cosmopolitan Purpose*

Whatever conception of the freedom of the will one may form in terms of metaphysics, the will's manifestations in the world of phenomena, i.e. human actions, are determined in accordance with natural laws, as is every other natural event. History is concerned with giving an account of these phenomena, no matter how deeply concealed their causes may be, and it allows us to hope that, if it examines the free exercise of the human will *on a large scale*, it will be able to discover a regular progression among freely willed actions. In the same way, we may hope that what strikes us in the actions of individuals as confused and fortuitous may be recognized, in the history of the entire species, as a steadily advancing but slow development of man's original capacities. Thus marriages, births, and deaths do not seem to be subject to any rule by which their numbers could be calculated in advance, since the free human will has such a great influence upon them; and yet the annual statistics for them in large countries prove that they are just as subject to constant natural laws as are the changes in the weather, which in themselves are so inconsistent that their individual occurrence cannot be determined in advance, but which nevertheless do not fail as a whole to sustain the growth of plants, the flow of rivers, and other natural functions in a uniform and uninterrupted course. Individual men and even entire nations little imagine that, while they are pursuing their own ends, each in his own way and often in opposition to others, they

* A passage printed this year among other brief notices in the twelfth issue of the *Gothaische Gelehrte Zeitungen*, based, no doubt, on a conversation of mine with a passing scholar, calls for the present elucidation, without which the passage referred to would be unintelligible.

are unwittingly guided in their advance along a course intended by nature. They are unconsciously promoting an end which, even if they knew what it was, would scarcely arouse their interest.

Since men neither pursue their aims purely by instinct, as the animals do, nor act in accordance with any integral, prearranged plan like rational cosmopolitans, it would appear that no law-governed history of mankind is possible (as it would be, for example, with bees or beavers). We can scarcely help feeling a certain distaste on observing their activities as enacted in the great world-drama, for we find that, despite the apparent wisdom of individual actions here and there, everything as a whole is made up of folly and childish vanity, and often of childish malice and destructiveness. The result is that we do not know what sort of opinion we should form of our species, which is so proud of its supposed superiority. The only way out for the philosopher, since he cannot assume that mankind follows any rational *purpose of its own* in its collective actions, is for him to attempt to discover a *purpose in nature* behind this senseless course of human events, and decide whether it is after all possible to formulate in terms of a definite plan of nature a history of creatures who act without a plan of their own. – Let us now see if we can succeed in finding a guiding principle for such a history, and then leave it to nature to produce someone capable of writing it along the lines suggested. Thus nature produced a Kepler who found an unexpected means of reducing the eccentric orbits of the planets to definite laws, and a Newton who explained these laws in terms of a universal natural cause.

FIRST PROPOSITION

All the natural capacities of a creature are destined sooner or later to be developed completely and in conformity with their end. This can be verified in all animals by external and internal or anatomical examination. An organ which is not meant for use or an arrangement which does not fulfil its purpose is a contradiction in the teleological theory of nature. For if we abandon this basic principle, we are faced not with a law-governed nature, but with an aimless, random process, and the dismal reign of chance replaces the guiding principle of reason.

SECOND PROPOSITION

In man (as the only rational creature on earth), *those natural capacities which are directed towards the use of his reason are such that they could be fully developed only in the species, but not in the individual.* Reason, in a creature, is a faculty which enables that creature to extend far beyond the limits of natural instinct the rules and intentions it follows in using its various powers, and the range of its projects is unbounded. But reason does not itself work instinctively, for it requires trial, practice and instruction to enable it to progress gradually from one stage of insight to the next. Accordingly, every individual man would have to live for a vast length of time if he were to learn how to make complete use of all his natural capacities; or if nature has fixed only a short term for each man's life (as is in fact the case), then it will require a long, perhaps incalculable series of generations, each passing on its enlightenment to the next, before the germs implanted by nature in our species can be developed to that degree which corresponds to nature's original intention. And the point of time at which this degree of development is reached must be the goal of man's aspirations (at least as an idea in his mind), or else his natural capacities would necessarily appear by and large to be purposeless and wasted. In the latter case, all practical principles would have to be abandoned, and nature, whose wisdom we must take as axiomatic in judging all other situations, would incur the suspicion of indulging in childish play in the case of man alone.

THIRD PROPOSITION

Nature has willed that man should produce entirely by his own initiative everything which goes beyond the mechanical ordering of his animal existence, and that he should not partake of any other happiness or perfection than that which he has procured for himself without instinct and by his own reason. For nature does nothing unnecessarily and is not extravagant in the means employed to reach its ends. Nature gave man reason, and freedom of will based upon reason, and this in itself was a clear indication of nature's intention as regards his endowments. For it showed that man was not meant to be guided by instinct or equipped and instructed by innate knowledge; on the contrary, he was meant to produce everything out of himself. Everything had to be entirely of his own making – the discovery of a suitable diet, of clothing, of external security and defence (for which nature gave him neither the bull's horns, the lion's claws, nor the dog's teeth, but only his hands), as well as all the pleasures that can make life agreeable, and even his insight and circumspection and the goodness of his will. Nature seems here to have taken pleasure in exercising the strictest economy and to have measured out the basic animal equipment so sparingly as to be just enough for the most pressing needs of the beginnings of existence. It seems as if nature had intended that man, once he had finally worked his way up from the uttermost barbarism to the highest degree of skill, to inner perfection in his manner of thought and thence (as far as is possible on earth) to happiness, should be able to take for himself the entire credit for doing so and have only himself to thank for it. It seems that nature has worked more with a view to man's rational *self-esteem* than to his mere well-being. For in the actual course of human affairs, a whole host of hardships awaits him. Yet nature does not seem to have been concerned with seeing that man should live agreeably, but with seeing that he should work his way onwards to make himself by his own conduct worthy of life and well-being. What remains disconcerting about all this is firstly, that the earlier generations seem to perform their laborious tasks only for the sake of the later ones, so as to prepare for them a further stage from which they can raise still higher the structure intended by nature; and secondly, that only the later generations will in fact have the good fortune to inhabit the building on which a whole series of their forefathers (admittedly, without any conscious intention) had worked without themselves being able to share in the happiness they were preparing. But no matter how puzzling this may be, it will appear as necessary as it is puzzling if we simply assume that one animal species was intended to have reason, and that, as a class of rational beings who are mortal as individuals but immortal as a species, it was still meant to develop its capacities completely.

FOURTH PROPOSITION

The means which nature employs to bring about the development of innate capacities is that of antagonism within society, in so far as this antagonism becomes in the long run the cause of a law-governed social order. By antagonism, I mean in this context the *unsocial sociability* of men, that is, their tendency to come together in society, coupled, however, with a continual resistance which constantly threatens to break this society up. This propensity is obviously rooted in human nature. Man has an inclination to *live in society*, since he feels in this state more like a man, that is, he feels able to develop his natural capacities. But he also has a great tendency to *live as an individual*, to isolate himself, since he also encounters in himself the unsocial characteristic of wanting to direct everything in accordance with his own ideas. He therefore expects resistance all around, just as he knows of himself that he is in turn inclined to offer resistance to others. It is this very resistance which awakens all man's powers and induces him to overcome his tendency to laziness. Through the desire for honour, power or property, it drives him to seek status among his fellows, whom he cannot *bear* yet cannot *bear to leave*. Then the first true steps are taken from barbarism to culture, which in fact consists in the social worthiness of man. All man's talents are now gradually developed, his taste cultivated, and by a continued process of enlightenment, a beginning is made towards establishing a way of thinking which can with time transform the primitive natural capacity for moral discrimination into definite practical principles; and thus a *pathologically* enforced social union is transformed into a *moral* whole. Without these asocial qualities (far from admirable in themselves) which cause the resistance inevitably encountered by each individual as he furthers his self-seeking pretensions, man would live an Arcadian, pastoral existence of perfect concord, self-sufficiency and mutual love. But all human talents would remain hidden for ever in a dormant state, and men, as good-natured as the sheep they tended, would scarcely render their existence more valuable than that of their animals. The end for which they were created, their rational nature, would be an unfilled void. Nature should thus be thanked for fostering social incompatibility, enviously competitive vanity, and insatiable desires for possession or even power. Without these desires, all man's excellent natural capacities would never be roused to develop. Man wishes concord, but nature, knowing better what is good for his species, wishes discord. Man wishes to live comfortably and pleasantly, but nature intends that he should abandon idleness and inactive self-sufficiency and plunge instead into labour and hardships, so that he may by his own adroitness find means of liberating himself from them in turn. The natural impulses which make this possible, the sources of the very unsociableness and continual resistance which cause so many evils, at the same time encourage man towards new exertions of his powers and thus towards further development of his natural capacities. They would thus seem to indicate the design of a wise creator – not, as it might seem, the hand of a malicious spirit who had meddled in the creator's glorious work or spoiled it out of envy.

FIFTH PROPOSITION

The greatest problem for the human species, the solution of which nature compels him to seek, is that of attaining a civil society which can administer justice universally. The highest purpose of nature – i.e. the development of all natural capacities – can be fulfilled for mankind only in society, and nature intends that man should accomplish this, and indeed all his appointed ends, by his own efforts. This purpose can be fulfilled only in a society which has not only the greatest freedom, and therefore a continual antagonism among its members, but also the most precise specification and preservation of the limits of this freedom in order that it can co-exist with the freedom of others. The highest task which nature has set for mankind must therefore be that of establishing a society in which *freedom under external laws* would be combined to the greatest possible extent with irresistible force, in other words of establishing a perfectly *just civil constitution*. For only through the solution and fulfilment of this task can nature accomplish its other intentions with our species. Man, who is otherwise so enamoured with unrestrained freedom, is forced to enter this state of restriction by sheer necessity. And this is indeed the most stringent of all forms of necessity, for it is imposed by men upon themselves, in that their inclinations make it impossible for them to exist side by side for long in a state of wild freedom. But once enclosed within a precinct like that of civil union, the same inclinations have the most beneficial effect. In the same way, trees in a forest, by seeking to deprive each other of air and sunlight, compel each other to find these by upward growth, so that they grow beautiful and straight – whereas those which put out branches at will, in freedom and in isolation from others, grow stunted, bent and twisted. All the culture and art which adorn mankind and the finest social order man creates are fruits of his unsociability. For it is compelled by its own nature to discipline itself, and thus, by enforced art, to develop completely the germs which nature implanted.

SIXTH PROPOSITION

This problem is both the most difficult and the last to be solved by the human race. The difficulty (which the very idea of this problem clearly presents) is this: if he lives among others of his own species, man is *an animal who needs a master*. For he certainly abuses his freedom in relation to others of his own kind. And even though, as a rational creature, he desires a law to impose limits on the freedom of all, he is still misled by his self-seeking animal inclinations into exempting himself from the law where he can. He thus requires a *master* to break his self-will and force him to obey a universally valid will under which everyone can be free. But where is he to find such a master? Nowhere else but in the human species. But this master will also be an animal who needs a master. Thus while man may try as he will, it is hard to see how he can obtain for public justice a supreme authority which would itself be just, whether he seeks this authority in a single person or in a group of many persons selected for this purpose. For each one of them will always misuse his freedom if he does not have anyone above him to apply force to him as the laws should require it. Yet the highest authority has to be just *in itself* and yet also a *man*. This is therefore the most difficult of all tasks, and a perfect solution is impossible. Nothing straight can be constructed from such warped wood as that which man is made of. Nature only requires of us that we should approximate to this idea.* A further reason why this task must be the last to be accomplished is that man needs for it a correct conception of the nature of a possible constitution, great experience tested in many affairs of the world, and above all else a good will prepared to accept the findings of this experience. But three factors such as these will not easily be found in conjunction, and if they are, it will happen only at a late stage and after many unsuccessful attempts.

SEVENTH PROPOSITION

The problem of establishing a perfect civil constitution is subordinate to the problem of a law-governed external relationship with other states, and cannot be solved unless the latter is also solved. What is the use of working for a law-governed civil constitution among individual men, i.e., of planning a *commonwealth?* The same unsociability which forced men to do so gives rise in turn to a situation whereby each commonwealth, in its external relations (i.e., as a state in relation to other states), is

* Man's role is thus a highly artificial one. We do not know how it is with the inhabitants of other planets and with their nature, but if we ourselves execute this commission of nature well, we may surely flatter ourselves that we occupy no mean status among our neighbours in the cosmos. Perhaps their position is such that each individual can fulfil his destiny completely within his own lifetime. With us it is otherwise; only the species as a whole can hope for this.

in a position of unrestricted freedom. Each must accordingly expect from any other precisely the same evils which formerly oppressed individual men and forced them into a law-governed civil state. Nature has thus again employed the unsociableness of men, and even of the large societies and states which human beings construct, as a means of arriving at a condition of calm and security through their inevitable *antagonism*. Wars, tense and unremitting military preparations, and the resultant distress which every state must eventually feel within itself, even in the midst of peace – these are the means by which nature drives nations to make initially imperfect attempts, but finally, after many devastations, upheavals and even complete inner exhaustion of their powers, to take the step which reason could have suggested to them even without so many sad experiences – that of abandoning a lawless state of savagery and entering a federation of peoples in which every state, even the smallest, could expect to derive its security and rights not from its own power or its own legal judgement, but solely from this great federation (*Fœdus Amphictyonum*), from a united power and the law-governed decisions of a united will. However wild and fanciful this idea may appear – and it has been ridiculed as such when put forward by the Abbé St Pierre and Rousseau (perhaps because they thought that its realization was so imminent) – it is none the less the inevitable outcome of the distress in which men involve one another. For this distress must force the states to make exactly the same decision (however difficult it may be for them) as that which man was forced to make, equally unwillingly, in his savage state – the decision to renounce his brutish freedom and seek calm and security within a law-governed constitution. All wars are accordingly so many attempts (not indeed by the intention of men, but by the intention of nature) to bring about new relations between states, and, by the destruction or at least the dismemberment of old entities, to create new ones. But these new bodies, either in themselves or alongside one another, will in turn be unable to survive, and will thus necessarily undergo further revolutions of a similar sort, till finally, partly by an optimal internal arrangement of the civil constitution, and partly by common external agreement and legislation, a state of affairs is created which, like a civil commonwealth, can maintain itself *automatically*.

Whether we should firstly expect that the states, by an Epicurean concourse of efficient causes, should enter by random collisions (like those of small material particles) into all kinds of formations which are again destroyed by new collisions, until they arrive *by chance* at a formation which can survive in its existing form (a lucky accident which is hardly likely ever to occur); or whether we should assume as a second possibility that nature in this case follows a regular course in leading our species gradually upwards from the lower level of animality to the highest level of humanity through forcing man to employ an art which is none the less his own, and hence that nature develops man's original capacities by a perfectly regular process within this apparently disorderly arrangement; or whether we should rather accept the third possibility that nothing at all, or at least nothing rational, will anywhere emerge from all these actions and counter-actions among men as a whole, that things will remain as they have always been, and that it would thus be impossible to predict whether the discord which is so natural to our species is not preparing the way for a hell of evils to overtake us, however civilized our condition, in that nature, by barbaric devastation, might perhaps again destroy this civilized state and all the cultural progress hitherto achieved (a fate against which it would be impossible to guard under a rule of blind chance, with which the state of lawless freedom is in fact identical, unless we assume that the latter is secretly guided by the wisdom of nature) – these three possibilities boil down to the question of whether it is rational to assume that the order of nature is *purposive* in its parts but *purposeless* as a whole.

While the purposeless state of savagery did hold up the development of all the natural capacities of human beings, it none the less finally forced them, through the evils in which it involved them, to leave this state and enter into a civil constitution in which all their dormant capacities could be developed. The same applies to the barbarous freedom of established states. For while the full development of natural capacities is here likewise held up by the expenditure of each commonwealth's whole resources on armaments against the others, and by the depredations caused by war (but most of all by the necessity of constantly remaining in readiness for war), the resultant evils still have a beneficial effect. For they compel our species to discover a law of equilibrium to regulate the essentially healthy hostility which prevails among the states and is produced by their freedom. Men are compelled to reinforce this law by introducing a system of united power, hence a cosmopolitan system of general political security. This state of affairs is not completely free from *danger*, lest human energies should lapse into inactivity, but it is also not without a principle of *equality* governing the *actions and counter-actions* of these energies, lest they should destroy one another. When it is little beyond the half-way mark in its development, human nature has to endure the hardest of evils under the guise of outward prosperity before this final step (i.e., the union of states) is taken; and Rousseau's preference for the state of savagery does not appear so very mistaken if only we leave out of consideration this last stage which our species still has to surmount. We are *cultivated* to a high degree by art and science. We are *civilized* to the point of excess in all kinds of social courtesies and proprieties. But we are still a long way from the point where we could consider ourselves *morally* mature. For while the idea of morality is indeed present in culture, an application of this idea which only extends to the semblances of morality, as in love of honour and outward propriety, amounts merely to civilization. But as long as states apply all their resources to their vain and violent schemes of expansion, thus incessantly obstructing the slow and laborious efforts of their citizens to cultivate their minds, and even deprive them of all support in these efforts, no progress in this direction can be expected. For a long internal process of careful work on the part of each commonwealth is necessary for the education of its citizens. But all good enterprises which are not grafted on to a morally good attitude of mind are nothing but illusion and outwardly glittering misery. The human race will no doubt remain in this condition until it has worked itself out of the chaotic state of its political relations in the way I have described.

EIGHTH PROPOSITION

The history of the human race as a whole can be regarded as the realization of a hidden plan of nature to bring about an internally – and for this purpose also externally – perfect political constitution as the only possible state within which all natural capacities of mankind can be developed completely. This proposition follows from the previous one. We can see that philosophy too may have its *chiliastic* expectations; but they are of such a kind that their fulfilment can be hastened, if only indirectly, by a knowledge of the idea they are based on, so that they are anything but overfanciful. The real test is whether experience can discover anything to indicate a purposeful natural process of this kind. In my opinion, it can discover *a little*; for this cycle of events seems to take so long a time to complete, that the small part of it traversed by mankind up till now does not allow us to determine with certainty the shape of the whole cycle, and the relation of its parts to the whole. It is no easier than it is to determine, from all hitherto available astronomical observations, the path which our sun with its whole swarm of satellites is following within the vast system of the fixed stars; although from the general premise that the universe is constituted as a system and from the little which has been learnt by observation, we can conclude with sufficient certainty that a movement of this kind does exist in reality. Nevertheless, human nature is such that it cannot be indifferent even to the most remote epoch which may eventually affect our species, so long as this epoch can be expected with certainty. And in the present case, it is especially hard to be indifferent, for it appears that we might by our own rational projects accelerate the coming of this period which will be so welcome to our descendants. For this reason, even the faintest signs of its approach will be extremely important to us. The mutual relationships between states are already so sophisticated that none of them can neglect its internal culture without losing power and influence in relation to the others. Thus the purpose of nature is at least fairly well safeguarded (if not actually furthered) even by the ambitious schemes of the various states. Furthermore, civil freedom can no longer be so easily infringed without disadvantage to all trades and industries, and especially to commerce, in the event of which the state's power in its external relations will also decline. But this freedom is gradually increasing. If the citizen is deterred from seeking his personal welfare in any way he chooses which is consistent with the freedom of others, the vitality of business in general and hence also the strength of the whole are held in check. For this reason, restrictions placed upon personal activities are increasingly relaxed, and general freedom of religion is granted. And thus, although folly and caprice creep in at times, *enlightenment* gradually arises. It is a great benefit which the human race must reap even from its rulers' self-seeking schemes of expansion, if only they realize what is to their own advantage. But this enlightenment, and with it a certain sympathetic interest which the enlightened man inevitably feels for anything good which he comprehends fully, must gradually spread upwards towards the thrones and even influence their principles of government. But while, for example, the world's present rulers have no money to spare for public educational institutions or indeed for anything which concerns the world's best interests (for everything has already been calculated out in advance for the next war), they will none the less find that it is to their own advantage at least not to hinder their citizens' private efforts in this direction, however weak and slow they may be. But eventually, war itself gradually becomes not only a highly artificial undertaking, extremely uncertain in its outcome for both parties, but also a very dubious risk to take, since its aftermath is felt by the state in the shape of a constantly increasing national debt (a modern invention) whose repayment becomes interminable. And in addition, the effects which an upheaval in any state produces upon all the others in our continent, where all are so closely linked by trade, are so perceptible that these other states are forced by their own insecurity to offer themselves as arbiters, albeit without legal authority, so that they indirectly prepare the way for a great political body of the future, without precedent in the past. Although this political body exists for the present only in the roughest of outlines, it none the less seems as if a feeling is beginning to stir in all its members, each of which has an interest in maintaining the whole. And this encourages the hope that, after many revolutions, with all their transforming effects, the highest purpose of nature, a universal *cosmopolitan existence*, will at last be realized as the matrix within which all the original capacities of the human race may develop.

NINTH PROPOSITION

A philosophical attempt to work out a universal history of the world in accordance with a plan of nature aimed at a perfect civil union of mankind, must be regarded as possible and even as capable of furthering the purpose of nature itself. It is admittedly a strange and at first sight absurd proposition to write a *history* according to an idea of how world events must develop if they are to conform to certain rational ends; it would seem that only a *novel* could result from such premises. Yet if it may be assumed that nature does not work without a plan and purposeful end, even amidst the arbitrary play of human freedom, this idea might nevertheless prove useful. And although we are too short-sighted to perceive the hidden mechanism of nature's scheme, this idea may yet serve as a guide to us in representing an otherwise planless *aggregate* of human actions as conforming, at least when considered as a whole, to a *system*. For if we start out from *Greek* history as that in which all other earlier or contemporary histories are preserved or at least authenticated,* if we next trace the influence of the Greeks upon the shaping and mis-shaping of the body politic of *Rome*, which engulfed the Greek state, and follow down to our own times the influence of Rome upon the *Barbarians* who in turn destroyed it, and if we finally add the political history of other peoples *episodically*, in

---

* Only an *educated public* which has existed uninterruptedly from its origin to our times can authenticate ancient history. Beyond that, all is *terra incognita*; and the history of peoples who lived outside this public can begin only from the time at which they entered it. This occurred with the *Jewish* people at the time of the Ptolemies through the Greek translation of the Bible, without which their *isolated* reports would meet with little belief. From this point, once it has been properly ascertained, their narratives can be followed backwards. And it is the same with all other peoples. The first page of Thucydides, as Hume puts it, is the only beginning of all true history.

so far as knowledge of them has gradually come down to us through these enlightened nations, we shall discover a regular process of improvement in the political constitutions of our continent (which will probably legislate eventually for all other continents). Furthermore, we must always concentrate our attention on civil constitutions, their laws, and the mutual relations among states, and notice how these factors, by virtue of the good they contained, served for a time to elevate and glorify nations (and with them the arts and sciences). Conversely, we should observe how their inherent defects led to their overthrow, but in such a way that a germ of enlightenment always survived, developing further with each revolution, and prepared the way for a subsequent higher level of improvement.

All this, I believe, should give us some guidance in explaining the thoroughly confused interplay of human affairs and in prophesying future political changes. Yet the same use has already been made of human history even when it was regarded as the disjointed product of unregulated freedom. But if we assume a plan of nature, we have grounds for greater hopes. For such a plan opens up the comforting prospect of a future in which we are shown from afar how the human race eventually works its way upward to a situation in which all the germs implanted by nature can be developed fully, and in which man's destiny can be fulfilled here on earth. Such a *justification* of nature – or rather perhaps of *providence* – is no mean motive for adopting a particular point of view in considering the world. For what is the use of lauding and holding up for contemplation the glory and wisdom of creation in the non-rational sphere of nature, if the history of mankind, the very part of this great display of supreme wisdom which contains the purpose of all the rest, is to remain a constant reproach to everything else? Such a spectacle would force us to turn away in revulsion, and, by making us despair of ever finding any completed rational aim behind it, would reduce us to hoping for it only in some other world.

It would be a misinterpretation of my intention to contend that I meant this idea of a universal history, which to some extent follows an *a priori* rule, to supersede the task of history proper, that of *empirical* composition. My idea is only a notion of what a philosophical mind, well acquainted with history, might be able to attempt from a different angle. Besides, the otherwise praiseworthy detail in which each age now composes its history must naturally cause everyone concern as to how our remote descendants will manage to cope with the burden of history which we shall bequeath to them a few centuries from now. No doubt they will value the history of the oldest times, of which the original documents would long since have vanished, only from the point of view of what interests *them*, i.e. the positive and negative achievements of nations and governments in relation to the cosmopolitan goal. We should bear this in mind, and we should likewise observe the ambitions of rulers and their servants, in order to indicate to them the only means by which they can be honourably remembered in the most distant ages. And this may provide us with another *small* motive for attempting a philosophical history of this kind.

Translated by H. B. Nisbet

FICHTE

The subsequent interpretation of Kant's work was marked by productive misunderstandings. Given the difficulty of Kant's revolutionary project, a growing number of interpreters was bound to appear. The first, however, to make a serious attempt not only to interpret Kant's philosophy, but also to complete and perfect it, was J. G. Fichte. He liked to emphasize the undiscovered spirit of the Kantian system that lay beneath its words. Fichte, however, did much more: he went beyond the limits of critical thought so clearly demarcated by Kant. He transformed the transcendental clarification of the conditions for the possibility of our knowledge into a conclusive explanation based on one single principle. This establishment of a firm methodological basis enabled him to deduce systematically and to connect homogeneously whatever Kant's reflection on the prerequisites of knowledge had explained without recourse to a strict system. With the help of only one single governing principle, all theoretical and practical consequences were to be developed. The persuasive power of Fichte's philosophy is ultimately also indebted to his uncompromising tone that so influences his audience that they are 'forced to understand', as he claimed in one of his later works.

Fichte called his systematic form a science of knowledge. He had in mind a supreme science as the basis of any other scientific endeavour. In times to come, it was supposed to contain the whole of philosophy. It is true that Fichte's predecessor, K. L. Reinhold, had already gone so far as to found the Kantian critique on a so-called elementary philosophy, in which the subject–object relation, so central to Kant's theory of knowledge, was expressed as the 'law of consciousness'. This means that, in consciousness, subject and object are related to, as well as separated from, each other. Kant had employed consciousness in his transcendental reflections without having disclosed its immanent structures. It was Reinhold who penetrated this structure by interpreting consciousness as always being a consciousness of something. With respect to subject and object, consciousness thus understood contains the two aspects of relating and distinguishing.

Fichte, on the other hand, saw a deeply rooted, and therefore only barely discernible, defect in the previous attempts at improving the foundation of Kant's philosophy. The ultimate principle itself, from which all knowledge is derived, cannot be taken as just another given fact; it would otherwise depend on further presuppositions. Hence, the only way to avoid a regress was by assuming the possibility of a principle that does not depend on any further presuppositions. Such a principle cannot be contained in the given structures of consciousness; it must be produced via the activity of consciousness. The science of knowledge, then, is not based on fact, but on action. The action in question is expressed in the statement 'I am I'. This statement might initially seem like an empty tautology, but it contains the heart of Fichte's philosophy.

Here, we have to proceed from a primordial act that does not already presuppose something else. This act must be freely posited with everything else posited alongside it. Fichte only knew of one such act, namely the act of saying 'I' to oneself. The ego, self or I does not exist before it actively seizes itself. And, by converting itself into a self, it makes reference to nothing else but its own identity. To say 'I' does not point out anything that already exists; it is not a subsequent or external feature of a given existence. To say 'I' means to posit one's own Being. Therefore, the principle of identity is created only with and not before the self that posits its Being as its own. Traditional logic's law of identity, 'A = A', is ultimately based on the self-identification 'I am I'. In designing the science of knowledge, Fichte proceeded from this assumption, and he grounded his uniform systematic intention in a primordial installation of identity itself.

Now, the self does not only posit itself. In saying 'I' to itself, it also posits everything else in contrast to itself. Thus, positing the self involves, at the same time, positing what is not the self. Negation is added to identity in one and the same act. By virtue of this negation, all reality in the course of its gradual development beyond the absolute primordial act can be explained with reference to precisely this act. A whole world is created, so to speak, by increasingly relativizing primordial unity. In this way, our consciousness of the world has to be transcendentally reconstructed.

With the self, Fichte gained the supporting principle of unity that enabled him to develop all parts of his philosophy in a stringent and complete fashion. After all, the act of the self is both action and knowledge at the same time. From the very beginning, it encompassed the theoretical and the practical aspect of philosophy. There was no longer any need for that complicated transition which Kant still had to deal with in order to mediate the two sides. Roughly speaking, the theoretical part describes the effect of that which is not the self on the self, i.e., the determination of the self by what is opposite it, while the practical part treats the effect that the self has on that which is not the self. In 1794, Fichte's *Foundation of the Entire Science of Knowledge* presented the first realization of his intentions. He held on to his systematic aim until the end of his life and rewrote the science of knowledge over and over again, defending it against objections and presenting it, as he saw it, with greater evidence.

The return to one principle which everyone can generate for themselves and in themselves by freely referring to themselves as 'I' lends a particular suggestiveness to Fichte's main insight. Besides the iron edifice of the system, a meditative tone of spiritual guidance and revivalist literature was brought to bear, a tone which the *Introductions to the Science of Knowledge* and those many ingenious works for a wider audience made good use of. Fichte was not so much interested in continuing philosophy along the lines of academic schools. True philosophy for him was a matter of leading the right kind of human existence. Every reader was supposed to feel called upon to participate in the real *Vocation of Man*. Fichte even provided an *Instruction for the Blessed Life*.

Of course, the difference between absolute self or absolute I and an individual consciousness must not be forgotten. It is the identity of the self that is at the basis of all consciousness. Whatever we know within our ordinary understanding of things and on the basis of scientific education is always and necessarily secondary to the primordial unifying action. Philosophy here established a hierarchy. Nevertheless, with the analysis of the self or I, it did not administer an esoteric theory that would have excluded others. On the contrary, Fichte spent a long time thinking through the role of the scholar in society.

This resulted in various investigations about the *Scholar's Vocation*, which finally also led the mature Fichte to contribute actively in the foundation of Berlin's new university. His lectures from the early years, which are reprinted below, may give an idea of how, in line with his basic philosophical thoughts, Fichte conceived of the scholar as the representative of a true mankind. Rousseau's inspirations, influential over the whole epoch, were taken up by Fichte and systematically expanded. The idealists' insights into education, learning and the public role of the scholar, which were later also to enrich Schelling and Humboldt, are part of a still living, though widely misunderstood, heritage in current concepts of school and university teaching.

The connection between self or I and society that was so important for Fichte is established almost automatically if the following is considered: free existence as a self, which philosophy recognizes as the essence of human beings, is only possible within society. To be a self presupposes recognition by one's equals. Only among people can people really become themselves. In his theory of law and morality, developed between 1796 and 1798 'according to the principles of the Science of Knowledge', Fichte deduced for the first time the concept of society. Kant had still considered society as a historical reality, while on the other hand, with his kingdom of ends, he had also postulated a coexistence of purely rational beings that is not of this world. With his influential analysis of master and slave in the *Phenomenology of Spirit*, Hegel later developed the assumption of a necessary recognition by equal others for the subject's existence as a self. Fichte deserves to be praised not simply for presupposing society but for making it plausible from within the concept of the self, mutual 'recognition' of subjects being the catchword.

Here, the apparently conclusive accusations, beginning with Fichte's contemporaries and frequently repeated, that his philosophy displayed an excessive egocentrism, can be refuted. It can be demonstrated that the innermost dimensions of his philosophy do not aim to emphasize individuality. Those who are acquainted with Fichte's early literary participation in the French Revolution (1793) and those who have followed the atheism debate about his allegedly dangerous influence on Jena's academic youth (1798–9) and those who have read the *Address to the German Nation* that contributed to the intellectual rebellion against Napoleon, do not need such a demonstration. Fichte in his philosophy proudly took it as a matter of course that science owed a general duty to mankind. He also did not doubt for a second, though, that society has to listen to the philosophical teachers of the people.

Fichte's thought never did things halfheartedly. Weighing matters carefully and assessing them realistically was not his way of doing things. As radically as he had advanced the transcendental reflection initiated by Kant beyond the dimension of critique and towards absolute principles, so unquestionably was he overcome by proselytism and dogmatism. He set German idealism on a course that was soon to make his own position outmoded. Ironically, this step was taken precisely with the aim of perfecting thought, an aim Fichte himself had been the first to swear by. The absolute aim upon which he had insisted was turned against him and his dogmatic onesidedness. The science of knowledge had, so to speak, not yet become sufficiently absolute. Later, Schelling attempted to perfect the system of thought, by continuing systematically along these lines.

THE TEXTS

The First Introduction to the *Science of Knowledge* confidently claims to be the only clarification of Kant's constantly misunderstood, revolutionary thought. Really, however, Fichte was introducing his own philosophy. It is called a science of knowledge in so far as it has to state conclusively the basis of all experience. Proceeding from any given experience in which subject and object are brought together, a basis can be sought from one side or the other. Proceeding in the direction of intelligence or the self leads to idealism; proceeding in the direction of the thing in itself leads to dogmatism. The dispute between their respective systems is absolutely irreconcilable because each claims the opposite of the other at any given time. At this point the argument cannot progress; it comes down to a matter of particular interests. In his transcendental dialectic (*Critique of Pure Reason*), in order to decide between determination by nature and the assumption of freedom, Kant had already made an appeal to the rational interest which, no doubt, aims at freedom. Fichte turned this theoretical dispute into a fundamental decision of human existence: 'What sort of philosophy one chooses depends, therefore, on what sort of man one is.' An inborn interest in freedom pleads for idealism. Idealism can be compelling because of the immediate obviousness of its principle, or in other words, because it relies on the dual character of consciousness and self-consciousness. In everything that it observes, the mind also observes itself. This is only achieved on the basis of free activity and can never be causally explained by dogmatism as brought about by things external. It is true, however, that the dogmatic standpoint of the empiricist is irrefutable because, in order for it to be refuted, it would have to have already accepted the idealist premise. Due to the reason mentioned above, however, this dogmatism fails in its project of establishing a conclusive concept of experience. Hence, this type of philosophy can be dismissed. In contrast to this position, idealism is based on an action that needs no prerequisites, an action that necessarily brings forth everything that follows, namely the free act of the self. Naturally, it presents its evidence in reversed fashion. It begins with a representation that can be generated in any individual consciousness, and it aims towards the conditions of representation as such, until it reaches an unconditioned beginning. The entire course of deduction embraces the three aspects of theory, praxis and faculty of judgement, i.e., the main topics of Kant's three critiques. These unconnected and undeduced aspects in Kant's critical philosophy were systematically aligned.

Fichte's fictitious letters, *On the Spirit and the Letter in Philosophy*, the most important of which is reprinted here, proceed from a distinction made by traditional interpretations of the scriptures, according to which the actual mental content of a word must be disclosed from beneath its mere letters. In one of the preceding letters, Fichte had already used the example of a work of art, and in this letter he summarizes considerations about the impact of art that are freely linked with the terminology in Kant's *Critique of Judgement*. Kant had credited the artistic genius with the otherwise inconceivable ability of producing something that arouses the same aesthetic experience in every spectator, irrespective of personal preferences. Art stimulates in a subject, via the reflective faculty of judgement in every individual, a uniform play of cognitive forces; something that could take place within any given subject in a structurally similar way. Art thereby establishes a community among people that expresses itself in a '*sensus communis*', a common sense. In reference to his own principle of the self-activity of the self or I, Fichte illuminated this universal sense further. He came upon the idea of a drive which revealed itself as a drive towards knowledge, as well as a drive towards action. This drive encompasses the fields of theory and praxis, and thereby it encompasses the entire system of the science of knowledge. Here, the free, disinterested harmony in man's nature on which Kant had based aesthetic judgements and which had no inner connection with knowledge, appeared as an aesthetic drive. This playful harmony represents the self to itself and thereby enriches its original activity. This helps explain the well-known fact that aesthetic ideas stimulate every person in a not exactly specifiable way. The text further responded to a contemporary reinterpretation of Kant's aesthetics as a programme of popular education, which Schiller had termed the 'aesthetic education of man'. For Schiller, the terror of enforced freedom should give way to the communal aspect of aesthetic experience. This seemed to open the possibility of political progress. Schiller thought that an aesthetic education would be especially capable of enhancing humanity. Fichte's letter was a response to this educational ideal which had become so attractive to the German bourgeoisie since the horrors of the French Revolution.

The influence of idealism on society was also the topic of *Some Lectures Concerning the Scholar's Vocation*. The scholar had a very special role in society, namely that of the 'highest and truest man'. The general vocation of man, when understood on the basis of Fichte's system as rational autonomy, free action and self-identity, is the first philosophical step in determining the vocation of the scholar. In a second step, Fichte tried to articulate the vocation of man in society. The drive to be in free harmony with oneself can only be realized in a community with other human beings. Fichte's terminology here still followed Kant's, whose 'kingdom of ends' referred to the purely rational community of all free agents who are free in a meta-empirical sense. Noticeable, too, is the teleological aspect of Kant's philosophy of history, namely that of mankind slowly perfecting itself. Only two years later, in his *Foundation of Natural Law*, Fichte made his breakthrough to the actual deduction of the Other on the basis of mutual recognition – a highly original thought that was to become influential through Hegel and Marx for the further development of practical and political philosophy. Before the position of the scholar could finally be scrutinized, Rousseau's question of how it was at all possible for the different classes among human beings to develop, needed an answer. The distinction of class corresponds to a social division of tasks under the conditions of an advanced culture which prevents people from equally developing all their constitutive features. Who is there to take care of the perfection of individual development and the satisfaction of all needs in the whole of society? It is a particular class of people who have the task of watching over the preservation of the commonwealth. The scholars are the ones who have the requisite knowledge. Within the framework of a historically developing society, they play a teacher's role similar to the leader's role of philosophers in Plato's utopian state. The scholars are supposed to be morally the most refined human beings of their epoch, at the peak of a universal human development, exemplary to the whole of society, while carrying a special rank. (The final lecture, which is not reprinted here, contains a treatment of Rousseau's first discourse *On the Arts and Sciences*.)

Rüdiger Bubner
Translated by Marcus Weigelt

Science of Knowledge

PREFATORY NOTE

De re, quae agitur, petimus, ut homines, eam non opinionem sed opus esse, cogitent, ac pro certo habeant, non sectae nos alicujus, aut placiti, sed utilitatis et amplitudinis humanae fundamenta moliri. Deinde, ut suis commodis aequi, in commune consulant, et ipsi in partem veniant. Baco de Verulamio

On a modest acquaintance with the philosophical literature since the appearance of the Kantian Critiques I soon came to the conclusion that the enterprise of this great man, the radical revision of our current conceptions of philosophy, and hence of all science, has been a complete failure; since not a single one of his numerous followers perceives what is really being said. Believing that I did, I decided to dedicate my life to a presentation, quite independent of Kant, of that great discovery, and will not relent in this determination. Whether I shall have greater success in making myself intelligible to my own generation, only time will tell. In any case, I know that nothing true or useful is lost again once it has entered the world of men; even if only a remote posterity may know how to use it.

In pursuit of my academic duties, I at first wrote for my students in the classroom, where I had it in my power to continue with verbal explanations until I was understood.

... in behalf of the matter which is in hand I entreat men to believe that it is not an opinion to be held, but a work to be done; and to be well assured that I am laboring to lay the foundation, not of any sect or doctrine, but of human utility and power. Next I ask that they fairly consult their common advantage ... and themselves participate in the remaining labors ...

Francis Bacon, *The Great Instauration*, Preface [my translation]

I need not here attest how many reasons I have for being satisfied with my students and for entertaining of very many of them the highest hopes for science. The manuscript in question also became known outside the university, and there are numerous ideas about it among the learned. Except from my students, I have neither read nor heard a judgment in which there was even a pretense of argument, but plenty of derision, abuse, and general evidence that people are passionately opposed to this theory, and also that they do not understand it. As to the latter, I take full responsibility for it, until people have become familiar with the content of my system in a different form and may find perchance that the exposition there is not, after all, so wholly unclear; or I shall assume the responsibility unconditionally and forever if this may incline the reader to study the present account, in which I shall endeavor to achieve the utmost clarity. I shall continue this exposition until I am convinced that I am writing wholly in vain. But I do write in vain, if no one examines my arguments.

I still owe the reader the following reminders. I have long asserted, and repeat once more, that my system is nothing other than the *Kantian*; this means that it contains the same view of things, but is in method quite independent of the *Kantian* presentation. I have said this not to hide behind a great authority, nor to seek an external support for my teaching, but to speak the truth and to be just.

After some twenty years it should be possible to prove this. Except for a recent suggestion, of which more anon, Kant is to this day a closed book, and what people have read into him is precisely what will not fit there, and what he wished to refute.

My writings seek neither to explain *Kant* nor to be explained by him; they must stand on their own, and *Kant* does not come into it at all. My aim – to express it directly – is not the correction and completion of the philosophical concepts now in circulation, whether anti-Kantian or Kantian; it is rather the total eradication and complete reversal of current modes of thought on these topics, so that in all seriousness, and not only in a manner of speaking, the object shall be posited and determined by the cognitive faculty, and not the cognitive faculty by the object. My system can therefore be examined on its own basis alone, not on the presuppositions of some other philosophy; it is to agree only with itself, it can be explained, proved, or refuted in its own terms alone; one must accept or reject it as a whole.

'If this system were true, certain propositions cannot hold' gets no reply from me: for I certainly do not consider that anything should hold, if this system contradicts it.

'I do not understand this work' means nothing more to me than just that; and I consider such an admission most uninteresting and uninstructive. My writings cannot be understood, and ought not to be understood, by those who have not studied them; for they do not contain the repetition of a lesson already learned beforehand, but, since *Kant* has not been understood, something that is quite new in our day.

Unreasoned disparagement tells me no more than that this theory is not liked, and such an avowal is also extremely unimportant; the question is not whether it pleases you or not, but whether it has been demonstrated. In order to assist the testing of its foundations, I shall add indications throughout this exposition as to where the system needs to be attacked. I write only for those who still retain an inner feeling for the certainty or dubiousness, the clarity or confusion of their knowledge, to whom science and conviction matter, and who are driven by a burning zeal to seek them. I have nothing to do with those who, through protracted spiritual slavery, have lost themselves and with themselves their sense of private conviction, and their belief in the conviction of others; to whom it is folly for anyone to seek independently for truth; who see nothing more in the sciences than a comfortable way of earning a living, and who shrink back from any extension of knowledge, as from a new burden of work; to whom no means are shameful to suppress the destroyer of their trade.

I would be sorry if they understood me. Until now it has gone according to my wishes with these people; and I hope even now that this exordium will so bewilder them that from now on they see nothing but letters on the page, while what passes for mind in them is torn hither and thither by the caged anger within.

INTRODUCTION

I

Attend to yourself: turn your attention away from everything that surrounds you and towards your inner life; this is the first demand that philosophy makes of its disciple. Our concern is not with anything that lies outside you, but only with yourself.

Even the most cursory introspection will reveal to anyone a remarkable difference between the various immediate modifications of his consciousness, or what we may also call his presentations. Some of them appear to us as completely dependent on our freedom, but it is impossible for us to believe that there is anything answering to them outside us, independently of our activity. Our imagination and will appear to us to be free. Others of our presentations we refer to a reality which we take to be established independently of us, as to their model; and we find ourselves limited in determining these presentations by the condition that they must correspond to this reality. In regard to the content of cognition, we do not consider ourselves free. In brief, we may say that some of our presentations are accompanied by the feeling of freedom, others by the feeling of necessity.

The question, 'Why are the presentations which depend on freedom determined precisely as they are, and not otherwise?' cannot reasonably arise, because in postulating that they depend on freedom all application of the concept of 'wherefore' is rejected; they are so because I have so determined them, and if I had determined them otherwise, they would be otherwise.

But the question, 'What is the source of the system of presentations which are accompanied by the feeling of necessity, and of this feeling of necessity itself?' is one that is surely worthy of reflection. It is the task of philosophy to provide an answer to this question, and in my opinion nothing is philosophy save the science which performs this task. The system of presentations accompanied by the feeling of necessity is also called *experience*, both internal and external.

Philosophy, in other words, must therefore furnish the ground of all experience.

Only three objections may be brought against the above. A person might deny that presentations occur in consciousness which are accompanied by the feeling of necessity and referred to a reality which is taken to be determined without our assistance. Such a person would either deny against his better knowledge or be differently constituted from other people; if so, there would actually be nothing there for him to deny, and no denial, and we could disregard his objection without further ado. Secondly, someone might say that the question thus raised is completely unanswerable, for we are, and must remain, in insurmountable ignorance on this issue. It is quite unnecessary to discuss arguments and counter-arguments with such a person. He is best refuted by providing the actual answer to the question, and then nothing remains for him to do but to examine our attempt and to indicate where and why it does not appear to him sufficient. Finally, someone might lay claim to the name and maintain that philosophy is entirely different from what has been indicated, or that it is something over and above this. It would be easy to show him that precisely what I have set forth has from the earliest been considered to be philosophy by all competent exponents, that everything he might wish to pass off as such has a different name already, and that if this word is to designate anything specific, it must designate precisely this science.

However, since we are not inclined to engage in this essentially fruitless controversy about a word, we have ourselves long ago surrendered this name and called the science which is expressly committed to solving the problem indicated, the *Science of Knowledge*.

2

One can ask for a reason only in the case of something judged to be contingent, viz., where it is assumed that it could also have been otherwise, and yet is not a matter of determination through freedom; and it is precisely the fact that he inquires as to its ground that makes it, for the inquirer, contingent. The task of seeking the ground of something contingent means: to exhibit some other thing whose properties reveal why, of all the manifold determinations that the explicandum might have had, it actually has just those that it does. By virtue of its mere notion, the ground falls outside what it grounds; both ground and grounded are, as such, opposed and yet linked to each other, so that the former explains the latter.

Now philosophy must discover the ground of all experience; thus its object necessarily lies outside all experience. This proposition holds good of all philosophy, and really did hold universally until the time of the Kantians and their facts of consciousness, and thus of inner experience.

There can be no objection at all to the proposition here established: for the premise of our argument is the mere analysis of our proposed concept of philosophy, and it is from this that our conclusion follows. Should someone say perhaps that the concept of ground ought to be explained in some other way, we certainly cannot prevent him from thinking what he likes in using this expression: however, it is our right to declare that under the above description of philosophy *we* wish nothing to be understood beyond what has been said. If this meaning be not accepted, the possibility of philosophy in our sense would accordingly have to be denied; and we have already attended to that alternative above.

3

A finite rational being has nothing beyond experience; it is this that comprises the entire staple of his thought. The philosopher is necessarily in the same position; it seems, therefore, incomprehensible how he could raise himself above experience.

But he is able to abstract; that is, he can separate what is conjoined in experience through the freedom of thought. *The thing*, which must be determined independently of our freedom and to which our knowledge must conform, and *the intelligence*, which must know, are in experience inseparably connected. The philosopher can leave one of the two out of consideration, and he has then abstracted from experience and raised himself above it. If he leaves out the former, he retains an intelligence in itself, that is, abstracted from its relation to experience, as a basis for explaining experience; if he leaves out the latter, he retains a thing-in-itself, that is, abstracted from the fact that it occurs in experience, as a similar basis of explanation. The first method of procedure is called *idealism*, the second *dogmatism*.

The present discussion should have convinced anyone that these two are the only philosophical systems possible. According to the former system, the presentations accompanied by the feeling of necessity are products of the intelligence which must be presupposed in their explanation; according to the latter, they are products of a thing-in-itself which must be assumed to precede them.

Should someone wish to deny this proposition, he would have to prove either that there is a way, other than that of abstraction, by which to rise above experience, or that the consciousness of experience consists of more constituents than the two mentioned.

Now in regard to the first system, it will indeed become clear later on that what is to rank as intelligence is not something produced merely by abstraction, but under a different predicate really has its place in consciousness; it will none the less emerge, however, that the consciousness thereof is conditioned by an abstraction, of a kind that is, of course, natural to man.

It is not at all denied that a person might fuse together a whole from fragments of these heterogeneous systems, or that idle work of this nature has in fact very often been done: but it is denied that, given a consistent procedure, there are any other systems possible besides these two.

4

Between the objects – we shall call the explanatory ground of experience that a philosophy establishes *the object of that philosophy*, since only through and for the latter does it appear to exist – between the object of *idealism* and that of *dogmatism*, there is, in respect of their relation to consciousness in general, a remarkable difference. Everything of which I am conscious is an object of consciousness. Such an object may stand in three relations to the subject. The object appears either as having first been created by the presentation of the intellect, or as existing without the aid of the intellect; and, in the latter case, either as determined in its nature, as well, or as present merely in its existence, while its essence is determinable by the free intellect.

The first relation amounts to a mere inventing, with or without an aim, the second to an object of experience, the third to a single object only, as we shall demonstrate forthwith.

I can freely determine myself to think this or that; for example, the thing-in-itself of the dogmatic philosophers. If I now abstract from what is thought and observe only myself, I become to myself in this object the content of a specific presentation. That I appear to myself to be determined precisely so and not otherwise, as thinking, and as thinking, of all possible thoughts, the thing-in-itself, should in my opinion depend on my self-determination: I have freely made myself into such an object. But I have not made myself as it is in itself; on the contrary, I am compelled to presuppose myself as that which is to be determined by self-determination. I myself, however, am an object for myself whose nature depends, under certain conditions, on the intellect alone, but whose existence must always be presupposed.

Now the object of idealism is precisely this self-in-itself.* The object of this system, therefore, actually occurs as something real in consciousness, not as a *thing-in-itself*, whereby idealism would cease to be what it is and would transform itself into dogmatism, but as a *self-in-itself*; not as an object of experience, for it is not determined but will only be determined by me, and without this determination is nothing, and does not even exist; but as something that is raised above all experience.

By contrast, the object of dogmatism belongs to those of the first group, which are produced solely by free thought; the thing-in-itself is a pure invention and has no reality whatever. It does not occur in experience: for the system of experience is nothing other than

---

* I have avoided this expression until now, in order not to engender the idea of a self as a *thing*-in-itself. My caution was in vain: for this reason I now abandon it, for I do not see whom I should need to protect.

thinking accompanied by the feeling of necessity, and not even the dogmatist, who like any other philosopher must exhibit its ground, can pass it off as anything else. The dogmatist wants, indeed, to assure to that thing reality, that is, the necessity of being thought as the ground of all experience, and will do it if he proves that experience can really be explained by means of it, and cannot be explained without it; but that is the very question at issue, and what has to be proved should not be presupposed.

Thus the object of idealism has this advantage over the object of dogmatism, that it may be demonstrated, not as the ground of the explanation of experience, which would be contradictory and would turn this system itself into a part of experience, but still in general in consciousness; whereas the latter object cannot be looked upon as anything other than a pure invention, which expects its conversion into reality only from the success of the system.

This is adduced only to promote clear insight into the differences between the two systems, and not in order to infer from it something against dogmatism. That the object of every philosophy, as the ground of the explanation of experience, must lie outside experience, is demanded simply by the nature of philosophy, and is far from proving a disadvantage to a system. We have not as yet found the reasons why this object should furthermore occur in a special manner in consciousness.

Should somebody be unable to convince himself of what has just been asserted, then, since this is only a passing remark, his conviction as to the whole is not yet made impossible thereby. Nevertheless, in accordance with my plan, I shall consider possible objections even here. One could deny the claim that there is immediate self-consciousness involved in a free action of the spirit. We would only have to remind such a person once more of the conditions of self-consciousness we have detailed. This self-consciousness does not force itself into being and is not its own source; one must really act freely and then abstract from objects and concentrate only upon oneself. No one can be compelled to do this, and even if he pretends to, one can never know if he proceeds correctly and in the requisite way. In a word, this consciousness cannot be demonstrated to anyone; each person must freely create it in himself. One could only object to the second assertion, viz., that the thing-in-itself is a sheer invention, by reason of having misunderstood it. We would refer such a person to the above description of the origin of this concept.

5

Neither of these two systems can directly refute its opposite, for their quarrel is about the first principle, which admits of no derivation from anything beyond it; each of the two, if only its first principle is granted, refutes that of the other; each denies everything in its opposite, and they have no point at all in common from which they could arrive at mutual understanding and unity. Even if they appear to agree about the words in a sentence, each takes them in a different sense.*

First of all, idealism cannot refute dogmatism. As we have seen, the former, indeed, has this advantage over the latter, that it is able to exhibit the presence in consciousness of the freely acting intellect, which is the basis of its explanation of experience. This fact, as such, even the dogmatist must concede, for otherwise he disqualifies himself from any further discussion with the idealist; but through a valid inference from his principle he converts it into appearance and illusion, and thereby renders it unfit to serve as an explanation of

---

* This is why *Kant* has not been understood and the Science of Knowledge has not found favor and is not soon likely to do so. The Kantian system and the Science of Knowledge are, not in the usual vague sense of the word, but in the precise sense just specified, idealistic; the modern philosophers, however, are one and all *dogmatists*, and firmly determined to remain so. *Kant* has been tolerated only because it was possible to make him into a dogmatist; the Science of Knowledge, which does not admit of such a transformation, is necessarily intolerable to these sages. The rapid diffusion of *Kantian* philosophy, once understood – as best it has been – is a proof not of the profundity, but of the shallowness of the age. In part, in its current form, it is the most fantastic abortion that has ever been produced by the human imagination, and it reflects little credit on the perspicacity of its defenders that they do not recognize this: in part, it is easy to prove that it has recommended itself only because people have thereby thought to rid themselves of all serious speculation and to provide themselves with a royal charter to go on cultivating their beloved, superficial empiricism.

anything else, since in his philosophy it cannot even validate itself. According to him, everything that appears in our consciousness, along with our presumed determinations through freedom and the very belief that we are free, is the product of a thing-in-itself. This latter belief is evoked in us by the operation of the thing, and the determinations which we deduce from our freedom are brought about by the same cause: but this we do not know, and hence we attribute them to no cause, and thus to freedom. Every consistent dogmatist is necessarily a fatalist: he does not deny the fact of consciousness that we consider ourselves free, for that would be contrary to reason; but he demonstrates, on the basis of his principle, the falsity of this belief. – He completely denies the independence of the self upon which the idealist relies, and construes the self merely as a product of things, an accident of the world; the consistent dogmatist is necessarily also a materialist. He could be refuted only on the basis of the postulate of the freedom and independence of the self; but it is precisely this that he denies.

The dogmatist is no less incapable of refuting the idealist.

The thing-in-itself, which is the fundamental principle of the dogmatist, is nothing and has no reality, as even its exponents must concede, apart from what it is alleged to acquire through the circumstance that experience can be explained only on its basis. The idealist destroys this proof by explaining experience in another way: thus he denies precisely what the dogmatist relies on. The thing-in-itself becomes completely chimerical; there no longer appears to be any reason at all to assume one; and with this the entire edifice of dogmatism collapses.

From what has been said the absolute incompatibility of the two systems appears at once, in that what follows from one of them annihilates the conclusions of the other; hence their fusion necessarily leads to inconsistency. Wherever it is attempted, the parts do not mesh, and at some juncture an immense hiatus ensues. Whoever would wish to take issue with what has just been asserted would have to demonstrate the possibility of such a combination, which presupposes a continued passage from matter to spirit or its reverse, or what is the same, a continued passage from necessity to freedom.

So far as we can yet see, from the speculative point of view the two systems appear to be of equal value: they cannot coexist, but neither one can make any headway against the other. In this light, it is interesting to ask what might motivate the person who sees this – and it is easy enough to see – to prefer one of the systems over the other, and how it is that skepticism, as the total surrender of the attempt to solve the problem presented, does not become universal.

The dispute between the idealist and the dogmatist is, in reality, about whether the independence of the thing should be sacrificed to the independence of the self or, conversely, the independence of the self to that of the thing. What is it, then, that motivates a reasonable man to declare this preference for one over the other?

From the given vantage point, which a person must necessarily adopt if he is to be counted a philosopher, and to which one comes sooner or later, even without meaning to, in the course of reflection, the philosopher finds nothing but *that he must present himself as free* and that there are determinate things outside him. It is impossible for a person to rest content with this thought; the thought of a mere presentation is only a half-thought, the fragment of a thought; something must be superadded which corresponds to the presentation independently of the presenting. In other words, the presentation cannot exist for itself alone: it is something only when conjoined with something else, and for itself it is nothing. It is precisely this necessity of thought which drives us on from that standpoint to the question, 'What is the ground of presentations?' or, what comes to the very same, 'What is it that corresponds thereto?'

Now the presentation of the independence of the self, and that of the thing, can assuredly coexist, but not the independence of both. Only one of them can be the first, the initiatory, the independent one: the second, by virtue of being second, necessarily becomes dependent on the first, with which it is to be conjoined.

Now which of the two should be taken as primary? Reason provides no principle of choice; for we deal here not with the addition of a link in the chain of reasoning, which is all that rational grounds extend to, but with the beginning of the whole chain, which, as an absolutely primary act, depends solely upon the freedom of thought.

Hence the choice is governed by caprice, and since even a capricious decision must have some source, it is governed by *inclination* and *interest*. The ultimate basis of the difference between idealists and dogmatists is thus the difference of their interests.

The highest interest and the ground of all others is self-interest. This is also true of the philosopher. The desire not to lose, but to maintain and assert himself in the rational process, is the interest which invisibly governs all his thought. Now there are two levels of humanity, and before the second level is reached by everyone in the progress of our species, two major types of man. Some, who have not yet raised themselves to full consciousness of their freedom and absolute independence, find themselves only in the presentation of things; they have only that dispersed self-consciousness which attaches to objects, and has to be gleaned from their multiplicity. Their image is reflected back at them only by things, as by a mirror; if these were taken from them, their self would be lost as well; for the sake of their self they cannot give up the belief in the independence of things, for they themselves exist only if things do. Everything they are, they have really become through the external world. Whoever is in fact a product of things, will never see himself as anything else; and he will be right so long as he speaks only of himself and of others like him. The principle of the dogmatists is belief in things for the sake of the self: indirect belief, therefore, in their own scattered self sustained only by objects.

The man who becomes conscious of his self-sufficiency and independence of everything that is outside himself, however – and this can be achieved only by making oneself into something independently of everything else – does not need things for the support of himself, and cannot use them, because they destroy that self-sufficiency, and convert it into mere appearance. The self which he possesses, and which is the subject of his interest, annuls this belief in things; he believes in his independence out of inclination, he embraces it with feeling. His belief in himself is direct.

This interest also explains the emotions which usually enter into the defense of philosophical systems. The attack on his system in fact exposes the dogmatist to the danger of losing his self; yet he is not armed against this attack, because there is something within him that sides with the attacker; hence he defends himself with passion and animosity. By contrast, the idealist cannot readily refrain from regarding the dogmatist with a certain contempt, for the latter can tell him nothing save what he has long since known and already discarded as erroneous; for one reaches idealism, if not through dogmatism itself, at least through the inclination thereto. The dogmatist flies into a passion, distorts, and would persecute if he had the power: the idealist is cool and in danger of deriding the dogmatist.

What sort of philosophy one chooses depends, therefore, on what sort of man one is; for a philosophical system is not a dead piece of furniture that we can reject or accept as we wish; it is rather a thing animated by the soul of the person who holds it. A person indolent by nature or dulled and distorted by mental servitude, learned luxury, and vanity will never raise himself to the level of idealism.

We can show the dogmatist the inadequacy and incoherence of his system, of which we shall speak in a moment: we can bewilder and harass him from all sides; but we cannot convince him, because he is incapable of calmly receiving and coolly assessing a theory which he absolutely cannot endure. If idealism should prove to be the only true philosophy, it is necessary to be born, raised, and self-educated as a philosopher: but one cannot be made so by human contrivance. Our science expects few converts, therefore, among those *already formed*; if it may have any hopes at all, they are set, rather, upon the young whose innate power has not yet foundered in the indolence of our age.

6

But dogmatism is completely unable to explain what it must, and this demonstrates its untenability.

It must explain the fact of presentation, and undertakes to render it intelligible on the basis of the influence of the thing-in-itself. Now it must not deny what our immediate consciousness tells us about presentation. – What, then, does it say about presentation? It is not my intention here to conceptualize what can only be intuited internally, nor to treat exhaustively of that to whose discussion a large part of the Science of Knowledge is dedicated. I merely wish to recall what everybody who has taken just one good look into himself must have discovered long ago.

The intellect as such *observes itself*; and this self-observation is directed immediately upon its every feature. The nature of intelligence consists in this *immediate unity* of being and seeing. What is in it, and what it is in general, it is *for itself*; and it is that, *qua* intellect, only in so far as it is that for itself. I think of this or that object: what, then, does this involve, and how, then, do I appear to myself in this thinking? In no other way than this: when the object is a merely imaginary one, I create certain determinations in myself; when the object is to be something real, these determinations are present without my aid: *and I observe that creation and this being*. They are in me only in so far as I observe them: seeing and being are inseparably united. – A thing, to be sure, is supposed to have a diversity of features, but as soon as the question arises: '*For whom*, then, is it to have them?' no one who understands the words will answer: 'For itself'; for we must still subjoin in thought an intellect *for* which it exists. The intellect is, by contrast, necessarily what it is for itself, and requires nothing subjoined to it in thought. By being posited as intellect, that for which it exists is already posited with it. In the intellect, therefore – to speak figuratively – there is a double series, of being and of seeing, of the real and of the ideal; and its essence consists in the inseparability of these two (it is synthetic); while the thing has only a single series, that of the real (a mere being posited). Intellect and thing are thus exact opposites: they inhabit two worlds between which there is no bridge.

It is by the principle of causality that dogmatism wishes to explain this constitution of intellect in general, as well as its particular determinations: it is to be an effect and the second member in the series.

But the principle of causality holds of a single *real* series, not of a double one. The power of the cause is transferred to something else that lies outside it, opposed to it, and creates a being therein and nothing more; a being for a possible intellect outside it and not for the being itself. If you endow the object acted upon with mechanical power only, it will transfer the received impulse to its neighbor, and thus the motion originating in the first member may proceed through a whole series, however long you wish to make it; but nowhere in it will you find a member which reacts upon itself. Or if you endow the object acted upon with the highest quality you can give to a thing, that of sensitivity, so that it governs itself on its own account and in accordance with the laws of its own nature, not according to the law given it by its cause, as in the series of mere mechanism, then it certainly reacts back upon the stimulus, and the determining ground of its being in this action lies not in the cause, but only in the requirement to be something at all; yet it is and remains a bare, simple being: a being for a possible intellect outside of itself. You cannot lay hold of the intellect if you do not subjoin it in thought as a primary absolute, whose connection with that being independent of it may be difficult for you to explain. – The series is simple, and after your explanation it remains so, and what was to be explained is not explained at all. The dogmatists were supposed to demonstrate the passage from being to presentation; this they do not, and cannot, do; for their principle contains only the ground of a being, but not that of presentation, which is the exact opposite of being. They take an enormous leap into a world quite alien to their principle.

They seek to conceal this leap in a variety of ways. Strictly – and that is the procedure of consistent dogmatism, which becomes materialism at once – the soul should not be a thing at all, and should be nothing whatever but a product, simply the result of the interaction of things among themselves.

But by this means there arises something in the things only, and never anything apart from them, unless an intellect, which observes things, is supplied in thought. The analogies the dogmatists present to make their system intelligible – that of harmony, for example, which arises out of the concord of several instruments – actually make its irrationality apparent. The concord and the harmony are not in the instruments; they are only in the mind of the listener who unifies the manifold in himself; and unless such a listener is supplied, they are nothing at all.

And yet, who is to prevent the dogmatist from assuming a soul as one of the things-in-themselves? This would then belong among the postulates he assumes for the solution of the problem, and only so is the principle of the action of things on the soul applicable, for in materialism there is only an interaction among things whereby thought is supposed to be produced. In order to make the inconceivable thinkable, he has sought to postulate the active thing, or the soul, or both, to be such that through their action presentations could result. The *acting thing* was to be such that its actions could become presentations, much like *God* in *Berkeley's* system (which is a dogmatic, and not at all an idealistic one). This leaves us no better off; we understand only mechanical action, and it is absolutely impossible for us to think of any other; the above proposal, therefore, consists of mere words without any sense. Or again, the soul is to be such that every action upon it becomes a presentation. But with this we fare exactly as with the previous principle: we simply cannot understand it.

This is the course dogmatism takes everywhere and in every form in which it appears. In the immense hiatus left to it between things and presentations, it inserts some empty words instead of an explanation. To be sure, these words can be memorized and repeated, but nobody at all has ever had, nor ever will have, a thought connected to them. For if one tries to conceive distinctly *how* the above occurs, the whole notion vanishes in an empty froth.

Thus dogmatism can only repeat its principle, and then reiterate it under various guises; it can state it, and then state it again; but it cannot get from this to the explanandum, and deduce the latter. Yet philosophy consists precisely of this deduction. Hence dogmatism, even from the speculative viewpoint, is no philosophy at all, but merely an impotent claim and assurance. Idealism is left as the only possible philosophy.

What is here established has nothing to do with the objections of the reader, for there is absolutely nothing to be said against the latter; its concern is, rather, with the absolute incapacity of many to understand it. Nobody who even understands the words can deny that all causation is mechanical and that no presentation comes about through mechanism. But this is precisely where the difficulty lies. A grasp of the nature of intelligence as depicted, upon which our entire refutation of dogmatism is founded, presupposes a degree of independence and freedom of mind. Now many people have progressed no further in their thinking than to grasp the simple sequence of the mechanism of nature; so it is very natural that presentations, if they wish to think of them, should also fall for them in this series, the only one that has entered their minds. The presentation becomes for them a kind of thing: a singular confusion, of which we find traces in the most famous of philosophical authors. Dogmatism is enough for such men; there is no hiatus for them, because for them the opposing world does not even exist. – Hence the dogmatist cannot be refuted by the argument we have given, however clear it may be; for it cannot be brought home to him, since he lacks the power to grasp its premise.

The manner in which we deal here with dogmatism also offends against the indulgent logic of our age, which, though uncommonly widespread in every period, has only in our own been raised to the level of a maxim expressed in words: one need not be so strict in reasoning, proofs are not to be taken so rigorously in philosophy as they are, say, in mathematics. Whenever thinkers of this type observe even a couple of links in the chain of reasoning, and catch sight of the rule of inference, they at once supply the remainder pell-mell by imagination, without further investigation of what it consists of. If an Alexander perforce tells them: Everything is determined by natural necessity: our presentations are dependent upon the disposition of things and our will upon the nature of our presentations; hence all our volitions are determined by natural necessity and our belief in free will is an illusion; they find this wonderfully intelligible and clear, and go off convinced and amazed at the brilliance of this demonstration, in spite of the fact that there is no sense to it. I beg to observe that the Science of Knowledge neither proceeds from nor counts upon this indulgent logic. If even a single member of the long chain that it must establish be not rigorously joined to the next, it will have proved nothing whatever.

7

As already stated above, idealism explains the determinations of consciousness on the basis of the activity of the intellect. The intellect, for it, is only active and absolute, never passive; it is not passive because it is postulated to be first and highest, preceded by nothing which could account for a passivity therein. For the same reason, it also has no *being* proper, no subsistence, for this is the result of an interaction and there is nothing either present or assumed with which the intellect could be set to interact. The intellect, for idealism, is an *act*, and absolutely nothing more; we should not even call it an *active* something, for this expression refers to something subsistent in which activity inheres. But idealism has no reason to assume such a thing, since it is not included in its principle and everything else must first be deduced. Now out of the activity of this intellect we must deduce *specific* presentations: of a world, of a material, spatially located world existing without our aid, etc., which notoriously occur in consciousness. But a determinate cannot be deduced from an indeterminate: the grounding principle, which is the rule of all deduction, is inapplicable here. Hence this primordial action of the intellect must needs be a determinate one, and, since the intellect is itself the highest ground of explanation, an action determined by the intellect and its nature, and not by something outside it. The presupposition of idealism will, therefore, be as follows: the intellect acts, but owing to its nature, it can act only in a certain fashion. If we think of this necessary way of acting in abstraction from the action itself, we shall call it, most appropriately, the law of action: hence there are necessary laws of the intellect. – This, then, also renders immediately intelligible the feeling of necessity that accompanies specific presentations: for here the intellect does not register some external impression, but feels in this action the limits of its own being. So far as idealism makes this one and only rationally determined and genuinely explanatory assumption, that the intellect has necessary laws, it is called critical, or also transcendental idealism. A transcendent idealism would be a system that deduced determinate presentations from the free and totally lawless action of the intellect; a completely contradictory hypothesis, for surely, as has just been remarked, the principle of grounding is inapplicable to such an action.

As surely as they are to be grounded in the unitary being of the intellect, the intellect's assumed laws of operation themselves constitute a system. This means that the fact that the intellect operates in just such a way under this specific condition can be further explained by the fact that it has a definite mode of operation under a condition in general; and the latter in turn may be explained on the basis of a single fundamental law: the intellect gives its laws to itself in the course of its operation; and this legislation itself occurs through a higher necessary action, or presentation. The law of causality, for example, is not a primordial law, but is merely one of several ways of connecting the manifold, and can be deduced from the fundamental law of this connection: and the law of this connection of the manifold, along with the manifold itself, can again be deduced from higher laws.

In accordance with this remark, critical idealism itself can now proceed in two different ways. On the one hand, it may really deduce the system of the necessary modes of operation, and with it concurrently the objective presentations created thereby, from the fundamental laws of the intellect, and so allow the whole compass of our presentations to come gradually into being before the eyes of its readers or listeners. On the other hand, it may conceive these laws as already and immediately applied to objects, that is, as applied somewhere, upon their lowest level (at which stage they are called categories), and then maintain that it is by means of them that objects are ordered and determined.

Now how can the critical philosopher of the latter sort, who does not deduce the accepted laws of the intellect from the nature thereof, obtain even a mere material knowledge of them – the knowledge that they are precisely these, viz., the laws of substantiality and causality? For I will not yet burden him with the question of how he knows that they are mere immanent laws of the intellect. They are the laws that are applied directly to objects: and he can have formed them only by abstraction from these objects, and hence only from experience. It avails nothing if he borrows them in some roundabout way from logic; for logic itself has arisen for him no otherwise than by abstraction from objects, and he merely does indirectly what, if done directly, would too obviously catch our eyes. Hence he can in no way confirm that his postulated laws of thought are really laws of thought, really nothing but immanent laws of the intellect. The dogmatist maintains against him that they are universal properties of things grounded in the nature of the latter, and it is past seeing why we should give more credence to the unproved assertion of the one than to the unproved assertion of the other. – This method yields no knowledge that the intellect must act precisely thus, nor why it must do so. In order to promote such understanding, something would have to be set forth in the premises that is the unique possession of the intellect, and those laws of thought would have to be deduced from these premises before our very eyes.

It is especially difficult to see, how, according to this method, the object itself arises; for, even if we grant the critical philosopher his unproved postulate, it explains nothing beyond the *dispositions* and *relations* of the thing; that, for example, it is in space, that it manifests itself in time, that its accidents must be related to something substantial, and so on. But whence comes that which has these relations and dispositions; whence the stuff that is organized in these forms? It is in this stuff that dogmatism takes refuge, and you have merely made a bad situation worse.

We know well enough that the thing comes into being surely through an action in accord with these laws, that it is nothing else but the *totality of these relations unified by the imagination*, and that all these relations together constitute the thing; the object is surely the original synthesis of all these concepts. Form and matter are not separate items; the totality of form is the matter, and it is through analysis that we first obtain individual forms. But the critical philosopher who follows the present method can only assure us of this; and it is in fact a mystery how he knows it himself, if indeed he does. So long as the thing is not made to arise as a whole in front of the thinker's eyes, dogmatism is not hounded to its last refuge. But this is possible only by dealing with the intellect in its total, and not in its partial, conformity to law.

Such an idealism is, therefore, unproved and unprovable. It has no other weapon against dogmatism save the assurance that it is right; and against the higher, perfected critical philosophy, nothing save impotent rage and the assertion that one can go no further, the assurance that beyond it there is no more ground, that from there one becomes unintelligible to *it*, and the like; all of which means nothing whatever.

Finally, in such a system only those laws are established whereby the purely subsumptive faculty of judgment determines the objects of external experience alone. But this is by far the smallest part of the system of reason. Since it lacks insight into the whole procedure of reason, this halfhearted critical philosophy gropes around in the sphere of practical reason and reflective judgment just as blindly as the mere imitator and copies out, just as artlessly, expressions totally unintelligible to it.*

In another place† I have already set forth in full clarity the methods of the perfected transcendental idealism established by the Science of Knowledge. I cannot explain how people could have failed to

---

* Such a critical idealism has been propounded by *Professor Beck* in his *Einzig möglichen Standpunkte* . . . Although I find in this view the weaknesses objected to above, that should not deter me from the public expression of due respect to the man who, on his own account, has raised himself out of the confusion of our age to the insight that the philosophy of Kant is not a dogmatism but a transcendental idealism, and that, according to it, the object is given neither in whole nor in half, but is rather made; and from expecting that in time he will raise himself even higher. I consider the above work as the most suitable present that could have been made to our age, and recommend it as the best preparation for those who wish to study the Science of Knowledge from my writings. It does not lead to this latter system; but destroys the most powerful obstacle which closes it off for many people. – Some have fancied themselves insulted by the tone of that work, and just recently a well-meaning reviewer in a famous journal demands in clear terms: *crustula, elementa velit ut discere prima*. For my part, I find its tone, if anything, too mild: for I truly do not think that we should, of all things, thank certain writers for having confused and debased the richest and noblest teaching for a decade or more, nor see why we should first ask their permission to be right. – As regards the hastiness with which the same author, in another group, which is far below him, pounces upon books that his own conscience ought to tell him he does not understand, and cannot even rightly know how deep their matter may go, I can feel sorry only on his own account.

† In the work, *Über den Begriff der Wissenschaftslehre*, Weimar, 1794.

understand that exposition; at any rate, it is asserted that some have not understood it.

I am forced, therefore, to repeat what has been said before, and warn that in this science everything turns on the understanding thereof.

This idealism proceeds from a single fundamental principle of reason, which it demonstrates directly in consciousness. In so doing it proceeds as follows. It calls upon the listener or reader to think a certain concept freely; were he to do so, he would find himself obliged to proceed in a certain way. We must distinguish two things here: the required mode of thinking – this is accomplished through freedom, and whoever does not achieve it with us will see nothing of what the Science of Knowledge reveals – and the necessary manner in which it is to be accomplished, which latter is not dependent on the will, being grounded in the nature of the intellect; it is something *necessary*, which emerges, however, only in and upon the occurrence of a free action; something *found*, though its discovery is conditioned by freedom.

So far idealism demonstrates its claims in our immediate consciousness. But that the above necessity is the fundamental law of all reason, that from it one can deduce the whole system of our necessary presentations – not only of a world whose objects are determined by the subsuming and reflective judgment, but also of ourselves as free practical beings under laws – this is a mere hypothesis. Idealism must prove this hypothesis by an actual deduction, and this precisely is its proper task.

In so doing it proceeds in the following fashion. *It shows that what is first set up as fundamental principle and directly demonstrated in consciousness, is impossible unless something else occurs along with it, and that this something else is impossible unless a third something also takes place, and so on until the conditions of what was first exhibited are completely exhausted, and this latter is, with respect to its possibility, fully intelligible.* Its course is an unbroken progression from conditioned to condition; each condition becomes, in turn, a conditioned whose condition must be sought out.

If the hypothesis of idealism is correct and the reasoning in the deduction is valid, the system of all necessary presentations or the entirety of experience (this identity is established not in philosophy but only beyond it) must emerge as the final result, as the totality of the conditions of the original premise.

Now idealism does not keep this experience, as the antecedently known goal at which it must arrive, constantly in mind; in its method it knows nothing of experience and takes no account of it at all; it proceeds from its starting point in accordance with its rule, unconcerned about what will emerge in the end. It has been given the right angle from which to draw its straight line; does it then still need a point to draw it to? In my opinion, all the points on its line are given along with it. Suppose that you are given a certain number. You surmise it to be the product of certain factors. Your task then is simply to seek out, by the rule well known to you, the product of these factors. Whether or not it agrees with the given number will turn out later, once you have the product. The given number is the entirety of experience; the factors are the principle demonstrated in consciousness and the laws of thought; the multiplication is the activity of philosophizing. Those who advise you always to keep an eye on experience when you philosophize are recommending that you change the factors a bit and multiply falsely on occasion, so that the numbers you get may, after all, match: a procedure as dishonest as it is superficial.

To the extent that these final results of idealism are viewed as such, as consequences of reasoning, they constitute the a priori in the human mind; and to the extent that they are regarded, where reasoning and experience really agree, as given in experience, they are called a posteriori. For a completed idealism the a priori and the a posteriori are by no means twofold, but perfectly unitary; they are merely two points of view, to be distinguished solely by the mode of our approach. Philosophy anticipates the entirety of experience and *thinks* it only as necessary, and to that extent it is, by comparison with real experience, a priori. To the extent that it is regarded as given, the number is a posteriori; the same number is a priori insofar as it is derived as a product of the factors. Anyone who thinks otherwise, simply does not know what he is talking about.

A philosophy whose results do not agree with experience is surely false, for it has not fulfilled its promise to deduce the entirety of experience and to explain it on the basis of the necessary action of the intellect. Either the hypothesis of transcendental idealism is, therefore, completely false, or it has merely been wrongly handled in the particular version which fails to perform its task. Since the demand for an explanation of experience is surely founded in human reason; since no reasonable man will accept that reason can impose a demand whose satisfaction is absolutely impossible; since there are only two roads to its satisfaction, that of dogmatism and that of transcendental idealism, and it can be proved without further ado that the former cannot fulfill its promise; for these reasons, the resolute thinker will always prefer the latter, holding that the hypothesis as such is completely right and that error has occurred only in the reasoning; nor will any vain attempt deter him from trying again, until finally success is achieved.

The course of this idealism runs, as can be seen, from something that occurs in consciousness, albeit only as the result of a free act of thought, to the entirety of experience. What lies between these two is its proper field. This latter is not a fact of consciousness and does not lie within the compass of experience; how could anything that did so ever be called philosophy, when philosophy has to exhibit the ground of experience, and the ground lies necessarily outside of what it grounds. It is something brought forth by means of free but law-governed thought. – This will become entirely clear as soon as we take a closer look at the fundamental assertion of idealism.

The absolutely postulated is impossible, so idealism shows, without the condition of a second something, this second without a third, and so on; that is, of all that it establishes nothing is possible alone, and it is only in conjunction with them all that each individual item is possible. Hence, by its own admission, only the whole occurs in consciousness, and this totality is in fact experience. Idealism seeks a closer acquaintance with this whole, and so must analyze it, and this not by a blind groping, but according to the definite rule of composition, so that it may see the whole take form under its eyes. It can do this because it can abstract; because in free thought it is surely able to grasp the individual alone. For not only the necessity of presentations, but also their freedom is present in consciousness: and this freedom, again, can proceed either lawfully or capriciously. The whole is given to it from the standpoint of necessary consciousness; it discovers it, just as it discovers itself. The series created by the unification of this whole emerges only through freedom. Whoever performs this act of freedom will come to be aware of it, and lay out, as it were, a new field in his consciousness: for one who does not perform it, that which the act conditions does not exist at all. – The chemist synthesizes a body, say a certain metal, from its elements. The ordinary man sees the metal familiar to him; the chemist, the union of these specific elements. Do they then see different things? I should think not! They see the same thing, though in different ways. What the chemist sees is the a priori, for he sees the individual elements: what the common man sees is the a posteriori, for he sees the whole. – But there is this difference here: the chemist must first analyze the whole before he can compound it, since he is dealing with an object whose rule of composition he cannot know prior to the analysis; but the philosopher can synthesize without prior analysis, because he already knows the rule that governs his object, reason.

No reality other than that of necessary thought falls, therefore, within the compass of philosophy, given that one wishes to think about the ground of experience at all. Philosophy maintains that the intellect can be thought only as active, and active only in this particular way. This reality is completely adequate for it; since it follows from philosophy that there is in fact no other.

It is the complete critical idealism here described that the Science of Knowledge intends to establish. What has just been said contains the concept of this former, and I shall entertain no objections to it, for no one can know better than I what I propose to do. Proofs of the impossibility of a project that will be accomplished, and in part already is so, are simply ridiculous. One has only to attend to the course of the argument, and examine whether or not it fulfills its promise.

Translated by Peter Heath and John Lachs

On the Spirit and the Letter in Philosophy

SECOND LETTER

You take up the question raised at the end of my previous letter and answer it in the following way:

'Nowhere else but in the depths of his own breast can the ingenious [*geistvolle*] artist have discovered what lies in mine, though it is hidden from my own eyes and from everyone else's. He reckons on the agreement of others, and he does so rightly. We see that under his influence the mass, if it be at all cultivated, actually comes together as one soul; that all individual differences in disposition and feeling disappear; that the same fear or the same pity or the same intellectual [*geistige*] pleasure lifts and moves all hearts. In as much as he is an artist he must have in him that which is common to all developed souls, and instead of the individual disposition which differentiates and divides others from it, the common disposition [*Universalsinn*] of collective humanity, as it were, and this alone must dwell in him at the moment of inspiration [*Begeisterung*]. We are all different from one another in many ways. No one person is exactly the same as another, neither as far as concerns his spiritual nor his physical character.

'Nevertheless we must all possess, to a greater or lesser extent, according to the degree of similarity or difference in education and experience, either on the surface of our mind [*Geist*] or in its more hidden depths, certain common characteristics. For we understand each other, we can communicate with each other, and all human intercourse from the beginning of time has been nothing but an uninterrupted struggle from generation to generation in which each individual tries to make every other with whom he comes into contact in the course of his life agree with him. What is not so easy for the ordinary man, and what he doesn't quite succeed in doing, the artist achieves by altering the ambition and giving up the idea of projecting his individuality on others. On the contrary he sacrifices it and takes instead those common characteristics which occur in each one of us, moulding them to form the individual character of his mind [*Geist*] and his work. Therefore what inspires him is called genius [*Genius*], and great genius, an essence from a higher sphere in which all lowly and earthly limitations determining the individual character of earthbound men can no longer be distinguished and merge together in a soft haze.

'Since the means which he uses to awaken and engage this common sense [*Gemeinsinn*], and to silence individuality for as long as he has us under his influence; – since these means and the necessary connection which exists between them and their effect cannot easily be discovered by reflection, nor by any reference to their purpose through concepts [*Begriffe*]: so only through experience, through his own inner experience of self, can the artist become acquainted with them. At least, any attempts to discover them by other routes have failed. The artist has already felt what he makes us feel after him, and the same forms which he conjures up before our eyes – regardless as to how they appeared before his own – have already lulled him into that sweet intoxication, that delightful madness which takes hold of us all at his singing, before his vibrant canvas, or at the sound of his flute. Cool self-possession [*Besonnenheit*] returns to him again and with sober artistry he portrays what he saw in his ecstasy in order to draw the whole of mankind into his delusion, the dear memory of which still fills him with sweet emotion, and to spread the burden of guilt which the founding of his kind placed upon him amongst the whole species. Wherever there are developed human beings the evidence of his long-extinguished inspiration [*Begeisterung*] will be celebrated by re-enactment to the end of time.'

Thus you solve the task in hand, and I think you are right. But let us jointly examine your argument further, break it down into its finer parts, and trace their development from the roots, so that we can form a definite idea of this common disposition [*Universalsinn*] which you use as the basis of your explanation. And let us see clearly how the impression, which you say is made on that faculty [*Sinn*] in the artist's mind, is created, and grasp – as far as it can be grasped – why it is able to communicate itself so easily and so universally.

You say that totally apart from all external experience and without any outside help the artist develops from the depths of his nature [*Gemüth*] what lies hidden from all in the human soul; that guided by his powers of divination he sets forth the characteristics common to the whole of humanity, which have not shown themselves as such in any previous experience. But the one thing in man which is independent and utterly incapable of being determined from outside we call 'drive' [*Trieb*]. This and this alone is the single and highest principle governing self-activity [*Selbstthätigkeit*] in us. This alone makes us independent, observing and acting beings. However much external things may influence us, they do not go so far as to bring out in us something which was not already present in them, nor do they produce an effect contrary to their underlying nature. Self-activity in man, which determines his character and distinguishes him from the rest of nature, placing him outside her laws, must itself be based on something peculiar to him. This peculiarity is drive. A human being is above all human because of drive, and what kind of a person he is depends on the greater or lesser force [*Kraft*] and effectiveness of drive, of the inner living and striving.

Only through drive is man an image-producing being [*vorstellendes Wesen*]. Even if, as some philosophers would have it, we could let objects provide him with the material of his representation [*Vorstellung*], letting images [*Bilder*] flow to him from all sides via things, he would still need self-activity to be able to grasp them and shape them into a representation, which the lifeless creatures in space around us are without, although the images floating through the whole universe must stream over them as they do over us. We need self-activity to arrange these representations in a motivated way: now to observe the outward form of a plant, so as to be able to recognize it again and distinguish it from other similar types; now to look into the laws which might have governed nature's formation of that plant; now to find out how it might be used as food or clothing or as medicine. We need self-activity in order unceasingly to intensify and extend our cognitive knowledge [*Erkenntniss*] of objects. Through it alone the star, which for the unschooled countryman remains a tiny lamp by the light of which to gather up his farm implements, becomes for the astronomer a large solid celestial body moving at immeasurable distances according to immutable laws.

To the extent that this kind of drive seeks the generation of knowledge we can call it, in this respect and for the sake of clarity and brevity, the 'knowledge-drive' [*Erkenntnisstrieb*], as if it were one particular *basic drive* [*Grundtrieb*], which it is not. It and all the other specific drives and forces which we may still call by this name are simply particular manifestations of the one indivisible primary force [*Grundkraft*] in man, and we must be very careful to refrain from interpreting such expressions in any other way, in this or in any other philosophical work. The knowledge-drive accordingly is always satisfied to a certain extent: every man has certain cognitions [*Erkenntnisse*], and without them he would be something other than a man. In general therefore this drive manifests itself in the effect it produces. From this we return to the cause in the self-active subject, and only in this way do we arrive at an idea [*Idee*] of the nature of this drive and a recognition [*Erkenntniss*] of its laws.

Drive is not always satisfied, in that it does not simply seek knowledge of the thing as it is, but looks for definition, variation and development of the thing as it ought to be. Then it is called 'practical' – and this in the narrowest sense, for strictly speaking all drive is practical in that it urges us to self-activity, so that in this sense everything in man is based on the practical drive, for there is nothing in him except through self-activity. Alternatively, when it goes in search of a certain particular representation purely for its own sake, and in no way for the sake of a thing which might correspond to it, or just for cognitive knowledge of this thing, then, since it does not yet have a name in its generality, we will provisionally give it one and call it the 'aesthetic', as a branch of it has been so named before. It is clear that an understanding [*Kenntniss*] of this drive and of the knowledge-drive cannot be reached by the same route, i.e., by tracing the cause from the effect. So the question arises as to how one does arrive at such an understanding. But before we answer this question let us make a sharper distinction between the drives themselves as put forward above.

The knowledge-drive aims at cognitive knowledge as such, and for the sake of cognition. It leaves us quite indifferent to the being [*Wesen*] of the thing, its outer or inner qualities. Under its guidance we want nothing more than to be aware of what these qualities are: we are aware, and we are satisfied. Here the representation has no other value and serves no other function beyond being fully in accordance with the fact [*Sache*]. It is the practical drive which seeks out the qualities of things, for the sake of qualities. We recognize this only too well when this drive is stimulated. But we are not satisfied with this. It must be different, and different in a determinate way. In the case of the knowledge-drive there is posited a thing which is completely self-determining, without any of our help, and the drive seeks to reproduce it in our mind, with these determinations and with no others, through free self-activity. In the case of the practical drive there is posited as fundamental a representation whose existence [*Daseyn*] and content are created through free self-activity in the soul, and the drive seeks to bring forward something that corresponds to it in the sensible world. In both cases the drive seeks neither the representation alone nor the thing alone, but a harmony between the two; only in the first case the representation ought to conform itself to the thing, and in the second case the thing to the representation.

It is quite a different matter with the drive which we have just named the aesthetic. It is directed towards a representation, and a particular [*bestimmte*] representation, exclusively for the sake of its determination [*Bestimmung*] and its determination as a pure representation. As far as this drive is concerned the representation is an end in itself. It does not derive its value from harmonizing with the object – on which no store is set in this connection – but has value in itself. It is not the replication of reality but a free unrestrained form of the image which is sought. Without any interdetermination [*Wechselbestimmung*] between it and an object such a representation stands isolated as the ultimate goal of the drive. It is not related to any thing which it governs or is governed by. Just as a representation whose very substance is created through absolute self-activity is at the basis of the practical determination [*Bestimmung*], so a representation created in the same way is at the basis of the aesthetic, with the difference that the latter need not, like the former, be presented with something that corresponds to it in the sensible world. Just as the knowledge-drive has as its ultimate goal a representation, and is satisfied when this is formed, so it is with the aesthetic, now with the difference that a representation of the first type should harmonize with the object, whereas the aesthetic representation does not have to harmonize with anything at all. It is possible that a presentation [*Darstellung*] of the aesthetic image should be called for in the sensible world; but this does not occur by means of the aesthetic drive, whose task is completed with the creation of the image in the soul, but rather by means of the practical drive, which for some reason intervenes in the order of representations and sets up a possible outward and extraneous focus for the replicated image [*Nachbildung*] in the real world. Likewise it can happen that a representation of an object which really exists harmonizes completely with the aesthetic drive, but in that case the ensuing satisfaction of this drive is in no way concerned with the empirical truth of the representation. The image created would be no less pleasing if it were empty, and it does not give any more pleasure because it happens at the same time to embody cognitive knowledge. It could not be otherwise – I remind you of this in passing, in order to make myself clearer, but not to draw any premature conclusions – it could not be otherwise if both these incompatible drives, one to leave things as they are and the other to work upon them everywhere and *ad infinitum*, are to unite and present to us a single indivisible man, according to our usual view of the matter. Or, looking at them in the manner described above, which strictly speaking is the only correct way: if both drives are one and the same and only the conditions of their expression are to be distinguished. Drive could not aim at the representation of the thing without aiming at the representation for its own sake. Just as impossible would be a drive which would work on the thing itself and modify it on the basis of a representation which lay beyond all experience or any possible experience, if there were no drive or faculty to create representations independent of the real nature of things.

How do these two drives just mentioned manifest themselves, if the aesthetic drive never produces, and the practical drive by no means always produces, actions [*Handlungen*] which would make it possible to observe them? Even so, the following means of tracking them down still remains. Since the drive, in the way it begins having an effect on man and then takes over, arouses and stimulates total self-activity and focusses it completely on something specific, whether it be an object outside him or a representation within him; so necessarily the fortuitous harmony in a sentient being, which man must certainly be, between the given and this tendency of self-activity, must be revealed in man's overwhelming awareness of self, of his force [*Kraft*] and of his range [*Ausbreitung*], which we call a feeling of pleasure. Conversely, the chance disharmony between the given and this same tendency must be revealed through an equally overwhelming feeling of impotence and constraint, which we call a feeling of displeasure. So let us conceive of a force in a magnet, and of a drive behind this force, a drive to attract anything made of iron which comes within its sphere of influence. Let it really attract a piece of iron: its drive expresses itself and is satisfied, and if we confer upon the magnet the power of feeling then a feeling of satisfaction, i.e., a feeling of pleasure, would necessarily be aroused in it. If on the other hand we allow the weight of the iron to exceed the force of the magnet, then the drive still remains inside it, since it really would attract the iron if we subtracted the amount by which the magnet is outweighed; but it is not satisfied, and if the magnet is once again given the power of feeling then it must necessarily feel a resistance to and a restriction and limitation of its force. In a word, it must feel displeasure. This is the sole source of all pleasure and displeasure.

Both drives, the practical as well as the aesthetic, express themselves in this way, but with a difference. As we have already said, the practical drive pursues an object outside man, one whose existence must be seen as independent of him in that no action ensues or could ensue. Certainly the as yet unshaped concept [*Begriff*] of this object is there in the soul. Something takes place in the mind

[*Gemüth*] through which the drive is expressed and signified for consciousness: namely, the concept of that towards which it is directed. The nature of the drive is characterized by this. It can be felt and is felt, and in this instance is called a 'desire' [*Begehren*] – a desire, in so far as the conditions in which the object can become real are not regarded as being within our power. If they do come within our power, and we decide to make the effort and the sacrifices necessary to make them real, then our desire is raised to the level of volition [*Wollen*]. When faced with an existing object, in this case one can predict what will arouse pleasure or displeasure, for only the actual existence of the object arouses such a feeling. One can therefore differentiate between the nature of the practical drive and the object, and thus between the satisfaction of this drive and the lack of it. The human spirit [*Geist*] takes on as it were something that belongs to it, an expression of its own actions outside itself, and with no difficulty it sees in the objects its own form, as if in a mirror. It is quite different with the aesthetic drive. It is not directed at anything outside man, but towards something which is only to be found within him. No prior representation of its objects is possible, because its object is itself only a representation. The nature of the drive is therefore not characterized by anything except by satisfaction or the lack of it. The one does not permit itself to be distinguished from the other, but both happen together. What is in us as the result of the aesthetic drive does not reveal itself through a desire, but only through an unexpectedly surprising but completely unmotivated and purposeless feeling of either well-being or discomfort, which bears no comprehensible relation to the other workings of our mind [*Gemüth*]. To continue the example: let us present to the magnet, which has a drive to attract a piece of iron outweighing the capacity of its force, the representation [*Vorstellung*] of this iron. Then it will *desire* to attract it. And if it can muster a force beyond its inherent capacity, to the extent of detracting as much from the iron as is in excess of its own capacity to attract; and if the urge to attract this iron is stronger than its antipathy (i.e. the refusal of the iron to have the weight reduced), then it will *experience volition* [*wollen*] to attract it. If we take away from the magnet this ability to posit [*vorzustellen*] both the iron outside itself and its ability to attract it, and simply leave it with drive, force, and self-sensation [*Selbstgefühl*], then it will experience a feeling of displeasure when the heaviness of the iron outweighs its own force, and a feeling of pleasure when, the weight having been taken away without its knowing, it is able to attract the iron. It cannot explain this feeling, which is not connected to anything it recognizes, and which is just like our feeling of aesthetic pleasure or displeasure – but does not stem from the same source. But imagine, as a fitting image for the aesthetic mood, the sweet songster of the night. Imagine, as you can well do along with the poet, that her soul is pure song; imagine her spirit as a striving to form the most perfect harmony, and its particular notes as the representative images [*Vorstellungen*] of this soul. Unaware of herself, the songster performs [*treibt*] up and down the octaves according to the inclination of her spirit; gradually it develops its whole capacity through the myriad of harmonies. Each new chord is on a new rung on the ladder of development and is in harmony with the basic drive of the songster, which she is unaware of; for we have given her no representations other than the notes themselves, so that she cannot make judgements about their connection with what is for her a chance harmony. In just the same way the direction of the aesthetic drive lies hidden from our eyes, and we similarly cannot compare the representations developing in us with that which obeys wholly other laws. All the same that harmony must arouse a pleasure in her which fills her whole being, the causes of which she could not for that very reason adduce. But she carries on her inner and secret life in the following tones: its development is not yet complete, this chord does not yet express her whole being, and that pleasure is turned to displeasure in a flash; then both dissolve into greater pleasure with the next note, but return again to drive the singer once more. Her life floats on the surging waves of aesthetic feeling, as does the life of art in every true genius.

So it is easy for the practical drive to make itself known to consciousness in all sorts of ways through its various functions, and it seems quite possible to learn to know it thoroughly and exhaustively by starting out from one's own inner experience. But as far as the aims of the aesthetic drive are concerned, more impediments arise.

There seems to be no way of penetrating far enough into the depths of our minds [*Geistes*] to reach it, other than by trying either to reach it through external experience regardless, waiting to see *whether* and *how* it will reveal itself in these conditions, or by leaving things to chance, blindly trusting one's imagination [*Einbildungskraft*] and waiting to see how its multifarious creations affect us. But in both cases one is still in danger of confusing a feeling of pleasure based on an obscure, undeveloped, perhaps completely empirical and individual practical consciousness with aesthetic pleasure proper. And so we are always left uncertain as to whether there is such a drive as that which we have described as the aesthetic, or whether all the things we take to be expressions of it are a subtle delusion. We could never guess with certainty, from previous actual experience, what would give pleasure; and the conclusions that what had given us pleasure must give everyone pleasure would remain without foundation.

Consider the position, that aesthetic representations can only develop first and foremost in and by means of experience which is directed towards cognitive knowledge: then you are confronted by a new difficulty. But looked at from another angle this becomes a relief, and the only thing that facilitates the transition from the sphere of knowledge to that of aesthetic feeling.

You see another difficulty: even knowledge is not in the first place sought for its own sake, but for a purpose beyond it. At the first level of development [*Bildung*], both of the individual and of the whole species, the practical drive in its baser expression outstrips all others, seeking the maintenance and external well-being of animal life. So likewise the knowledge-drive begins by serving this need, in order by so doing to develop the capacity for an independent subsistence. Because of the harshness of nature, or because of the advance of our fellow men against us in struggle, we have no time to linger in contemplation of the things around us. We seize busily on their useful qualities in order to get the best out of them, with constant misgivings about the disadvantages in practice which might follow from a false view of them. Hastily we hurry away from this hard-won cognitive knowledge to the exploitation of these things, and are very careful not to lose a moment in gaining the tools which we could use for the immediate attainment of our ends. Mankind must first attain a certain external well-being and security. The cry of want from within must first be silenced, and strife from without must be settled, before we can observe and linger over our contemplations, and abandon ourselves during this leisurely and liberal contemplation to aesthetic impressions, even if it must be coldbloodedly, without reference to the needs of the moment, and even with the danger of going astray. Thus the calm surface of the water captures the beautiful image of the sun; the outlines drawn in pure light dance and are thrown together and engulfed in the mighty face of the inconstant waves.

Hence the periods and regions of serfdom [*Knechtschaft*] are also those of tastelessness [*Geschmacklosigkeit*]; and if it is on the one hand inadvisable to allow men to be free before their aesthetic sense is developed, so on the other hand it is impossible to develop it before they are free. Thus the idea [*Idee*] of elevating men through aesthetic education [*ästhetische Erziehung*] to be worthy of freedom, and to freedom itself, will get us into a vicious circle if we do not find beforehand a means of arousing the courage of the individual amongst the throng to be neither the master nor the slave of anyone. In such a time it is all that the oppressed one can do to keep himself alive under the boot of the oppressor, to get enough air and not let himself be completely trodden down. The oppressor himself can only maintain his equilibrium, and not lose his balance during the twistings and turnings of the victim. The burden and the pressure on him are increased because of his unnatural and irremediable position. Because of this the contortions of the victim only get more panic-stricken and daring, and the repression of the other more severe, so that through a very understandable interaction the evil increases in a dismal progression. Neither of the two has time – and they will have increasingly less time – to breathe, to look calmly around himself and let his senses open up to the delightful influence of beneficent nature. Both retain all their lives the taste [*Geschmack*] they embraced then, when nothing confined them but their swaddling-clothes: the taste for garish colours which violently stimulate the dulled eye, and for the gloss of precious metals. The needy craftsman hurries to appease this taste in the one person who is well-off, in order to reap the scant reward which he needs to live. Thus art declined during the Roman empire at the same rate as freedom, until under Constantine it became a slave to barbarian pomp. Thus the emperor of China's elephants are clad in heavy gold ornaments, and the horses of the kings of Persia drink from cups of solid gold.

No more depressing, but more repugnant and more disturbing for art, is the sight of those under freer skies and milder men of power, who stand in the centre between the two extremes, and who are allowed by the world to be free, but who do not make use of this last remnant of freedom, which, it seems, a genius watching over mankind has thrown into the constitution as seed for harvesting by future generations. No, they press their attentions on the rulers, who are themselves tired of the eternal uniformity, against their will, and grieve that no one acknowledges their bowing and scraping, nor gives them a political importance which they do not in themselves have. Then, with mathematical precision, all forms of culture [*Bildung*] are estimated according to their future use: speculation which wanders harmlessly at will is asked what it has to offer before it crosses the threshold; novels and plays are searched for their fine morals; one has no chagrin in publicly admitting that one finds an Iphigenia or an epistle in the same vein unpoetic; and Homer himself would probably be called an insipid poetaster if he were not excused for the sake of his Greekness.

But just that aforementioned condition that we must begin our life with experience, as we have said before, reveals to us the only possible transition to spiritual life. As soon as that pressing urgency is removed, no longer driving us to snatch up greedily any possible mental acquisition [*Geisteserwerb*] only to be able to expend it when the need dictates, then the drive for cognitive knowledge is aroused for the sake of knowledge itself. We begin by letting our inner [*geistig*] eye wander over objects and linger awhile; we look at them from several angles without considering a possible use for them, and take the risk of making a dubious assumption only to await the right explanation in peace. We are seized by the single noble avarice of collecting the wealth of the spirit [*Geistesschätze*] for the sake of having it and to delight in looking at its items, since we do not need them to live and they are not imprinted with the stamp of the mint which alone has currency. We dare to invest our riches in attempts which could fail, being more indifferent to the possible loss. We have taken the first step in separating ourselves from the animal in us. Liberalmindedness [*Liberalität der Gesinnungen*] comes into being – the first degree of humanity.

During this peaceful and unmotivated contemplation of objects, when our mind [*Geist*] is secure and not keeping a watch on itself, our aesthetic sense develops with reality as its guide without our having anything to do with it. But after both have gone down the same path for a distance, it breaks loose at the parting of the ways and continues independent of and unaccompanied by reality. Thus your eye often rested on the land to the west of your country dwelling. If you could look at it completely disinterestedly, not trying to see how you might escape the night attacks of bands of thieves, then you would not just see the green grass and beyond that the different sorts of clover and beyond that the tall corn, and commit to memory what was there; but your contemplative eye would linger with pleasure on the fresh green of the grass, would look further at the numerous blossoms of the clover, and would glide softly over the rippling waves of the corn towards the heights beyond. There ought, you would say, to be a little village at the top under some trees, or perhaps a wood. But you would not desire to have a house in the village, nor to walk in the wood. It would have been just the same to you if, without your knowing it, someone had conjured up what you wished for by means of an optical illusion. How did this come about? Well, your aesthetic sense had already been aroused in the contemplation of the first objects, in that they satisfied it unexpectedly; but it was offended that this view should cease so abruptly, and that your eye should sink into empty space beyond the heights. According to its requirements the view should have resolved itself in a suitable manner, in order to complete and round off the beautiful whole that had been begun; and your imagination [*Einbildungskraft*], guided up to now by the aesthetic sense, was able to meet this need itself.

You see in this example a short history of the development of our whole aesthetic faculty [*Vermögen*]. During peaceful contemplation, which no longer concerns itself with knowledge of what has been long recognized, but which extends as it were further out beyond the object, the aesthetic sense develops in the soul at rest, when intellectual curiosity [*Wissbegierde*] has been stilled and the knowledge-drive has been satisfied. One object has our approval quite without interest, i.e. we judge it to be in conformity with a certain rule (which we will not go into any further) without attaching any greater value to it. Another object does not receive this approval, and would not unless we took great pains to make it other than it is. It now remains to be shown that we likewise possess a certain sense and a certain awareness [*Kenntniss*] which is no more than that, which will not lead to anything, and which cannot be used for anything. This faculty is called taste [*Geschmack*], and the same term chiefly applies to the skill in making correct and generally acceptable judgements in this respect; its opposite is tastelessness.

Out of this contemplation, which still continues to hold on to the thread of reality but wherein we are no longer concerned with the real nature of things, but rather with their oneness with our spirit, the imagination, born to be free, soon attains total freedom. Having arrived in the sphere of the aesthetic drive it remains there, even when the drive deviates from nature and portrays forms not as they are but as they ought to be according to the requirements of this drive. This free creative ability is called 'spirit' [*Geist*]. Taste judges the given, but spirit creates. Taste is the complement and fulfilment of liberality, spirit that of taste itself. One can have taste without spirit, but not spirit without taste. Through spirit the sphere of taste, which is confined within the bounds of nature, is enlarged. The products of spirit create new objects and further develop taste, albeit without elevating it to the status of spirit itself. Everyone can cultivate taste, but it is doubtful whether everyone can raise himself to the level of spirit.

The infinite and unlimited objective of our drive is called the 'idea' [*Idee*], and in as much as a part of it may be presented as a sensible image [*Bild*], then it is called the 'ideal' [*Ideale*]. Spirit is therefore a faculty of the ideal.

Spirit leaves the bounds of reality behind it, and in its own special sphere there are no bounds. The drive to which it is entrusted passes into the infinite; through it the spirit is led ever onwards from one vista to another, and when it has attained the goal it had in view new horizons open up to it. In the pure, clear aether of the land of its birth there are no vibrations other than those it creates with its own wings.

Translated by Elizabeth Rubinstein

Some Lectures Concerning the Scholar's Vocation

PREFACE

These lectures were delivered this past summer semester before a considerable number of our students. They provide entry into a whole which the author wishes to complete and to lay before the public at the proper time. External circumstances, which can contribute nothing to the correct evaluation or understanding of these pages, have induced me to have these first five lectures printed separately and, moreover, to have them printed exactly in the form in which they were first delivered, without altering one single word. This may excuse several careless expressions. Owing to my other work, I was from the beginning unable to polish them in the way I would have liked. Declamation can be used to assist an oral delivery, but revising them for publication would have conflicted with my secondary aim in publishing them.

Several expressions found in these lectures will not please every reader, but for this the author should not be blamed. In pursuing my inquiries I did not ask whether something would meet with approval or not, but rather, whether it might be true; and what, according to the best of my knowledge, I considered to be true I expressed as well as I could.

In addition, however, to those readers who have their own reasons to be displeased by what is said here, there may be others for whom what is said here will seem to be useless, because it is something which cannot be achieved and which fails to correspond to anything in the real world as it now exists. Indeed, I am afraid that the majority of otherwise upright, respectable, and sober persons will judge these lectures in this way. For although the number of persons capable of lifting themselves to the level of ideas has always been a minority in every age, this number (for reasons which I can certainly leave unmentioned) has never been smaller than it is right now. It may be true that, within that area to which ordinary experience assigns us, people have never thought for themselves more widely or judged more correctly than they do now; however, just as soon as they are supposed to go any distance beyond this familiar area, most persons are completely lost and blind. If it is not possible to rekindle the higher genius in such persons once it has been extinguished, then we must permit them to remain peacefully within the circle of ordinary experience. And in so far as they are useful and indispensable within this circle, we must grant them their undiminished value in and for this area. They are, however, guilty of a great injustice if they try to pull down to their own level everything which they cannot themselves reach: if, for example, they demand that everything which is published should be as easy to use as a cookbook or an arithmetic book or a book of rules and regulations, and if they decry everything which cannot be employed in such a manner.

That ideals cannot be depicted within the real world is something that we others know just as well as such persons do – perhaps we know this better than they. All we maintain is that reality must be judged in accordance with ideals and must be modified by those who feel themselves able to do so. Supposing that such persons cannot be convinced that this is true, still, since they are what they are, they lose very little by not being convinced, and mankind loses nothing. It merely becomes clear from this that they cannot be counted on to contribute anything to the project of improving mankind. Mankind will undoubtedly continue on its way. May a kindly nature reign over such persons, may it bestow upon them rain and sunshine at the proper time, wholesome food and undisturbed circulation, and in addition – intelligent thoughts!

Jena, Michaelmas 1794

FIRST LECTURE
CONCERNING THE VOCATION OF MAN AS SUCH

You are already somewhat acquainted with the purpose of the series of lectures which I am beginning today. I would like to answer – or rather, I would like to prompt you to answer – the following questions: What is the scholar's vocation? What is his relationship to mankind as a whole, as well as to the individual classes of men? What are his surest means of fulfilling his lofty vocation?

The scholar is a scholar only in so far as he is distinguished from other men who are not scholars. The concept of the scholar arises by comparison and by reference to society (by which is understood here not merely the state, but any aggregate whatsoever of rational men, living alongside each other and thus joined in mutual relations).

It follows that the scholar's vocation is conceivable only within society. The answer to the question What is the scholar's vocation? thus presupposes an answer to another question: What is the vocation of man within society?

The answer to this latter question presupposes, in turn, an answer to yet another, higher one: What is the vocation of man as such? That is to say, what is the vocation of man considered simply qua man, merely according to the concept of man as such – man isolated and considered apart from all the associations which are not necessarily included in the concept of man?

If I may assert something without proof, something which has undoubtedly already been demonstrated to many of you for a long time and something which others among you feel obscurely, but no less strongly on that account: All philosophy, all human thinking and teaching, all of your studies, and, in particular, everything which I will ever be able to present to you can have no purpose other than answering the questions just raised, and especially the last and highest question: What is the vocation of man as such, and what are his surest means for fulfilling it?

For a clear, distinct, and complete insight into this vocation (though not, of course, for a feeling of it), philosophy in its entirety – and moreover a well-grounded and exhaustive philosophy – is presupposed. Yet the vocation of man as such is the subject of my lecture for today. You can see that, unless I intend to treat philosophy in its entirety within this hour, I will be unable to deduce what I have to say on this topic completely and from its foundations. What I can do is to build upon your feelings. At the same time you can see that the *last* task of all philosophical inquiry is to answer that question which I wish to answer in these public lectures: What is the vocation of the scholar? or (which amounts to the same thing, as will become evident later), What is the vocation of the highest and truest man? And you can see as well that the *first* task of all philosophical inquiry is to answer the question What is the vocation of man as such? I intend to establish the answer to this latter question in my private lectures. All I wish to do today is to indicate briefly the answer to this question – to which I now turn.

The question concerning what the genuinely spiritual element in man, the pure I, might be like, considered simply in itself, isolated and apart from any relation to anything outside of itself, is an unanswerable question, and taken precisely it includes a self-contradiction. It is certainly not true that the pure I is a product of the not-I (which is my name for everything which is thought to exist outside of the I, everything which is distinguished from the I and opposed to it). The assertion that the pure I is a product of the not-I expresses a transcendental materialism which is completely contrary to reason. However, it certainly is true (and, at the appropriate place, will be strictly demonstrated) that the I is never conscious of itself nor able to become conscious of itself, except as something empirically determined – which necessarily presupposes something outside of the I. Even a person's body (which he calls 'his' body) is something apart from the I. Yet apart from this connection with a body he would not be a person at all, but would be something quite inconceivable (if one can still refer to a thing which is not even conceivable as 'something'). Thus neither here nor anywhere else does the expression 'man considered in himself and in isolation' mean man considered as a pure I and apart from all relationship to anything at all apart from his pure I. Instead, this expression means merely man conceived of apart from all relationship to rational beings like himself.

What is man's vocation when he is conceived of in this manner? What is there in the concept of man which pertains to him but not to the nonhumans among those beings with which we are acquainted? What distinguishes man from all those beings with which we are acquainted but which we do not designate as human?

I must begin with something positive, and since I cannot here begin with what is absolutely positive, that is, with the proposition 'I am', I will have to propose a hypothetical proposition, one which is indelibly etched in human feeling – a proposition which is at the same time the result of all philosophy, a proposition which can be strictly demonstrated and which will be demonstrated in my private lectures. The proposition in question is the following: Just as certainly as man is rational, he is his own end, that is, he does not exist because something else should exist. Rather, he exists simply because *he* should exist. His mere existence is the ultimate purpose of his existence, or (which amounts to the same thing) it is contradictory to inquire concerning the purpose of man's existence: he is *because* he is. This quality of absolute being, of being for his own sake, is the characteristic feature, the determination or vocation of man, in so far as he is considered merely and solely as a rational being.

But absolute being, being purely and simply, is not all that pertains to man. Various particular determinations of this absolute being also pertain to him. It is not simply that *he is; he also is something*. He does not say merely 'I am'; he adds, 'I am this or that'. He is a rational being in so far as he exists at all. But what is he in so far as he is something or other? This is the question we have to answer now.

To begin with, it is not because *one* exists that one is *what* one is; rather, one is what one is because *something else exists in addition to oneself*. As we have already said above and will demonstrate in the proper place, empirical self-consciousness, that is, the consciousness of any specific determination or vocation within ourselves at all, is impossible apart from the presupposition of a not-I. This not-I must affect man's passive faculty, which we call 'sensibility'. Thus, to the extent that man is something [definite] he is a sensuous being. But according to what we have already said, man is a rational being at the same time, and his reason should not be canceled by his sensibility. Reason and sensibility are supposed to coexist alongside each other. In this context the proposition 'man is because he is' is transformed into the following: *man ought to be what he is simply because he is*. In other words, all that a person is ought to be related to his pure I, his mere being as an I. He ought to be all that he is simply because he is an I, and what he cannot be because he is an I, he ought not to be at all. This formula, which remains obscure, will become clear at once.

The pure I can be represented only negatively, as the opposite of the not-I. The characteristic feature of the latter is multiplicity, and thus the characteristic feature of the former is complete and absolute unity. The pure I is always one and the same and is never anything different. Thus we may express the above formula as follows: Man is always supposed to be at one with himself; he should never contradict himself. Now the pure I cannot contradict itself, since it contains no diversity but is instead always one and the same. However, the empirical I, which is determined and determinable by external things, can contradict itself. And if the empirical I contradicts itself, this is a sure sign that it is not determined in accordance with the form of the pure I, and thus that it is not determined by itself but rather by external things. But this should not be, since man is his own end. A person ought to determine himself and not permit himself to be determined by something foreign. He ought to be what he is because this is what he wills to be and what he ought to will to be. The empirical I ought to be determined in a manner in which it could be eternally determined. Therefore, I would express the principle of morality in the formula (which I mention only in passing and for the purpose of illustration): 'Act so that you could consider the maxims of your willing to be eternal laws for yourself.'

The ultimate characteristic feature of all rational beings is, accordingly, absolute unity, constant self-identity, complete agreement with oneself. This absolute identity is the form of the pure I and is its only true form; or rather, in the conceivability of identity we *recognize* the expression of the pure form of the I. Any determination which can be conceived to endure forever is in accordance with the pure form of the I. This should not be understood only halfway and one-sidedly. It is not simply that the will ought always to be one with itself (though this is all that moral theory is concerned with), but rather that all of man's powers, which in themselves constitute but one power and are distinguished from each other merely in their application to different objects, should coincide in a complete identity and should harmonize with each other.

At least for the most part, however, the empirical determinations of our I do not depend upon us, but upon something external to us. The will is of course free within its own domain, that is, in the realm of objects to which, once man has become acquainted with them, it can be related. This will be demonstrated at the proper time. But feeling, as well as representation (which presupposes feeling), is not something free, but depends instead upon things external to the I – things whose characteristic feature is not identity at all, but rather multiplicity. If the I nevertheless ought always to be at one with itself in this respect too, then it must strive to act directly upon those very things upon which human feeling and representation depend. Man must try to modify these things. He must attempt to bring them into harmony with the pure form of the I, in order that the representation of these things, to the extent that this depends upon the properties of the things, may harmonize with the form of the pure I. But it is not possible purely by means of the will alone to modify things in accordance with our necessary concepts of how they should be. A certain skill is also needed, a skill acquired and sharpened by practice.

Furthermore, and even more important, the unhindered influence of things upon the empirically determinable I, an influence to which we naturally entrust ourselves so long as our reason has not yet been awakened, gives a particular bent to our empirically determinable I. And since this bent is derived from things outside of us, it is impossible for it to be in harmony with the form of our pure I. Mere will is not sufficient for removing these distortions and restoring the original pure shape of our I; we require, in addition, that skill which we acquire and sharpen through practice.

The skill in question is in part the skill to suppress and eradicate those erroneous inclinations which originate in us prior to the awakening of our reason and the sense of our own spontaneity, and in part it is the skill to modify and alter external things in accordance with our concepts. The acquisition of this skill is called 'culture', as is the particular degree of this skill which is acquired. Culture differs only in degree, but is susceptible of infinitely many gradations. In so far as man is considered as a rational, sensuous creature, then culture is the ultimate and highest means to his final goal: complete harmony with himself. In so far as man is considered merely as a sensuous creature, then culture is itself his ultimate goal. Sensibility ought to be cultivated: that is the highest and ultimate thing which one can propose to do with it.

The net result of all that has been said is the following: Man's ultimate and supreme goal is complete harmony with himself and – so that he can be in harmony with himself – the harmony of all external things with his own necessary, practical concepts of them (i.e., with those concepts which determine how things ought to be). Employing the terminology of the Critical Philosophy, this agreement is what Kant calls 'the highest good'. From what has already been said it follows that this 'highest good' by no means consists of two parts, but is completely unitary: the highest good is the *complete harmony of a rational being with himself*. In the case of a rational being dependent upon things outside of himself, the highest good may be conceived as twofold: as harmony between *the willing* [of such a being] and the idea of an eternally valid willing (i.e., as *ethical goodness*), or as the harmony of our willing (it should go without saying that I am here speaking of our rational willing) with *external things* (i.e., as *happiness*). And thus we may note in passing that it is not true that the desire for happiness destines man for ethical goodness. It is rather the case that the concept of happiness itself and the desire for happiness first arise from man's moral nature. Not *what makes us happy is good*, but rather, *only what is good makes us happy*. No happiness is possible apart from morality. Of course, feelings of *pleasure* are possible without morality and even in opposition to it, and in the proper place we will see why this is so. But pleasurable feelings are not happiness; indeed, they often even contradict happiness.

Man's final end is to subordinate to himself all that is irrational, to master it freely and according to his own laws. This is a final end which is completely inachievable and must always remain so – so long, that is, as man is to remain man and is not supposed to become God. It is part of the concept of man that his ultimate goal be unobtainable and that his path thereto be infinitely long. Thus it is not man's vocation to reach this goal. But he can and he should draw nearer to it, and his true vocation qua *man*, that is, in so far as he is a rational but finite, a sensuous but free being, lies in *endless approximation toward this goal*. Now if, as we surely can, we call this total harmony with oneself 'perfection', in the highest sense of the word, then *perfection* is man's highest and unattainable goal. His vocation, however, is to *perfect himself without end.* He exists in order to become constantly better in an ethical sense, in order to make all that surrounds him better *sensuously* and – in so far as we consider him in relation to society – *ethically* as well, and thereby to make himself ever happier.

Such is man's vocation in so far as we consider him in isolation, that is, apart from any relation to rational beings like himself. We do not, however, exist in isolation; though I cannot turn today to a consideration of the general connection between rational beings, I must, nevertheless, cast a glance upon that particular association with you which I enter upon today. What I would like to help many aspiring young men to grasp clearly is that lofty vocation which I have indicated briefly to you today. It is this vocation which I would like for you to make the most deliberate aim and the most constant guide of your lives – you young men who are in turn destined to affect mankind in the strongest manner, and whose destiny it is, through teaching, action, or both – in narrower or wider circles – to pass on that education which you have received and on every side to raise our fellowmen to a higher level of culture. When I teach something to you, I am most probably teaching unborn millions. Some among you may be well enough disposed toward me to imagine that I sense the dignity of my own special vocation, that the highest aim of my reflections and my teaching will be to contribute toward advancing culture and elevating humanity in you and in all those with whom you come into contact, and that I consider all philosophy and science which do not aim at this goal to be worthless. If this is how you judge me, then allow me to say that you are right about my intentions. Whether or not I have the power to live up to this wish is not entirely up to me. It depends in part on circumstances beyond our control; it depends in part upon you as well – upon your attentiveness, which I hereby request; upon your own efforts, which I cheerfully count upon with complete confidence; and upon your confidence in me, to which I commend myself and will seek by my actions to commend to you.

SECOND LECTURE
CONCERNING MAN'S VOCATION WITHIN SOCIETY

Before it can become a science and a *Wissenschaftslehre*, philosophy must answer a number of questions, questions the dogmatists, who have made up their minds about everything, have forgotten to ask, and which the skeptics have dared to raise only at the risk of being accused of irrationality or wickedness – or both at once.

I have no desire to be superficial and to treat shallowly a subject concerning which I believe myself to possess better-founded knowledge. Nor do I wish to conceal and pass over in silence difficulties which I see clearly. Yet it remains my fate in these public lectures to have to touch upon several of these still almost entirely untouched questions and to touch upon them without being able to treat them in an exhaustive manner. At the risk of being misunderstood or misinterpreted I will be able to provide nothing but *hints* for further reflection and *directions* toward further information concerning matters I would prefer to have treated fundamentally and exhaustively. If I suspected that among you there were many of those 'popular philosophers' who resolve every difficulty easily and without any effort or reflection, merely with the aid of what they call their own 'healthy common sense' – if this is what I thought, then I would seldom stand here before you without quailing.

Among the questions which philosophy has to answer we find the following two in particular, which have to be answered before, among other things, a well-founded theory of natural rights is possible. First of all, by what right does a man call a particular portion of the physical world '*his* body'? How does he come to consider this to be his body, something which belongs to his I, since it is nevertheless something completely opposed to his I? And then the second question: How does a man come to assume that there are rational beings like himself apart from him? And how does he come to recognize them, since they are certainly not immediately present to his pure self-consciousness?

What I have to do today is to establish what the vocation of man within society is, and before this task can be achieved the preceding questions have to be answered. By 'society' I mean the relationship in which rational beings stand to each other. The concept of society presupposes that there actually are rational beings apart from oneself. It also presupposes the existence of some characteristic features which permit us to distinguish these beings from all of those who are not rational and thus are not members of society. How do we arrive at this presupposition, and what are these characteristic features of rational beings? This is the initial question which I have to answer.

Persons still unaccustomed to strict philosophical inquiry might well answer my question as follows: 'Our knowledge that rational beings like ourselves exist apart from us and our knowledge of the signs which distinguish rational beings from nonrational ones have both been derived from experience.' But such an answer would be superficial and unsatisfying. It would be no answer at all to *our* question, but would pertain to an altogether different one. Egoists also have these experiences to which appeal is being made, and they have still not been thoroughly refuted on that account. All that experience teaches us is that our consciousness contains *the representation* of rational beings outside of ourselves. No one disputes this and no egoist has ever denied it. What is in question is whether there is anything *beyond this representation* which corresponds to it, that is, whether rational beings exist independently of our representations of them and would exist even if we had no such representations. And in regard to this question we can learn nothing from experience, just as certainly as experience is experience, that is, the system of our representations.

The most that experience can teach is that there are effects which resemble the effects of rational causes. It cannot, however, teach us that the causes in question actually exist as rational beings in themselves. For a being in itself is no object of experience.

We ourselves first introduce such beings into experience. It is *we* who explain certain experiences by appealing to the existence of rational beings outside of ourselves. But *with what right* do we offer this explanation? The *justification* needs to be better demonstrated before we can use this explanation, for its validity depends upon such a justification and cannot be based simply upon the fact that we actually make use of such explanations. Our investigation would not be advanced a single step thereby. We are left facing the question previously raised: How do we come to assume that there are rational beings outside of us, and how do we recognize them?

The thorough investigations of the Critical philosophers have unquestionably exhausted the theoretical realm of philosophy. All remaining questions must be answered on the basis of practical principles (a point which I mention merely for its historical interest). We must now see whether the proposed question can actually be answered from practical principles.

According to our last lecture, man's highest drive is the drive toward identity, toward complete harmony with himself, and – as a means for staying constantly in harmony with himself – toward the harmony of all external things with his own necessary concepts of them. It is not enough that his concepts *not* be *contradicted* (in which case he could be indifferent to the existence or nonexistence of objects *corresponding* to his concepts); rather [in order to achieve the harmony desired] there really ought to be something which corresponds to these concepts. All of the concepts found within the I should have an expression or counterpart in the not-I. This is the specific character of man's drive.

Man also possesses the concepts of reason and of rational action and thought. He necessarily wills, not merely to realize these concepts within himself, but to see them realized outside of him as well. One of the things that man requires is that rational beings like himself should exist outside of him.

Man cannot bring any such beings into existence, yet the concept of such beings underlies his observation of the not-I, and he expects to encounter something corresponding to this concept. The first, though merely negative, distinguishing characteristic of rationality, or at least the first one that suggests itself, is efficacy governed by concepts, that is, purposeful activity. What bears the distinguishing features of purposefulness may have a rational author, whereas that to which the concept of purposefulness is entirely inapplicable surely has no rational author. Yet this feature is ambiguous. The distinguishing characteristic of purposefulness is the harmony of multiplicity in a unity. But many types of such harmony are explicable merely by natural laws – not *mechanical* laws, but *organic* ones certainly. In order, therefore, to be able to infer convincingly from a particular experience to its rational cause we require some feature in addition [to purposefulness]. Even in those cases where it operates purposefully, nature operates in accordance with *necessary laws*. Reason always operates *freely*. The freely achieved harmony of multiplicity in a unity would thus be a certain and nondeceptive distinguishing feature of rationality within appearances. The only question is how one can tell the difference between an effect one has experienced which occurs necessarily and one which occurs freely.

I can by no means be directly conscious of a free being outside of myself. I cannot even become conscious of freedom within me, that is, I cannot become conscious of my own freedom. For freedom in itself is the ultimate explanatory basis for all consciousness, and thus freedom itself cannot belong to the realm of consciousness. What I can become conscious of, however, is that I am conscious of no cause for a certain voluntary determination of my empirical I other than my will itself. As long as one has explained oneself properly in advance, one might well say that this very lack of any consciousness of a cause is itself a consciousness of freedom – and we wish to call it such here. *In this sense* then, one can be conscious of one's own free action.

Suppose now that the manner of behavior of that substance which is presented to us through appearance is altered, altered by *our* free action (of which we are conscious in the sense just indicated), and altered so that it no longer remains explicable by *that* law in accordance with which it operated previously, but can only be explained by that law upon which *we* have based *our own* free action – a law which is quite opposed to the previous law. The only way in which we could account for the alteration in this case is by assuming that the cause of the effect in question was also rational and free. Thus there arises, to use the Kantian terminology, an *interaction governed by concepts*, a purposeful community. And this is what I mean by 'society' – the concept of which is now completely determined.

One of man's fundamental drives is to be permitted to assume that rational beings like himself exist outside of him. He can assume this only on the condition that he enter into society (in the sense just specified) with these beings. Consequently, the social drive is one of man's fundamental drives. It is man's *destiny* to live in society; he *ought* to live in society. One who lives in isolation is not a complete human being. He contradicts his own self.

You can see how important it is not to confuse society as such with that particular, empirically conditioned type of society which we call 'the state'. Despite what a very great man has said, life in the state is not one of man's absolute aims. The state is, instead, only a *means for establishing a perfect society*, a means which exists only under specific circumstances. Like all those human institutions which are mere means, the state aims at abolishing itself. *The goal of all government is to make government superfluous.* Though the time has certainly not yet come, nor do I know how many myriads or myriads of years it may take (here we are not at all concerned with applicability in life, but only with justifying a speculative proposition), there will certainly be a point in the a priori foreordained career of the human species when all civic bonds will become superfluous. This is that point when reason, rather than strength or cunning, will be universally recognized as the highest court of appeal. I say 'be recognized' because even then men will still make mistakes and injure their fellowmen thereby. All they will then require is the goodwill to allow themselves to be convinced that they have erred and, when they are convinced of this, to recant their errors and make amends for the damages. Until we have reached this point we are, speaking quite generally, not even true men.

According to what we have said, the positive distinguishing feature of society is *free interaction*. This interaction is its own end, and it operates *purely and simply* in order to operate. But when we maintain that society is its own end, we are not by any means denying that the manner in which it operates might be governed by an additional, more specific law, which establishes a more specific goal for the operation of society.

The fundamental drive was the drive to discover rational beings like ourselves, that is, *men*. The concept of man is an idealistic concept, because man's end qua man is something unachievable. Every individual has his own particular ideal of man as such. Though all of these ideals have the same content, they nevertheless differ in degree. Everyone uses his own ideal to judge those whom he recognizes as men. Owing to the fundamental human drive, everyone wishes to find that everyone else resembles this ideal. We experiment and observe the other person from every side, and when we discover him to lie *below* our ideal of man, we try to raise him to this ideal. The winner in this spiritual struggle is always the one who is the higher and the better man. Thus the *improvement of the species* has its origin within society, and thus at the same time we have discovered the vocation of all society as such. Should it appear as if the higher and better person has no influence upon the lower and uneducated person, this is partly because our own judgement deceives us. For we frequently expect fruit at once, before the seed has been able to germinate and develop. And perhaps it is partly because the better person stands upon a level which is so much higher than that of the uneducated person that the two do not have enough points of mutual contact and are unable to have sufficient effect upon each other – a situation which retards culture unbelievably and the remedy for which will be indicated at the proper time. But on the whole the better person will certainly be victorious, and this is a source of reassurance and solace for the friend of mankind and truth when he witnesses the open war between light and darkness. The light will certainly win in the end. Admittedly, we cannot say how long this will take, but when darkness is forced to engage in public battle this is already a guarantee of impending victory. For darkness loves obscurity. When it is forced to reveal itself it has already lost.

Thus the following is the result of all of our deliberations so far: Man is destined for society. *Sociability* is one of those skills which man ought to perfect within himself in accordance with his vocation as a man, as this was developed in the previous lecture.

However much man's vocation for society as such may originate from the innermost and purest part of his nature, it is, nevertheless, merely a drive, and as such it is subordinate to the supreme law of self-harmony, that is, the ethical law. Thus the social drive must be further determined by the ethical law and brought under a fixed rule. By discovering what this rule is we discover what *man's* vocation within *society* is – which is the object of our present inquiry and of all our reflections so far.

To begin with, the law of absolute self-harmony determines the social drive *negatively*: this drive must not contradict itself. The social drive aims at *interaction, reciprocal* influence, *mutual* give and take, *mutual* passivity and activity. It does not aim at mere causality, at the sort of mere activity to which the other person would have to be related merely passively. It strives to discover *free, rational* beings outside of ourselves and to enter into community with them. It does not strive for the *subordination* characteristic of the physical world, but rather for *coordination*. If one does not permit the rational beings he seeks outside of himself to be free, then he is taking into account only their *theoretical ability*, but not their free practical rationality. Such a person does not wish to enter into society with these other free beings, but rather to *master* them as one masters talented beasts, and thus he places his social drive into contradiction with itself. Indeed, rather than saying that such a person places his social drive into contradiction with itself, it is far more true to say that he does not possess such a higher drive at all, that mankind has not yet developed that far in him, that it is he himself who still stands on the lower level of the half human, the level of slavery. He is not yet mature enough to have developed his own sense of freedom and spontaneity, for if he had then he would necessarily have to wish to be surrounded by other free beings like himself. Such a person is a slave and wishes to have slaves. Rousseau has said that many a person who considers himself to be the master of others is actually more of a slave than they are. He might have said, with even more accuracy, that anyone who considers himself to be a master of others is himself a slave. If such a person is not a slave in fact, it is still certain that he has a slavish soul and that he will grovel on his knees before the first strong man who subjugates him. The only person who is himself free is that person who wishes to liberate everyone around him and who – by means of a certain influence whose cause has not always been remarked – really does so. We breathe more freely under the eyes of such a person. We feel that nothing constrains, restrains, or confines us, and we feel an unaccustomed inclination to be and to do everything which is not forbidden by our own self-respect.

Man may employ mindless things as means for his ends, but not rational beings. One may not even employ rational beings as means for their own ends. One may not work upon them as one works upon dead matter or animals, that is, using them simply as a means for accomplishing one's ends, without taking their freedom into account. One may not make any rational being virtuous, wise, or happy against his own will. Quite apart from the fact that the attempt to do so would be in vain and that no one can become virtuous, wise, or happy except through his own labor and effort – even apart from this fact, one ought not even wish to do this, even if it were possible or if one believed that it were; for it is wrong, and it places one into contradiction with oneself.

The law of complete, formal self-harmony also determines the social drive *positively*, and from this we obtain the actual vocation of man within society. All of the individuals who belong to the human race differ among themselves. There is only one thing on which they are in complete agreement: their ultimate goal – perfection. Perfection is determined in only one respect: it is totally self-identical. If all men could be perfect, if they could all achieve their highest and final goal, then they would be totally equal to each other. They would constitute but one single subject. In society, however, everyone strives to improve the others (at least according to his own concept) and to raise them to the ideal which he has formed of man. Accordingly, the ultimate and highest goal of society is the complete unity and unanimity of all of its members. But the achievement of this goal presupposes the achievement of the vocation of man as such, the achievement of absolute perfection. The former, therefore, is just as inachievable as the latter, and it remains inachievable so long as man is not supposed to cease to be man and to become God. The *final goal* of man within society is thus the complete unity of all individuals, but this is not the *vocation* of man within society.

Man can and should approximate endlessly to this goal. Such approximation to total unity and unanimity may be termed 'unification'. The true vocation of man within society is, accordingly, unification, a unification which constantly gains in internal strength and expands its perimeter. But since the only thing on which men are or can be in agreement is their ultimate vocation, this unification is possible only through the search for perfection. We could, therefore, just as well say that our social vocation consists in the process of communal perfection, that is, perfecting ourselves by freely making use of the effect which others have on us and perfecting others by acting in turn upon them as upon free beings.

In order to fulfill this vocation and to do so ever more adequately, we require a skill that is acquired and increased only through culture. This skill has two aspects: the skill of *giving*, or affecting others as free beings, and the capacity for *receiving*, or for making the most of the effect which others have upon us. We will specifically discuss both of these skills at the proper place. One must make a particular effort to maintain the latter skill alongside a high degree of the former, for otherwise one remains stationary and thus regresses. Rarely is anyone so perfect that he cannot be further educated in some respect by almost anyone – perhaps concerning something that seems unimportant to him or that he has overlooked.

I am acquainted with few ideas more lofty than this idea of the way the human species works upon itself – this ceaseless living and striving, this lively give and take which is the noblest thing in which man can participate, this universal intermeshing of countless wheels whose common driving force is freedom, and the beautiful harmony which grows from this. Everyone can say: 'Whoever you may be, because you bear a human face, you are still a member of this great community. No matter how countlessly many intermediaries may be involved in the transmission, I nevertheless have an effect upon you, and you have an effect upon me. No one whose face bears the stamp of reason, no matter how crude, exists for me in vain. But I am unacquainted with you, as you are with me! Still, just as it is certain that we share a common calling – to be good and to become better and better – it is equally certain that there will come a time (it may take millions or trillions of years – what is time!) when I will draw you into my sphere of influence, a time when I will benefit you too and receive benefit from you, a time when my heart will be joined with yours by the loveliest bond of all – the bond of free, mutual give and take.'

THIRD LECTURE
CONCERNING THE DIFFERENCE BETWEEN CLASSES WITHIN SOCIETY

We have now presented man's vocation *qua man* as well as his vocation *within society*. The scholar exists as a scholar only within the context of society. Accordingly, we could now turn to an investigation of the particular vocation within society of the scholar. However, the scholar is not merely a member of society; he is at the same time a member of a particular class within society. At least one speaks of 'the learned class'. Whether such talk is justified is something which we will see at the proper time.

Thus our main inquiry concerning the scholar's vocation presupposes not only the two inquiries we have just completed, but also a third, an investigation of the following important question: How does the difference between the various classes of men arise in the first place? Or, what is the origin of inequality among men? Even without any preliminary investigation, we understand by the word *class* not something which originated accidentally and without any help from us, but rather something determined and arranged by free choice and for a purpose. Nature may be responsible for that *physical inequality* which arises accidentally and without our assistance, but the *inequality of classes* appears to be a moral inequality. Concerning this moral inequality the following question naturally arises: What is the justification for the existence of different classes?

Many attempts have already been made to answer this question. Some persons, proceeding from first principles derived from experience, have seized upon and rhapsodically enumerated the various purposes which are served by the difference between classes and the many advantages we derive from this. By this means, however, we would sooner answer any other question whatsoever than the one just raised. The *advantage* which someone derives from a particular arrangement does nothing to *justify* it. The question raised was by no means the historical question concerning the purposes which may have led to this arrangement, but rather the moral question concerning the permissibility of making such an arrangement, whatever purposes it might have had. This question has to be answered on the basis of principles of pure reason, indeed, on the basis of principles of pure practical reason. So far as I know, no one has ever even attempted to provide such an answer. I must preface my own attempt with a few general principles from the *Wissenschaftslehre*.

All laws of reason have their foundation in the nature of our mind, but we first become empirically conscious of these laws through an experience to which they are applicable. The more often we have occasion to apply them, the more intimately they become interwoven with our own consciousness. This is how it is with *all* laws of reason, and specifically, with the laws of practical reason – laws which, unlike those of theoretical reason, do not aim at a mere *judgement*, but rather at external efficacy. These practical laws are present to consciousness in the form of *drives*. All drives have their foundation in our nature – but no more than their foundation. Every drive has to be *awakened* by experience before we can become conscious of it. Furthermore, in order for a drive to become an *inclination* and in order for its satisfaction to become a *need*, the drive in question has to be *developed* through frequently repeated experiences of the same type.

Experience, however, is not dependent upon us; neither, therefore, is the awakening and the development of our own drives at all dependent upon us.

The independent not-I, considered as the basis of experience, that is, *nature*, is something manifold. Not one of its parts is totally identical to any other part (a proposition which is also affirmed by the Kantian philosophy and can be strictly demonstrated within that philosophy). From this it follows that nature affects the human mind in a variety of very different ways and never develops the mind's capacities and aptitudes in the same way twice. What we call 'individuals', as well as their particular empirical individual nature, is determined by the different ways in which nature acts upon them. Thus we can say that no individual, with respect to his awakened and developed abilities, is completely the same as anyone else. From this there arises a physical inequality to which we have contributed nothing and which we are unable to remove by the exercise of our freedom. For before we can freely resist nature's influence upon us, we must have become conscious of our freedom and able to use it. This state, however, can be attained in no other manner except by the awakening and development of our drives – something which does not depend upon us.

The highest law of mankind and of all rational beings is the law of total self-harmony or absolute identity. But to the extent that this law becomes something positive and obtains some content by being applied to nature, it demands that all of an individual's talents ought to be developed equally and that all of his abilities ought to be cultivated to the highest possible degree of perfection. This demand cannot be fulfilled by the mere law alone, because, according to what has just been said, its fulfillment does not depend merely upon this law, nor upon *our will* (which is, of course, determinable by this), but rather, depends upon *the free operation of nature*.

If we assume that there are several rational beings and relate this law [of self-harmony] to society, then the demand that *every person* ought to cultivate all of his talents equally contains at the same time the demand *that all of the various rational beings ought to be cultivated or educated equally*. Since all talents have their foundation entirely within pure reason, they are all equal in themselves; therefore, they all ought to be cultivated to the same extent – which is what is required by this demand. Equal results must always follow from the equal cultivation of equal talents. And thus we arrive by another route at the conclusion established in our last lecture: the final aim of all society is *the complete equality of all of its members*.

We have already shown in the previous lecture and by another route that the mere law can no more fulfill this demand [for the complete equality of all the members of society] than it can fulfill the above demand upon which this lecture is based [i.e., the demand for the equal cultivation of all of one's talents, as well as the equal cultivation of all of the members of society]. Nevertheless, the free will *ought to* and *can* strive for an ever closer approximation to this end.

This is where the efficacy of the social drive enters in. For the social drive aims at this same end and will provide the means for the endless approximation which has been demanded. Included within the social drive, or the drive to interact with other free, rational beings and to interact with them qua free, rational beings, are the following two drives: *the drive to communicate*, that is, the drive to cultivate in other persons that aspect of personality in which *we* ourselves are especially strong and, in so far as it is possible, to make everyone else equal to our own better self; and also *the drive to receive*, that is, the drive to allow others to cultivate in us that aspect in which they are especially strong and we are especially weak. Nature's mistakes are in this way corrected by reason and freedom, and that one-sided development with which nature has furnished each individual becomes the common property of the entire species. In return, the entire species cultivates the individual. On the supposition that all of the individuals who are possible under a specific set of natural conditions actually do exist, then the species will provide the individual with all the education which is possible in such circumstances. Nature develops everyone one-sidedly, but it does so at every point at which it comes into contact with any rational being. What reason does is to unify these points, thus presenting a solid and extended front to nature. In this manner reason compels nature to cultivate every talent in the species at least, since it did not wish to do so in the individual. Through these drives [to communicate and to receive], *reason* itself sees to the equitable distribution of the desired education among the individual members of society; and *reason* will continue to see to this, since the realm of nature does not extend this far.

Reason will see to it that every individual obtains *indirectly from the hands of society* that complete education which he could not obtain *directly* from nature. Thus from the advantages possessed by each individual, society will accumulate a common store for the free use of everyone, thereby multiplying the advantages by the number of individuals. Reason will make the individual's deficiencies into a common burden and will thus infinitely reduce them. Expressed differently and in a manner which more easily lends itself to some applications: the aim of all cultivation of skill is the subordination of nature (in the sense specified) to reason and the agreement of experience (to the extent that it is independent of the laws of our faculty of representation) with our necessary practical concepts of experience. Reason is, accordingly, engaged in a constant struggle with nature, a war that can never end – so long as we are not supposed to become gods. However, nature's influence should and can become weaker and weaker, whereas reason's dominion should and can become stronger and stronger. Reason ought to gain one victory after another over nature. Perhaps an individual may struggle successfully against nature at that particular point where he comes into contact with it, although in every other aspect he is governed by nature. But society now joins together and assumes joint responsibility: what the individual could not accomplish by himself can be accomplished by the united strength of all. Of course, everyone struggles alone, but all of us share in the weakening of nature through the common struggle and in that victory over nature separately achieved by each person in his own field. Hence physical inequality even serves to strengthen that bond that unites all men in a single body. The compulsion of our needs and the much sweeter compulsion to satisfy these needs binds men more closely together. In seeking to weaken the power of reason, nature succeeds only in strengthening it.

So far everything has proceeded naturally. We have shown that there is a great variety of different *personal characters*, in accordance with the various types and levels of development, but we have not yet shown that there are any distinct *classes*. We have not yet shown this because we have been unable so far to indicate *any particular free determination*, that is, any voluntary choice of a particular sort of education. One should not misunderstand or only partially understand the claim that we have been unable so far to indicate any particular free determination. The social drive as such certainly does involve freedom: it merely urges; it does not compel. One may resist and suppress this drive. Out of misanthropic egoism one can isolate himself completely and can refuse to accept anything from society, in order not to have to render anything to it. Out of crude bestiality one can overlook the freedom of society and can consider it to be subordinate to his mere caprice, because he thinks of himself as subordinate to the caprice of nature. But this does not concern us here. If we are responsive to the social drive at all, then this drive requires us to share the good that we possess with those who need it and to receive what we lack from those who have it. For this no special new determination or modification of the social drive is required – which is all that I meant to say.

The characteristic difference [between the distinction between persons and the distinction between classes, i.e., between natural and social inequality] is as follows: *Under the circumstances which have been set forth so far*, I, as an individual, surrender myself to nature for the development of any particular talent which I may have. I do so *because I must*. I do not have any choice in the matter, but involuntarily follow the guidance of nature. I accept all that nature provides, but I cannot accept what she does not wish to provide. Though I neglect no opportunity to cultivate as many aspects of my personality as possible, I create no such opportunities at all, because I cannot do so. But if, *on the other hand*, as linguistic usage indicates, a class is something which is supposed to be freely chosen, then before *I can choose* a class – if I am to do so – I must have *previously* surrendered myself to nature. For in order to make such a choice, various drives have to have been awakened within me, and I have to have become conscious of various talents. Nevertheless, *in the choice itself* I resolve that from now on I will pay no heed to certain opportunities which nature may provide, and I will do this so that I will henceforth be able to devote all of my strength and all of my natural gifts *exclusively to developing one or more specific skills*. My class is determined by the particular skill to the development of which I freely dedicate myself.

The question arises: *Ought* I to select a particular class? Or, if I am not morally *obliged* to do so, *may* I dedicate myself solely to one particular class, that is, to cultivating only one aspect of myself? If, as a matter of unconditional duty, I ought to choose some specific class, then it must be possible to derive from the supreme law of reason a drive which has as its object this choice of a class – in the same way in which it is possible to derive from this law a drive whose object is society as such. If I am merely permitted to choose a class, then no such drive can be derived from the law of reason, and all that can be so derived is the permission to make such a choice. In this latter case it must be possible to indicate some empirical datum which determines the will to make the actual choice which the law merely permits. Such an empirical datum would specify a merely prudential rule, but not a law. We will see how this works in the course of our investigation.

The law commands: 'Cultivate all of your talents completely and equally, in so far as you are able to do so.' But the law does not specify whether I should exercise these talents directly upon nature, or whether I should exercise them indirectly through community with others. This choice, accordingly, is left entirely to my own discretion. The law commands: 'Subordinate nature to your aims.' But the law does not say that if I discover that nature has already been sufficiently molded by others for some of my purposes, then I ought to mold it further for all possible human purposes. Thus the law does not prohibit me from choosing a particular class, though neither am I enjoined by it to make such a choice simply because I am not forbidden to do so. Here I find myself in the realm of free choice. I may choose a class, and in order to decide whether or not I should do so (though not in order to decide which particular class to choose – something which I will discuss on another occasion), I have to base my decision on quite different grounds than those which can be immediately derived from this law.

As matters now stand, man is born into society. He no longer encounters nature in its native state; instead, he finds it already prepared in various ways for his possible purposes. He discovers a multitude of men in various fields busily cultivating nature on every side for the use of rational beings. He discovers that many things which he would otherwise have had to do for himself have already been accomplished. He may be able to lead a very comfortable life without directly applying his own strength to nature at all, and perhaps he could attain a certain sort of perfection merely by enjoying what society has already achieved, in particular, by enjoying what society has contributed to his own cultivation. But this is not permissible. He must at least try to pay his own debt to society. He must take his place. He must at least strive in some way to improve society, which has done so much for him.

There are two ways in which he may attempt to do this: On the one hand, he can try to cultivate every aspect of nature by himself. But then it might take him his entire lifetime – and, if he had them, several lifetimes – to learn what had already been accomplished by those who preceded him and what still remained to be done. Such an effort would be superfluous, and thus from the standpoint of the human species his entire life would be lost, certainly not through the fault of his evil will, but rather because of his lack of good sense. Or, on the other hand, he can seize upon some particular speciality – perhaps the one which for the time being he is most interested in completely exhausting and for whose cultivation he is already best prepared by nature and society – and dedicate himself exclusively to it. The cultivation of his other talents he leaves up to society, while at the same time he intends, strives, and wishes to contribute to the cultivation of society within his own speciality. In making this decision, he has selected a class, and this choice, considered in itself, is perfectly legitimate. Yet, like all free acts, this one too is subject to the ethical law, insofar as the ethical law regulates our behavior. That is, this act is subject to the categorical imperative, which I express as follows: 'Never will things which contradict each other.'

So expressed, this is a law which everyone can obey satisfactorily, since what we will depends not in the least upon nature, but only upon us.

The choice of a class is a free choice. Thus we may not compel any person to join any particular class, nor may we deny him admission to any class. Every individual action, as well as every general institution, which aims at such compulsion is illegitimate. This is so quite apart from the fact that it is stupid to compel a man to join a particular class or to bar him from another, since nobody can be totally acquainted with anyone else's special talents. A member of society who is assigned to the wrong place in this manner is often totally lost for society. Apart from this, such compulsion is wrong in itself, because it places our own action in contradiction with our practical concept of it. We desired a *member* of society, and we produce a *tool* of society. We desired a *free fellow worker* on our great project, and we produce a *coerced, passive instrument* of the same. Thus, as far as we were able, we have killed the man within the person we have treated in this manner; we have wronged him, and we have wronged society.

We selected a particular class as well as a specific talent for further cultivation *because we wanted to be able to repay society for all that it has done for us.* Consequently, everyone is bound actually to apply his education for the benefit of society. No one has the right to work merely for his own private enjoyment, to shut himself off from his fellowmen and to make his education useless to them; for it is precisely the labor of society which has put him in a position to acquire this education for himself. In a certain sense education is itself the product and the property of society, and thus the man who does not want to benefit society robs it of its property. Everyone has the duty not only to want to be generally useful to society, but also the duty, according to the best of his knowledge, to bend all of his efforts toward society's final end: the constant improvement of the human species – liberating it more and more from natural compulsion, and making it ever more independent and autonomous. And thus, from this new inequality [of classes] there arises a new equality: the equitable advancement of culture in every individual.

I am not claiming that things are always actually as I have just described them. But according to our practical concepts of society and of different social classes, this is how things ought to be, and we can and should work to make them so. At the proper time we shall see how vigorously the scholarly class in particular can work toward this end and how many means to this end it has in its power.

If we only contemplate the idea just presented, even apart from all relation to ourselves, we can at least catch a glimpse beyond ourselves of an association in which one cannot work for himself without working at the same time for everyone, nor work for others without working for himself; for the successful progress of any member is the successful progress of them all, and one person's misfortune is everyone's misfortune. Simply through the harmony which it reveals in the most diverse things, this spectacle pleases us sincerely and exhaults our spirit mightily.

Our interest in this spectacle only increases when we take ourselves into account and consider ourselves as members of this great and intimate association. Our sense of our own dignity and power increases when we say to ourselves what every one of us can say: 'My existence is not in vain and without any purpose. I am a necessary link in that great chain which began at that moment when man first became fully conscious of his own existence and stretches into eternity. All these people have labored for my sake. All that were ever great, wise, or noble – those benefactors of the human race whose names I find recorded in world history, as well as the many more whose services have survived their names: I have reaped their harvest. Upon the earth on which they lived I tread in the footsteps of those who bring blessings upon all who follow them. Whenever I wish, I can assume that lofty task which they had set for themselves: the task of making our fellowmen ever wiser and happier. Where they had to stop, I can build further. I can bring nearer to completion that noble temple that they had to leave unfinished.'

'But,' someone may say, 'I will have to stop too, just like they did.' Yes! and this is the loftiest thought of all: Once I assume this lofty task I will never complete it. Therefore, just as surely as it is my vocation to assume this task, I can never cease *to act* and thus I can never cease *to be*. That which is called 'death' cannot interrupt my work; for my work must be completed, and it can never be completed in any amount of time. Consequently, my existence has no temporal limits: I am eternal. When I assumed this great task I laid hold of eternity at the same time. I lift my head boldly to the threatening stony heights, to the roaring cataract, and to the crashing clouds in their fire-red sea. 'I am eternal!' I shout to them, 'I defy your power! Rain everything down upon me! You earth, and you, heaven, mingle all of your elements in wild tumult. Foam and roar, and in savage combat pulverize the last dust mote of that body which I call my own. Along with its own unyielding project, my will shall hover boldly and indifferently above the wreckage of the universe. For I have seized my vocation, and it is more permanent than you. It is eternal, and so too am I!'

FOURTH LECTURE
CONCERNING THE SCHOLAR'S VOCATION

I must speak to you today about the vocation of the scholar.

I find that I am in a peculiar situation in regard to this subject. For all of you, or at least most of you, have chosen the sciences as your life's work, and so have I. Presumably, you devote your entire energies to the goal of being respected members of the scholarly class, and so have and so do I. I am thus supposed to speak as a scholar before prospective scholars on the subject of the scholar's vocation. I am supposed to examine this subject thoroughly and, if possible, exhaustively – omitting from my presentation nothing which is true. Suppose that I should discover that the vocation of this class is a very honorable and lofty one, more distinguished than that of any other class: how can I say this without being immodest, without depreciating the other classes, and without seeming to be blinded by conceit? Yet I am speaking as a philosopher, and as such I am obliged to specify precisely the meaning of every concept. So what can I do if the concept which comes next in the series happens to be the concept of the scholar? It is impermissible for me to suppress anything which I recognize to be true: it remains true in any case. Even modesty is subordinate to truth, and it is a false modesty which stands in the way of the truth. For the time being let us investigate our subject impartially, as if it had no relation to ourselves and were a concept borrowed from a world totally alien to us. Let us demand all the more precision in our proofs. And let us not forget something which I intend to present with no less force in its proper place: that every class is necessary and deserves our respect, that an individual's merit is not determined by the class to which he belongs, but rather by the way he fulfills his role as a member of that class. For every person deserves to be honored only in so far as he approximates to fulfilling his role completely. For this reason, the scholar has reason to be the humblest person of all: since the goal which is set for him must always remain very distant, and since he has to achieve a very lofty ideal – one from which he normally remains very distant.

We have seen that men possess various drives and talents and that the vocation of every individual is to cultivate all of his talents to the best of his ability. One of man's drives is the social drive. This drive offers man a new, special type of education, that is, education for society, as well as an extraordinary facility for education as such. It is up to each person to decide whether he shall cultivate all of his talents immediately within nature or whether he shall cultivate them indirectly through society. The first course is difficult and does nothing to advance society; therefore, within society every individual quite legitimately selects his own special branch of general education, leaving the other branches to his fellow members of society in the expectation that they will share the benefits of *their* education with *him*, just as he will share the benefits of *his* with *them*. This is the origin of and the justification for the difference between the various classes within society.

Such were the results of my previous lectures. A classification of the various classes according to pure concepts of reason (which is entirely possible) would have to be based upon an exhaustive enumeration of all of man's natural talents and needs – not counting those needs which are purely artificial. A specific class can be dedicated to the cultivation of each specific talent or – which amounts to the same thing – to the satisfaction of each of man's natural needs (i.e., each need which has its origin in a basic human drive). We will reserve this investigation for some future time in order to devote this hour to a topic which lies nearer to us.

If someone were to ask about the relative perfection of a society organized according to the above first principles (and as our investigation of the origin of society has made clear, every society, in accordance with man's natural drives, is organized in this way by itself and without any guidance), then in order to answer this question we would first have to investigate the following question: Are *all* needs cared for in the society in question? Are they all developed and satisfied, and are they developed and satisfied *equally*? If they are, then the society in question is perfect qua society. This does not mean that it would attain its goal (which, according to our previous deliberations is impossible), but rather that it would be so organized that it would necessarily have to *approximate* more and more closely to its goal. If all needs are not equally cared for in this manner, then it would of course remain possible for the society in question to make cultural progress through a fortunate accident. This, however, could not be counted on with any certainty; the society might just as well regress through an unfortunate accident.

The first presupposition for seeing to the equal development of all of man's talents is an acquaintance with all of his talents: a scientific knowledge of all of his drives and needs, a complete survey of his entire nature. Yet such complete knowledge of man in his totality is something which is itself based upon a talent, one which must itself be developed. Man certainly has a drive to *know*, in particular, he has a drive to know his own needs. The development of this drive, however, requires all of one's time and energy. If there is any common need which urgently demands that a special class of persons be dedicated to its satisfaction, it is this one.

But the *acquaintance* with man's talents and needs would be an extremely sad and depressing thing without the scientific knowledge of how to *develop* and *satisfy* them. It would also be something empty and quite useless. It is most unkind of someone to show me my shortcomings without at the same time showing me the means by which I may overcome them, or to produce within me a sense of my own needs without putting me in a position to satisfy them. It would be far better for him to leave me in my state of animal ignorance. In short, such knowledge could not be the sort which society desires and for the sake of which society requires a special class possessing such knowledge; for such knowledge does not have the aim it is supposed to have, namely, the improvement, and thereby the unification, of the species. Accordingly, this knowledge of men's needs must be joined with a knowledge of the *means for satisfying them*. Both sorts of knowledge are the business of the same class, because neither sort of knowledge can be complete, much less efficacious and vigorous, without the other. Knowledge of the first sort is based on principles of pure reason; it is *philosophical* knowledge. Knowledge of the second sort is partly based on experience; to that extent it is *philosophical-historical* knowledge (not merely historical knowledge, since before I can evaluate as means to ends the objects given in experience, I must first be acquainted with the ends to which these objects refer, and such ends can only be recognized philosophically). The knowledge in question is supposed to be useful to society. It is, therefore, not enough merely to know what talents man has and the means for developing them. Such knowledge would still always remain entirely fruitless. In order to obtain the desired utility, an additional step is required: one must know the particular cultural level of one's society at a particular time, as well as the particular level it has to reach next and the means it has to employ to do so. Using reason alone and assuming only the existence of experience as such, one can certainly determine in advance of any particular experience the course which the human species will follow. One can specify in an approximate manner the various steps it has to climb in order to reach a particular stage of development. One cannot, however, determine the level of a particular society at a particular time solely on the basis of reason. For this one has to examine experience as well. One has to study the events of former ages, albeit with an eye purified by philosophy. One must look around oneself and observe one's contemporaries. The last element in the knowledge which society requires is thus purely *historical*.

Taken together (and if they are not, they are of much less use) the three types of knowledge just indicated constitute what is – or at least should be – called 'learning'; the person who dedicates his life to the acquisition of such knowledge is called a 'scholar'.

Every individual scholar does not have to master the entire field of human knowledge in all three of these respects. Such total mastery would be for the most part impossible, and just for this reason the attempt to gain it would be fruitless and would lead to the waste, without any gain for society, of a person's entire life – a life which could have been useful to society. Individuals may stake out for themselves individual portions of the domain of knowledge, but in his own area each person should cultivate all three: philosophical and philosophical-historical, as well as purely historical knowledge. In saying this, I wish to indicate in a merely provisional manner something which I will discuss more fully at a later time. I wish to assert here (on my own testimony at least) that the study of a properly grounded philosophy does not make it superfluous to acquire empirical knowledge – not, at least, if such knowledge is thorough. On the contrary, such a philosophy demonstrates in the most convincing manner the indispensability of empirical knowledge. We have already shown that the purpose of all human knowledge is to see to the equal, continuous, and progressive development of all human talents. It follows from this that the true vocation of the scholarly class is the *supreme supervision of the actual progress of the human race in general and the unceasing promotion of this progress*. Only with great effort do I here restrain my feelings from being carried away by the lofty idea which is now before us, but the path of cold investigation is not yet at an end. Yet I must at least mention in passing what it is that those who attempt to hinder the advance of science would actually do. (I say '*would* do', for how can I know whether there really are any such persons?) The whole progress of the human race depends directly upon the progress of science. Whoever retards the latter also retards the former. And what public image does the person who retards the progress of mankind present to his age and to posterity? With actions louder than a thousand words, he screams into the deafened ears of his own and later ages: 'So long as I am alive, at least, my fellowmen shall become no wiser and no better. For if mankind were to advance, then, despite all my resistance, I too would be forced to advance at least in some respect, and this I abhor. I do not wish to become more enlightened or ennobled. My element is darkness and perversity, and I will summon up my last ounce of strength in order to keep from being budged from this element.' Mankind can dispense with, can be robbed of, everything without risk of losing its true dignity – it can dispense with everything, that is, except for the possibility of improvement. Like that foe of mankind whom the Bible depicts, these misanthropes have deliberated and calculated coldly and cunningly; they have explored the most sacred depths in order to choose where mankind has to be attacked in order to be nipped in the bud. They have found the spot. With indignation mankind turns away from the spectacle presented by such persons, and we return to our inquiry.

Science itself is only one branch of human development – every branch of which must be advanced if all of man's talents are to be further cultivated. Hence, like every person who has chosen a particular class, every scholar strives to advance science, specifically, that area of science which he has chosen. He has to do what everyone has to do in his special area, and he has to do far more than this. He is supposed to supervise and promote the progress of the other classes, but is he himself *not* supposed to make any progress? The progress of all of the other special areas of development depends upon the progress of the scholar. He must always proceed in advance of the other areas in order to clear and explore the path and then to guide them along it, but is he himself supposed to stay behind? From that moment he would cease to be what he is supposed to be, and thus – since he is nothing else but this – he would be nothing at all. I am not saying that every scholar *actually has to advance* his own area; perhaps he cannot do so. But I am saying that every scholar must *strive* to do so, and that he may not rest or believe himself to have discharged his duty until he has advanced his area of science. And so long as he lives he can continue to advance it further. If he is overtaken by death before he has achieved his purpose then he is of course released from his duty within this world of appearances, and his sincere attempt will be counted as his accomplishment would have been. If the following rule applies to all men, it applies especially to the scholar: he ought to forget his accomplishments as soon as they are completed and he always ought to think only of what he still has to accomplish. The person whose field is not enlarged with every step that he takes has not yet advanced very far.

The scholar is especially destined for society. More than any other class, his class, in so far as he is a scholar, properly exists only through and for society. Accordingly, it is his particular duty to cultivate to the highest degree within himself the social talents of *receptivity* and the *art of communication*. If he has acquired the appropriate empirical knowledge in the appropriate manner, then his receptivity should already be highly cultivated. He should be familiar with his scientific predecessors. And this familiarity cannot have been produced merely by rational reflection, but has to have been learned through oral or written instruction. By constantly learning something new he should preserve his receptivity and try to guard against that total lack of openness to foreign opinions and ways of thinking which one often encounters, occasionally even among excellent and independent thinkers. For no one is so well instructed that he could not always learn something new and occasionally something very essential, and seldom is anyone so ignorant that he could not tell even the most knowledgeable man something new. The scholar always needs skills of communication, since he does not possess his knowledge for himself, but rather for society. He has to practice this art from childhood and has to preserve it in all of his activities. At the proper time we will examine *the means by which* he does this.

The scholar should now actually apply for the benefit of society that knowledge which he has acquired for society. He should awaken in men a feeling for their true needs and should acquaint them with the means for satisfying these needs. This does not imply that all men have to be made acquainted with those profound inquiries which the scholar himself has to undertake in order to find something certain and sure. For that would mean he would have to make all men scholars to the same extent that he himself is a scholar, and this is neither possible nor appropriate. Other things also have to be done, and this is why there are other classes of men. If these others were to devote their time to scholarly investigations, then even the scholars would soon have to cease being scholars. But then how can and how should the scholar disseminate his knowledge? Society could not continue to exist without trust in the integrity and the ability of others, and accordingly, this trust is deeply etched in our hearts. Moreover, we are especially favored by nature in that our trust is the greatest precisely in those areas in which we are most dependent upon the integrity and ability of others. Once he has acquired it as he should, the scholar may count on this trust in his integrity and ability. In addition, all men have a sense for what is true. By itself, of course, this sense is not sufficient. It has to be developed, scrutinized, and purified, and this is precisely the scholar's task. Such a sense or feeling for truth is not sufficient to lead the uneducated person to all the truths that he needs; but, unless it has been artificially falsified (something which is often done by persons who think of themselves as scholars), it is always enough to permit him to recognize the truth after another has guided him to it – even if he does not see the deeper reasons why it is true. Likewise, the scholar may rely upon this sense of truth. To the extent that we have developed the concept of the scholar so far, we can say that it is the vocation of the scholar to be the *teacher* of the human race.

But the scholar does not merely have to make men generally acquainted with their needs and the means for satisfying them. He has to direct their attention to the needs which confront them under the specific circumstances inherent in each particular time and place, as well as the specific means for achieving each purpose as it arises. He does not look only at the present; he looks toward the future as well. He does not see only the present standpoint; he also sees the direction in which the human race must now proceed if it is to continue on the path toward its final goal and is not to stray from this path or go backward on it. He cannot demand that the human race proceed at once to that point which shines before his eyes. No step along this path can be skipped. The scholar simply has to see to it that we do not remain standing in one place or turn back. In this respect the scholar is the *educator* of mankind. I wish to mention explicitly at this point that when engaged in this activity, as in all of his occupations, the scholar is subject to the ethical law, which commands harmony with oneself. The scholar exercises an influence upon society. Society is based upon the concept of freedom; it and all of its members are free. Thus the scholar may employ none but moral means to influence society. He will not be tempted to use *compulsory means* or physical force to get men to accept his convictions. In our era one should not have to waste any further words on such folly. But neither should the scholar employ *deception*. Quite apart from the fact that in doing so he would wrong himself and that his duty as a person would in any case be higher than his duty as a scholar, he would wrong society at the same time. For every individual in society ought to act on the basis of free choice and on the basis of a conviction which *he himself has judged adequate*. In each of his actions he ought to be able to think of himself as an end and ought to be treated as such by every other member of society. A person who is deceived is being treated as a mere means to an end.

The final aim of every individual person, as well as of society as a whole, and thus the final aim of all of the scholar's work for society, is the ethical improvement of the whole person. It is the scholar's duty always to keep this final aim in view and to have it before his eyes in all that he does within society. But no one who is not himself a good man can work successfully for ethical improvement. We do not teach by words alone; we also teach – far more forcefully – by example. Everyone who lives in society owes it to society to set a good example, because the power of example originates only through our life in society. How much greater is the scholar's obligation to set a good example – the scholar, who is supposed to surpass the other classes in every aspect of culture! How can he think that others will follow his teachings if he contradicts them before everyone's eyes in every action of his life? (The words addressed by the founder of Christianity to his followers apply quite aptly to the scholars: 'Ye are the salt of the earth, but if the salt has lost its savor wherewith shall it be salted?' When the elect among men have been corrupted, where should one search to find ethical goodness?) Considered, therefore, in this last respect, the scholar ought to be the *ethically best* man of his time. He ought to represent the highest level of ethical cultivation which is possible up to the present.

This is the vocation we have in common, the fate we share. It is a happy fate to have a particular calling which requires one to do just that which one has to do for the sake of one's general calling as a human being. It is a happy fate to be required to apply one's time and energy only to something for which one would otherwise have to make time and save up energy with prudent economy. And it is a happy fate to have for one's work, one's business, one's own daily task, something which for other persons is a pleasant relaxation from labor. Here is an invigorating thought, one which elevates the soul and which each of you who is worthy of his vocation can have: 'Within my special area the culture of my age and of future ages is entrusted to me. My labors will help determine the course of future generations and the history of nations still to come. I am called to testify to the truth. My life and destiny do not matter at all, but infinitely much depends upon the results of my life. I am a priest of truth. I am in its pay, and thus I have committed myself to do, to risk, and to suffer anything for its sake. If I should be pursued and hated for the truth's sake, or if I should die in its service, what more would I have done than what I simply had to do?'

I realize how much I have now said and realize equally well that an emasculated age which has lost its nerve cannot endure this feeling and cannot bear to have it expressed. And I realize that, with a timorous voice which betrays its inner shame, such an age will call anything to which it cannot rise 'muddled enthusiasm'. Anxiously, it will avert its gaze from a picture in which it sees only its own enervation and shame, and something strong and elevated will make no more impression upon such an age than a touch makes upon those who are crippled in every limb. I know all this, but I also know where I am speaking. I am speaking before an audience of young men whose very age protects them from such utter enervation. I would like to provide you with a manly ethical theory, and at the same time and by means of this, I would like to place in your soul feelings which will protect you against such enervation in the future.

I frankly admit that I would like to use this position in which providence has placed me in order to disseminate a more manly way of thinking, a stronger sense of elevation and dignity, and a more intense desire to fulfill one's vocation despite every danger. I would like to broadcast this in every direction, as far as the German language extends and even farther if I could. This I would like to do, so that after you have left this place and have scattered in all directions I could know that in all those places you are scattered there live men whose chosen friend is truth: men who will cling to truth in life and in death; men who will provide a refuge for truth when all the world thrusts it out; men who will publicly defend the truth when it is slandered and maligned; men who will gladly suffer the cleverly concealed hatred of the great, the insipid smiles of the conceited, and the pitying shrugs of the narrow-minded – all for the sake of truth. This is why I said what I have said, and this will remain my ultimate object in saying all that I will ever say to you.

Translated by Daniel Breazeale

SCHELLING

In the final years of the eighteenth century, hopes that philosophy might achieve a definitive completion created a fervour of intellectual activity. Fichte's advance towards the active structure of a self that fundamentally unified the commonly separated sides of subject and object was a real revelation. It seemed to be time to take a less fainthearted philosophical approach and to set out confidently to thematize the Absolute. A true theory of the Absolute would align philosophy with its oldest tasks, and with the wisdom of Plato, Spinoza or Leibniz. Such a theory would have to succeed in unfolding all essential branches of knowledge from one single centre.

Fortuitously, the most promising young minds, who were all pursuing the same objectives, were united in Tübingen's theological seminary. Hölderlin, whose philosophical significance was eclipsed by his tragic existence as a poet, may well have been the secret stimulus. Schelling certainly was the shining light who gained early fame with his ingenious essays. The slowly maturing Hegel was initially unnoticed, but in the end he surpassed them all. We have, with the thoughtful fragment of 1795 known as the *Oldest Programme of the Idealist System*, an exciting document from this early period of friendly co-operation. It already contained the seeds of all the important concepts and systematic complexities which determined the philosophical development of the decades to follow. The intellectual scope of the text went even beyond the idealist school in the strict sense and went so far as to demand the realization of theory in praxis that is characteristic of Hegel's pupils.

Schelling was the first to articulate a convincing account of what had merely been sketched in the early *Programme*, whose authorship, by the way, is still subject to philosophical dispute. The preface to the book that discusses *Ideas about a Philosophy of Nature* supports the idea that metaphysics needs to be restored from practical philosophy, given Kant's destruction of metaphysics in theoretical philosophy. Since Fichte's reflections were exclusively focused on the most abstract aspect of self-consciousness, the lack of a well-founded philosophy of nature became very apparent. Thus, Schelling's contemporaries were initially impressed with his essays on the philosophy of nature. Conquering the material realm, as opposed to the realm of spirit or mind, was counted, in the process of perfecting the system, as a necessary counterpart to the exploration of spirit in the immanence of the self. Trying to understand the essence of nature through the essence of mind or spirit was the striking solution by which Schelling managed to rehabilitate a tradition that had come to be discredited in Kant's critical philosophy.

Fichte's absolute self and Spinoza's infinite substance still had to be combined in thought. Self-consciousness always originates in an act of reflection and it therefore needs something else, an Other, a non-I, in contrast to which it can define itself. This division had to be overcome by finding a way back to the undivided basis that produces and bears all limitations and definitions in itself. Schelling drew attention to Leibniz's monadology, where we find a world of self-defining individuals which are no longer determined from the outside and which are thus in harmony with one another. Schelling's philosophy of nature inserted in this metaphysical framework, retrieved from this great tradition, knowledge drawn from contemporary scientific and naturalistic research. Today, the details of his deductions from various phenomena associated with life, electricity, mechanics, chemistry, etc., appear dated and slightly awkward. The idea, however, of philosophically understanding nature from within itself, a nature prior to its scientistic conversion into the sphere of external objects, can still serve to balance the dogmas of an epoch totally committed to its faith in science.

Deriving the essence of spirit and the essence of nature from one and the same source led to the next stage in Schelling's thought, the philosophy of identity in *The System of Transcendental Idealism* (1800). If spirit and matter become understandable via identical explanatory principles, then the final principle we have to assume is identity itself, an identity where subject and object cannot be differentiated. That which may only be determined in contrast to something else must first be preceded by an original unity divided successively into determinations. The explanatory model here traces a development. Philosophy reconstrues an evolutionary history of the general level of consciousness as already encountered in prephilosophical thought, a history that must not be mistaken for empirical history. Explanation by way of historical development was the model for Hegel's later *Phenomenology of Spirit*.

In order to illustrate the original unity that precedes all determinate existence and that thereby itself fades away in indeterminacy, Schelling turned towards art. We have to imagine an original identity that resembles the way subjective and objective elements create an indistinguishable unity in a work of art, the way that form and what is formed are completely mediated. Schelling's philosophical system needed an instrument in order to elucidate itself, and this instrument was art. Given that art and philosophy mirror each other, Schelling's philosophy of art gained insights into the peculiarities of the aesthetic sphere that remain, half hidden, in our present time.

In order to tackle a problem that had been left unsolved, Schelling's profound late work, *Philosophical Investigations Concerning the Essence of Human Freedom* (1809), took up both the approach of his philosophy of nature and the basic thoughts of his philosophy of identity. What is it that actually impels the primary basis of everything, that undifferentiated unity, to come out of itself and go beyond itself? What does it mean that this basis does not persist in its closed state and that it founds something that is necessarily distinct from it? Schelling had to borrow elements from mystical theology in order to discuss the paradoxical relation of freedom and necessity, a relation that is exhibited in the inner separation of the cause, or basis, from what is caused, or based. Primordial unity does not only release finite determinations from itself, it must also desire the process in which what is created departs from its basis and becomes independent. The necessity by which the finite emerges from its basis must harmonize with the freedom that is contained in such a separation.

In the old doctrine of God this contradiction had, since Augustine, been discussed under the heading of theodicy, in terms of how it is possible for evil to enter the world. There had to be a defence for the all-encompassing grace of the creator despite the obviously degenerate nature of his creation. God cannot be culpable if evil is explained as the fall of the creature away from God, or as subordinates mistakenly insisting on their independence. It is the wilfulness of human beings that goes astray because it loses contact with the necessity of a divine order.

The background of Schelling's text was the traditional doctrine of sin. The assumption, however, that freedom could not be thought of except in correspondence with necessity, formulated a credo of German idealism as a whole. In Kant's ethics, freedom had emerged in the submission to a binding moral law. Hegel's philosophy of right later removed an abstractness that had still been attached to this demand of submission in Kant's formal ethics, and also lifted the spell of rationalized theology that makes Schelling's text so attractive. The concrete presentation in Hegel's historically oriented philosophy lends particular strength to the postulate of the correspondence between freedom and necessity. Hegel's answer was that reason, the principle of freedom, is realized in the necessary context of history.

As he got older, Schelling was led further and further away from a philosophical autonomy of reason and towards the old truths of religion and myth. His late philosophy wanted to be understood as a protest against the unacknowledged one-sidedness that he claimed to be the price that idealism had paid for its perfection. Schelling coined the expression 'negative philosophy' for a philosophy which, according to him, had come to power after the idealist systems were complete. The negative needed to be followed by a positive philosophy, one that Schelling himself still wanted to present. After a brilliant start, Schelling was forced into the role of an outsider, giving private lectures while Hegel's career was approaching its peak. Even so, he still had his say in concluding the philosophical development of idealism.

Schelling believed he had provided the actual impulse for the movement, which his former comrade-in-arms and later competitor,

Hegel, managed to develop only incompletely. Schelling's main argument claimed that Hegel's logic, the hard core of his system, had only managed to reach the concept of Being, while beyond it, the actual reality of Being had remained unexplained. The demanding task of determining Being not only externally, but in its own reality as the basis for the possibility of all existence, was initiated by Schelling with good reason. However, he did not so much work towards results as merely anticipate them, for his later works often adopt an obscure or visionary tone.

After being in Hegel's shadow for a long time, it must have been a triumph for Schelling, after Hegel's death, to be named his successor at the university of Berlin. His distinguished audience, tired of disputes between various Hegelian cliques, expected substantial revelations, but soon gave up in disappointment. Schelling failed in his attempt to surpass Hegel after his death. He died in isolation, away from the philosophical stage, by now regarded as an obscure figure. Only in recent years has criticism of Hegel's idealism, either from a materialist perspective or in line with Heidegger's doctrine of Being, brought about a re-evaluation of the late Schelling's position.

THE TEXTS

In his *Ideas about a Philosophy of Nature, as Introduction to the Study of this Science*, Schelling sketched out the specific task of this discipline, which had been neglected in the philosophical development of his time. In Kant's epistemological critique, experience had been guided by nature. Kant had ruled out any assumptions about the realm of things in themselves, beyond the way in which reality as appearance confronts our experience. The gap was supposed to be filled by understanding Kant's critical question as a reflection. Reflection means a division, the separation of subject and object that tears us away from an immediately given, unreflected unity of intuition. Although philosophical investigation must adopt this special role in contrast to our everyday attitudes, it must also grasp the relativity of its reflection. Schelling wanted to overcome this division and restore an original unity. His solution was not that we should refrain from taking the first step of philosophical reflection, but rather that a resolute second step would need to follow. If reflection claims to be definitive, it misunderstands itself. In a true philosophy, reflection is recognized as merely a means to be followed by further intellectual activity.

Hence, overcoming mere reflection is a philosophical task in its own right, which at the same time changes the view of the world created by reflection. Schelling's new perspective on reality no longer kept spirit (mind) and matter artificially divided. Likewise, an understanding of spirit that is not strictly separated from our understanding of nature became possible. 'Nature should be the Mind made visible, Mind the invisible Nature.' Philosophy must try to go backwards to reach this point of inner unity preceding the separation caused by reflection. In view of this project, Schelling needed to reconsider old traditions that went back to Spinoza and Leibniz, but that were superseded by critical philosophy. In determining individual mechanical, chemical or organic phenomena, his philosophy of nature unfolded the basic thought of matter not as opposed to, but as affiliated with, the intellect.

The difficult lecture text *On the Nature of Philosophy as Science* presupposes the early idealist debates about the status of philosophy as a system. Principally, it implicitly criticizes Hegel's construction of the unity of philosophical knowledge, a unity produced by the different forms in which this idea of unity itself appears historically. Hegel's demand for systematic unity had arisen only because we have to presuppose an irresolvable conflict in human knowledge. If it weren't for this deep disunity, there would be no tendency towards a system. These are the conditions for the system. What shape, then, must its principle take? Since this must be the principle of all individual determinations encompassed and supported by the system, it cannot be determined the same way they are. The tricky determination of this principle, which is itself indeterminable due to its role of making determination possible, is reworked over the course of this text. We must not be led to think of it as something indeterminate which is, paradoxically, nevertheless determinate, like Spinoza's infinite substance and Fichte's absolute self. Simply negating determinateness as such, however, is equally insufficient because such a negation can itself only be expressed with reference to determination. The only possibility left is to think of this principle as the freedom to be determinate, or as the original potential to accept determinations. This infinite basis for creating the finite is expressed, borrowing from the terminology of the mystics, as a personal ability, will or desire, until a quite daring etymological leap turns it into the 'eternal magic'.

These expressions, however, vacillating between caution and audacity, must not take the focus away from the central problem. Without misleading reifications and restrictions, the principle that is responsible for concrete and determinate existence had to be named. With a constant eye on the problem, Schelling then tested existing idealist and mainly Fichtean proposals, such as absolute subject, self-knowledge, transcendental intuition, etc. Here he employed the concept of ecstasy, later revived in Heidegger's existential philosophy. Ecstasy stands for precisely the kind of relation which a subject has to itself when it perceives and knows itself. The ecstatic relation as such, 'keeping absolute subject and our knowledge separate', comes first. In contrast, determinations like subject and object are only derivatives. Schelling wanted to take the tension between unity and separation, appearing in an already reified form in the idealist concept of the subject in so far as it meant the identity of subject and object, back to this original basis of an ecstatic relation. Just as we can discover the truth of the philosophy of the ego or self in a primordial ecstatic relation, so we can discover the truth of dialectics in the restlessness within this tension. Schelling had very obviously assimilated the classical topics of contemporary philosophy in order to articulate them more profoundly. He wanted to return the developed philosophical idea to an 'unpreconceivable' origin which had been lost from sight in the process of its rational treatment.

Rüdiger Bubner
Translated by Marcus Weigelt

Ideas for a Philosophy of Nature

PREFACE TO THE FIRST EDITION

What the previous philosophical speculation of our age has left us as its net result is briefly the following: 'The former theoretical philosophy (under the name of metaphysics) was a mixture of quite heterogeneous principles. One part of it contained laws, which pertain to the possibility of *experience* (general *natural laws*), another, fundamental principles which extend over all experience (essentially metaphysical principles).

'Now, however, it has been established that only a *regulative* use can be made of the latter in theoretical philosophy. Only our moral nature raises us above the phenomenal world, and laws which, in the realm of ideas, are of *constitutive* use are for that very reason *practical* laws. So nothing remains hereafter of what was previously metaphysical in theoretical philosophy, except the practical alone. What are left to theoretical philosophy are only the general principles of a possible experience, and instead of being a science which *follows* physics (metaphysics), it will in future be a science which *precedes* physics.'

But now theoretical and practical philosophy (which in deference to the schools perhaps we may separate, but which are originally and necessarily united in the human mind) fall apart as *pure* and *applied*.

The *pure* theoretical philosophy concerns itself only with the investigation into the reality of our knowledge *as such*; it belongs, however, to the *applied*, under the name of a Philosophy of Nature, to derive from principles a *determinate* system of our knowledge (that is, the system of experience as a whole).

What *physics* is for *theoretical* philosophy, *history* is for the *practical*, and so the two main branches of our empirical knowledge develop out of these two main parts of philosophy.

Thus in working out the *Philosophy of Nature* and the *Philosophy of Man*, I hope to embrace the whole of *applied* philosophy. From the former natural science, from the latter history, should receive a scientific foundation.

The following essay is intended only to be the beginning of an execution of this plan. I shall explain in the Introduction the *idea* of a Philosophy of Nature on which this essay is based. So I must expect that the test of the philosophical principles of this work will issue from this Introduction.

But so far as the *execution* is concerned, as the title already indicates, this work contains no scientific system, but only *ideas* for a Philosophy of Nature. One may regard it as a series of individual discussions on this subject.

The present first part of this work divides into two, the empirical and the philosophical. I considered it necessary to begin with the first, because what follows in the text very often takes cognizance of more recent discoveries and investigations in physics and chemistry. However, this involved the inconvenience that much had to remain in doubt which I believed myself able to decide, on philosophical principles, only at a later stage. With regard to many statements of the first Book, therefore, I must refer to the second (especially the eighth chapter). With respect to questions as yet still to some extent in dispute concerning the nature of heat and the phenomena of combustion, I have followed the basic rule of admitting absolutely no hidden elemental substances in bodies, the reality of which can in no way be established by experience.

In all these investigations concerning heat, light, electricity and the like, writers have recently mingled more or less philosophical principles without first distancing themselves from the empirical context, principles which are already alien to the experimental sciences in and for themselves, and usually so indefinite that intolerable confusion arises as a result. In physics nowadays the concept of force is played with in this way more frequently than ever, especially since doubts have begun to be entertained about the materiality of light, etc.; the question has already several times been raised whether electricity might not perhaps be *life-force*. All these vague ideas introduced illegitimately into physics I have had, in the first part of the work, to leave in their indefiniteness, since they can be rectified only philosophically. Otherwise I have sought to keep myself always within the limits of physics and chemistry in this part – and therefore also to speak their picture-language.

In the section on light, I wished especially to give opportunity for inquiries into the influence of light on our atmosphere. That this influence is not merely of the mechanical kind is already inferrable from the relationship of light to vital air. Further investigations into this topic could perhaps produce more detailed conclusions even about the nature of light and its propagation in our atmosphere. The matter is doubly important since we now know indeed that the atmospheric air is a mixture, but do not know how Nature can maintain this relation of different kinds of air constant, despite the innumerable changes in the atmosphere. What I have said about this, in the section on the kinds of air, is far from sufficient to afford a final conclusion on this point. The hypothesis which I have proposed concerning the origin of electrical phenomena, and have supported with evidence, I should like all the more to see tested, since, if it is true, it must extend its influence still further (for instance, to physiology).

The *philosophical* part of this work is concerned with *dynamics* as the basic science of a theory of Nature, and *chemistry* as following from it. The part which follows next will include the principles of the theory of organic nature, or so-called physiology.

It will be apparent from the Introduction that my purpose is not to *apply* philosophy to natural science. I can think of no more pitiful, workaday occupation than such an application of abstract principles to an already existing empirical science. My object, rather, is first to allow natural science itself to *arise* philosophically, and my philosophy is itself nothing else than natural science. It is true that chemistry teaches us to *read* the *letters*, physics the *syllables*, mathematics *Nature*; but it ought not to be forgotten that it remains for philosophy to interpret what is read.

INTRODUCTION

What philosophy is as such cannot just be answered immediately. If it were so easy to agree about a definite concept of philosophy, one would only need to analyse this concept to see oneself at once in possession of a philosophy of universal validity. The point is this: Philosophy is not something with which our mind, without its own agency, is originally and by nature imbued. It is throughout a work of freedom. It is for each only what he has himself made it; and therefore the idea of philosophy is also only the result of philosophy itself, which, as an infinite science, is at the same time the science of itself.

Instead, therefore, of prescribing an arbitrary concept of philosophy in general or of the Philosophy of Nature in particular, in order thereafter to resolve it into its parts, I shall endeavour to let such a concept itself first *come into being* before the eyes of the reader.

Meanwhile, as one must, after all, have some starting point, I shall provisionally presuppose that a Philosophy of Nature *ought* to deduce the possibility of Nature, that is of the all-inclusive world of experience, from first principles. But I shall not deal with this concept analytically, or presuppose that it is correct and derive consequences from it, but before all else I shall investigate whether reality belongs to it as such, and whether it expresses anything that admits of *development*.

On the Problems which a Philosophy of Nature has to Solve

Whoever is absorbed in research into Nature, and in the sheer enjoyment of her abundance, does not ask whether Nature and experience be possible. It is enough that she is there for him; he has made her real by his very *act*, and the question of what is possible is raised only by one who believes that he does not hold the reality in his *hand*. Whole epochs have been spent in research into Nature, and yet one does not weary of it. Some have devoted their entire lives to this avocation and have not ceased to pray to the veiled goddess. Great spirits have lived in their own world, untroubled about the principles of their discoveries; and what is the whole reputation of the shrewdest doubter against the life of a man who has carried a world in his head and the whole of Nature in his imagination?

How a world outside us, how a Nature and with it experience, is possible – these are questions for which we have *philosophy* to thank; or rather, *with* these questions philosophy came to be. Prior to them mankind had lived in a (philosophical) state of nature. At that time man was still at one with himself and the world about him. In obscure recollection this condition still floats before even the most wayward thinker. Many never lose it and would be happy in themselves, if the fateful example did not lead them astray; for Nature releases nobody willingly from her tutelage, and there are no *native* sons of freedom. Nor would it be conceivable how man should ever have forsaken that condition, if we did not know that his spirit, whose element is *freedom*, strives to make *itself* free, to disentangle itself from the fetters of Nature and her guardianship, and must abandon itself to the uncertain fate of its own powers, in order one day to return, as victor and by its own merit, to that position in which, unaware of itself, it spent the childhood of its reason.

As soon as man sets himself in opposition to the external world (how he does so we shall consider later), the first step of philosophy has been taken. With that separation, reflection first begins; he separates from now on what Nature had always united, separates the object from the intuition, the concept from the image, finally (in that he becomes his own *object*) himself from himself.

But this separation is only *means*, not *end*. For the essence of man is action. But the less he reflects upon himself, the more active he is. His noblest activity is that which is not aware of itself. As soon as he makes himself object, the *whole* man no longer acts; he has suspended one part of his activity so as to be able to reflect upon the other. Man is not born to waste his mental power in conflict against the fantasy of an imaginary world, but to exert all his powers upon a world which has influence upon him, lets him feel its forces, and upon which he can react. Between him and the world, therefore, no rift must be established; contact and reciprocal action must be possible between the two, for only so does man become man.

Originally in man there is an absolute equilibrium of forces and of consciousness. But he can upset this equilibrium through freedom, in order to re-establish it through freedom. But only in equilibrium of forces is there health.

Mere reflection, therefore, is a spiritual sickness in mankind, the more so where it imposes itself in domination over the whole man, and kills at the root what in germ is his highest being, his spiritual life, which issues only from Identity. It is an evil which accompanies man into life itself, and distorts all his intuition even for the more familiar objects of consideration. But its preoccupation with dissection does not extend only to the phenomenal world; so far as it separates the spiritual principle from this, it fills the intellectual world with chimeras, against which, because they lie beyond all reason, it is not even possible to fight. It makes that separation between man and the world permanent, because it treats the latter as a thing in itself, which neither intuition nor imagination, neither understanding nor reason, can reach.

In contrast to this stands the true philosophy, which regards reflection as such merely as a means. Philosophy *must* presuppose that original divorce, because without it we should have no need to philosophize.

Therefore it assigns to reflection only *negative* value. It proceeds from that original divorce to unite once more, through freedom, what was originally and *necessarily* united in the human mind, i.e., forever to cancel out that separation. And so far as philosophy itself was made necessary only by that separation – was itself only a necessary evil, a discipline of errant reason – so it works in this respect for its own destruction. That philosopher who might employ his life, or a part of it, in pursuing the philosophy of reflection in its endless dichotomizing, in order to eliminate it in its ultimate ramifications, would earn for himself the most worthy place by this service, which, although it remains negative, may be respected equally with the highest, even if he were not himself to have the satisfaction of seeing philosophy in its absolute form resurrect itself self-consciously out of the dismembering activities of reflection. The simplest expression of complicated problems is always the best. He who first attended to the fact that he could distinguish himself from external things, and therewith his ideas from the objects, and conversely, the latter from the former, was the first philosopher. He first interrupted the mechanics of his thinking, upset the equilibrium of consciousness, in which subject and object are most intimately united.

In that I envisage the object, object and idea are one and the same. And only in this inability to distinguish the object from the idea during the envisaging itself lies the conviction, for the ordinary understanding, of the reality of external things, which become known to it, after all, only through ideas.

This identity of object and idea the philosopher now does away with, by asking: How do ideas of external things arise in us? By this question we displace the things *outside* of ourselves, suppose them to be independent of our ideas. At the same time there ought to be connection between them and our ideas. But we are acquainted with no *real* connection between *different* things other than that of *cause* and *effect*. So the first endeavour of philosophy is to put object and idea into the relationship of cause and effect.

But now we have expressly posited things as *independent of ourselves*. On the other hand, we feel *ourselves* to be dependent upon the objects. For our idea is itself only *real* in so far as we are compelled to assume agreement between it and the things. So we cannot make the things the effects of our ideas. Nothing remains, therefore, but to make the ideas dependent upon the things and to regard the latter as causes, the former as effects.

Now, however, one can see at first glance that by this move we essentially cannot achieve what we wanted. We wanted to explain how it comes about that in us the object and the idea are inseparably united. For only in this union lies the reality of our knowledge of external things. And it is just this reality that the philosopher is supposed to establish. But if the things are *causes* of ideas, then they *precede* the ideas. Consequently the separation between the two becomes permanent. But we wanted, after we had separated object and idea through freedom, to unite them again through freedom, we wanted to know that, and why, there is *originally* no separation between them.

Further, we know the things only through and in our ideas. There-fore, what they are, in so far as they precede our ideas, and so are not presented – of that we have no conception whatever.

Again, in asking: How does it come about that I have ideas? I raise myself *above* the idea and become, *through* this very question, a being that feels itself to be *free ab origine* with respect to all ideation, who surveys the ideation itself and the whole fabric of his ideas *beneath* him. Through this question itself I become an entity which, independent of external things, has *being in itself*.

Thus, with this question itself, I step out of the series of my ideas, release myself from connection with the things, adopt a position where no external force can reach me any longer; now, for the first time, the two hostile beings *mind* and *matter* separate. I place each of them in different worlds, between which no further connection is possible. In that I step out of the series of my ideas, even *cause* and *effect* are concepts which I survey from above. For they both arise only in the necessary succession of my ideas, from which I have released myself. How, then, can I subordinate myself again to these concepts, and allow things external to me to affect me?*

Or let us make the attempt the other way round, allow external things to affect us, and now explain how, despite this, we come to the question how ideas are possible in us.

Indeed, how things affect *me* (a free being) is not at all conceivable. I conceive only how things affect things. So far as I am *free*, however (and I *am* free, in that I raise myself above the interconnection of things and ask how this interconnection itself has become possible), I am not a *thing* at all, not an *object*. I live in a world entirely my own; I am a being that exists, not for other beings, but *for itself*. There can be only deed and act in me; from me effects can only *proceed*; there can be no *passivity* in me, for there is passivity only where there is effect and counter-effect, and this is only in the interconnection of

---

* Some ingenious members of the Kantian school have opposed this from the start. This philosophy allows all concepts of cause and effect to arise only in our minds, in our ideas, and yet the ideas themselves again, to be *caused* in me, according to the law of causality, by external things. Nobody wanted to hear of it at the time; but now surely it must be heard.

things, above which I have raised myself. But let it be the case that I am a *thing*, which is itself caught up in the series of causes and effects, and is itself, together with the entire system of ideas, a mere result of the manifold effects which impinge upon me from without; in short, suppose I am myself a mere piece of mechanism. But what is caught up in mere mechanism cannot step out of the mechanism and ask: How has all this become possible? *Here*, in the midst of the series of phenomena, absolute necessity has assigned to it its place; if it leaves this place, it is no longer this thing. It is inconceivable how any external cause whatsoever could affect this self-dependent being, whole and complete in itself.

In order to be able to philosophize, therefore, one must be capable of asking that very question with which all philosophy begins. This question is not such as one can, without further ado, address to others. It is one brought forth freely, a problem self-given. *That* I am capable of posing this question is proof enough that I am, as such, independent of external things; for how otherwise could I have asked how these things themselves are possible *for me*, in my consciousness? One would therefore have to think that anyone who so much as raises this question is by that very fact refusing to explain his ideas as effects of external things. But this question has fallen among those who were completely incapable of devoting themselves to it. As it passed into their mouths, it also took on another sense, or rather, it lost all sense and meaning. *They* are beings who know themselves in no other way than so far as laws of cause and effect have power and dominion over them. *I*, in that I raise this question, have exalted myself above these laws. *They* are caught up in the mechanism of their thinking and representing; *I* have broken through this mechanism. How would they wish to understand me?

One who for himself is nothing other than what things and circumstances have made him, who, without dominion over his own ideas, is seized by, and dragged along with, the stream of causes and effects – how will he wish to know whence he comes, or whither he goes, or how he has become what he is? Does the wave know this, that drives hence in the stream? He has not even the right to say that he is a result of the collective effect of external things; for in order to be able to say this, he must presuppose that he knows *himself*, that he is therefore also something *for himself*. But this he is not. He exists only for other rational beings – not for himself – is a mere *object* in the world; and it is advantageous for him and for science that he should never hear of anything else or imagine anything other.

From time immemorial the most ordinary people have refuted the greatest philosophers with things understandable even to children and striplings. One hears, reads, and marvels that such common things were unknown to such great men and that people admittedly so insignificant could master them. It does not occur to anybody that perhaps the philosophers were also aware of all that; for how else could they have swum against the stream of evidence? Many are convinced that Plato, if he could only have read Locke, would have gone off ashamed; many a one believes that even Leibniz, if he arose from the dead to go to school for an hour with him, would be converted, and how many greenhorns have not sung triumphal songs over Spinoza's grave?

What was it, then, you ask, that drove all these men to forsake the common ways of thinking of their age and to invent systems opposed to everything that the great mass of people have always believed and imagined? It was a free inspiration, which elevated them into a sphere where *you* no longer even understand their task, while on the other hand many things became inconceivable to them, which seem very simple and understandable to you.

It was impossible, for them, to join and bring into contact things which, in you, Nature and mechanism have always united. They were also unable to deny the world outside them, or that there was a mind within them, and yet there appeared to be no possible connection between the two. To you, if you ever think about these problems, there can be no question of converting the world into a play of concepts, or the mind within you into a dead mirror of things.

Long since, the human spirit (still youthful, vigorous and fresh from the gods) had lost itself in mythology and poetic fictions about the origin of the world. The religions of entire peoples were founded on that conflict between spirit and matter, before a happy genius – the first philosopher – discovered the concepts in which all succeeding ages grasped and held firm both ends of our knowledge. The greatest thinkers among the ancients did not venture beyond this contradiction. Plato still sets matter, as an other, over against God. The *first* who, with complete clarity, saw mind and matter as one, thought and extension simply as modifications of the same principle, was *Spinoza*. His system was the first bold outline of a creative imagination, which conceived the finite immediately in the idea of the infinite, purely as such, and recognized the former only in the latter. *Leibniz* came, and went the opposite way. The time has come when his philosophy can be re-established. His mind despised the fetters of the schools; small wonder that he has survived amongst us only in a few kindred spirits and among the rest has long become a stranger. He belonged to the few who also treat science as a free activity. He had in himself the universal *spirit of the world*, which reveals itself in the most manifold forms; and where it enters, life expands. It is therefore doubly insufferable that only now are the right words for his philosophy supposed to have been found, and that the Kantian school should force its inventions upon him – alleging that he says things the precise opposite of everything he taught. There is nothing from which Leibniz could have been more remote than the speculative chimera of a world of *things-in-themselves*, which, known and intuited by no mind, yet affects us and produces all our ideas. The first thought from which he set out was: 'that the ideas of external things would have arisen in the soul by virtue of her own laws *as in a particular world*, even though nothing were present but God (the infinite) and the soul (the intuition of the infinite)'. He still asserted in his latest writings the absolute impossibility that an external cause should produce an effect upon the inwardness of a mind; he asserted, accordingly, that all alterations, all change of perceptions and presentations in a mind, could proceed only from an inner principle. When Leibniz said this, he spoke to philosophers. Today some people have intruded into philosophizing, who have a feeling for all else, but not for philosophy. Accordingly, if among ourselves it is said that no ideas could arise in us through external causes, there is no end of astonishment.

Nowadays it is valid in philosophy to believe that the monads have windows, through which things climb in and out.*

It is quite possible to drive even the most convinced adherent of things-in-themselves as the causes of our ideas into a corner by all sorts of questions. One can say to him, I understand how matter affects matter, but neither how one in-itself affects another, since there can be no cause and no effect in the realm of the intelligible, nor how this law of one world extends into another altogether different from it, in fact completely opposed to it. You would then have to admit, if I am dependent on external impressions, that I myself am nothing more than matter – as it were, an optical glass, in which the light-ray of the world refracts. But the optical glass does not itself see; it is merely an instrument in the hand of a rational being. And what is that in me which judges it to be an impression that has impinged upon me? Again, my own self, which surely, in so far as it judges, is not passive, but active – and thus something in me which feels itself free from the impression, and which nevertheless knows about the impression, apprehends it, raises it to consciousness.

Further, during the intuiting, no doubt arises concerning the reality of the external perception. But now comes the understanding and begins to divide and divides endlessly. Is matter outside you real? If so, it must *consist* of infinite parts. If it consists of infinitely many parts, it must have been put together out of these parts. But for this assembling our imagination has only a finite measure. Therefore an endless putting together must have occurred in finite time. Or the putting together must have begun somewhere, which means there are ultimate parts of matter, so I must (in the dividing) encounter such ultimate parts; but I only ever find bodies of the same kind and never penetrate beyond the surface; the real seems to flee before me, or to vanish under my hand, and matter, the first foundation of all experience, becomes the most insubstantial thing we know.

Or does this conflict exist simply to enlighten us about ourselves? Is perception, as it were, only a dream, which mirrors reality in front of all rational beings, and is understanding given to them only in

* Leibnitii Princip. Philosoph. #7.

order to awaken them from time to time – to remind them what they are, so that their existence (for obviously enough we are intermediate beings) may thereby be divided between sleeping and waking? But I cannot understand any such primordial dream. All dreams are but shadows of reality, 'recollections from a world, which previously was actual'. If one wished to assume that a higher Being was causing these shadow-images of actuality in us, even here the question would recur as to the real possibility of the concept of such a relationship (since I know of simply nothing in this sphere, which would follow according to cause and effect); and since that Being surely produced what it imparted to me out of itself, then presuming, as is necessary, that it can have no transitive effect on me, there would be no other possibility than that I had received that shadow-show merely as a limitation, or modification, of its absolute productivity, and thus again, within these limits, always through production.

Matter is not insubstantial, you say, for it has original *forces*, which cannot be annihilated by any subdivision. 'Matter has forces.' I know that this expression is very common. But how? 'Matter has' – here then it is presupposed as something that exists for itself and independently of its forces. So would these forces be merely accidental to it? Because matter is at hand *outside you*, so also it must owe its forces to an external cause. Are they, as it were, as some Newtonians say, implanted in it by a higher hand? But you have no conception of influences by which forces are *implanted*. You know only how matter, i.e., force itself, works against force; and how effects can be produced on something which originally is not *force*, we have no conception at all. One may say something of the sort; it can pass from mouth to mouth; but never yet has it actually entered any human head, because no human head can think any such thing. Therefore, you cannot conceive matter at all without force.

Further: Those forces are forces of attraction and repulsion. 'Attraction and repulsion' – do these, then, take place in empty space? Do they not themselves already presuppose occupied space, that is, matter? So you must admit that neither forces without matter nor matter without forces can be conceived. But now matter is the final substratum of your knowledge, beyond which you cannot go;

and as you cannot explain those forces *from* the matter, so you cannot explain them at all empirically, that is, by something *outside yourself*, as surely you must do according to your system.

Irrespective of this it is asked in philosophy how matter *is possible* external to us, thus also, how those forces are possible outside us. One can abjure all philosophizing (would to God those who do not understand it would be pleased to do so), but if you do wish to philosophize, you cannot neglect those questions. Now, however, you can in no way make intelligible what a force might be independent of you. For force as such makes itself known only to your *feeling*. Yet feeling alone gives you no objective concepts. At the same time you make objective use of those forces. For you explain the movement of celestial bodies – universal gravitation – by forces of attraction and maintain that in this explanation you have an absolute principle of these phenomena. In your system, however, the force of attraction ranks as nothing more or less than a *physical* cause. For as matter independent of you exists outside you, so likewise you can only know what forces belong to it through experience. As physical ground of explanation, however, the force of attraction is nothing more and nothing less than an occult quality. All the same, let us first see whether empirical principles can be adequate at all to explain the possibility of a world system. The question answers itself in the negative; for the ultimate knowledge from experience is this, that a universe exists; this proposition is the limit of experience itself. Or rather, that a universe exists is itself only an *idea*. Even less, therefore, can the universal equilibrium of world forces be anything that you could have concocted from experience. For you could not even extract this idea from experience for the individual system if it is everywhere idea; but it is transferred to the whole only by analogical inferences; such inferences, however, give no more than probability. Whereas ideas like that of a universal equilibrium, true in themselves, must for that reason be products of something, or must be grounded in something, which is itself absolute and independent of experience.

Accordingly, you would have to admit that this idea itself reaches over into a higher region than that of mere natural science. Newton, who never wholly abandoned himself to that, and himself still sought after the *effective cause of attraction*, saw only too well that he stood at the frontier of Nature and that here two worlds diverge. Seldom have great minds lived at the same time without working from altogether different angles towards the same objective. Whereas Leibniz based the system of the spiritual world on the pre-established harmony, Newton found the system of a material world in the equilibrium of world forces. But if, after all, there is unity in the system of our knowledge, and if we ever succeed in uniting the very last extremes of that system, we must hope that even here, where Leibniz and Newton diverged, an all-embracing mind will at some time find the midpoint round which the *universe of our knowledge* moves – the two worlds between which our knowledge is at present still divided; and Leibniz's pre-established harmony and Newton's system of gravitation still appear as one and the same, or merely as different aspects of one and the same totality.

I go farther. Raw matter, that is, matter in so far as it is thought of as merely filling space, is only the firm ground and basis on which the edifice of Nature is first constructed. Matter has to be something real. But what is real only permits of being sensed. How then is sensation possible in me? As you say, it is not enough that I should be affected from without. There must be something in me which *senses*, and between this and what you assume to be outside me no contact is possible. Or, if this external thing works on me as matter on matter, then I can only react upon this externality (as it were, by repulsive force), but not *upon myself*. And yet this has to occur, for I have to *sense*, have to raise the sensation to consciousness.

What you sense of matter you call *quality*, and only in so far as it has a determinate quality is it said to be real for you. That it has quality *at all* is *necessary*, but that it has this *determinate* quality appears to you as *contingent*. If so, then matter as such cannot have one and the same quality: There must, therefore, be a multiplicity of *determinations* with all of which you are nevertheless acquainted through mere sensation. What then is it that causes sensation? 'Something *internal*, an inner constitution of matter'. These are words, not facts. For where then is the inside of this matter? You can divide endlessly and yet come no farther than to the surfaces of bodies. All this has long been obvious to you; so you have long since explained what is merely sensed as something which has its basis only in the manner of your sensing. But this is the very least. For it does not make sensation any more intelligible that nothing which exists outside of you should be in itself sweet or sour; in any case, you always assume a *cause* actually outside you, which produces these sensations in you. But suppose we allow you the inner effects of outer causation, what then have colours, scents, and the like, or the causes external to you of these sensations, in common with your mind? You investigate very meticulously how light reflected from bodies affects your optical nerves, also indeed how the inverted image on the retina is not inverted in your soul, but appears upright. But then again what is that in you which sees this image on the retina itself, and investigates how indeed it can have come into the soul? Obviously it is something which to this extent is completely independent of the external impression, and to which nevertheless this impression is not unknown. How then did the impression reach *this* region of your soul in which you feel wholly free and independent of impressions? However many intervening factors you insert between the effects on your nerves, brain, etc., and the idea of an external thing, you only deceive yourself; for the transition from the body to the soul, according to your own submissions, cannot occur continuously, but only by a leap, which you profess you would rather avoid.

Moreover, that one mass works upon another by virtue of its mere motion (by impenetrability) is what you call impact or *mechanical* movement.

Or else, one material thing works on another without the condition of a previously received motion, so that movement proceeds from rest through attraction, and this is your *gravity*.

You conceive of matter as *inert*, that is, as something which does not move self-actively, but can only be moved by external causes.

Again, the gravity which you ascribe to bodies, you set equal to the quantity of matter (irrespective of its volume) as specific weight.

Now you find, however, that one body can impart motion to another without being moved itself, that is, *without* acting upon it by *impact*.

You observe, further, that two bodies can mutually attract one another altogether independent of the relation of their masses, that is to say, *independent* of the laws of *gravity*.

You therefore assume that the ground of this attraction can be sought neither in the weight nor on the surface of the body so moved; the ground must be something internal and must depend on the *quality* of the body. Only you have never yet explained what you understand by the *inner nature* of a body. Moreover, it has been demonstrated that quality has legitimate sense only in relation to your sensation. But here we are speaking, not of your sensation, but of an objective fact, which occurs outside you, which you apprehend with your senses, and which your understanding seeks to translate into intelligible concepts. Now, assume that we admit quality to be something which has a ground, not merely in your sensation, but in the body outside you; what then do the words mean: One body attracts another by virtue of its qualities? For what is *real* in this attraction, that is, what enables you to perceive it, is merely – the motion of the body. Motion, however, is a pure mathematical magnitude, and can be defined purely phoronomically. How then does this external movement combine with an inner quality? You are borrowing pictorial expressions, which are taken from living natures, for example, family relationship. But you would be very hard put to convert this image into an intelligible concept. Further, you heap elementary stuff on elementary stuff, but these are nothing else than just so many refuges of your ignorance. For what do you think of under these terms? Not matter itself, e.g., carbon, but something that is contained in this matter, as if hidden, and first imparts these qualities to it. But where then is this elementary stuff in the body? Has anyone ever found it by division or separation? As yet there is not one of these stuffs which you could present to the senses. But even if we presume their existence, what do we gain? Is the quality of matter somehow explained thereby? I conclude thus: Either the quality which they impart to the body belongs to the elementary stuffs themselves, or it does not. In the first case, you have explained nothing, for the question was just that, how do qualities arise? In the other case, again nothing is explained, for I understand how one body could (mechanically) strike the other and so impart motion to it; but how a body completely devoid of qualities could impart quality to another, this nobody understands, and nobody can make it intelligible. For quality as such is something of which so far you have been in no position to give any objective conception, and yet of which you make objective use (in chemistry, at least).

These are the elements of our empirical knowledge. For if we may once presuppose matter and with it forces of attraction and repulsion, besides an endless multiplicity of kinds of matter, which are all distinguished from one another by qualities, we have, according to the guidance of the table of categories:

1. *Quantitative* motion, which is proportional only to the quantity of matter – gravity;
2. *Qualitative* motion, which is appropriate to the inner constitution of matter – *chemical* motion;
3. *Relative* motion, which is transmitted to bodies by influence from without (by impact) – *mechanical* motion.

It is these three possible motions from which natural science engenders and develops its entire system.

The part of physics which is concerned with the *first* is called *statics*. That which is concerned with the *third* is called *mechanics*. This is the main part of physics; for basically the whole of physics is nothing but applied mechanics.* That part, which is concerned with the *second* kind of motion, serves in physics only as ancillary, namely *chemistry*, whose object is essentially to trace the specific difference of matter; it is the science which first creates for mechanics (in itself a wholly formal science) content and diverse application. It requires,

---

* In mechanics the universal properties of bodies, like elasticity, solidity, density, etc., in so far as they have influence on *mechanical* movement, can likewise be included. However, *universal* kinematics does not at all belong among the empirical sciences – I believe that, according to this division, physics acquires a far simpler and more natural coherence than it has hitherto received in most textbooks.

that is to say, very little trouble to derive from the principles of chemistry the main objects which physics (with respect to its mechanical and dynamical motions) investigates; for example, for chemical attraction between bodies to take place, one may say, there must be a matter which extends them, which works against inertia – light and heat – also substances which mutually attract one another and, so that there may be the greatest simplicity, *one* fundamental substance, which all others attract. And, as Nature itself requires many chemical processes for its continuance, these conditions of chemical processes, and so vital air, as the product of light and that fundamental stuff, must be present everywhere. And as this air would promote the violence of combustion all too readily and exhaust the strength of our organs excessively, a mixture of it with another kind of air directly opposed to it is needed – atmospheric air, and so forth.

This is more or less the way in which the theory of Nature attains completeness. But our present concern is not how we might present such a system, once it exists, but how in general such a system could exist. The question is not whether and how that assemblage of phenomena and the series of causes and effects, which we call the course of Nature, has become actual *outside us*, but how they have become actual *for us*, how that system and that assemblage of phenomena have found their way to our minds, and how they have attained the necessity in our conception with which we are absolutely compelled to think of them. For it is presupposed, as undeniable fact, that the representation of a succession of causes and effects external to us is as necessary for our mind as if they belonged to its very being and essence. To explain this necessity is a major problem of all philosophy. The question is not whether this problem as such ought to exist, but how, once it exists, it must be solved.

First of all, what does it mean to say: We must think of a succession of phenomena which is absolutely *necessary*? Obviously this: These phenomena could follow one another only in this *particular* succession, and *vice versa*, only in these *particular* phenomena can this succession proceed.

For that our ideas follow one another in this precise order, that for example the lightning precedes the thunder, does not follow it, and so on, for this we do not seek the reason *in us*; it does not matter *to us* how we let the ideas follow one another; the reason must, therefore, lie in *the things*, and we declare that this particular succession is a succession of the *things themselves*, not merely of our ideas of them. Only in so far as the phenomena *themselves* follow one another thus and not otherwise are we compelled to represent them in this order; only because and in so far as this succession is *objectively* necessary is it also *subjectively* necessary.

Now from this it follows further that this particular succession cannot be divorced from these particular phenomena; the succession must thus come to be and arise together with the phenomena, and conversely the phenomena must come about and arise together with the succession; therefore, both succession and phenomena are in mutual relation, both are mutually necessary in regard to each other.

One has only to analyse the commonest judgements that we pass at every moment about the connection of phenomena, in order to discover that the above presuppositions are contained in them.

Now, if neither the phenomena can be separated from their succession nor the succession from its phenomena, only the two following cases are possible:

Either succession and phenomena both arise together and inseparably *outside* us.

Or succession and phenomena both arise together and inseparably *within* us.

Only in these two cases is the succession, which we represent to ourselves, an actual succession of things, not merely an ideal sequence of our presentations one after another.

The first assertion is that of the common human understanding, and even of philosophers formally opposed to Hume's scepticism, Reid and Beattie, among others. In this system the things in themselves follow one another; we have only to look at them; but how the representation of them got into us is a question pitched much too high for this system. But we do not want to know how the succession is possible outside us, but how this particular succession, since it proceeds quite independently of us, yet is represented *as* such by us, and in so far as it is so, with absolute necessity. Now of this question that system takes no account. It is therefore not susceptible of any philosophical critique; it has not one point in common with philosophy from which one could proceed to investigate, test or contest it, for it is altogether oblivious of the question which it is the essential business of philosophy to solve.

That system should first be made philosophical before one could even test it. But then one runs the risk of fighting against a mere fabrication, for the common understanding is not so consistent, and such a system as that consistent with common sense has in fact never yet existed in any human head; for as soon as one seeks to give it philosophical expression, it becomes wholly unintelligible. It speaks of a succession, which, *independently* of me, is supposed to take place *outside* me. I understand how a succession (of ideas) takes place *within* me; but a succession which goes on in the things themselves, independent of the finite ideas, is wholly unintelligible to me. For if we were to posit a Being who was not finite, and accordingly not bound to the succession of presentations, but who grasped everything, present and future, together in one intuition, for such a Being there would be no succession in the things external to him: It is therefore a succession, as such, only under the condition of the finitude of the representation. But if the succession were also grounded in the things-in-themselves, independently of all presentation, there would have to be a succession for such a Being as we have assumed as well, which is self-contradictory.

For this reason, all philosophers up to the present have unanimously declared that succession is something which cannot be conceived at all apart from the presentations of a finite mind. Now we have established that, if the presentation of a succession is to be necessary, it must arise together with the things, and *vice versa*; the succession must be as little possible without the things as the things without the succession. If, therefore, succession is something possible only in our ideas, there is a choice between only two alternatives.

Either one insists that things exist outside us independently of our ideas. Then, by so doing, the objective necessity, with which we represent to ourselves a particular succession of *things*, is explained away as mere illusion, in as much as one denies that the succession takes place in the things themselves.

Or one adheres to the assertion that the very phenomena themselves, together with the succession, come to be and arise only in our ideas, and that only to that extent is the order in which they follow one another a genuinely objective order.

Now the first assertion obviously leads to the most fantastical system that has ever existed, and which even today would be maintained only by a handful, without their even knowing it. *Here* now is the place to dispose completely of the axiom that things affect us from without. For let us just ask what things outside us and independent of these ideas might be. First we must divest them of everything that belongs only to the peculiarities of our faculty of representation. To that belongs, not only succession, but also all conception of cause and effect and, if we wish to be consistent, also all representation of space and extension, both of which are utterly inconceivable without time, from which we have removed the things-in-themselves. Nevertheless these things-in-themselves, although altogether inaccessible to our faculty of intuition, must still be actually present – one knows not how or where – probably in the *twilight worlds* of Epicurus – and these things have to *affect* me in order to occasion my ideas. True it is that nobody has ever yet entered into the question what idea we actually frame of such things. To say that they are not conceivable is one way out, but that is soon cut off. If we speak of them, we must have an idea of them, or else we speak as we should not. One has, indeed, an idea even of nothing; one thinks of it at least as the absolute void, as something purely formal, and so on. One might think that the idea of things-in-themselves were a similar notion. But the idea of nothing can, after all, still be made palpable through the schema of empty space. Things-in-themselves, however, are expressly excluded from space and time, for the latter belong, of course, only to the peculiar form of representation of finite beings. So nothing is left but an idea which floats midway between something and nothing, i.e., which does not even have the virtue of being absolutely nothing. It is, in fact, scarcely credible that such a nonsensical conglomeration of things, which, bereft of all sensible characteristics, are nevertheless supposed to function as sensible things, should ever have come into anybody's head.*

Indeed, if everything that belongs to the presentation of an objective world is eliminated beforehand, what is there left for me to understand? Clearly, only *myself*. So all ideas of an external world would have to develop out of *me*, myself. For if succession, cause, effect, and the rest, first attach to things in my representation of them, one can as little conceive what those concepts could be without the things, as what the things could be without the concepts. Hence the venturesome explanation which this system is constrained to give of the origin of representation. In opposition to things-in-themselves it sets up a mind, and this mind contains in itself certain *a priori* forms, which have only this advantage over things-in-themselves, that one can at least represent them as something absolutely empty. In representing the things, we apprehend them in these forms. Thereby the formless objects acquire structure; the empty forms, content. How it happens that things come to be represented at all, about that there is the deepest silence. It is enough that we represent things as external to us. Only in the representation, however, do we first carry space and time over to them, and further, the concepts of substance and accident, cause and effect, and so on. Thus the succession of our ideas arises in us, and indeed a necessary succession; and this self-made succession, first brought forth in consciousness, is called the course of Nature.

This system requires no refutation. To propound it is to overturn it from the bottom up. In fact, the *Humean* scepticism is vastly superior and not at all comparable to it. Hume (faithful to his principles) leaves it altogether undecided whether our ideas correspond to things outside us or not. In every case, however, he has to assume that the *succession* of appearances takes place only in our ideas; but that we take just this *particular* succession as *necessary* he declares to be pure illusion. But what one can justly demand of Hume is that he at least

---

* The truth is that the idea of things-in-themselves had come down to Kant through the tradition and had lost all meaning in the course of inheritance. [This note is lacking in the first edition.]

explain the source of this *illusion*. For that we do actually think of a sequence of causes and effects as necessary – that thereon rest all our empirical sciences, theory of Nature and history (in which he was himself so great a master), he cannot deny. But whence this illusion itself? Hume answers: 'From custom; *because hitherto the appearances have followed one another in this order*, the imagination has accustomed itself to expect the same order also in the future, and this expectation has, like every long habituation, ultimately become for us a *second nature*.' But this explanation turns in a circle, for the very thing that had to be explained was *why things have hitherto followed one another in this order* (which Hume does not deny). Was this sequence perhaps something in the things outside us? But apart from our ideas, there is no succession. Or, if it was merely the succession of our ideas, then a reason for the persistence of this succession must also be given. What exists independent of me I am unable to explain; but for what goes on only *in me* the reason must be found also in me. Hume can say: It is so, and that satisfies me. But this is not to philosophize. I do not say that a Hume *ought* to philosophize, but once a man *proclaims* that he wants to philosophize, he can no longer dismiss the question, Why?

So nothing remains but the attempt to derive the necessity of a succession of presentations from the *nature* of our mind, and so of the finite mind as such, and, in order that this succession may be genuinely *objective*, to have the things themselves, together with this sequence, arise and come into being in it.

Among all previous systems I know only two – the Spinozistic and the Leibnizian – which not only undertook this attempt, but whose entire philosophy is nothing else but this attempt. Now because there is still at present much doubt and discussion about the relation of these two systems – whether they contradict each other, or how they cohere – it seems useful to say something about them at the outset.

Spinoza, as it seems, was worried at a very early stage about the connection of our ideas with things outside us, and could not tolerate the separation which had been set up between them. He saw that ideal and real (thought and object) are most intimately united in our nature. That we have ideas of things outside us, that our ideas even reach out *beyond* the things, he could explain to himself only in terms of our *ideal nature*; but that these ideas correspond to actual *things*, he had to explain in terms of the *affections* and *determinations* of the ideal in us. Therefore we could not become aware of the real, save in contrast to the ideal, or of the ideal, save in contrast to the real. Accordingly, no separation could occur between the actual things and our ideas of them. Concepts and things, thought and extension, were, for this reason, one and the same for him, both only modifications of one and the same ideal nature.

However, instead of descending into the depths of his self-consciousness and descrying the emergence thence of the two worlds in us – the ideal and the real – he passed himself by; instead of explaining from our nature how finite and infinite, originally united in us, proceed reciprocally from each other, he lost himself forthwith in the idea of an infinite outside us. In this infinity there arose, or rather originally were – one knows not whence – affections and modifications, and with these an endless series of finite things. For, because there was no transition in his system from infinite to finite, a beginning of *becoming* was for him as inconceivable as a beginning of *being*. Yet that this endless succession is envisaged by me, and is envisaged with *necessity*, followed from the fact that the things and my ideas were originally one and the same. I myself was only one of the Infinite's thoughts, or rather just a constant succession of presentations. But Spinoza was unable to make it intelligible how I myself in turn become aware of this succession.

For, generally speaking, as it came from his hand, his system is the most unintelligible that ever existed. One must have taken this system up into oneself, have put oneself in the place of his infinite Substance, in order to know that infinite and finite – do not *arise*, but – *exist* originally together and inseparably, not *outside us*, but *in us*, and that the nature of our mind and of our whole mental existence rests on just this original union. For we know immediately only our own essence, and only ourselves are intelligible to us. How affections and determinations are and can exist in an Absolute external to me, I do not understand. But I do understand that even within me there could be nothing *infinite* unless there were at the same time a *finite*.

For that necessary union of ideal and real, of the absolutely active and absolutely passive (which Spinoza displaced into an infinite Substance outside me) exists *within me* originally without my co-operation, and that is just what *my* nature consists in.*

Leibniz followed this route, and here is the point where he diverges from Spinoza and connects with him. It is impossible to understand Leibniz without having stationed oneself at this point. *Jacobi* has shown that his whole system sets out from the concept of *individuality* and reverts to it. In the concept of individuality alone, there is an original union of what all other philosophy separates, the positive and the negative, the active and the passive in our nature. How there can be *determinations* in an infinite external to us, Spinoza knew no way of making intelligible, and he sought in vain to avoid a transition from the infinite to the finite. This transition is absent only where finite and infinite are *originally* united, and this *original* union exists nowhere except in the essence of an individual nature. Leibniz, therefore, went over neither from the infinite to the finite nor from the latter to the former, but both were made actual for him at the same time – as if through one and the same unfolding of our nature – through one and the same operation of the mind.

That ideas in us *follow* one another is the necessary consequence of our finitude, but that this series is *endless* proves that they proceed from a being in whose nature finitude and infinity are united.

That this succession is *necessary* follows, in Leibniz's philosophy, from the fact that the things together with the ideas arise by virtue of the mere laws of our nature, according to an inner principle in us, as in a world of its own. What alone Leibniz held to be originally real and actual *in themselves* were *perceptual beings*; for in these alone was that *unification* original, out of which everything else that is called actual *develops* and *goes forth*. For everything which is actual outside us is finite, and so not conceivable without a positive, which gives it

---

* But closer consideration will at once teach anyone that every positing-in-me of the absolute identity of finite and infinite, like the positing-outside-me, is again only *my* positing, so that the former *in itself* is neither an in-me nor an outside-me. [This note is added in the second edition.]

reality, and a negative, which sets its limit. This unification of positive and negative activity, however, is nowhere *original* except in the nature of an individual. External things *were* not actual *in themselves*, but have only *become* actual through the mode of presentation of spiritual natures; but that from whose nature all existence first *emerges*, that is, the ideating being alone, would have had to be something which bears the source and origin of its existence in itself.

If now the whole succession of ideas springs from the *nature* of the finite mind, so likewise the whole series of our experiences must be derivable from it. For that all beings like ourselves perceive the phenomena of the world in the same necessary serial order is conceivable only and solely from our common nature. To explain this agreement of our nature, however, by a pre-established harmony is actually not to explain it. Because this word only says *that* such agreement occurs, but not how and why. It is, however, implicit in Leibniz's system itself that this agreement should follow from the *essence* of finite natures as such. Because if this were not so, the mind would cease to be absolutely *self-explanatory* of its knowledge and cognition. Nevertheless it would still have to seek the ground of its ideas *outside itself*. We should have reverted once again to the same point from which we began; the world and its order would be *contingent* for us, and the representation thereof would come to us only from without. But with that we are inevitably swept beyond the limits within which alone we understand ourselves. For if a superior hand had so contrived us in the first place that we were compelled to envisage such a world and such an order of phenomena, then, discounting the fact that this hypothesis is wholly unintelligible to us, this whole world is once again an illusion: One thrust of that hand is able to wrest it from us, or to translate us into an entirely different order of things; it is then wholly doubtful even that beings of our own kind (with similar ideas to ours) exist outside us. Leibniz, therefore, could not have associated with the pre-established harmony the idea that one usually couples with it. For he explicitly asserts that no mind could have *come to be*; that is, the concepts of cause and effect are altogether inapplicable to a mind. It is, therefore, absolutely self-explanatory of its being and knowing, and just because it exists at all, is also *what it is*, i.e., a being to whose *nature* this particular system of ideas of external things also belongs.

Philosophy, accordingly, is nothing other than a *natural history of our mind*. From now on all dogmatism is overturned from its foundations. We consider the system of our ideas, not in its *being*, but in its *becoming*. Philosophy becomes *genetic*; that is, it allows the whole necessary series of our ideas to arise and take its course, as it were, before our eyes. From now on there is no longer any separation between experience and speculation. The system of Nature is at the same time the system of our mind, and only now, once the great synthesis has been accomplished, does our knowledge return to analysis (to *research* and *experiment*). But this system does not yet exist. Many faint-hearted spirits have misgivings at the outset, for they speak of a system of *our nature* (the magnitude of which they do not know), no otherwise than as if they were speaking about a *syllabus** of our *concepts*.

The dogmatist, who assumes everything to be originally *present* outside us (not as *coming to be* and *springing forth from* us) must surely commit himself at least *to this*: that what is *external* to us is also to be explained by *external* causes. He succeeds in doing this, as long as he remains within the nexus of cause and effect, despite the fact that he can never make it intelligible how this nexus of causes and effects has *itself* arisen. As soon as he raises himself above the individual phenomenon, his whole philosophy is at an end; the limits of mechanism are also the limits of his system.

But now mechanism alone is far from being what constitutes Nature. For as soon as we enter the realm of *organic nature*, all mechanical linkage of cause and effect ceases for us. Every organic product exists *for itself*; its being is dependent on no other being. But now the cause is never the *same as* the effect; only between quite *different* things is a relation of cause and effect possible. The organic, however, produces *itself*, arises *out of itself*; every single plant is the product only of an individual *of its own kind*, and so every single organism endlessly

---

* In the writings and translations from the earliest times of German purism one finds the expressions: *Syllabus of essences*, *Syllabus of Nature*. It is a shame that our modern philosophers have allowed these expressions to go out of use.

produces and reproduces only *its own species*. Hence no organization progresses *forward*, but is forever turning back always into *itself*. Accordingly, an organization as such is neither *cause* nor *effect* of anything outside it, and so is nothing that intrudes into the nexus of mechanism.

Every organic product carries the reason of its existence in *itself*, for it is cause and effect of itself. No single part could *arise* except in this whole, and this whole itself consists only in the *interaction* of the parts. In every other object the parts are *arbitrary*; they exist only in so far as I *divide*. Only in organized beings are they *real*; they exist without my participation, because there is an *objective* relationship between them and the whole. Thus a *concept* lies at the base of every organization, for where there is a necessary relation of the whole to the part and of the part to the whole, there is *concept*. But this concept dwells in the *organization itself*, and can by no means be separated from it; it *organizes itself*, and is not simply, say, a work of art whose concept is to be found *outside* it in the understanding of the artist. Not only its form but its *existence* is purposive. It could not organize itself without already being organized. The plant nourishes itself and subsists through assimilation of external matter, but it can assimilate nothing to itself unless it is already organized. The maintenance of the living body depends on respiration. The vital air it inhales is decomposed by its organs in order to flow through the nerves as electric fluid. But to make this process possible, organization must already have been present, which yet, on the other hand, does not survive without this process. Thus organization constructs itself only out of organization. In the organic product, for this very reason, form and matter are inseparable; this particular matter could only arise and come to be along with this particular form, and *vice versa*. Every organization is therefore a *whole*; *its unity lies in itself*; it does not depend on our choice whether we think of it as one or as many. Cause and effect is something evanescent, transitory, mere *appearance* (in the usual sense of the word). The organism, however, is not mere appearance, but is *itself* object, and indeed an object subsisting through itself, in itself whole and indivisible, and because in it the form is inseparable from the matter, the *origin* of an organism, as such, can no more be explained mechanically than the origin of matter itself.

So if the purposiveness of the organic product is to be explained, the dogmatist finds himself completely deserted by his system. Here it no longer avails to separate concept and object, form and matter, as it pleases us. For *here*, at least, both are originally and necessarily united, not in our idea, but in the *object* itself. I should like one of those who take playing with concepts for philosophy, and fantasies of things for real things, to venture with us into *this* field.

First of all you must concede that here the talk is of a *unity*, which is absolutely inexplicable in terms of *matter*, as such. For it is a unity of the *concept*, a unity that exists only in relation to an intuiting and reflecting being. For that there is absolute individuality in an organism, that its parts are possible only through the whole, and the whole is possible, not through assembling, but through interaction, of the parts, is a *judgement* and cannot be judged at all save only by a mind, which relates whole and part, form and matter, reciprocally one to another, and only through and in this relation does all purposiveness and attunement to the whole arise and come to be in the first place. What indeed have these parts, which are but matter, in common with an *Idea*, which is originally alien to matter, and to which they are nevertheless attuned? Here no relation is possible except through a third thing, to whose ideas both, matter and concept, belong. Such a third thing, however, is only an intuiting and reflecting mind. So you have to admit that organization as such is conceivable only in relation to a *mind*.

Even those who will have it that the organic product itself arises from a wonderful collision of atoms admit this. For in that they derive the origin of these things from blind chance, they also promptly abolish all purposiveness in them and with it all conception of organization itself – that is to say, if consistently thought out. For since purposiveness is conceivable only in relation to a judging intellect, the question must be answered how the organic products arise independently *of me*, as if there were no relation at all between them and a judging intelligence, that is, as if there were no purpose in them anywhere.

Hence the first thing that you grant is this: Any conception of purpose can arise only in an intelligence, and only in relation to such an intelligence can anything be called purposive.

At the same time, you are no less compelled to concede that the purposiveness of natural products dwells in *themselves*, that it is *objective* and *real*, hence that it belongs, not to your *arbitrary*, but to your *necessary* representations. For you can very easily distinguish what is arbitrary and what is necessary in the conjunction of your concepts. Whenever you conjoin things which are separated in space in *a single* aggregate, you act quite freely; the unity which you bestow on them you transfer to them simply from your thoughts; there is no reason residing in the *things themselves* which required you to think of them as one. But when you think of each plant as an individual, in which everything concurs together for one purpose, you must seek the reason for that in the *thing outside you*: you feel yourself constrained in your judgement; you must therefore confess that the unity with which you think it is not merely *logical* (in your thoughts), but *real* (actually outside you).

It is now incumbent upon you to answer the question, how it happens that an idea, which obviously exists merely in you, and can have reality only in relation to yourself, must yet be actually intuited and represented by you, as itself outside you.

Certainly there are philosophers who have *one* universal answer to all these questions, which they repeat at every opportunity and cannot repeat enough. That which is form in the things, they say, we initially impose on the things. But I have long sought to know just how you could be acquainted with what the things are, without the form which you first impose on them, or what the form is, without the things on which you impose it. You would have to concede that, *here* at least, the form is absolutely inseparable from the matter, and the concept from the object. Or, if it rests with your choice whether or not to impose the idea of purposiveness on things outside you, how does it come about that you impose this idea only on *certain* things, and not on *all*, that further, in this representing of purposeful products, you feel yourself in no way *free*, but absolutely constrained? You could give no other reason for either than that this purposive form just belongs to certain *things* outside you, originally and without assistance from your choice.

This granted, what was valid before is also valid here: The form and matter of these things could never be separated; both could come into being only together and reciprocally, each through the other. The concept which lies at the base of this organization has no reality *in itself*, and, conversely, this particular matter is not *organized matter*, *qua* matter, but only because of the indwelling *concept*. This particular object, therefore, could arise only together with this concept; and this particular concept, only together with this particular object.

All previous systems must be judged according to this principle.

In order to comprehend this union of concept and matter, you assume a higher divine intelligence, who designed his creations in ideal forms and brought forth Nature in accordance with these ideals. But a being in whom the concept *precedes* the act, the design the execution, cannot *produce*, but can only form or model, matter already there, can only stamp the impress of the understanding and of purposiveness upon the matter from without. What he produces is purposive, not *in itself*, but only in relation to the understanding of the artificer, not *originally* and *necessarily*, but only contingently. Is not the understanding a dead faculty? And has it any other use than to grasp and apprehend the actual when it is present? And, instead of creating the actual, does it not borrow its own reality from actuality itself? And is it not merely the slavishness of this faculty, its capacity for describing the *outlines* of the real, which sets up an accommodation between itself and the reality? But here the question is how the *actual* arises, and with it the ideal (the purposive), which is simply inseparable from it. Not that the things of Nature, as such, are purposive, as every work of art is also purposive, but that this purposiveness is something which could not be imparted to them at all from without, that they are purposive originally *through themselves* – this is what we want to see explained.

You therefore take refuge in the *creative* power of a divinity, from which the actual things together with their ideas proceeded and sprang forth. You realized that you had to allow the actual to arise together with the purposive, the purposive together with the actual, if you wished to assume something outside you that is purposive in and through itself.

But let us assume for a moment what you allege (although you yourself are in no position to make it intelligible); let us assume it is through the creative power of a divinity that the whole system of Nature arose and with it all the diversity of purposive products external to us. Have we in fact advanced even a single step farther than before, and do we not find ourselves once again at the same point from which we set out at the beginning? How organic products external to, and independent of, me have actually come to be was not at all what I required to know; for how could I even form a clear idea of that for myself? The question was: how the *representation* of purposive products outside me had got *into me*, and how, *although it pertains to things only in relation to my understanding*, I am nevertheless compelled to think of this purposiveness as *actually outside me* and necessary. This question you have not answered.

For as soon as you regard the things of Nature as actual outside you and hence as the work of a creator, no purposiveness can inhere in them, because this is of course valid only in relation to *your* understanding. Or do you also wish to presuppose concepts of purpose and the like in the creator of the things? But as soon as you do this, he ceases to be a creator and becomes merely an artificer, he is at most the architect of Nature. However, you *destroy* all idea of *Nature* from the very bottom, as soon as you allow the purposiveness to enter her from without, through a transfer from the intelligence of any being whatever. As soon as you make the idea of the creator *finite*, therefore, he ceases to be creator; extend it to *infinity*, and you then lose all conception of purposiveness and understanding, and only the idea of an absolute power remains. From now on everything finite is merely a modification of the infinite. But you no more comprehend how a modification may be possible in the infinite as such, than you comprehend how this modification of the infinite, that is, how the whole system of finite things, could have got into your consciousness, or how the unity of things, which can only be *ontological* in the Infinite Being, can have become *teleological* in your understanding.

You could, of course, seek to explain this by the peculiar nature of a finite mind. But if you do that, you no longer need the infinite as something external to you. You could, from now on, allow everything to arise and come to be simply in your mind. For if you also presuppose things *outside* and independent of you, which *in themselves* are purposive, you must nevertheless still explain how your *ideas* agree with these external things. You would have to take refuge in a pre-established harmony, would have to assume that a mind, analogous to your own, reigns in the very things outside you. For only in a mind able to create can concept and actuality, ideal and real, so interpenetrate and unite that no separation is possible between them. I cannot think otherwise than that Leibniz understood by substantial form a mind *inhering in* and regulating the organized being.

This philosophy must accept, therefore, that there is a hierarchy of life in Nature. Even in mere organized matter there is *life*, but a life of a more restricted kind. This idea is so old, and has hitherto persisted so constantly in the most varied forms, right up to the present day – (already in the most ancient times it was believed that the whole world was pervaded by an animating principle, called the world-soul, and the later period of Leibniz gave every plant its soul) – that one may very well surmise from the beginning that there must be some reason latent in the human mind itself for this natural belief. And so it is. The sheer wonder which surrounds the problem of the origin of organic bodies, therefore, is due to the fact that in these things necessity and contingency are most intimately united. *Necessity*, because their very *existence* is *purposive*, not only their form (as in the work of art), *contingency*, because this purposiveness is nevertheless actual only for an intuiting and reflecting being. For that reason, the human mind was early led to the idea of a *self*-organizing matter, and because organization is conceivable only in relation to a mind, to an original union of mind and matter in these things. It saw itself compelled to seek the reason for these things, on the one hand, in Nature herself, and on the other, in a principle exalted above Nature; and hence it very soon fell into thinking of mind and Nature as one. Here for the first time there emerged from its sacred obscurity that ideal being in which the mind supposes concept and deed, design and execution, to be one. Here first a premonition came over man of his own nature, in which intuition and concept, form and object, ideal and real, are originally one and the same. Hence the peculiar aura which surrounds this problem, an aura which the philosophy of mere reflection, which sets out only to *separate*, can never develop, whereas the pure intuition, or rather, the creative imagination, long since discovered the symbolic language, which one has only to construe in order to discover that Nature speaks to us the more intelligibly the less we think of her in a merely reflective way.

No wonder that language, used dogmatically, soon lost sense and meaning. So long as I myself am *identical* with Nature, I understand what a living nature is as well as I understand my own life; I apprehend how this universal life of Nature reveals itself in manifold forms, in progressive developments, in gradual approximations to freedom. As soon, however, as I separate myself, and with me everything ideal, from Nature, nothing remains to me but a dead object, and I cease to comprehend how a *life outside* me can be possible.

If I question the common understanding, it believes that *life* is to be seen only where there is *free movement*. For the capacities of animal organs – sensibility, irritability, and the like – themselves presuppose an impulsive principle, without which the animal would be incapable of reacting to external stimulation, and only through this free reactivity of the organs does the stimulus from without become excitation and impression. Here the most complete reciprocity prevails: Only through excitation from without is the animal determined to movement, and conversely, only through this capacity to produce movement in itself does external impression become a stimulus. (Hence there can be neither irritability without sensibility nor sensibility without irritability.)

But all these functions of the organs, purely as such, are insufficient to explain *life*. For we could very well imagine an arrangement of fibres, nerves, and so on, in which (as, for example, in the nerves of a dissected organic body, by electricity, metallic stimulation, etc.) free movements could be produced by external stimuli, without our being able to attribute *life* to this composite thing. One might perhaps retort that nevertheless the coordination of *all* these movements would bring about life; but that involves a higher principle, which we can no longer explain in terms of matter alone, a principle that orders all individual movements, holds them together, and so first creates and brings forth a whole out of a multiplicity of motions which agree with one another, and mutually produce and reproduce themselves. So here again, we meet that absolute unification of Nature and Freedom in one and the same being. The living organism is to be a product of *Nature*: but in this natural product an ordering and coordinating *mind* is to rule. These two principles shall in no way be separated in it, but most intimately united. In intuition the two are not to be distinguishable at all; there must be neither *before* nor *after*, but absolute simultaneity and reciprocity between them.

As soon as philosophy removes this internal conjunction, two systems arise directly opposed to each other, of which neither can refute the other, because both entirely destroy all idea of life, which flees all the farther from them the nearer they think to approach it.

I am not speaking of that so-called philosophy of those who would hold that even thought, imagery and will spring up in us, now from a chance collision of already organized particles, now through an actually artificial conjunction of muscles, fibres, membranes and ligaments which hold the body together, and fluid substances which flow through it, and so on. I maintain, however, that we as little understand empirically a life *outside us* as we do a consciousness *outside us*, that neither the one nor the other is explicable from physical causes, that in this respect it is completely indifferent whether the body is regarded as an accidental aggregate of organized particles, or as a hydraulic machine, or as a chemical laboratory. Assume, for instance, that all the movements of a living body were explicable by changes in the composition of its nerves, its sinews, or the fluid that is taken to circulate in them; then not only is it a question of how those changes are caused, but also of what principle holds all these changes harmoniously together.

Or if at last a philosophical purview of Nature as a system, which nowhere stands still but progresses, discovers that with living matter Nature oversteps the limits of inorganic chemistry, so that (because otherwise chemical processes in the body would be unavoidable and because the dead body is destroyed by genuine chemical dissolution) there must be in the living body a principle which exempts it from chemical laws, and if this principle is now called *Life-force*, then I maintain on the contrary that Life-force, taken in this sense (and however prevalent this expression may be), is a completely self-contradictory concept. For we can think of force only as something finite. But no force is finite by *nature* except in so far as it is limited by one opposing it. Where we think of force (as in matter), therefore, we must also presume a force *opposed* to it. Between opposing forces, however, we can only conceive a double relationship. Either they are in *relative* equilibrium (in absolute equilibrium they would both be completely eliminated); then they are thought of as at *rest*, as in matter which is therefore said to be inert. Or one thinks of them as in perpetual, never-settled conflict, where each in turn prevails and submits; but then, again, a third must be present which keeps this conflict going and maintains the work of Nature in this conflict of alternately prevailing and submissive forces. Now this third cannot itself be a force, for otherwise we should return to the previous alternative. So it must be something that is higher than just *force*; yet *force* is the ultimate (as I shall prove) to which all our physical explanations must return; so that third would have to be something which lies right outside the limits of empirical research into Nature.

But now beyond and above Nature, in the ordinary notion of it, nothing higher is acknowledged than mind. However, if we now want to conceive the Life-force as a spiritual principle, then we totally abolish that concept in so doing. For *force* means what, at least as a *principle*, we can put at the apex of natural science, and what, although not itself presentable, yet, in the *way it works*, is definable by physical laws. But how a mind can act physically we have not the slightest idea; for that reason also, a mental principle cannot be called *Life-force*, an expression by which one always at least suggests the hope of allowing that principle to work according to physical laws.*

* This one sees very clearly from the utterances of many defenders of the *Life-force*. Herr Brandis, for example (in his *Experiments on the Life-force*, 81), asks, 'Should electricity (which seems to co-operate in phlogistical processes generally) also participate in the phlogistical life-processes (which the author assumes), or *might electricity be the life-force itself*? I consider it *more than likely*.'

But if we forgo, as we are then compelled to do, this concept (of a Life-force), we are now obliged to take refuge in a completely antithetical system, in which at once mind and matter stand opposed to each other, regardless of the fact that we now understand how mind affects matter as little as we could previously understand how matter affects mind.

Mind, considered as the principle of life, is called *soul*. I shall not repeat the objections that have long since been brought against the philosophy of the dualists. It has hitherto been contested for the most part from principles which had as little content as the contested system itself. We do not ask how in general a connection is possible between soul and body (a question to which one is not entitled, because the questioner himself does not understand it) but rather – what one can understand and must answer – how the idea of such a connection has arisen *in us*. That I think, imagine, will, and that this thinking, etc., can so little be a result of my body, that on the contrary the latter only becomes *my* body through these capacities to think and to will, I know full well. Let it meanwhile be permitted, moreover, for the sake of speculation, to distinguish the principle of motion from the moved, the soul from the body, despite the fact that as soon as the talk is of action we completely forget this distinction. Now with all these assumptions, at least this much is obvious, that if there is in me life and soul, the last as something distinct from the body, I can become aware of either only through *immediate* experience. That I *am* (think, will, etc.) is something that I must know, if I know anything at all. Thus I understand how an idea of my own being and life arises in me, because if I understand anything whatsoever, I must understand this. Also, because I am immediately aware of my own being, the inference to a soul in me, even if the conclusion should be false, at least rests on *one* indubitable premise, that I *am, live, imagine, will*.

But how do I now come to transfer *being, life*, etc., to things *outside* me? For just as soon as this happens, my immediate knowledge is converted into *mediate*. But now I maintain that there can be only an *immediate* knowledge of being and life, and that what *is* and *lives* only is and lives in so far as it first and foremost exists *for itself*, is aware of its life through being alive. Suppose, then, that there appears to me in my perception an organic being, freely self-moving, then I certainly know that this being *exists*, that it is *for me*, but not that it *exists for itself* and *in itself*. For life can as little be represented outside life as consciousness outside consciousness.* So even an empirical conviction that something lives outside me is absolutely impossible. For the Idealist can say that your representing to yourself organized, free, self-moving bodies can just as well belong simply to the necessary peculiarities of your faculty of representation; and even the philosophy which bestows life on everything external to me does not permit the idea of this life outside me to come into me from *outside*.

But if this idea arises only *in me*, how can I be persuaded that anything corresponds to it outside me? It is also obvious that I am persuaded of a life and self-existence outside me only *practically*. I must in practice be *compelled* to acknowledge beings outside me, who are like me. If I were not compelled to enter into the company of people outside me and into all the practical relationships associated with that; if I did not know that beings, who resemble me in external shape and appearance, have no *more* reason to acknowledge freedom and mentality in me than I have to acknowledge the same in them; in fine, if I were not aware that my moral existence only acquires purpose and direction through the existence of other moral beings outside me, then left to mere speculation, I could of course doubt whether humanity dwelt behind each face and freedom within each breast. All this is confirmed by our commonest judgements. Only of beings external to me, who put themselves on an equal footing with me in life, between whom and myself giving and receiving, doing and suffering, are fully reciprocal, do I acknowledge that they are spiritual in character. On the other hand, if the rather curious question is brought up, whether animals also have souls, a person of common sense is at once taken aback, because, with the affirmation of that, he would consider himself committed to something he cannot immediately know.

If in the end we go back to the original source of the dualistic

* Jacobi's *David Hume* [Breslau, 1787], p. 140.

belief, that a soul distinct from the body dwells at least in *me*, then what is it in me which itself in turn judges that I consist of body and soul, and what is this *I* which is supposed to consist of body and soul? Here, clearly, there is something still higher, which, freely and independently of the body, gives the body a soul, conceives body and soul together, and does not itself enter into this union – a higher principle, as it seems, in which body and soul are themselves again identical.

Finally, if we persist in this dualism, we now have close at hand the antithesis from which we began: mind and matter. For the same incomprehensibility, as to how connection is possible between matter and mind, continues to oppress us. One can conceal from oneself the finality of this antithesis by deceptions of all kinds, can insert between mind and matter any number of physical intermediaries, which come to be ever more and more tenuous. But sometime, somewhere, a point must surely come where mind and matter are one, or where the great leap we have so long sought to avoid becomes inevitable; and in this all theories are alike.

Whether I allow animal spirits, electrical fluids, or types of gas to suffuse or fill the nerves, and thereby to propagate impressions from outside into the sensorium, or whether I pursue the soul into the uttermost (and still more problematical) humours of the brain (a project which at least has the merit of having done the *uttermost*) is, with respect to the *matter in hand*, altogether indifferent. It is clear that our critique has come full circle, but not that we have become in any degree wiser than we were to begin with, about that antithesis from which we started. We leave behind man, as evidently the most devious problem of all philosophy, and our critique ends here in the same extremity with which it began.

If, finally, we gather up Nature into a single Whole, *mechanism*, that is, a regressive series of causes and effects, and *purposiveness*, that is, independence of mechanism, simultaneity of causes and effects, stand confronting each other. If we unite these two extremes, the idea arises in us of a purposiveness of the whole; Nature becomes a circle which returns into itself, a self-enclosed system. The series of causes and effects cease entirely, and there arises a reciprocal connection of *means* and *end*; neither could the individual become *real* without the whole, nor the whole without the individual.

Now this absolute purposiveness of the whole of Nature is an Idea, which we do not think arbitrarily, but *necessarily*. We feel ourselves forced to relate every individual to such a purposiveness of the whole: where we find something in Nature that seems purposeless or quite contrary to purpose, we believe the whole scheme of things to be torn apart, or do not rest until the apparent refractoriness to purpose is converted to purposiveness from another viewpoint. It is therefore a necessary maxim of the reflective reason, to presuppose everywhere in Nature a connection by end and means. And although we do not transform this maxim into a constitutive law, we still follow it so steadfastly and so naïvely that we openly assume that Nature will, as it were, voluntarily come to meet our endeavour to discover absolute purposiveness in her. Similarly, we proceed with complete confidence in the agreement of Nature with the maxims of our reflective reason, from special subordinate laws to general higher laws; nor do we cease to assume *a priori*, even of phenomena which still stand isolated in the series of our perceptions, that *they* too are interconnected through some common principle. And we only believe in a Nature external to us where we discern multiplicity of effects and unity of means.

What then is that secret bond which couples our mind to Nature, or that hidden organ through which Nature speaks to our mind or our mind to Nature? We grant you in advance all your explanations of how such a purposive Nature has come to be actual *outside us*. For to explain this purposiveness by the fact that a divine intelligence is its author is not to philosophize, but to propound pious opinions. By that you have explained to us virtually nothing; for we require to know, not how such a Nature arose outside us, but how even the very *idea* of such a Nature has got *into us*; not merely how we have, say, arbitrarily generated it, but how and why it originally and *necessarily* underlies everything that our race has ever thought about Nature. For the existence of such a Nature *outside me* is still far from explaining the existence of such a Nature *in me*; for if you assume that a predetermined harmony occurs between the two, indeed that is just the object of our question. Or if you maintain that we simply *impose* such an idea on Nature, then no inkling of what Nature is and ought to be for us has ever entered your soul. For what we want is not that Nature should coincide with the laws of our mind *by chance* (as if through some *third* intermediary), but that *she herself*, necessarily and originally, should not only *express*, but *even realize*, the laws of our mind, and that she is, and is called, Nature only in so far as she does so.

Nature should be Mind made visible, Mind the invisible Nature. Here then, in the absolute identity of Mind *in us* and Nature *outside us*, the problem of the possibility of a Nature external to us must be resolved. The final goal of our further research is, therefore, this idea of Nature; if we succeed in attaining this, we can also be certain to have dealt satisfactorily with that problem.

These are the main problems, whose solution is to be the purpose of this essay.

But this essay does not begin *from above* (with the establishment of principles), but *from below* (with experimental findings and the testing of previous systems).

Only when I have reached the goal which I have set myself will it be permissible for me to retrace in reverse the course which has been run.

Translated by Errol E. Harris and Peter Heath

On the Nature of Philosophy as Science

The idea or the endeavour of finding a system of human knowledge, or, put differently and more appropriately, of contemplating human knowledge within a system, within a form of coexistence, presupposes, of course, that originally and of itself it does not exist in a system, hence that it is an ἀσύστατον [*asystaton*] – something whose elements do not coexist, but rather something that is in inner conflict. In order to recognize this *asystasy*, this non-existence, this disunity, this *bellum intestinum*, so to speak, in human knowledge (for this inner conflict must become apparent), the human spirit must already have searched in every possible direction. Hence in Greece, for example, the idea of the system had to be preceded by a) the simple physicists, who believed that everything can be explained in terms of natural causes, b) Anaxagoras' dualism, and c) the Eleats' doctrine which, in order to resolve all existing conflicts, posited mere *unity*, while it would be equally legitimate to posit opposition or disunity, and while the true system can only be the one that establishes the unity of unity and opposition, i.e. the one that shows how unity can coexist with opposition and opposition with unity, and how the one is indeed necessary for the benefit of the other. All this had to take place before even the true *idea* of a system could appear in Plato. In terms of time, then, the systems are prior to the system. The need for harmony arises first of all in disharmony.

Finally, for there really to be an endeavour to find a system, one must have come to see that this conflict between opinions is not something incidental, grounded in subjective imperfections such as superficial or erroneous thinking by individuals, or, as some shallow minds would have it, in mere logical fabrications. One must have understood that this conflict has an objective basis, that it is grounded in the nature of the matter itself, namely in the primary roots of all existence. One must have given up all hopes that this conflict, this *bellum omnium contra omnes*, might come to an end, that one individual view could become absolute master over the others, that one system could subjugate the others. This can, of course, often seem to be the case. For although all exclusive systems have in common that they are not the system and that they are therefore something partial or subordinate, one of them can still be on a higher level than another. Or actually – for this deserves to be explained more precisely – the problem has to be understood in the following way. Within all contradictions between the systems, there is ultimately only one great contradiction, one original discord. This can be expressed by saying that according to one assertion A equals B, and according to the other it equals C. Now it can happen that both systems, the one positing A = B and the one positing A = C, have to be comprehended as competing on a very subordinate level. In the meantime, someone appears who goes beyond this subordinate standpoint, and who, rather than putting forth something that could unify A = B with A = C on a higher level, only repeats A = B, but on a higher level, raising it to a higher power. Frequently, however, this onesidedness becomes even more accentuated, for once the analysis begins, it naturally follows its course and finally reaches the point where it is a matter of individual choice. Thereby, however, we only admit that neither is the absolute master of the other. If, however, A = B has really advanced (without being otherwise essentially altered), while A = C has not advanced, then A = B openly becomes the master of A = C. This does not last very long, though, as A = C will become aware of its disadvantage and will also advance, such that, again, but only at the higher standpoint, the two confront each other in just the same way as on the lower.

Another, even more incidental possibility is the following: if A = B and A = C perfectly balance each other, the outcome will depend on which of the two is the better combatant. Alas, this is the kind of victory that does not decide anything.

Hence, one system can become the other's master only in appearance and for a short time, while in reality or in the long run it is impossible. Each system actually has the same authority, the same claim to validity, and this insight has to precede the system in the wider sense – the system *par excellence*. So long as the materialist does not acknowledge the legitimacy of the intellectualist, or the idealist the legitimacy of the realist, the system κατ' ἐξοχήν [*kat' exochen; par excellence*] is inconceivable. I wish to point out, by the way, that only those systems which constitute genuine elements of our intellectual development are mentioned here, as opposed to those which are only so called by their authors; even to consider such people capable of an *error* would be to give them too much credit. Those who can *err* must at least be on some track. But those who never even set out and just stay sitting at home, cannot err. Those who dare set out to sea can certainly, due to storms or by their lack of skill, lose their way and be led astray, but those who never even leave port and whose entire endeavour, rather, consists in not leaving port and in preventing philosophy from ever beginning, by endless philosophizing about philosophy, those, of course, have no dangers to fear.

Hence the idea of the system as such presupposes the necessary and irresolvable conflict of the systems: without the latter the former would not arise.

Philosophy has often been reproached for this asystasy, this inner conflict. Kant, in various parts of his writings, as well as others later, for the purposes of instruction and improvement, compared metaphysics unfavourably with mathematics. 'Look here,' they say, 'how in geometry, for example, everyone is in agreement, going back to Euclid and beyond him to Thales and to the Egyptian priests, while in philosophy the motto is still: *quot capita, tot sensus*, as many systems as there are heads, and every day brings a new one.' Concerning those systems that spring up overnight, I have already given my opinion. If one holds philosophy in low esteem, however, because it has systems and geometry does not, then I say: certainly there are no systems in geometry, because there is no system – and there must be systems in philosophy precisely because there is a system. It is as though one preferred a stereometrically regular crystal to the human body for the reason that the former has no possibility of falling ill, while the latter hosts germs of every possible illness. Illness is related to health, namely, in roughly the same way as the individual system is related to the system κατ' ἐξοχήν. In the human organism as well, doctors distinguish between different systems. Now, if someone suffers from one of these systems, or if one of these systems is particularly prominent, then they are tied to that system, restrained in their freedom, and are actually its slave. Healthy individuals do not feel any of these systems in particular. They do not *know*, as we say, that they have a digestive, etc., system; they are free from all systems. Why? Not because those systems would not be part of their organism, as this would not serve much to their benefit, but because they each live only in the whole, in the total system, in which all individual systems, so to speak, fall silent and become impossible (the word 'healthy' probably means the same as *whole*). The same happens in philosophy. Those who manage to get through to the end find themselves in complete freedom, they are free from the systems – *above* all systems.

We have, then, determined the following by this point. 1) The *external possibility of the system*, the matter, so to speak, the fabric of it, is precisely that irresolvable inner conflict in human knowledge. 2) This conflict must have become apparent; it must have shown itself and developed in every possible direction. 3) One must understand that there is nothing accidental in this conflict and that everything is grounded in the primary principles themselves. 4) One must give up the hope of ever terminating this conflict by having one system become master over another. If, however, a one-sided subjugation of one by the other is impossible then 5) we must not – and this is a new element – we must not imagine finding a unity in which they all *annihilate* one another either, because in this way, too, the concept of the system would perish, and the task consists precisely in having them all truly *coexist*. In the first case (where they would annihilate one another), instead of the system, one would only be confronted with a bottomless pit into which everything sinks and within which nothing can be distinguished any longer. The systems, however, are not supposed to be annihilated, they are supposed to coexist, like the different systems of one organism, and in this coexistence they are supposed to produce a perspective that goes beyond the individual systems, a healthy perspective which gives pleasure to man, the same way as in a healthy human body all differences between the organs and functions blend into *one* inseparable life whose feeling is well-being.

The desire to annihilate, to destroy any real system would precisely defeat the purpose. For where does the onesidedness of the systems come from? The answer: it comes, as *you* must already clearly grasp, not from where it was claimed to have come from, but from where it was *denied* to have come from. Leibniz already says somewhere, very naïvely: 'I have found that for the most part the sects are right in a fair share of what they claim, but not so much in what they deny.' Leibniz must have felt that in exclusion there is falsity, but he himself still set up an obviously onesided system when he claimed that everything in the world could be traced back to powers of representation: 'The deeper we penetrate into the basis of all things, the more truth can be discovered in the doctrines of most sects. We finally arrive at a central viewpoint in which we find everything united. If we step into this centre, we only see regularity and correspondence. If we withdraw from it, and the further we withdraw from it, the more confused everything becomes, lines shift and one aspect covers another.' But here, too, he adds: 'The mistake so far has been the sect mentality. People have restricted themselves by dismissing what others had taught.' Hence here, too, the mistake is supposed to consist in the act of dismissing. But why did the same Leibniz make the same mistake? The answer: his system, indeed, rested on a high level and so it, too, contained, though with only a partial perspective, a certain centre from which many doctrines and claims resting on a lower level could seem to be in correspondence with each other.

So far I have talked about the external reason of the system, or about the ambition of regarding human knowledge in a system – in coexistence. This external reason is a conflict in human knowledge which is, in itself, irresolvable. I have not demonstrated or proven it; I have presupposed it and I had to presuppose it. Instead of the system itself, I would have otherwise also had to present the preparations – the propaedeutic – for it. Namely, the best propaedeutic is the one which follows the necessary contradiction in which the awakening consciousness, or the awakening reflection, gets entangled, and the one which follows it from its primary roots, through all its branches, towards the desperation which, so to speak, forces man to form the idea of a superior whole. In this superior whole, by coexisting, the conflicting systems create a higher consciousness that frees man from all systems again, that takes him beyond all systems. This is actually the purpose of mere dialectics, and although dialectics is by no means the science itself, it is nevertheless the preparation for it.

So, the external reason for the system is an original ἀσυστασία [asystasy] of human knowledge. But what is the *principle* of its possibility? We do grasp the desirability of such a whole that brings all conflicting elements into harmony, but how is it possible and which presuppositions make it conceivable? The first presupposition for it is indisputably 1) the general idea of progression, of *movement* within the system. For it is certainly impossible that conflicting assertions could be true, as one would commonly say, *at the same time* – namely at one and the same evolutionary moment. It is quite possible, though, that at a certain point in the evolution, the statement 'A is B' is true, while at another 'A is not B is true'. Here the movement keeps conflicting statements separate. 2) This movement, however, requires a subject of movement and of progress, understood as that which moves and progresses, and about this subject two assumptions are made. a) It is only *one* subject that proceeds through everything. For if there were one subject in B and another in C, then B and C would be completely separated and there would be no connection. In the same way as it is only one and the same subject that lives in the different elements of an organism, so it has to be only one subject that proceeds through all the aspects of the system – it is not true, however, that therefore the elements through which it proceeds are one and the same also. But b) this one subject must proceed through everything and cannot remain in anything. For wherever it would remain, life and evolution would be inhibited. *Proceeding through everything and not being anything*, namely not being anything such that it could not also be something else – this is the requirement.

What is this subject that is in everything and that does not remain in anything? What should we call it? (Let me remark in passing, this question is identical to the common question of what the principle of philosophy is. The principle of philosophy is something that is not only principle at the beginning and then ceases to be principle. It is something always and everywhere, in the beginning, middle and end, equally principle. Furthermore, others also used to conceive of this principle as a supreme law. Since philosophy was regarded only as presenting a chain of laws deriving from one another, it was thought that there must be a supreme element in this chain – a first law, from which a second one is derived, and from this a third, and so on. In this way, Descartes had a supreme law in his *cogito ergo sum*. Fichte: I am I. In a living system, however, one that is not a sequence of laws, but of aspects of progression and evolution, the existence of such a supreme law is out of the question.) *What* then is the system's principle, the one subject that proceeds through everything and does not remain in anything? What should we call it, what can we say about it? First, we want to see what the question itself, '*What* is it?', means. 'To characterize it as *something* that it really is.' Now, this is easy. Should I say then: A is B? Of course! But it is not only B. What I require, then, is that it be more precisely determined, I require that its concept be paraphrased within fixed limits, that it be *defined*. If one requires a definition, then one wants to know what the subject definitely is, and not merely what it is in such a way that it could also be something else, or even the opposite of it. This is the case here. I can neither say for certain that A is B, nor that it is not B. It is B as well as not B, and it is neither B nor not B. It is not in such a way B that it would not also be not B, and it is not in such a way not B that it can in no way and by no means also be B. And the same would be the case with any other determination, with C, with D and so on. What, then, remains? Should I utter the entire sequence, should I say: 'It is A, B, C, D, and so on'? But, gentlemen, this is precisely the entire science, this is precisely already the system itself. So, what remains? The answer: the indefinable itself, the aspect of the subject which cannot be defined, has to be made the definition. What does it mean to define something? According to the word itself:

to confine something within certain limits. Nothing can therefore be defined which by nature is not confined within certain limits. For this reason, the definition of a geometrical figure is something very simple because its essence precisely consists in delimiting. Here the *definiendum* is already a *definitum* – I do not actually define it, it already is defined, and when I say that I am giving a definition, e.g., of the ellipse, it just means this much: I only become aware of the definition of the ellipse, of a definition that is contained in the ellipse itself. For this reason, geometry = definable science. When we look at philosophy as the subject, however, things are very different. It is simply indefinable. For 1) it is nothing – not *something*, and even this would at least be a negative definition. But it is also not nothing, i.e., it is everything. Only it is nothing individual, static, particular; it is B, C, D, and so on, only in so far as each of these elements belongs to the flow of an inseparable movement. There is nothing that it would be and nothing that it would not be. It is in constant motion, it cannot be restricted to one form, it is the incoercible, the ungraspable, the truly infinite. Those who want to gain a command of the completely free and self-generating science must rise to its level. Here we have to depart from everything finite, from everything that is still an entity, and our last attachments must dwindle. Here we have to leave *everything* – not only, as one commonly says, wife and children, but that which merely *exists*, even *God*. For from this standpoint God, too, is only an entity. Here, where we first mention this concept (God), we may use it as the supreme example for demonstrating what was said earlier. We said: there is nothing that the absolute subject would not be, and there is nothing that this subject would be. Namely, the absolute subject is not not God, and it is not God either, it is also that which is not God. Hence, in this respect it is above God – since one of the most splendid mystics of early times dared speak of a superdivinity, this will also be permitted to us too. I want to make this point here, so that the Absolute – that absolute subject – will not be straightforwardly mistaken for God. This distinction is very important. Those, then, who want to find themselves at the starting point of a truly free philosophy, have to depart even from God. Here the motto is: whoever wants to preserve it will lose it, and whoever abandons it will find it. Only those have reached the ground in themselves and have become aware of the depths of life, who have at one time abandoned everything and have themselves been abandoned by everything, for whom everything has been lost, and who have found themselves alone, face-to-face with the infinite: a decisive step which Plato compared with death. That which Dante saw written on the door of the inferno must be written in a different sense also at the entrance to philosophy: 'Abandon all hope, ye who enter here.' Those who look for true philosophy must be bereft of all hope, all desire, all longing. They must not wish anything, not know anything, must feel completely bare and impoverished, must give everything away in order to gain everything. It is a grim step to take, it is grim to have to depart from the final shore. This we can infer from the fact that so few have ever been capable of it. How high does Spinoza rise when he teaches us that we ought to separate ourselves from all particular and finite things and to reach for the infinite. And how deeply does he sink again when he turns this infinite into a substance, i.e., into something dead, stagnant. When he tries to explain this substance as the unity of the realms of extension and thought, it is as if he attaches two weights with which he drags substance down completely into the finite sphere. Fichte, he who stood here on this spot before I did, and who was the first to take up again the emphatic call for freedom, he to whom philosophy is indebted for being able to start freely and from the beginning again, did something similar in our time. Far below himself he saw all existence, existence which for him was merely an inhibition of free activity. However, when all external and objective existence disappeared for him, in the moment when one expected him to go beyond all mere existence, he clung to his own self. Those who want to climb up to the free ether, however, have to abandon not only objects, but also themselves. Man is granted, by means of a great resolution in the middle of time, the opportunity to begin his moral life anew. Should this not also be possible in the spiritual realm? In this case, however, he would quite simply have to be born again.

I said that precisely the indefinable aspect of the absolute subject would itself have to be made the definition. However, on closer inspection, it strikes us that *with this characterization* we have gained nothing of the absolute subject except a negative concept. And so, apart from everything else, there seems to be a danger of getting caught up in negation. For even the word *infinite* really only expresses the negation of finiteness. And in the same way: indefinable, incoercible, ungraspable. So we actually only know what this subject is not, and not what it is. This, however, is no reason for us to give up at this point, and with all our available means we shall strive to provide an affirmative concept of it.

Let us look at the reason why we got into this danger of negation. What did we do? Resolutely and categorically we said to ourselves that the absolute subject was the indefinable, the ungraspable, the infinite. Precisely in doing so, however, we acted against our own maxim, namely that nothing can be affirmed of this absolute subject without qualification, without the opposite being possible also. This must also be applied to the concept of the indefinable. For it is not indefinable in such a way that it could not also become definable, not infinite in such a way that it could not also become finite, and not ungraspable in such a way that it could not also become graspable. And if, gentlemen, *you* firmly keep this in mind, *you* have the positive concept. Namely, in order to be able to adopt one form it must of course be beyond all form, though its positive element is not that it is beyond all form or ungraspable, but, rather, that it can adopt a form, that it can make itself graspable, thus that it is free to adopt or not to adopt a form. For even at the very outset, it was not claimed that it was simply without shape or form, but only that it did not remain in any particular form, was not tied down by any given one. Hence, we explicitly presupposed that it *would* adopt a certain form. For only in adopting and then successfully divesting itself of each form, does it present itself as in itself ungraspable, infinite. It would not be free, however, to divest itself of each form if it had not been free from the very beginning to adopt or not to adopt form. I say from the very beginning – for after it has adopted form once, it might not be able to break through to its eternal freedom again immediately, but, rather, only by going through all forms. Originally, however, it is free to adopt or not to adopt a form.

I do not, however, wish to express it like this: it is that which is free to adopt form. For this way freedom would appear as a *quality*, presupposing a subject different from and independent of it. Freedom, however, is the *essence* of the subject, or the subject itself is *nothing but the eternal freedom*.

This freedom, however, is not mere independence from external determination. It is precisely the freedom to adopt a form. It is the eternal freedom, but not in the sense that it could not also not be eternal freedom, namely by making the transition to a different form. And here we notice what the duplicity of its existence and its non-existence originates in, its *natura anceps* [dual nature], that is, in being pure absolute freedom itself. If it were freedom only in such a way that it could not also become non-freedom, that it would have to remain freedom, then freedom itself would impose a barrier, a necessity, and it would not really be absolute freedom.

Now we finally have the whole and complete concept, in such a way that we cannot lose it any more. Anything that we could still add would merely be unwrapping and explaining, and this is how *you* should understand it. Instead of essential freedom, we can also say: 1) it is eternal, pure ability – not the ability to do something (which would restrict it), but ability for the sake of ability, an ability free of object and intention. It is the supreme ability, and when we catch sight of it we feel as though exposed to a flash of that original freedom. 2) It is will, not the will belonging to a being distinct from it, nothing apart from will, nothing but pure will itself. It is also not the will of something (for that would restrict it), but will in itself. It is not the will that really wills, but also not the will that does not will and that repels, but it is will in so far as it neither wills nor does not will, and which is in complete indifference (an indifference that includes itself and non-indifference). And *you* may know, at least historically, that this indifference used to be claimed as the form of the Absolute.

The way this eternal freedom first adopts a particular form – an existence – and the way, proceeding through everything and remaining in nothing, it finally breaks through to eternal freedom again – as the eternally struggling, but never defeated, forever invincible force that ends up consuming each form it adopts, and, hence, rising from each one like a phoenix transfigured by its death in the flames – this is the *content* of the supreme science.

But *how can we become aware of this eternal freedom*, how can we know its movement? This, then, is the next question.

It is an ancient doctrine that something can only be recognized by something similar to it, that like is only known by like.* That which knows must have a likeness with that which is known, and that which is known must have a likeness with that which knows. So, too, is the eye similar to the light according to that ancient dictum which Goethe incorporated into the preface of his theory of colours:

> If the eye were not like the sun
> How could we ever see the light?
> If God's own strength lived not in us
> How could we delight in his divinity?

Here we are not especially faced with a historical knowledge of that movement, but with a shared knowledge, a co-knowledge, *conscientia*. It follows then, that in us must lie something similar or equal to eternal freedom. Or more precisely: this eternal freedom itself must lie in us, this eternal freedom must be that which in us recognizes itself.

How is this possible? I ask: is the concept of eternal freedom really so distant from our knowledge? What is this eternal freedom? As we have already seen, it a) = eternal pure *ability*. Every ability, however, is *knowledge*, even though the reverse does not hold true. b) When ability is effective, it is will. Before the will makes the transition to its effect, it is will at rest. The will, in so far as it does not will, is indifference. But what does each act of the will do? It attracts, it makes something its object, i.e. it is a form of knowledge. For knowledge, too, makes something its object, and if eternal freedom in its indifference is the will at rest, then knowledge at rest also = knowledge that does not know. (I am, by the way, not claiming that will and knowledge are one and the same, but only that in every act of the will there is

* Sextus Empiricus, *Adversus Grammaticos*, Lib. I, c. 13.

knowledge, for the will cannot be conceived of without knowledge.)

c) The concepts of ability and will are united in the word 'to desire'. I do not want to = I do not desire to. 'May one blind man desire to show the way to another' = 'May one blind man be able etc.' Eternal freedom is eternal desire, not the desire for something, but desire in itself or, as it can also be expressed, eternal magic. I am using this expression because it expresses my concept; true, it is a strange word, but when we use it for ourselves it is in our possession again. Saying eternal ability or eternal magic is one and the same. This expression, however, suggests itself because it expresses the capacity both to adopt any form and not remain in any given one. This is precisely the case with knowledge, too. Even knowledge at rest is, in itself, infinite and can adopt any form. For as long as it is ineffective, magic = knowledge at rest. By becoming effective and adopting a form, it becomes knowing, it receives knowledge, and thus goes from form to form, proceeds from knowledge to knowledge, but only in order to, in the end, break through to the bliss of ignorance again (which at that point is a knowing ignorance). This movement, then, produces science (I am, of course, not talking about human science here). Science originally develops only when a principle departs from its original state of ignorance and becomes knowledge and, after it has gone through all forms, returns to its original ignorance. That which is the absolute beginning cannot know itself. In its transition to knowledge it ceases to be the beginning and it therefore has to proceed until it rediscovers itself as the beginning. The beginning, restored as a beginning that knows itself, is the end of all knowledge.

The *original* magic contains more than mere knowledge, that is, objective production. In order to distinguish *this* knowledge, which is at the same time objective production and creation, from mere knowledge, which is only an ideal repetition of original knowledge, its proper linguistic expression had to be found: *wisdom*. Wisdom is more than knowledge, it is *active* knowledge, the knowledge belonging to life and action, and thus it is also practical. This is why eternal freedom can also be called *wisdom*, wisdom *par excellence* in the high sense of the word, especially as used by the Orientals, and in particular by the Old Testament. The origin of the Hebrew word for wisdom indicates domination, power, strength. Only in wisdom is there power and strength, for wisdom is that which is in everything, but for this very reason also that which is above everything. Only in unity, however, is there strength, while in separation there is weakness. Of this wisdom an old Oriental poem asks: 'But where shall wisdom be found, and where is the place of understanding? Man knoweth not the price thereof; neither is it found in the land of the living. The depth saith, It is not in me: and the sea saith, It is not with me.'* This means that wisdom is in nothing *individual*, it does not dwell in the land of the living, for it never remains anywhere at all. It moves through everything, like the wind whose whistle we may hear, but whose place no one knows. The way the poem continues illuminates that this is the meaning: 'It is denied to the eyes of all men; destruction and death say, We have heard the fame thereof with our ears', i.e. it has passed us by, we have only heard of it *in transitu*, in passing. 'Only God understandeth the way thereof', for it does not, *according to its nature*, stand still, and even when it is with God, it cannot stand still. 'Only God understandeth the place thereof. For he looketh to the ends of the earth', i.e. of all human life, and wisdom is not in the beginning, nor in the middle, nor in the end alone, it is in the beginning, middle, and end.

Thus here wisdom = eternal freedom.

This wisdom, though, is no longer in man. There is no objective production, but only ideal reproduction in him. He is not the magic mover of all things. In him remains *only* knowledge. In this knowledge, however, he *searches* for eternal freedom or wisdom. How could he search for it, *unless it was searching for itself in him*? For that which is known must be like that which knows. *But how could eternal freedom search for itself in his subjective knowledge when it could also search for itself objectively?* For its entire movement is certainly a search for itself. If it searches for itself in man, in subjective knowledge, then this is only due to having been inhibited in its objective search. This is precisely the case. We have characterized it as not remaining in anything.

* Job 28.

223

Now, we *see* that it does not remain in anything and that it destroys each form. What it replaces the destroyed form with, however, is nothing but the same form again. Here, then, we cannot recognize any progress, but only inhibition. Reluctantly, it drives each form towards self-destruction (e.g. a plant towards producing seeds), always hoping that something new will arise. The root of this standstill cannot be determined, but the state of the world is proof of its existence. The regular course of the stars, the recurrent circle of general phenomena refers to it. The sun rises in order to set, and sets in order to rise. The water runs into the sea in order to evaporate from it. One generation comes, the other goes, everything works in order to exhaust and destroy itself, and yet nothing new arises. Objectively, then, progress is inhibited. *Only* in knowledge is there still an open space, and here wisdom can still search for and still find itself. This is why it is of interest to man to internalize it. The active, the objectively producing ingredient, no doubt, has disappeared from this knowledge; the magic is gone. Whatever in it was objective movement, action and life is now, in man, nothing more than knowledge. This knowledge, though, is still essentially the same. It is eternal freedom that is contained in us in the form of knowledge. It is the same magic that produces everything, that is master in all the arts, but that is now, in man, restricted to knowledge, to the merely ideal repetition of the process.

How can *we* know this absolute subject, or eternal freedom? This question is founded on a more general one: How can it be known *at all*? That is:

1) There is a contradiction in the idea of knowing eternal freedom. It is absolute subject = primordial state. How, then, can it become object? It is impossible for it to become object *as* absolute subject, for, as such, it has no object-like relation to anything; it is contained in its primordial state and nothing can interfere with it, and thus far it is truly the transcendent. Instead of absolute subject, it can also be called pure knowledge, and as such it cannot be that which is known. This must be demonstrated for all concepts that we have compared with the concept of absolute subject or eternal freedom.

We said, for example, that it was eternal pure ability. Pure ability, however, is removed from everything, it is not concrete, it is absolute inwardness. The same is the case for pure will and pure desire.

Now, if eternal magic as absolute subject is not concrete, then everything depends on it *becoming* concrete, i.e. an object. This is certainly possible. Since it is *absolute* freedom, i.e. freedom also to not be freedom (to not be subject), it *can* step outside itself as subject. *As* object, of course, it can then be known. We can perceive it in all its forms, but not *as* eternal freedom, not *as* subject, not *as it is in itself*.

It seems, then, that it cannot be known anywhere, or by any means. As absolute subject it is beyond all knowledge; as object it is not in itself. Only in one way can the absolute subject, nevertheless, be known *as* such. It could be known if, after being an object, it were restored as a subject. Then it would no longer be *merely* subject, or object such that it would be lost as subject. Then it would as object be subject and as subject be object, without therefore being two. Then *as* that which is known it would be that which knows, and *as* that which knows be that which is known. Then eternal freedom would come to know itself in the way it was known.

Since the possibility of a *self-knowledge* of eternal freedom is contained only in this transformation from object to subject, the absolute subject, too, does not know itself, a) in the *beginning* – for there it is merely pure knowledge (knowledge at rest = knowledge that does not know). Similarly, it does not know *itself* b) in the *middle* or in the transition, where it knows itself, but as something different, not *as* eternal freedom. Only c) in the end does it know itself *as itself*.

Certainly it should know itself, as this is its aim; what else would there be for it to know other than *itself, when nothing is outside it*? Thus, it *ought* to be subject and object of itself, even though the two poles are kept separate throughout the movement. Precisely this, however, creates the movement, and the two ends must not coincide, for as soon as they meet, the movement stops. This can be clarified by the example of a magnetic needle: if the two poles in the magnetic needle were to coincide, its life would cease.

Thus, the *entire* movement is only a movement towards self-knowledge. The imperative, the impulse of the entire movement, is Γνῶθι Σεαυτόν [*gnoti seauton*], know thyself, the practice of which is *generally* regarded as wisdom. Know what you are, and *be* what you have come to know yourself as, this is the supreme rule of wisdom.

Thus, eternal freedom in indifference is wisdom *at rest*, in motion it is never-resting wisdom at search, and in the end it is wisdom realized. Since wisdom searching for itself is present in the entire movement, the entire movement is a striving for wisdom, it is – objectively – philosophy.

Now it could be said: here (in the end), eternal freedom is recognizable as the absolute subject. Certainly, but *only for itself*. Only eternal freedom, therefore, can actually know itself; there is no knowledge of it aside from the one in which *the same* knows *the same*. Thus, for man there seems to be no knowledge of eternal freedom. We do, though, demand such a knowledge, an immediate knowledge. The only way for it to be possible is that the self-knowledge of eternal freedom be *our consciousness*, and vice versa, that *our consciousness* be a *self-knowledge of eternal freedom*. Or, since this self-knowledge is based on a transition from the objective to the subjective realm, what if this transition took place *in us*, i.e., what if we ourselves were eternal freedom restored as a subject after being the object?

This thought must not startle us. For a) in man alone we find this unfathomable freedom again. In the middle of time he is outside time, he is permitted to be another beginning, he is the beginning restored. b) An obscure memory of having once been the beginning, the power, the absolute centre of everything, very clearly stirs in man. He would be this centre in a twofold way, 1) in so far as he is the same, but returned, eternal freedom that had been there in the beginning. Thus, he would be the absolute centre in the form of this beginning, and he would be this centre 2) in the form of freedom returned.

But *if* man, too, were only freedom come to itself – as he really is, for man with respect to his interior is nothing but *ego*, *consciousness*, and any consciousness presupposes that one has come to oneself – and if man were also this beginning returned, then, in fact, *he does not know himself as that beginning*. For if he knew himself as such, if he knew himself as freedom come to itself, then the question of how to recognize this eternal freedom would not be necessary. We would know it *immediately*, we would *be* only this self-knowledge of eternal freedom. Since we are, none the less, this knowledge of eternal freedom and do not know it, we will first of all have to be led, by science, into knowing this knowledge. Science too, however, must follow the same path and cannot reach this knowledge other than *by proceeding from eternal freedom*. It cannot proceed, however, from the latter without knowing it. Here we are confronted with an obvious circularity. We would already need to have the result of science in order to begin science. At this point, the difficulties which had until now remained in darkness are revealed to us. What is left? Should we use *anticipation* as a remedy? Anticipation, however, is an imperfect kind of knowledge. It really only refers to the future. It is undeniable that with the first step in philosophy comes also the anticipation of its end; there is no science without divination. It is, however, not the same to divine the *end* in the beginning and anticipate the beginning itself in the beginning, for the latter is a contradiction. The same is the case with *belief*. I honour belief, but to begin with believing in the *principle* would be ridiculous. Or should we start with a *hypothesis* which only achieves certainty at the end? This sounds good, but it is not enough. In any case, here *I* would always be the one to posit science or the principle. What matters in philosophy, though, is rising above all knowledge that begins merely *with oneself*. What would have to be done then? What should we begin with? Here, then, what prevents most people from even taking up philosophy must be pointed out. It is the idea of dealing with a demonstrative science, which at the very beginning proceeds from one piece of knowledge in order to reach another piece of knowledge, and another from that one, etc. Philosophy, however, is not a demonstrative science. Philosophy is, to put it straightforwardly, a *free act of the spirit*. Its first step does not yield knowledge, but, rather more explicitly, ignorance. It is the surrender of all that is *knowledge* to man. As long as *he* still desires knowledge, the absolute subject will, for him, turn into an object, and for this very reason he will not come to know it in itself. But by saying I, as myself, cannot know, *I* – do not *want* to know, by disposing of knowledge, *he* creates space for knowledge, that is for the absolute subject, which was precisely shown to be knowledge itself. In this act of revoking knowledge, and being content with not knowing, the absolute subject is established *as* knowledge. In this act of establishing, of course, I become aware of it as something that is exuberant. This act of becoming aware might also be referred to as knowledge. It must, however, immediately be added that it is a kind of knowledge which is, in view of myself, better referred to as ignorance. The absolute subject is only there as long as I do not make it an object, i.e. as long as I have no knowledge, or have given up my knowledge. But as soon as this ignorance tries to become knowledge, the absolute subject disappears again because it *cannot* be an object.

Attempts have been made to articulate this peculiar relation using the expression *intellectual perception*. It was called perception because it was assumed that in perceiving something, or (since this word has become so common) in attending to something, the subject loses itself, is placed outside itself. It was called *intellectual* perception in order to express that the subject is not lost in sensory perception, i.e., in a real object, but that it is lost in, or gives itself up in, something that *cannot* be an *object*. Precisely because this expression needs first of all to be clarified, however, it is better to set it aside completely. More appropriately, we could use the term *ecstasy* for this relation. Our ego, namely, is placed *outside* itself, i.e. outside its role. Its role is to be subject. Confronted with the absolute subject, it cannot remain a subject, for the absolute subject cannot behave like an object. It must, then, give up its *place*, it must be placed outside itself, as something that no longer exists. Only in this state of having abandoned itself can the absolute subject appear to it in its state of self-abandonment, and so we also behold it in *amazement*. The benevolent Plato uses this gentle expression when he says: 'This is the primary affection of the philosopher – amazement τὸ θαυμάζειν [*to thaumazein*],' and when he adds, 'for there *is* no other beginning of philosophy than amazement.'* It is a wonderful expression with which *you* should profoundly inscribe your souls, especially since there

* *Theaetetus*, 155d.

are so many half-wits who always advise beginners in philosophy to turn inward – to go into their most profound depths, which only means as much as deeper and deeper into their own limitations. What man needs is not to be placed inside himself, but outside himself. It was precisely by going into himself that he originally lost what he was supposed to be. Indeed, *he* was the eternal freedom that had lost itself and then searched the whole of nature for itself – he was this freedom that had returned to itself and he was supposed to remain this. By wanting only to see himself in it, however, to fathom it, to attract it, i.e. to turn himself into a subject, he did continue to be a subject, of course, but the eternal freedom also continued to be a mere object for him. What else could he do so as to become again what he used to be – the wisdom, namely the self-knowledge of eternal freedom – other than dislodge himself from this place, place himself outside himself?

I wish to remark here that Ἔκστασις [*ekstasis; ecstasy*] *is a vox anceps* [ambivalent expression], to be taken for better or for worse. Namely, there is ecstasy whenever something is removed or dislodged from its place. What matters, though, is whether something is removed from a place that it merits or from a place that it does not merit. In the latter case, we have a beneficial ecstasy which brings us back to our senses, while the former leads us into senselessness.

But how can man be brought to this ecstasy – a question that is synonymous with: how can man be brought to his senses? I want to demonstrate this in a general way here (not by going through the entire development).

When man turns original freedom into his object and wants to obtain knowledge about it, a necessary contradiction follows: he wants to know and feel eternal freedom as eternal freedom, but, by turning it into an object, it imperceptibly becomes non-freedom, and, none the less, he searches for and desires it *as* freedom. He wishes to become aware of it as freedom, but ruins it by thus attracting it. Therefore, man begins to drift internally, in a rotating movement, in which he constantly searches for freedom and in which freedom escapes him. This inner drift is the state of the most nagging doubt, of an eternal restlessness. Not only does freedom disappear; he who

wants to know it also finds himself in a state of supreme unfreedom
– in constant tension with the freedom that he eternally searches for
and that constantly escapes him. This tension, which is also there in
man (no tension = freedom), finally reaches its highest point, an
ἀκμή [*akme*], which must be succeeded by an eruption in which he
who attempted to know eternal freedom *within itself* is cast out –
placed on to the periphery – and released into complete *ignorance*.
Only here does he feel well again. This crisis is, however, only a
beginning, a condition for the actual process, which now must be
described. As a result of the separation, two elements are now posited,
on one side our consciousness in the state of absolute ignorance, and
on the other side the absolute subject, which is now revealed to
consciousness as eternal freedom and which declares itself as that of
which the other is ignorant. Although these two are set apart, they
do not remain separated. They had only abandoned a *false unity*
under which they had laboured in order to gain the true, right and
free unity. But precisely *because* they are discharged from one and the
same unity, they continuously behave, so to speak, like sympathizing
organs, whereby no change can occur in one of them without being
reflected in the other. A change, though, is necessary, for the absolute
subject cannot remain in such narrow confines (the absolute
inwardness); immediately it begins to move again. Its movement has,
like every movement, three main stages. 1) The *first* stage is the one
in which the absolute subject finds itself in absolute inwardness = A.
This corresponds with the stage of knowledge in which it is absolute
outwardness, i.e. ignorance = B. The absolute subject, however,
cannot persevere in this absolute in-itself. It necessarily makes the
transition to outwardness, or A becomes object = B. Thus 2) the
second stage, A becomes B. In the first stage, knowledge could not
help but exist as absolutely ignorant; in the second, where A becomes
B, absolute ignorance makes the transition to knowledge = A. The
knowledge that was posited as absolute ignorance, as B, as outward,
ventures to become inwardness again – knowledge – = A. The transition from subject to object is reflected in the transition from object
to subject. This is why we need the expression 'reflection'. Similar
to the way an object is mirrored in water, the absolute subject is

inversely related to consciousness. The absolute subject leaves only absolute ignorance behind. If, however, A becomes B then in the same fashion B becomes A, i.e., knowledge.

The absolute subject, however, does not rest at the stage of its outwardness, at 3) the *third* stage it turns back into A from B again, it is re-established as subject, only it is now A restored from B. Similarly, the knowledge that stands in communication with it will also change its relation. When the absolute subject is restored, knowledge must wither away into ignorance; B that had become A becomes B again, i.e., *ignorance*, but as brought back from knowledge it is no longer just ignorance, it is a knowing ignorance. It is not, as in the beginning, an outward ignorance, but an inward ignorance. It has assimilated, *internalized* again the eternal freedom from which it had been discharged in that crisis. Or it has remembered eternal freedom for itself. Now it knows this freedom, knows it indeed immediately, namely *as* that which itself is the interior of it, of ignorance. Hence, the ancient doctrine that all philosophy consists in remembrance. (In order to return to itself as the original inside of eternal freedom – for it was generated *in* this freedom – it had to be placed outside itself.)

This relation of knowledge and absolute subject can also be illustrated by two lines. Imagine two lines:

$$
\begin{array}{c}
\text{B} \\
\text{A}\!\!-\!\!-\!\!-\!\!-\!\!-\!\!-\!\!\text{B} = \text{A} \\
\text{A} \\
\text{B}\!\!-\!\!-\!\!-\!\!-\!\!-\!\!-\!\!\text{A} = \text{B}
\end{array}
$$

On the first line, the absolute subject (A) is the beginning, and on the second line, the knowledge in ignorance (B) is the beginning. Both are correlates. At one point in its movement, the absolute subject makes the transition to object (B). At the same moment, B of the upper line is reflected in the lower line as A, or ignorance makes the transition to knowledge (A). At a third moment, however, the absolute subject of the upper line (A), that had become the object (B) in the second moment, makes the transition back from object to subject again. Or in other words: B becomes A again, and at the same moment, the B = A of the upper line is reflected in the lower line and appears as A = B, or as knowledge united with ignorance.

So much for general remarks. This is the outline of a proper theory of philosophy.

Now for a few explanations and corollaries.

The process is based on *keeping separate* absolute subject and our knowledge, whereby, however, the two are in constant communication, so that with each movement of the absolute subject, the state of knowledge also changes. On this basis, the question is no longer how we can be certain of the *reality of this knowledge*. For a) in that state of self-abandonment, in that ecstasy, where I, as I, know myself as complete ignorance, the absolute subject immediately becomes supreme reality for me. I *posit* the absolute subject due to my ignorance (in that ecstasy). For me, it is not an *object* that I knowingly know, but the absolute subject that I ignorantly know and that I posit precisely due to my ignorance. This communication between my knowledge and the absolute subject, by means of which there is as much reality in the absolute subject as there is non-reality in my knowledge, is only possible, however, because the two are originally one, because eternal freedom is originally lodged in our consciousness or *is our* consciousness, because, truly, apart from our consciousness, there is no place at all for eternal freedom to come to itself. b) Whatever holds true of the first positing of the absolute subject, namely that the absolute subject as such posits me as ignorant, and vice versa, that I, as ignorant, posit the absolute subject, also holds true of every *individual* form of knowledge in this progression. That is to say α) knowledge undergoes constant change, it is *always different but still the same*. But β) it is not my knowledge that changes; my knowledge is *being* changed. Each of *its* particular forms is only a reflex (the *opposite*, hence reflection!) of the given form of eternal freedom and γ) I immediately apperceive *that* form through the reflex in myself, i.e. through the changes in my knowledge. Thus δ), all knowledge unfolds only inwardly. We are not only the *idle* spectators, but we ourselves undergo constant change until we reach the form of perfect knowledge. This is not a superficial, but a deep-reaching process that leaves the indelible marks of its movement inside us. This is also the way it has to be. Nothing that is given to man reaches him just externally. The light of science has to arise in us through internal separation and liberation.

In philosophy, nothing begins as a pure and finished law. A complete concept is only produced gradually. In connection with the above-mentioned crisis, whose consequence is the separation of absolute subject and consciousness, I will go back again to the process already described. For originally, human consciousness is the interior, that which underlies, bears, and is the subject of eternal freedom coming to itself, as the silent, i.e. ignorant, non-active, non-emerging interior. That eternal freedom comes to itself is based on its transition from object back to subject, from B to A. Hence, B is the underlying phenomenon, that which was, so to speak, placed underneath A. Now B is an individual form or shape – that of man. Thus, man or human consciousness is that silent interior of eternal freedom come to itself, and the *individual* consciousness is only the basis of absolute or universal consciousness. This, however, is not yet the complete picture. Otherwise, *although eternal freedom would know itself, it would not be known by man.* Man, therefore, must attract this eternal freedom that characterizes him (to which he is the subject). He must desire it *for himself.* The particular principle, the *individual* human consciousness, is only the *basis* of the Absolute or universal consciousness, and man, hence, would like to have universal consciousness as *his* individual consciousness. Thereby, however, he suspends universal consciousness. For this had been based on B being *in* A, on B being the silent, hidden, unnoticeable interior of A. Thus, by attracting pure consciousness, he destroys it. Here, then, emerges the contradiction of man destroying what he wants *by* wanting it. From this contradiction arises that drifting movement, because that which the searcher searches for escapes him, so to speak, in constant flight. Hence, that final crisis in which the unity, expressed as B transformed into A – i.e. the consciousness of eternal freedom (= the primordial consciousness) – is torn apart. By way of this crisis, we are placed right at the beginning again. A is pure, absolute subject again, subject so much so that it does not even know of itself. The only new thing that is left intact, as the ruin of the preceding process so to speak, is B, placed outside itself and brought to ignorance. It had become free by being placed outside, thereby having its first moment of gaining consciousness, and for the first time enjoying the freedom and the bliss of ignorance. It is now – to employ a positive expression – what we can call *free thought*. Thought means abandoning knowledge. Knowledge is bound, thought is in complete freedom, and already the *word* suggests that all free thought is the result of a separation, a crisis, a tension that was lifted. The word, indeed, either derives α) from stretching, or β) from the Hebrew word [זיז] or γ) from δίνος [*dinos*], that which has escaped a turbulent movement. It always refers back to an origin in conflict. We get the same result when we go back to an old use of the word 'to think', as is still manifest e.g. in the following saying: 'Those who are distinguished think for a long time', i.e. their memory lasts for a long time. Here too, thought is characterized as that which is placed outside and preceded by knowledge.

The elements now separated are nothing but separated primordial consciousness itself. When they were together as one, primordial consciousness *was* in them, and it is still contained in their separation, but only as something torn apart attempting to restore itself, only *potentially*, as a seed, as something that can be restored. This primordial consciousness itself in its potentiality, in its mere capacity to be restored, is *reason*. Or more emphatically, primordial consciousness which strives to restore itself in this separation, which we only perceive as a stimulus, as a signal, as an aspect of us, is *reason*. This illuminates the potential, the merely suffering nature of reason, but this also shows that reason cannot be the active principle in science.

Since both free ignorant thought and the absolute subject opposed to it contain the separated primordial consciousness, they are both a mere discharge of this primordial consciousness. Only as such, as correlate of my ignorant, objectless knowledge, can primordial consciousness at all be posited, and in so far as this ignorant knowledge is free thought, I can say: *it is posited by my free thought*, it is my thought, not in the sense that a chimera is also my thought, but in the sense that it was originally together and one with what is now thought. This is why it is discharged *in* thought from the same primordial consciousness which also had been *my* consciousness. I can say: it is my *concept*. But a) this does not mean that it is the *object* corresponding to my concept, but, rather, that it is the concept itself. b) It is not, as one says, *mere* concept, but it is the eternal freedom itself which is only called my concept because it is *originally* conceived in primordial consciousness, which was also my consciousness. Every concept, though, is only something discharged from my consciousness, and can be called 'concept' because it was conceived in consciousness. We must also not imagine that *thought* precedes and posits the absolute subject, but that both emerge in one and the same act – in the same decision. Both are born together and emerge at the same time from a primordial unity. Free thought, which rebuffs all knowledge, is now confronted with the absolute subject. It is a great moment, the actual birth of philosophy.

Primordial unity, however, tries incessantly to produce itself. For its separation, too, is a forced condition – that is to say the two opponents are related in such a way that what was posited as absolute subject, as A, tries to emerge in B = A, i.e. in that which knows itself. It cannot persist in this kind of abstraction, for it has lost its interior, its fulfilment. It is pure knowledge itself, the knowledge that does not know, it is the empty essence of consciousness that strives for fulfilment. Its fulfilment, however, is precisely in B. A, too, wants to *remember* its knowledge, i.e. to reinternalize B, which used to be its *subject*, its *knowledge*. But now A, the absolute subject, is only being preserved in its abstraction by B, by the power of an ignorant knowledge, a knowledge that rejects all its knowledge. With respect to its nature it does not endure one single moment, because it is *natura anceps*, a freedom which it is and which it also is not, and hence it must make a decision immediately. So it is, I can say, my concept, but it is a concept that is stronger than I am, a living, a driving concept. It is by nature the most agile thing, indeed it is agility itself. Ignorant knowledge now relates to it as the force that slows down and retards its movement. And precisely because it is only being sustained in its abstraction by the power of ignorant knowledge, precisely for this reason it cannot move, as is usually said, without the knowledge or permission of this knowledge that does not want to give up the freedom of ignorance. And in this way my knowledge is a free, quietly observing witness that accompanies the movement step by step. Now I must not ask any more about *how I know this movement*. For the movement itself and my knowledge of this movement, each moment of the movement and my knowledge of this moment are one in each instant, and this slowing, retarding, reflecting knowledge is actually the philosopher's knowledge, is what he can call *his own* in this process. For the movement takes place entirely independently of him, and – *very importantly* – it is not he who moves in his knowledge and thereby generates knowledge (knowledge thus generated is subjective, a mere conceptual knowledge devoid of reality), but on the contrary, *his* knowledge is in itself immobile. It is not merely ignorance, but sets itself against knowledge, resists the movement, stops it, and thereby compels the movement to hold its ground at all moments, to linger and not to jump over any one moment. This retarding force is the actual force of the philosopher. The masters of this art are those who remain prudent and calm, who are capable of stopping the movement, of compelling it to linger, who so to speak do not allow the movement to take any steps other than the necessary ones and who always allow it only *that* step which is necessary, not a bigger or smaller one. *This* is what the art of philosophy consists in; just as true artists in general can be recognized by a force that slows down and retards, rather than by a force that produces, drives, or accelerates.

It could be said: the philosopher or this knowledge is in constant communication with the driving element which, as it were, desires knowledge incessantly. He must make every step difficult for it, he has to struggle with it for every step of the way. Here is this inner contact, this constant conversation between two principles. The first is knowledge itself, knowledge as essence but which does not know; the other *knows* but is not the essence, not *knowledge itself* but only ignorant knowledge. The first wants to remember and the other helps it remember. It is this art of inner communication of which the outward communication, which is called *only* its dialectic, is the copy and – when turned into mere form – the empty appearance and the shadow. This relation was represented as it were in person by a divine man, divine not meant in the usual hyperbolic sense, but a truly divine man, the understanding of whose inner greatness and glory alone could indicate the path towards true philosophy – Socrates, doubtless the brightest star in all of antiquity, in whom providence wanted to show what the original splendour of nature was capable of, Socrates, who, when he said that he knew only that he did not know, wanted thereby to express his relation to that which actually produces knowledge and which he strove to stimulate everywhere and whenever he could. He himself said that he was not going to give birth any more – just as this is not the task of an ignorant knowledge, one that is dead as it were, for fertility is to be found only in eternal freedom. He was not going to give birth any more, but would help others give birth, would induce it, comparing himself with his mother, who had been a midwife. In the same way as an intelligent midwife does not rush the process, but urges the child-bearing mother to hold out and to endure in the pains of labour until the hour comes to give birth, so he acted as the guide who does not rush but slows down the movement or birth by means of constant contradiction.

When the original unity $B = A$ (to describe the movement further in a few words), when this original unity is restored, B, standing in communication with it, can no longer act a) as being completely ignorant (for it is no longer merely subject), or b) as having knowledge, for it does not have an object any longer. Thus there is no space at all for B, but since it cannot be extinguished, there is nothing left for it other than to let itself be completely absorbed into $B = A$, i.e. to know *itself* as B transformed into A and thus to become internal to A again. Now, a) it is what it was to begin with, the silent interior of eternal freedom (for it does not need to attract eternal freedom any more), and yet at the same time it is that which has knowledge of eternal freedom, because from its very movement it brings the whole and complete knowledge back with itself – for it has seen eternal freedom in all its moments. And b) it knows *itself*, for it has experienced itself in all its depths. But this was exactly what was to be achieved – that it would know itself *as* the interior of eternal freedom. Beforehand, it *was* the interior of eternal freedom, but ignorant.

The goal is thus *immediate* knowledge of eternal freedom. In order to reach this goal, however, as in the original movement, the poles must be kept separate.

Part of substantiating philosophy as science is also demonstrating its *necessity*. Basically this has already been achieved by what has so far been said. The necessity of philosophy immediately emerges from the inevitable inner conflict that was mentioned above. I say inevitable. For human consciousness cannot stop at being the silent interior, the mere basis of the eternal movement, the movement of eternal freedom itself. Though not exactly forced, man will still, necessarily and inevitably, attract the eternal freedom that he is and desire it for himself, so as to be productive with it upon his own initiative. For it must not be thought that this would have occurred only at the beginning of things. Each individual human consciousness is a return of eternal freedom to itself. In every human consciousness, though, the same attraction occurs again.

Could it be said, then, that each human being undergoes this inner movement of drift? And is this not also the case, that we must admit that the greater part of people wander about in an unconscious state? Even if the tension accompanied by inner activity does not appear as such, it is still present in its result, the unconsciousness. And if we do not perceive this tension in most people any more, it is only because they do not even reach the point of inner tension, but are lulled, prematurely distracted and removed from their inwardness, into an agreeable daze. The inner confrontation does not break out in most people, or at least does not reach that level of tension at which a decision becomes necessary. That the reason and the occasion of the inner conflict lie in human nature can be illuminated by the fact that in almost every epoch there are unlettered and uneducated people in whom this inner confrontation arises involuntarily and by itself, and who, despite opposition from academic scholars, produce a philosophy of their own accord, and master a more or less happy crisis. Wherever this inner conflict is originally stirred up, however, without being resolved through this crisis and separation into a level-headed knowledge, it necessarily produces what we call *errors*. All errors are only the products of those inner spiritual forces that are locked in violent combat.

Errors are neither trivial nor mere deficiencies. They are an inversion of knowledge (belonging to the category of evil, sickness). If all errors were plainly and simply wrong, that is devoid of all truth, they would be harmless. Some claims are of this harmless kind, but it would be giving them too much honour to call them errors. For even errors have something honourable, they always contain a grain of truth. These very distortions, however, these inversions of truth, these marks of original truth still recognizable or obscurely felt in even the most terrible errors, are what makes them so dreadful. The most gentle force, one that is active in the formations of organic beings, produces, if it is inhibited, something monstrous. This is so terrifying, not because of its dissimilarity, but precisely because of its similarity with the true formation, as the human form is still recognizable. The inner rotation, too, is produced by an inhibition, an attraction, where the moving force does not stop, for it flows from an eternal source.

It could be said that error arises by merely *wanting* to know. So only by not *wanting* to know are we safe from error. True, this is the household remedy that most people employ. But *wanting* to know does not depend on man. He *wants* to know before he knows that he wants to know. For already each individual consciousness arises in man from an attraction, from turning that which he is into his object. Man is by nature already in knowledge – in the knowledge that he acquires by making himself a knowing subject in opposition to the eternal freedom which he ought to have been. Since this knowledge was generated by turning eternal freedom into an object, as it were, by displacing it, its only consequence is a *distortion* of knowledge. A *mixture* of truths and falsities, then, had to arise in knowledge. In this mixed, impure knowledge we live by nature – hence also our 'natural' knowledge. People who, without being cleansed beforehand, approach philosophy, as it were, covered in the impurity of this knowledge, must necessarily fall into an even greater confusion than the one they are in to begin with. Of course, all their thoughts and endeavours can only serve to assert and defend this false knowledge as though it were their own lives – and rightfully so, because their lives exist only in this knowledge. This is why whatever is found in this knowledge they establish as universally valid eternal truths. For example: 'The natural is outside the supernatural.' Of course this is so, and we feel this separation painfully. Indeed, it was from this very pain that we demanded to be freed by a higher kind of knowledge. But since these people are completely captivated by the present, by what is at a standstill, they fail to see that there existed a point where the natural was in the supernatural (that eternal freedom, from which everything stems, is beyond all nature), as well as a point where it will be within it again, as it should be within it in man. That wonderful connection of freedom and necessity in man does not tell them anything. The two are infinitely far away from each other, and infinitely close. Freedom estranged from itself is nature, nature withdrawn back into itself is freedom. What is missing is only a reinversion. Man has fallen into error precisely because he has separated the natural from the supernatural. Those, then, who fight for this dualism, are basically fighting for the *guilt* of man, and they want to project what only man is guilty of on to nature, the object itself.

Even better than these attempts at trying to reach science with unpurified and mixed knowledge, is the otherwise desolate doctrine according to which we are unable ever to know anything. One can see that with *this* knowledge nothing can be known, but one still does not want to give up trying to master this crisis. Kant calls his philosophy *critical*, and if it had really made it to the point of this crisis, it might well and justly bear that name. It is, however, only the beginning of the actual crisis, for when Kant says, for example, that we cannot know the transcendent, the divine, with the forms of our finite reason, he is quite right and has not actually said anything apart from what is obvious. He always presupposes, however, that it would have to be known in these forms if it is knowable at all.

Man is supposed to die away from this natural knowledge. In philosophy, man is not the one who knows, but the one who resists what actually generates knowledge, and who in free thought and in constant contradiction stops this generating element, reflects it. For this very reason, however, he also wins it for himself. That which generates knowledge, however, is *capable* of everything, for it is the spirit that permeates everything, the eternal magic, the wisdom that is the master of all arts. In this wisdom, according to one of the later occidental books,* lies the spirit that is understanding, unified and yet manifold (this a very important characteristic), and that goeth through all *spirits*, however understanding, acute and sincere they may be – thus also through the supreme spirit. For the divinity itself, though purity itself, is not more pure than spirit is. It goes through all spirits, for it is the most agile being, or, as this fundamental Greek text puts it: ʽπάσης γὰρ κινήσεως κινητικώτερον σοφία, διήκει δὲ καὶ χωρεῖ διὰ πάντων κ. τ. λ.' – more agile than everything that can move – which corresponds with what I have already said: it is agility itself and therefore more agile than every individual movement. It is unitary and can do – it is able to do – and indeed does everything. It remains what it is and yet renews everything, i.e. it constantly produces one new thing from another. This constant existence as one and yet as always another is the characteristic of knowledge. Knowledge is neither in what is always one and never emerges from itself, nor in what straightforwardly falls apart, in what lacks unity and coherence. Knowledge is coherence, one and yet many, always another and yet always one.

This wisdom is not far from man, for it is only what was discharged from primordial consciousness, which was originally also his consciousness. Man was supposed to be the silent interior of eternal freedom that had come to itself, which precisely through this coming-to-itself was realized wisdom. While this coming-to-itself went undisturbed, the freedom that had come to itself in man and thus knew itself was also in control of itself. Likewise, the freedom that we see in nature and that is not in control of itself became calm freedom; and the eternal freedom that knew itself – and through it man – was the calm power or magic of all things. But man interfered with this coming-to-itself by desiring eternal freedom for himself. He could only, however, attract *the freedom* that he *was*, i.e. the freedom that

---

* The Wisdom of Solomon, 7, 24.

had come to itself in him, not the freedom which was to be subordinated to this very freedom and thereby become free also. This freedom, then, remained outside, where it still produces its miracles. It is useless in so far as it keeps on wearing out and destroying its productions, only to produce the same again – as it were in an idle bustle, which does not come from *its will*, though, and in which it is caught up against its will.

He pushed aside, however, the eternal freedom that he was. Precisely by trying to attract it and thus by becoming the subject opposed to it, he excluded it (this the oft-mentioned contradiction). This is why wisdom is constantly presented as *excluded* in that old occidental book – 'it lamenteth in the streets'* – and those who look for it find it easily, they find it 'in front of their doors, waiting for them'.† Constantly it calls upon man to give up that inner tension, to place, as far as possible, *himself* and thereby wisdom, too, into freedom again, which happens in the very crisis that we said marked the beginning of philosophy, i.e. of the love of wisdom.

The freedom, too, that was external to him and had remained in nature is in agreement with the freedom locked up in man for whose liberation it is waiting. It appears to be in agreement with the inner freedom by making man's outward life as difficult as the other freedom makes his inward life. He who is inexperienced is attracted by its involuntary charm – involuntary, for this freedom would like to cover its charm, but itself urges him to hand himself over, and teaches him painful lessons, teaches him to step back from this abyss with a shudder. It does not hide it or keep it secret from him but tells him directly that it only deceives him. And, since in being at a *standstill* it is properly speaking a product of man, it shows in every possible way that it is not in the least grateful to him.

Everything, then, calls upon man to give up his knowledge, to make this separation through which he would first of all see *himself* in complete freedom, but also see, opposite him, the antecedent freedom in its original purity.

* Proverbs 1, 20.
† The Wisdom of Solomon, 6, 15.

With these words I wish to conclude this investigation into the nature of philosophy as science. It is always already a lasting reward to know what true philosophy is and how it relates to man and to his other endeavours. The concept of wisdom is not futile even for those who want to remain outside actual philosophy. The love of wisdom is revealed not only in what is called thus by the academies. Wisdom is in everything; it emerges from everything for those who look for it. It is hidden in all possible objects, in all the sciences, and this love, this search for wisdom ennobles every study. Those who find it are in possession of a genuine treasure. It ennobles the most common thing and turns the highest and noblest thing into something common, something to be treated like daily bread. But it only gives itself to pure souls. For only to the pure is the pure revealed.

Translated by Marcus Weigelt

HEGEL

Hegelian philosophy is commonly regarded as the culmination of idealism. Hegel himself understood and accounted for his philosophy this way. True, during his lifetime the Absolute Professor was already mocked for his hubris, and after his death, it was swiftly asserted throughout the scientifically minded world of nineteenth-century philosophy that idealism had collapsed. However, Hegel himself had claimed that the task of philosophy was to 'comprehend its time in thought'. He had subjected his own intellectual efforts to a historical premise and had thereby acknowledged thought as finite. Only as a consequence of his theory, in which the human quest for knowledge was historically relativized, did Hegel assume a specific duty to truly free thought. By assimilating its historical relativity, Hegel's philosophy tried to remove this relativity. Hence, the absolute claim of Hegel's philosophy was based not so much on an overestimation of himself, but rather on reflective reasoning.

Hegel found himself confronted with a number of philosophical systems, all of which claimed to be valid and true. In spite of these fiercely competing alternatives, we must still, according to Hegel, adhere to the idea of a philosophical truth. Nevertheless, the historical dimension necessarily contained in this idea simply cannot be denied. The undiminished demand for truth, therefore, must be combined with the acceptance of historical relativity. The history in which philosophical truth is manifested must itself become a philosophical issue: not as one among others, but, rather, as that on which the justification of systematic philosophy itself is based. Philosophy has no prospects of solving its original task conclusively unless the initially separated realms of system and history are mediated with each other. Only once this problem of history is settled, a problem that directly affects systematic philosophy as a whole, could the hopes for a new philosophical beginning, cherished since Kant, be fulfilled.

Therefore, in contrast to the high-spirited systematic projects of his predecessors, Hegel's beginnings were critically directed at the level of thought reached by his contemporaries. Even the so-called early theological writings of the young graduate from the seminary in Tübingen, edited from posthumous fragments only in our century and offering considerable revisions to the commonly accepted view of Hegel, are filled with critique. The critique is directed against Kant's concept of morality and its abstraction and distance from practical political life, as well as against the positive theology that resulted from an atrophied living spirit of Christianity in the course of history. Under the given state of affairs, it was only possible to articulate the desired unity of subject and object critically, i.e. against a historically formed separation. During his time as a university lecturer at Jena, Hegel's critical work still played an important role. Hegel, the academic novice, initially sought his way alongside Schelling, his younger friend and fellow student from his Tübingen days, who had advanced to a professorship a long time before. For a while, he subscribed to Schelling's system. Gradually, though, he began to articulate his own systematic projects, which finally led to a break with Schelling.

Hegel's new conception was published in the form of the *Phenomenology of Spirit*, conceived as an extensive introduction to his own intellectual edifice. The *Phenomenology*, finished in the decisive historical moment of Napoleon's conquest of Jena, initially confused its audience because it concerned itself entirely with the historical appearance of human spirit. Its introductory function was lost from sight, especially since Hegel, due to the external circumstances of his own life, took a long time to execute the project as a whole. Only in 1812–13, did the *Science of Logic* finally appear, which according to Hegel contained a metaphysics of absolute spirit. It was followed by the elements of a material philosophy of nature and of spirit. A condensed survey was presented by the *Encyclopedia of the Philosophical Sciences*, written in Heidelberg in 1817.

It is difficult to perceive the systematic coherence established across various texts. In particular, the heart of the system, the *Logic*, makes immense demands on the reader. Hegel's interpreters, therefore, have tended to prefer the *Phenomenology*, in which he illustrated much more lucidly the forms of human spirit in their historical sequence. The still prevailing preference for the *Phenomenology* is even backed by a famous statement by Marx. Marx thought that the secret of Hegel's dialectics lay in its phenomenological concretion, whereas the speculative parts of the system seemed to him to be ideological inversions. We do, however, have to remind ourselves that the *Phenomenology* only represents the theory of phenomenal appearances of spirit, and it becomes deceptive once it is taken as the whole truth. The complicated procedure of the *Phenomenology*, as laid out by the Introduction, makes sense only in terms of a very specific aim: to make transparent the historical forms in which spirit appears. The *Phenomenology* has to make these forms transparent with respect to what is merely an appearance in them. It only tries to reach a preliminary goal, one that has to be followed by an unrestricted substantive presentation of the Absolute. The Absolute, however, cannot be presented in an unrestricted way, unless the entire sphere of its historical restriction has been traversed.

In his speculative logic, Hegel tried to present the truth of spirit, as opposed to its manifold appearances. What does the ambitious title *Science of Logic* mean? Logic here is not what one would ordinarily take it to be, namely the instrument that determines the formal rules of thought. Logic is science, just as metaphysics had, since Aristotle, been the supreme science which grounded all other sciences. Hegel called this basic science a logic because it did not deal with objects that could be distinguished from concepts, that is, because it dealt with the pure concepts themselves, concepts that have to be grasped precisely with respect to their own objective or substantial content. After Kant's destruction of traditional metaphysics, Hegel tried to reprocess the entire metaphysical stock of problems. What metaphysics had wanted to achieve when it was still freely talking about Being, Nothingness, Becoming, Essence, Idea and so forth, could be developed strictly methodologically from the concepts which spirit, historically enlightened as to its origin, had at that point acquired.

The *Logic* gave conceptual stability to the treatises of a material philosophy concerning the truth of nature and of spirit. Thus, they could acquire the status of philosophical sciences that, according to Hegel, was still lacking in the tentative attempts of his forerunners. The realm of nature was completely determined by its opposition to spirit, while the realm of spirit dialectically unfolded the process of coming to itself. Quite obviously, the essence of nature remained insufficiently determined when explained in reference to the primacy of spirit. Hegel's philosophy of nature will, therefore, probably not be counted among the strongest parts of his *œuvre*. The situation is very different for his philosophy of spirit, which dealt with the realities of individual, society and history. It is these parts in particular that have secured the lasting appeal of Hegel's philosophy. An adequate understanding of isolated parts, however, will hardly be possible without considering the clearly devised systematic coherence.

Hegel's philosophy of right and his philosophy of history, however, have constantly been subject to precisely this restricted focus on isolated parts. Since their topics were of immediate interest, both theories enjoyed a particular prominence in debates about Hegel. The debate over the status of his *Elements of the Philosophy of Right* (1821), for example, still continues today. This book, written in a politically reactionary period and published by a professor who had been appointed to Berlin only a few years before, represented for some the dogmatic glorification of Prussian monarchy, while for others it was the most advanced theory of law and politics, one which unified inherited ancient traditions and modern consciousness. Does the famous statement from the Preface, 'What is rational is actual; and what is actual is rational', mean that everything that exists should be justified as rational, or that only that which passes the test of reason should be allowed to determine reality? This question already divided the Left- from the Right-Hegelians.

Ever since the Hegelian school of the 1830s and 1840s, passions have been equally inflamed when it comes to assessing the master's construction of history. Hegel, no doubt, interpreted world history as progress in the consciousness of freedom, a kind of earthly revelation of God. Here, the significance of everyday struggles and interests was reduced in the name of the ruling world spirit. Hegel's pupils regretted that his promising theory, to which they had temporarily attached eschatological expectations, had not turned to practice. Marxism tried to stick to a teleological scheme, but sought to ground it in economic reality. The historicism that permeated the entire nineteenth century refrained from an optimistic view of historical progress, but preserved the principle of historical self-understanding. In the train of historicism, both the hermeneutic school and the methodology of the humanities today still argue in an implicitly Hegelian fashion, in so far as they want to understand historical events or facts as fundamentally meaningful.

It is not surprising that Hegel is still a source of key-words for the philosophical theories of society and history. It was he who raised these topics to the level of philosophical investigation. Meanwhile, reception of Hegel has also drawn attention to other parts of his work. His aesthetic theory, having remained in oblivion for a long time alongside the theory of absolute spirit, is more frequently discussed today. Now that efforts of reconstruction have managed to shed light on the organization of the system, the lucid as well as enigmatic *Logic* has justifiably become a centre of interest. The idea of dialectics, formerly set aside as abstruse compared to the content of his historical thinking, is newly appreciated in its methodological and logical significance. Even today's philosophy of science is accommodating, when it is open to philosophical reflection and not inhibited by orthodoxy. Hegel's impact, then, is diverse and by no means over with.

Hegel and Kant share the reputation of having again and again stimulated the thought of those who came after the decline of classical or idealist philosophy. It may even be possible to write the history of philosophy from then on as a hidden conflict between Kantian and Hegelian motifs. Kant has been summoned against Hegel whenever speculative exuberance needed reminding of its limits, by reference to science and experience. Hegel is used as the main witness whenever conceptual work is done on the phenomena of social and historical life. Although the comprehensive encyclopedic claim of the Hegelian system has become an irrevocable part of the past, idealism in its

Hegelian perfection is not a lifeless corpse from which the living spirit has long departed.

THE TEXTS

The instigation for the text that aimed to determine the *Difference between Fichte's and Schelling's System of Philosophy* (1801) was provided by K. L. Reinhold's publications. Reinhold had followed the drifting spirit of his time and had finally, after being a Kantian and later a Fichtean, landed on the logic of Bardili. The worthy Swabian schoolmaster Bardili had stood up to the latest philosophies of subjectivity in general, by insisting on an abstract principle of logical identity. Hegel intended to put things straight, to clarify the difference between Fichte and Schelling, and to point out the higher authority of his friend Schelling. Apart from the polemics peculiar to the time in which this text was written, Hegel also discussed the basic relation of each philosophy to its time. All those systems of various epochs have to be interpreted as appearances of one and the same absolute reason. Thereby their particularity is overcome and, in the process of overcoming it, the Absolute is portrayed. Philosophy is not independent of the given conditions of an epoch. The epochs precisely contain a need for true philosophy, because the ever more developed rational culture no longer corresponds to the unifying tendencies of life.

Hegel recognized a generally prevailing division in the phenomena of his epoch. The ancient ideal of a living mediation was long gone, while at the same time the demand for the reconstitution of a rational totality in reality became more urgent. This tension arose with the reflective activity of reason, in which subject and object were thematized in strict opposition. Philosophical reason had to break with this dogmatism and treat reflection as a means. This involved reflecting on reflection itself. On the basis of this idea, Hegel elaborated the basic concept of speculation. This concept of speculation, which was later to support the entire system, was here more closely connected to Schelling's idea of transcendental intuition. With the idea of determination by epoch as a premise, a philosophy of the Absolute can initially only be determined by means of reflection rather than reason. This inadequate transposition of the absolute theme into concepts of division, however, is the key to solving the problematic relation of history and system. Within the imperfect medium of reflection, the true and historically final philosophy is paving its own path by interpreting the historically conditioned forms of philosophy as appearances of itself. This system of reflection is suspended once reason performs the renewed reflection on reflection. After involving itself with reflection, philosophy can also dialectically overcome it.

The basic scheme of the *Phenomenology of Spirit* is thereby already sketched. The *Phenomenology* describes the entire history of human consciousness as an ordered sequence of the appearances of absolute spirit. Comprehensively executing the process of investigation also means overcoming the sphere of mere appearances, thereby preparing the systematic presentation of the Absolute itself. The Introduction explains the method that is to be employed. It unconditionally rejects the Kantian ideal of a critical philosophy of reflection. Hegel thinks that it is wrong to separate the means and instruments used by our knowledge from the objects themselves. We would otherwise be caught within an opposition of reflection and would never make headway towards the Absolute, which is supposed to be the ultimate object of philosophy. Still, the common ideas of natural consciousness cannot simply be dismissed. As given prerequisites of true philosophy, they have to be taken seriously, but only with the intention of being overcome. Sceptical doubt about our immediate knowledge of things must start doubting itself; its act of negating must itself be subjected to qualifications. Negation is not thereby lost in complete nothingness, but, as a determinate negation, it also acquires a content. The slow acquisition of what is contained in the negating experiences of consciousness is the same as the process of going through all the disguises and distortions of reflection and of advancing towards actual knowledge. Once this process has been set in motion, it proceeds unerringly by virtue of the forces of consciousness itself. It ends where no further mediation between consciousness and its object will be necessary because their division will have been immanently overcome. It is then that the standpoint of absolute knowledge will be reached. Along the path to this standpoint, the philosopher's only job is 'observation'. The philosopher beholds the dialectical process that takes place in consciousness itself, and thereby merely produces order and coherence. In this sense, the phenomenological perspective is preparatory for strictly systematic work.

An essential part of the encyclopedic system of the philosophical sciences is the philosophy of right, which applies the purely speculative principles to political reality. The Preface to the *Elements of the Philosophy of Right* takes up clear positions on a variety of prejudices and opinions about philosophy in general and about the philosophy of right in particular. The state has to be understood as a reality of spirit. It is more than the sum total of the vain pursuits of contingent individuals and it has, no less than nature, a substantial meaning. The traditional topic in natural law concerning a foundation of norms built on the intrinsic nature of law and state gets prominent treatment by Hegel. The law as the rationality of the thing itself is above the privacy of sentiments and it must also be defended against sophist trends of reasoning. The corrupting force of reflection must be opposed by the reality of morality embodied in the order of the state, a morality that goes necessarily unnoticed in any utopian construction of the world. Only this kind of reconciliation between reason and reality can meet the claims of free subjectivity, because it neither projects these claims on to an empty moral 'ought', nor merely subjugates them to some crude existing reality.

Hegel's philosophy of right terminates with a perspective on the philosophy of history, because reason that reaches practical reality always realizes itself historically. The last text to be reprinted here is a late lecture that introduces Hegel's *Philosophy of World History*. This, too, has to be seen as an element in the material philosophy of the system, as opposed to the phenomenological structuring of the forms of consciousness that is preliminary to the systematic standpoint. Philosophical world history has to be written in the name of absolute spirit. The philosopher can do nothing but regard events rationally, and this implies systematically extracting from these events the element of reason that alone endures in their infinite variety. Of course, history must be taken as it comes, and events must not be fitted into an external *a priori* scheme. In the course of rationally inspecting the historical material, that which is contingent will separate itself from that which is purposeful. Ultimately, however, only reason itself is purposeful, and so the eye of the philosophical historian necessarily discovers a teleological development. Historical changes, then, appear as meaningful, and a plan of divine providence seems to structure the whole. Hegel did not hesitate to talk about a revelation of God through the essential structures of history, in which a spiritual substance confronts the rational observer. The theological overestimation of history has always provoked opposition and has often been dismissed as a philosophical attempt at glossing over reality. The methodological conviction, however, that meaningful structures are only revealed in a retrospective understanding, is something every theory of history has inherited from Hegel.

Rüdiger Bubner
Translated by Marcus Weigelt

The Difference Between Fichte's and Schelling's System of Philosophy

PREFACE

In those few public utterances in which a feeling for the difference between Fichte's and Schelling's systems of philosophy can be recognized, the aim seems to be more to hide their distinctness or to get round it than to gain a clear awareness of it. Neither the systems as they lie before the public for direct inspection nor, among other things, Schelling's answer to Eschenmayer's idealistic objections against the philosophy of nature have brought the distinctness of the two systems out into open discussion. On the contrary, *Reinhold*, for example, is so far from an inkling of it that he takes the complete identity of both systems for granted. So his view of Schelling's system is distorted in this way too [as well as in other ways]. The occasion for the following treatise is this confusion of Reinhold's, rather than his revolution of bringing philosophy back to logic – a revolution that he has not merely threatened us with, but has proclaimed as already accomplished.

The Kantian philosophy needed to have its spirit distinguished from its letter, and to have its purely speculative principle lifted out of the remainder that belonged to, or could be used for, the arguments of reflection. In the principle of the deduction of the categories Kant's philosophy is authentic idealism; and it is this principle that Fichte extracted in a purer, stricter form and called the spirit of Kantian philosophy. The things in themselves – which are nothing but an objective expression of the empty form of opposition – had been hypostasized anew by Kant, and posited as absolute objectivity like the things of the dogmatic philosophers. On the one hand, he made the categories into static, dead pigeonholes of the intellect; and on the other hand he made them into the supreme principles capable of nullifying the language that expresses the Absolute itself – e.g., 'substance' in Spinoza. Thus he allowed argumentation to go on replacing philosophy, as before, only more pretentiously than ever under the name of critical philosophy. But all this springs at best from the form of the Kantian deduction of the categories, not from its principle or spirit. Indeed, if we had no part of Kant's philosophy but the deduction, the transformation of his philosophy [from speculation into reflection] would be almost incomprehensible. The principle of speculation is the identity of subject and object, and this principle is most definitely articulated in the deduction of the forms of the intellect [*Verstand*]. It was Reason [*Vernunft*] itself that baptized this theory of the intellect.

However, Kant turns this identity itself, which is Reason, into an object of philosophical reflection, and thus this identity vanishes from its home ground. Whereas intellect had previously been handled by Reason, it is now, by contrast, Reason that is handled by the intellect. This makes clear what a subordinate stage the identity of subject and object was grasped at. The identity of subject and object is limited to twelve acts of pure thought – or rather to nine only, for modality really determines nothing objectively; the nonidentity of subject and object essentially pertains to it. Outside what is objectively determined by the categories there remained an enormous empirical realm of sensibility and perception, an absolute *a posteriori* realm. For this realm the only a priori principle discovered is a merely subjective maxim of the faculty of reflecting judgement. That is to say, nonidentity is raised to an absolute principle. Nothing else was to be expected, once the identity, i.e., the rational, had been removed from the Idea, which is the product of Reason, and the Idea had been posited in absolute opposition to being. Reason as a practical faculty had been presented as it must be conceived by finite thought, i.e., by the intellect: not as absolute identity, but in infinite opposition, as a faculty of the pure unity [typical] of the intellect. Hence there arises this contrast: there are no absolute objective determinations for the intellect [i.e., in critical philosophy], but they are present for Reason [i.e., in speculative philosophy].

The principle of Fichte's system is the pure thinking that thinks itself, the identity of subject and object, in the form Ego = Ego. If one holds solely and directly to this principle and to the transcendental principle at the basis of Kant's deduction of the categories, one has the authentic principle of speculation boldly expressed. However, as soon as [Fichte's] speculation steps outside of the concept that it establishes of itself and evolves into a system, it abandons itself and its principle and does not come back to it again. It surrenders Reason to the intellect and passes over into the chain of finite [acts and objects] of consciousness from which it never reconstructs itself again as identity and true infinity. Transcendental intuition, the very principle [of speculation], thereby assumes the awkward posture of something that is in opposition to the manifold deduced from it. The Absolute of the system shows itself as apprehended only in the form in which it appears to philosophical reflection. This determinacy which is given to the Absolute by reflection is not removed – so finitude and opposition are not removed. The principle, the Subject–Object, turns out to be a subjective Subject–Object. What is deduced from it thereby gets the form of a conditioning of pure consciousness, of the Ego = Ego; and pure consciousness itself takes on the form of something conditioned by an objective infinity, namely the temporal progression *ad infinitum*. Transcendental intuition loses itself in this infinite progression and the Ego fails to constitute itself as absolute self-intuition. Hence, Ego = Ego is transformed into the principle 'Ego *ought* to be equal to Ego.' Reason is placed in absolute opposition, i.e., it is degraded to the level of intellect, and it is this degraded Reason that becomes the principle of the shapes that the Absolute must give itself, and of the Sciences of these shapes.

These are the two sides of Fichte's system. On the one hand it has established the pure concept of Reason and of speculation and so made philosophy possible. On the other hand, it has equated Reason with pure consciousness and raised Reason as apprehended in a finite shape to the status of principle. That these two sides should be distinguished must be shown to be an inner necessity of the problem itself [*die Sache selbst*], even though the external occasion for making the distinctions is a need of the time and is now provided by a bit of contemporary flotsam in time's stream, namely Reinhold's *Contributions* to a Survey of the State of Philosophy at the Beginning of the New Century. In these *Contributions* the aspect of authentic speculation and hence of philosophy in Fichte's system is overlooked; and so is the aspect of Schelling's system that distinguishes it from Fichte's – the distinction being that in the philosophy of nature Schelling sets the objective Subject–Object beside the subjective Subject–Object and presents both as united in something higher than the subject.

As to the need of the times, Fichte's philosophy has caused so much of a stir and has made an epoch to the extent that even those who declare themselves against it and strain themselves to get speculative systems of their own on the road, still cling to its principle, though in a more turbid and impure way, and are incapable of resisting it. The most obvious symptoms of an epoch-making system are the misunderstandings and the awkward conduct of its adversaries. However, when one can say of a system that fortune has smiled on it, it is because some widespread philosophical need, itself unable to give birth to philosophy – for otherwise it would have achieved fulfilment through the creation of a system – turns to it with an instinct-like propensity. The acceptance of the system seems to be passive but this is only because what it articulates is already present in the time's inner core and everyone will soon be proclaiming it in his sphere of science or life.

In this sense one cannot say of Fichte's system that fortune has smiled on it. While this is partly due to the unphilosophical tendencies of the age, there is something else that should also be taken into account. The greater the influence that intellect and utility succeed in acquiring, and the wider the currency of limited aims, the more powerful will the urge of the better spirit be, particularly in the more open-minded world of youth. A phenomenon such as the *Speeches on Religion* may not immediately concern the speculative need. Yet they and their reception – and even more so the dignity that is beginning to be accorded, more or less clearly or obscurely, to poetry and art in general in all their true scope – indicate the need for a philosophy that will recompense nature for the mishandling that it suffered in

Kant and Fichte's systems, and set Reason itself in harmony with nature, not by having Reason renounce itself or become an insipid imitator of nature, but by Reason recasting itself into nature out of its own inner strength.

This essay begins with general reflections about the need, presupposition, basic principles, etc. of philosophy. It is a fault in them that they are general reflections, but they are occasioned by the fact that presupposition, principles, and such like forms still adorn the entrance of philosophy with their cobwebs. So, up to a point it is still necessary to deal with them until the day comes when from beginning to end it is philosophy itself whose voice will be heard. Some of the more interesting of these topics will be more extensively treated elsewhere.

Jena, July 1801

VARIOUS FORMS OCCURRING IN CONTEMPORARY PHILOSOPHY

Historical View of Philosophical Systems

An age which has so many philosophical systems lying behind it in its past must apparently arrive at the same indifference which life acquires after it has tried all forms. The urge toward totality continues to express itself, but only as an urge toward completeness of information. Individuality becomes fossilized and no longer ventures out into life. Through the variety of what he has, the individual tries to procure the illusion of being what he is not. He refuses the living participation demanded by science, transforming it into mere information, keeping it at a distance and in purely objective shape. Deaf to all demands that he should raise himself to universality, he maintains himself imperturbably in his self-willed particularity. If indifference of this sort escalates into curiosity, it may believe nothing to be more vital than giving a name to a newly developed philosophy, expressing dominion over it by finding a name for it, just as Adam showed his dominance over the animals by giving names to them. In this way philosophy is transposed to the plane of information. Information is concerned with alien objects. In the philosophical knowledge that is only erudition, the inward totality does not bestir itself, and neutrality retains its perfect freedom [from commitment].

No philosophical system can escape the possibility of this sort of reception; every philosophical system can be treated historically. As every living form belongs at the same time to the realm of appearance, so too does philosophy. As appearance, philosophy surrenders to the power capable of transforming it into dead opinion and into something that belonged to the past from the very beginning. The living spirit that dwells in a philosophy demands to be born of a kindred spirit if it is to unveil itself. It brushes past the historical concern which is moved by some interest to [collect] information about opinions. For this concern it is an alien phenomenon and does not reveal its own inwardness. It matters little to the spirit that it is forced to augment the extant collection of mummies and the general heap of contingent oddities; for the spirit itself slipped away between the fingers of the curious collector of information. The collector stands firm in his neutral attitude towards truth; he preserves his independence whether he accepts opinions, rejects them, or abstains from decision. He can give philosophical systems only one relation to himself: they are opinions – and such incidental things as opinions can do him no harm. He has not learned that there is truth to be had.

The history of philosophy [seems to] acquire a more useful aspect, however, when the impulse to enlarge science takes hold of it, for according to Reinhold, the history of philosophy should serve as a means 'to penetrate more profoundly than ever into the spirit of philosophy, and to develop the idiosyncratic views of one's predecessors about the grounding of the reality of human cognition further in new views of one's own'. Only if this sort of information concerning previous attempts to solve the problem of philosophy were available could the attempt actually succeed in the end – if mankind is fated to succeed in it at all.

As can be seen, the project of such an investigation presupposes an image of philosophy as a kind of handicraft, something that can be improved by newly invented turns of skill. Each new invention presupposes acquaintance with the turns already in use and with the purposes they serve; but after all the improvements made so far, the principal task remains. Reinhold evidently seems to think of this task as the finding of a universally valid and ultimate turn of skill such that the work completes itself automatically for anyone who can get acquainted with it. If the aim were such an invention, and if science were a lifeless product of alien ingenuity, science would indeed have the perfectibility of which mechanical arts are capable. The preceding philosophical systems would at all times be nothing but practice studies for the big brains. But if the Absolute, like Reason which is its appearance, is eternally one and the same – as indeed it is – then every Reason that is directed toward itself and comes to recognize itself, produces a true philosophy and solves for itself the problem which, like its solution, is at all times the same. In philosophy, Reason comes to know itself and deals only with itself so that its whole work and activity are grounded in itself, and with respect to the inner essence of philosophy there are neither predecessors nor successors.

Nor is it any more correct to speak of *personal views* entertained in philosophy than of its steady improvement. How could the rational be a personal idiosyncrasy? Whatever is thus peculiar in a philosophy must *ipso facto* belong to the form of the system and not to the essence of the philosophy. If something idiosyncratic actually constituted the essence of a philosophy, it would not be a philosophy, though even where the system itself declared its essence to be something idiosyncratic it could nevertheless have sprung from authentic speculation which suffered shipwreck when it tried to express itself in the form of science. One who is caught up in his own idiosyncrasy can see in others only their idiosyncrasies. If one allows personal views to have a place in essential philosophy, and if Reinhold regards what he has recently turned to as a philosophy peculiar to himself, then it is indeed possible generally to regard all preceding ways of presenting and solving the problem of philosophy as merely personal idiosyncrasies and mental exercises. But the exercises are still supposed to prepare the way for the attempt that finally succeeds – for though we see that the shores of those philosophical Islands of the Blest that we yearn for are only littered with the hulks of wrecked ships, and there is no vessel safe at anchor in their bays, yet we must not let go of the teleological perspective.

Fichte dared to assert that Spinoza could not possibly have believed in his philosophy, that he could not possibly have had a full inner living conviction; and he said of the ancients that it is even doubtful that they had a clear conception of the task of philosophy. This, too, must be explained in terms of the idiosyncratic form in which his philosophy expressed itself.

In Fichte, the peculiar form of his own system, the vigor that characterizes it as a whole produces utterances of this sort. The peculiarity of Reinhold's philosophy, on the other hand, consists in its founding and grounding concern with different philosophical views, making a great to-do about the historical investigation of their idiosyncrasies. His love of, and faith in, truth have risen to an elevation so pure and so sickening that in order to found and ground the step into the temple properly, Reinhold has built a spacious vestibule in which philosophy keeps itself so busy with analysis, with methodology and with storytelling, that it saves itself from taking the step altogether; and in the end, as a consolation of his incapacity to do philosophy, Reinhold persuades himself that the bold steps others have taken had been nothing but preparatory exercises or mental confusions.

The essence of philosophy, on the contrary, is a bottomless abyss for personal idiosyncrasy. In order to reach philosophy it is necessary to throw oneself into it *à corps perdu* – meaning by 'body' here, the sum of one's idiosyncrasies. For Reason, finding consciousness caught in particularities, only becomes philosophical speculation by raising itself to itself, putting its trust only in itself and the Absolute which at that moment becomes its object. In this process Reason stakes nothing but finitudes of consciousness. In order to overcome these finitudes and construct the Absolute in consciousness, Reason lifts itself into speculation, and in the groundlessness of the limitations and personal peculiarities it grasps its own grounding within itself. Speculation is the activity of the one universal Reason directed upon itself. Reason, therefore, does not view the philosophical systems of different epochs and different heads merely as different modes [of doing philosophy] and purely idiosyncratic views. Once it has liberated its own view from contingencies and limitations, Reason necessarily finds itself throughout all the particular forms – or else a mere manifold of the concepts and opinions of the intellect; and such a manifold is no philosophy. The true peculiarity of a philosophy lies in the interesting individuality which is the organic shape that Reason has built for itself out of the material of a particular age. The particular speculative Reason [of a later time] finds in it spirit of its spirit, flesh of its flesh, it intuits itself in it as one and the same and yet as another living being. Every philosophy is complete in itself, and like an authentic work of art, carries the totality within itself. Just as the works of Apelles or Sophocles would not have appeared to Raphael and Shakespeare – had they known them – as mere preparatory studies, but as a kindred force of the spirit, so Reason cannot regard its former shapes as merely useful preludes to itself. Virgil, to be sure, regarded Homer to be such a prelude to himself and his refined era, and for this reason Virgil's work remains a mere postlude.

The Need of Philosophy

If we look more closely at the particular form worn by a philosophy we see that it arises, on the one hand, from the living originality of the spirit whose work and spontaneity have re-established and shaped the harmony that has been rent; and on the other hand, from the particular form of the dichotomy from which the system emerges. Dichotomy is the source of *the need of philosophy*; and as the culture of the era, it is the unfree and given aspect of the whole configuration. In [any] culture, the appearance of the Absolute has become isolated from the Absolute and fixated into independence. But at the same time the appearance cannot disown its origin, and must aim to constitute the manifold of its limitations into one whole. The intellect, as the capacity to set limits, erects a building and places it between man and the Absolute, linking everything that man thinks worthy and holy to this building, fortifying it through all the powers of nature and talent and expanding it *ad infinitum*. The entire totality of limitations is to be found in it, but not the Absolute itself. [The Absolute is] lost in the parts, where it drives the intellect in its ceaseless development of manifoldness. But in its striving to enlarge itself into the Absolute, the intellect only reproduces itself *ad infinitum* and so mocks itself. Reason reaches the Absolute only in stepping out of this manifold of parts. The more stable and splendid the edifice of the intellect is, the more restless becomes the striving of the life that is caught up in it as a part to get out of it, and raise itself to freedom. When life as Reason steps away into the distance, the totality of limitations is at the same time nullified, and connected with the Absolute in this nullification, and hence conceived and posited as mere appearance. The split between the Absolute and the totality of limitations vanishes.

The intellect copies Reason's absolute positing and through the form [of absolute positing] it gives itself the semblance of Reason even though the posits are in themselves opposites, and hence finite. The semblance grows that much stronger when intellect transforms and fixes Reason's negating activity [as distinct from its positing activity] into a product. The infinite, in so far as it gets opposed to the finite, is a thing of this kind, i.e., it is something rational as posited by the intellect. Taken by itself, as something rational, it merely expresses the negating of the finite. By fixing it, the intellect sets it up in absolute opposition to the finite; and reflection which had risen to the plane of Reason when it suspended the finite, now lowers itself again to being intellect because it has fixed Reason's activity into [an activity of] opposition. Moreover, reflection still pretends to be rational even in its relapse.

The cultures of various times have established opposites of this kind, which were supposed to be products of Reason and absolutes, in various ways, and the intellect has labored over them as such. Antitheses such as spirit and matter, soul and body, faith and intellect, freedom and necessity, etc. used to be important; and in more limited spheres they appeared in a variety of other guises. The whole weight of human interests hung upon them. With the progress of culture they have passed over into such forms as the antithesis of Reason and sensibility, intelligence and nature and, with respect to the universal concept, of absolute subjectivity and absolute objectivity.

The sole interest of Reason is to suspend such rigid antitheses. But this does not mean that Reason is altogether opposed to opposition and limitation. For the necessary dichotomy is One factor in life. Life eternally forms itself by setting up oppositions, and totality at the highest pitch of living energy [*in der höchsten Lebendigkeit*] is only possible through its own re-establishment out of the deepest fission. What Reason opposes, rather, is just the absolute fixity which the intellect gives to the dichotomy; and it does so all the more if the absolute opposites themselves originated in Reason.

When the might of union vanishes from the life of men and the antitheses lose their living connection and reciprocity and gain independence, the need of philosophy arises. From this point of view the need is contingent. But with respect to the given dichotomy the need is the necessary attempt to suspend the rigidified opposition between subjectivity and objectivity; to comprehend the achieved existence [*das Gewordensein*] of the intellectual and real world as a becoming. Its being as a product must be comprehended as a producing. In the infinite activity of becoming and producing, Reason has united what was sundered and it has reduced the absolute dichotomy to a relative one, one that is conditioned by the original identity. When, where and in what forms such self-reproductions of Reason occur as philosophies is contingent. This contingency must be comprehended on the basis of the Absolute positing itself as an objective totality. The contingency is temporal in so far as the objectivity of the Absolute is intuited as a going forth in time. But in so far as it makes its appearance as spatial compresence, the dichotomy is a matter of regional climate. In the form of fixed reflection, as a world of thinking and thought essence in antithesis to a world of actuality, this dichotomy falls into the Northwest.

As culture grows and spreads, and the development of those outward expressions of life into which dichotomy can entwine itself becomes more manifold, the power of dichotomy becomes greater, its regional sanctity is more firmly established and the strivings of life to give birth once more to its harmony become more meaningless, more alien to the cultural whole. Such few attempts as there have been on behalf of the cultural whole against more recent culture, like the more significant beautiful embodiments of far away or long ago, have only been able to arouse that modicum of attention which remains possible when the more profound, serious connection of living art [to culture as a living whole] can no longer be understood. The entire system of relations constituting life has become detached from art, and thus the concept of art's all-embracing coherence has been lost, and transformed into the concept either of superstition or of entertainment. The highest aesthetic perfection, as it evolves in a determinate religion in which man lifts himself above all dichotomy and sees both the freedom of the subject and the necessity of the object vanish in the kingdom of grace, could only be energized up to a certain stage of culture, and within general or mob barbarism. As it progressed, civilization has split away from it [i.e., this aesthetic religious perfection], and juxtaposed it to itself or vice versa. Because the intellect has grown sure of itself, both [intellect and the aesthetic religious perfection] have come to enjoy a measure of mutual peace by separating into realms that are completely set apart from one another. What happens in one has no significance in the other.

However, the intellect can also be directly attacked by Reason in its own realm. These attempts to nullify the dichotomy, and hence the absoluteness of intellect, through reflection itself are easier to understand. Dichotomy felt itself attacked, and so turned with hate and fury against Reason, until the realm of the intellect rose to such power that it could regard itself as secure from Reason. – But just as we often say of virtue that the greatest witness for its reality is the semblance that hypocrisy borrows from it, so intellect cannot keep Reason off. It seeks to protect itself against the feeling of its inner emptiness, and from the secret fear that plagues anything limited, by whitewashing its particularities with a semblance of Reason. The contempt for Reason shows itself most strongly, not in Reason's being freely scorned and abused, but by the boasting of the limited that it has mastered philosophy and lives in amity with it. Philosophy must refuse friendship with these false attempts that boast insincerely of having nullified the particularities, but which issue from limitation, and use philosophy as a means to save and secure these limitations.

In the struggle of the intellect with Reason the intellect has strength only to the degree that Reason forsakes itself. Its success in the struggle therefore depends upon Reason itself, and upon the authenticity of the need for the reconstitution of totality, the need from which Reason emerges.

The need of philosophy can be called the *presupposition* of philosophy if philosophy, which begins with itself, has to be furnished with some sort of vestibule; and there has been much talk nowadays about an absolute presupposition. What is called the presupposition of philosophy is nothing else but the need that has come to utterance. Once uttered, the need is posited for reflection, so that [because of the very nature of reflection] there must be two presuppositions.

One is the Absolute itself. It is the goal that is being sought; but it is already present, or how otherwise could it be sought? Reason produces it, merely by freeing consciousness from its limitations. This suspension of the limitations is conditioned by the presupposed unlimitedness.

The other presupposition may be taken to be that consciousness has stepped out of the totality, that is, it may be taken to be the split into being and not-being, concept and being, finitude and infinity. From the standpoint of the dichotomy, the absolute synthesis is a beyond, it is the undetermined and the shapeless as opposed to the determinancies of the dichotomy. The Absolute is the night, and the light is younger than it; and the distinction between them, like the emergence of the light out of the night, is an absolute difference – the nothing is the first out of which all being, all the manifoldness of the finite has emerged. But the task of philosophy consists in uniting these presuppositions: to posit being in non-being, as becoming; to posit dichotomy in the Absolute, as its appearance; to posit the finite in the infinite, as life.

Still, it is clumsy to express the need of philosophy as a presupposition of philosophy, for the need acquires in this way a reflective form. This reflective form appears as contradictory propositions, which we shall discuss below. One may require of propositions that they be justified. But the justification of these propositions as presuppositions is still not supposed to be philosophy itself, so that the founding and grounding gets going before, and outside of, philosophy.

Reflection as Instrument of Philosophizing

The form that the need of philosophy would assume, if it were to be expressed as a presupposition, allows for a transition from the need of philosophy to the *instrument of philosophizing*, to *reflection* as Reason. The task of philosophy is to construct the Absolute for consciousness. But since the productive activity of reflection is, like its products, mere limitation, this task involves a contradiction. The Absolute is to be posited in reflection. But then it is not posited, but cancelled; for in having been posited it was limited [by its opposite]. Philosophical reflection is the mediation of this contradiction. What must be shown above all is how far reflection is capable of grasping the Absolute, and how far in its speculative activity it carries with it the necessity and possibility of being synthesized with absolute intuition. To what extent can reflection be as complete for itself, subjectively, as its product must be, which is constructed in consciousness as the Absolute that is both conscious and non-conscious at the same time?

Reflection in isolation is the positing of opposites, and this would be a suspension of the Absolute, reflection being the faculty of being and limitation. But reflection as Reason has connection with the Absolute, and it is Reason only because of this connection. In this respect, reflection nullifies itself and all being and everything limited, because it connects them with the Absolute. But at the same time the limited gains standing precisely on account of its connection with the Absolute.

Reason presents itself as the force of the negative Absolute, and hence as a negating that is absolute; and at the same time, it presents itself as the force that posits the opposed objective and subjective totality. Reason raises the intellect above itself, driving it toward a whole of the intellect's own kind. Reason seduces the intellect into producing an objective totality. Every being, because it is posited, is an opposite, it is conditioned and conditioning. The intellect completes these its limitations by positing the opposite limitations as conditions. These need to be completed in the same way, so the intellect's task expands *ad infinitum*. In all this, reflection appears to be merely intellect, but this guidance toward the totality of necessity is the contribution and secret efficacy of Reason. Reason makes the intellect boundless, and in this infinite wealth the intellect and its objective world meet their downfall. For every being that the intellect produces is something determinate, and the determinate has an indeterminate before it and after it. The manifoldness of being lies between two nights, without support. It rests on nothing – for the indeterminate is nothing to the intellect – and it ends in nothing. The determinate and the indeterminate, finitude and the infinite that is to be given up for lost, are not united. The intellect stubbornly allows them to subsist side by side in their opposition. And stubbornly it holds fast to being as against not-being; yet being and not-being are equally necessary to it. The intellect essentially aims at thoroughgoing determination. But what is determinate for it is at once bounded by an indeterminate. Thus its positings and determinings never accomplish the task; in the very positing and determining that have occurred there lies a non-positing and something indeterminate, and hence the task of positing and determining recurs perpetually.

If the intellect fixes these opposites, the finite and the infinite, so that both are supposed to subsist together as opposed to each other, then it destroys itself. For the opposition of finite and infinite means that to posit the one is to cancel the other. When Reason recognizes this, it has suspended the intellect itself. Its positing then appears to Reason to be non-positing, its products to be negations. If Reason is placed in opposition to the objective infinite, this nullification of the intellect or Reason's pure positing without opposing is subjective infinity: the realm of freedom as opposed to the objective world. But in this form, the realm of freedom is itself something opposite and conditioned. In order to suspend opposition absolutely, Reason must also nullify the independence of this realm. It nullifies both of the opposed realms by uniting them; for they only are in virtue of their not being united. Within the union, however, they subsist together; for what is opposite and therefore limited is, in this union, connected with the Absolute. But it does not have standing on its own account, but only in so far as it is posited in the Absolute, that is, as identity. The limited is either necessary or free, according to whether it belongs to one or the other of the mutually opposed and therefore relative totalities. In so far as the limited belongs to the synthesis of both totalities, its limitation ceases: it is free and necessary at the same time, conscious and nonconscious. This conscious identity of the finite and infinite, the union of both worlds, the sensuous and the intelligible, the necessary and the free, in consciousness, is *knowledge*. Reflection, the faculty of the finite, and the infinite opposed to it are synthesized in Reason whose infinity embraces the finite within it.

So far as reflection makes itself its own object, its supreme law, given to it by Reason and moving it to become Reason, is to nullify itself. Like everything else, reflection has standing only in the Absolute; but as reflection it stands in opposition to it. In order to gain standing, therefore, reflection must give itself the law of self-destruction. The immanent law, the law through which reflection by its own power would constitute itself as absolute, would be the law of contradiction: namely that, being posited, reflection shall be and remain posited. Reflection would thus fix its products as absolutely opposed to the Absolute. It would have as its eternal law to remain intellect and not to become Reason and to hold fast to its own work, which, as limited, is opposed to the Absolute and as opposed to the Absolute, is nothing.

When placed in an opposition, Reason operates as intellect and its infinity becomes subjective. Similarly, the form which expresses the activity of reflecting as an activity of thinking, is capable of this very same ambiguity and misuse. Thinking is the absolute activity of Reason itself and there simply cannot be anything opposite to it. But if it is not so posited, if it is taken to be nothing but reflection of a purer kind, that is, a reflection in which one merely abstracts from the opposition, then thinking of this abstracting kind cannot advance beyond the intellect, not even to a Logic supposed capable of comprehending Reason within itself, still less to philosophy.

Reinhold sets up identity as 'the essence or inward character of thinking as such': 'the infinite repeatability of one and the same as one and the same, in and through one and the same'. One might be tempted by this semblance of identity into regarding this thinking as Reason. But because this thinking has its antithesis (a) in an application of thinking and (b) in absolute materiality [*Stoffheit*], it is clear that this is not the absolute identity, the identity of subject and object which suspends both in their opposition and grasps them within itself, but a *pure* identity, that is, an identity originating through abstraction and conditioned by opposition, the abstract intellectual concept of unity, one of a pair of fixed opposites.

Reinhold sees the fault of all past philosophy in 'the habit, so deeply rooted and widespread among contemporary philosophers, of regarding thinking both in general and in its application as something merely subjective'. If Reinhold were truly serious about the identity and non-subjectivity of this thinking, he could not make any distinction between thinking and its application. If thinking is true identity, and not something subjective, where could this application that is so distinct from it come from, let alone the stuff that is postulated for the sake of the application? To the analytic method an activity must appear to be synthetic precisely because it is to be analysed. The elements that originate in the analysis are unity and a manifold opposed to it. What analysis presents as unity is called subjective; and thinking is characterized as a unity of this sort opposed to the manifold, that is, it is an abstract identity. In this way thinking has become something purely limited, and its activity is an application [of the identity] to some independently extant material, an application which conforms to a law and is directed by a rule, but which cannot pierce through to knowledge.

Only so far as reflection has connection with the Absolute is it Reason and its deed a knowing. Through this connection with the Absolute, however, reflection's work passes away; only the connection persists, and it is the sole reality of the cognition. There is therefore no truth in isolated reflection, in pure thinking, save the truth of its nullification. But because in philosophizing the Absolute gets produced by reflection for consciousness, it becomes thereby an objective totality, a whole of knowledge, an organization of cognitions. Within this organization, every part is at the same time the whole; for its standing is its connection with the Absolute. As a part that has other parts outside of it, it is something limited, and is only through the others. Isolated in its limitation the part is defective; meaning and significance it has solely through its coherence with the whole. Hence single concepts by themselves and singular cognitions [*Erkenntnisse*] must not be called knowledge. There can be plenty of singular empirical known items [*Kenntnisse*]. As known from experience they exhibit their justification in experience, that is, in the identity of concept and being, of subject and object. Precisely for this reason, they are not scientific knowledge: they find their justification only in a limited, relative identity. They do not justify themselves as necessary parts of a totality of cognitions organized in consciousness, nor has speculation recognized the absolute identity in them, i.e., their connection with the Absolute.

Relation of Speculation to Common Sense

What the so-called common sense takes to be the rational, consists similarly of single items drawn out of the Absolute into consciousness. They are points of light that rise out of the night of totality and aid men to get through life in an intelligent way. They serve as correct standpoints from which one takes off and to which one returns.

In fact, however, men only have this confidence in the truth of these points of light because they have a feeling of the Absolute attending these points; and it is this feeling alone that gives them their significance. As soon as one takes these truths of common sense by themselves and isolates them as cognitions of the intellect, they look odd and turn into half-truths. Reflection can confound common sense. When common sense permits itself to reflect, the proposition it states for the benefit of reflection claims to be by itself knowledge and valid cognition. Thus sound sense has given up its strength, the strength of supporting its pronouncements and counteracting unsteady reflection solely by the obscure totality which is present as feeling. Although common sense expresses itself for reflection, its dicta do not contain the consciousness of their connection with the absolute totality. The totality remains inward and unexpressed.

For this reason, speculation understands sound intellect well enough, but the sound intellect cannot understand what speculation is doing. Speculation acknowledges as the reality of cognition only the being of cognition in the totality. For speculation everything determinate has reality and truth only in the cognition of its connection with the Absolute. So it recognizes the Absolute in what lies at the basis of the pronouncements of sound sense too. But since, for speculation, cognition has reality only within the Absolute, what is cognized and known in the reflective mode of expression and therefore has a determinate form, becomes nothing in the presence of speculation. The relative identities of common sense which pretend to absoluteness in the limited form in which they appear, become contingencies for philosophical reflection. Common sense cannot grasp how what has immediate certainty for it, can at the same time be nothing to philosophy. For in its immediate truths it only feels their connection with the Absolute, and it does not separate this feeling from their appearance, wherein they are limitations, and yet they are supposed as such to have standing and absolute being. But in the face of speculation they vanish.

Common sense cannot understand speculation; and what is more, it must come to hate speculation when it has experience of it; and, unless it is in the state of perfect indifference that security confers, it is bound to detest and persecute it. For common sense, the essential and the contingent in its utterances are identical and this identity is absolute; and, just as it cannot separate the limits of appearance from the Absolute, so what it does separate in its consciousness, becomes absolutely opposed, and what it cognizes as limited it cannot in consciousness unite with the unlimited. Limited and unlimited are, to be sure, identical for common sense, but this identity is and remains something internal, a feeling, something unknown and unexpressed. Whenever it calls the limited to mind, and the limited is raised into consciousness, the unlimited is for consciousness absolutely opposed to the limited.

In this relation or connection of the limited with the Absolute there is consciousness of their opposition only; there is no consciousness at all of their identity. This relation is called *faith*. Faith does not express the synthesis inherent in feeling or intuition. It is, rather, a relation of reflection to the Absolute, and one in which reflection is certainly Reason. But though it nullifies itself as something that sunders and is sundered, and also nullifies its product too – an individual consciousness – it still preserves the form of sundering. The immediate certitude of faith, which has been much talked of as the ultimate and highest consciousness, is nothing but the identity itself, Reason, which, however, does not recognize itself, and is accompanied by the consciousness of opposition. Speculation, however, lifts the identity of which sound sense is not conscious into consciousness. In other words, speculation constructs conscious identity out of what, in the consciousness of the ordinary intellect, are necessarily opposites; and this synthesis of what is sundered in faith is an abomination to faith. In its consciousness the holy and the divine only have standing as objects. So the healthy intellect sees only destruction of the divine in the suspended opposition, in the identity brought into consciousness.

In particular, ordinary common sense is bound to see nothing but nullification in those philosophical systems that satisfy the demand for conscious identity by suspending dichotomy in such a way that one of the opposites is raised to be the absolute and the other nullified. This is particularly offensive if the culture of the time has already fixed one of the opposites otherwise. Speculation, as philosophy, has here indeed suspended the opposition, but speculation, as system, has elevated something which in its ordinary familiar form is limited, to absolute status. The only aspect here relevant is the speculative, and this is simply not present for ordinary common sense. Viewed from this speculative aspect, the limited is something totally different from what it appears to ordinary common sense; having been elevated into being the Absolute, it is no longer the limited thing that it was. The matter of the materialist is no longer inert matter which has life as its opposite and its formative agent; the Ego of the idealist is no longer an empirical consciousness which, as limited, must posit an infinite outside itself. The question that philosophy has to raise is whether the system has truly purified all finitude out of the finite appearance that it has advanced to absolute status; or whether speculation, even at its furthest distance from ordinary common sense with its typical fixation of opposites, has not still succumbed to the fate of its time, the fate of positing absolutely one form of the Absolute, that is, something that is essentially an opposite. But even where speculation has actually succeeded in freeing from all forms of appearance the finite which it has made infinite, ordinary common sense primarily takes offense over the name though it may take no other notice of the business of speculation. Speculation does indeed elevate finite things – matter, the Ego – to the infinite and thus nullifies them: matter and Ego so far as they are meant to embrace totality, are no longer matter and Ego. Yet the final act of philosophical reflection is still lacking: that is to say, the consciousness of the nullification of these finite things. And even though the Absolute within the system has still preserved a determinate form, in spite of the fact that this nullification has actually been accomplished, still the genuinely speculative tendency is unmistakable anyway. But ordinary common sense understands nothing about it, and does not even see the philosophic principle of suspending the dichotomy. It only sees the systematic principle by which one of the opposites is raised to the Absolute and the other nullified. So it has an advantage over the system with respect to the dichotomy. For there is an absolute opposition present in both of them. But in ordinary common sense there is *completeness* of opposition [whereas the system makes one of the opposites explicitly absolute]; and hence common sense is enraged on two counts.

Nevertheless, apart from its philosophical side, there accrues to a philosophical system of this kind, encumbered as it is with the defect of raising to the Absolute something that is still in some respect an opposite, another advantage and a further merit, which are not only incomprehensible but must be abhorrent to the ordinary intellect. The advantage is that by raising something finite to an infinite principle, the system has struck down with one stroke the whole mass of finitudes that adhere to the opposite principle. And the merit with regard to culture consists in having made the dichotomy that much more rigid and hence strengthened the urge toward unification in totality in the same measure.

Common sense is stubborn; it stubbornly believes itself secure in the force of its inertia, believes the non-conscious secure in its primordial gravity and opposition to consciousness; believes matter secure against the difference that light brings into it just in order to reconstruct the difference into a new synthesis at a higher level. In northern climates this stubbornness perhaps requires a longer period of time to be so far conquered that the atomic matter itself has become more diversified, and inertia has first been set in motion on its own ground by a greater variety of their combination and dissolution and next by the multitude of fixed atoms thus generated. Thus the human intellect becomes more and more confused in its own proper doings and knowings, to the point where it makes itself capable of enduring the suspension of this confusion and the opposition itself.

The only aspect of speculation visible to common sense is its nullifying activity; and even this nullification is not visible in its entire scope. If common sense could grasp this scope, it would not believe speculation to be its enemy. For in its highest synthesis of the conscious and the non-conscious, speculation also demands the nullification of consciousness itself. Reason thus drowns itself and its knowledge and its reflection of the absolute identity, in its own abyss: and in this night of mere reflection and of the calculating intellect, in this night which is the noonday of life, common sense and speculation can meet one another.

Principle of a Philosophy in the Form of an Absolute Basic Proposition

Philosophy, as a totality of knowledge produced by reflection, becomes a system, that is, an organic whole of concepts, whose highest law is not the intellect, but Reason. The intellect has to exhibit correctly the opposites of what it has posited, as well as its bounds, ground and condition. Reason, on the other hand, unites these contradictories, posits both together and suspends them both. One might demand that the system as an organization of propositions should present the Absolute which lies at the basis of reflection in the fashion of reflection, that is, as the highest, or absolutely fundamental proposition. But such a demand at once entails its own nullity. For a proposition, as something posited by reflection, is something limited and conditioned on its own account. It requires another proposition as its foundation, and so on *ad infinitum*. Suppose that the Absolute is expressed in a fundamental proposition, validated by and for thinking, a proposition whose form and matter are the same. Then either mere sameness is posited, and the inequality of form and matter is excluded, so that the fundamental proposition is conditioned by this inequality. In this case the fundamental proposition is not absolute but defective; it expresses only a concept of the intellect, an abstraction. Or else the fundamental proposition also contains both form and matter as inequality, so that it is analytic and synthetic simultaneously. In that case the fundamental proposition is an antinomy, and therefore not a proposition. As a proposition it is subject to the law of the intellect, the law that it must not contradict itself, that it cannot suspend itself, that it be something posited. As an antinomy, however, it does suspend itself.

It is a delusion that something merely posited for reflection must necessarily stand at the summit of a system as the highest or absolute and basic proposition; or that the essence of any system is expressible as a proposition that has absolute validity for thinking. This delusion makes the business of judging a system easy. For of any thought expressed by a proposition it can be shown very easily that it is conditioned by an opposite and therefore is not absolute: and one proves for this opposite that it must be posited, hence that the thought expressed by the fundamental proposition is a nullity. The delusion accounts itself all the more justified if the system itself expresses the Absolute which is its principle, in the form of a proposition or definition which is basically an antinomy, and for this reason suspends itself as something posited for mere reflection. For example, Spinoza's concept of substance, defined as both cause and effect, concept and being, ceases to be a concept because the opposites are united in a contradiction.

No philosophical beginning could look worse than to begin with a definition as Spinoza does. This offers the starkest contrast to 'founding and grounding', or the 'deduction of the principles of knowledge', or the laborious reduction of all philosophy to the 'highest facts of consciousness', etc. But when Reason has purified itself of the subjectivity of reflection, then Spinoza's artlessness which makes philosophy begin with philosophy itself, and Reason come forward at once with an antinomy, can be properly appreciated too.

If the principle of philosophy is to be stated in formal propositions for reflection, the only thing that is present, at the outset, as the object of this task is knowledge, i.e., in general terms the synthesis of the subjective and objective, or absolute thinking. But reflection cannot express the absolute synthesis in one proposition, if this proposition has to be valid as a proper proposition for the intellect. Reflection must separate what is one in the absolute Identity; it must express synthesis and antithesis separately, in two propositions, one containing the identity, the other dichotomy.

In $A = A$, as principle of identity, it is connectedness that is reflected on, and in this connecting, this being one, the equality, is contained in this pure identity; reflection abstracts from all inequality. $A = A$, the expression of absolute thought or Reason, has only one meaning for the formal reflection that expresses itself in the propositions of the intellect. This is the meaning of pure unity as conceived by the intellect, or in other words a unity in abstraction from opposition.

Reason, however, does not find itself expressed in this onesidedness of abstract unity. It postulates also the positing of what in the pure equality had been abstracted from, the positing of the opposite, of inequality. One A is subject, the other object; and the expression of their difference is $A \neq A$, or $A = B$. This proposition directly contradicts the first. It abstracts from pure identity and posits the non-identity, the pure form of non-thinking, just as the first proposition is the form of pure thinking, which is not the same thing as absolute thinking, or Reason. Only because non-thinking, too, is thought, only because $A \neq A$ is posited through thinking, can it be posited at all. In $A \neq A$, or $A = B$ there also is the identity, the connection, the '=' of the first proposition, but it is here only subjective, that is, only in so far as non-thinking is posited by thinking. But if non-thinking is posited for thinking this is entirely incidental to the non-thinking, it is a mere form for the second proposition. One must abstract from this form in order to have its matter pure.

This second proposition is as unconditioned as the first and *qua* unconditioned it is condition of the first, as the first is condition of the second. The first is conditioned by the second in that it is what it is through abstraction from the inequality that the second proposition contains; the second conditioned by the first, in that it is in need of a connection in order to be a proposition.

The second proposition has also been stated in the subordinate form of the principle of sufficient reason. Or rather, it was first brought down to this extremely subordinate meaning when it was turned into the principle of causality. A has a ground means: to A pertains an existence that is not an existence of A: A is a being posited that is not the being posited of A. Hence, $A \neq A$, $A = B$. If one abstracts from A's being something posited, as one must in order to have the second proposition in its purity, it expresses A's not being posited. To posit A as something posited and also as something not posited is already the synthesis of the first and second propositions.

Both propositions are principles of contradiction, but in an inverse sense. The first, the principle of identity, states that contradiction is $= 0$. The second proposition, in so far as one relates it to the first, states that contradiction is as necessary as non-contradiction. Taken separately (*für sich*) both propositions are posits on the same level. [But] if the second one is so stated that the first proposition is connected with it at the same time, then it is the highest possible expression of Reason by the intellect. This connection of the two propositions expresses the antinomy; and as an antinomy, as an expression of the absolute identity, it makes no difference whether we posit $A = A$ or $A = B$ as long as each of them, $A = B$ and $A = A$, is taken as connection of both propositions. $A = A$ contains the difference of A as subject and A as object together with their identity, just as $A = B$ contains the identity of A and B together with their difference.

The intellect has not grown into Reason if it does not recognize the antinomy in the principle of sufficient reason which is a connection of both propositions. In that case the second proposition is not, *formaliter*, a new one for it: for the mere intellect $A = B$ does not say more than the first proposition and consequently it conceives A's being posited as B only as a repetition of A. That is to say, the intellect just holds fast to the identity and abstracts from the fact that when A is repeated as B or as posited in B, something else, a non-A, is posited and posited as A, hence, A is posited as non-A. If one reflects only on the formal aspect of speculation and holds fast to the synthesis of knowledge [only] in analytic form, then antinomy, that is, the contradiction that cancels itself, is the highest formal expression of knowledge and truth.

Once antinomy is acknowledged as the explicit formula of truth, Reason has brought the formal essence of reflection under its control. The formal essence still has the upper hand, however, if thought, [conceived merely] in its character of abstract unity, i.e., exclusively in the form of the first proposition as opposed to the second, is posited as the first truth of philosophy, and a system of the reality of cognition is supposed to be erected by analysis of the application of thinking. In that case, the entire course of this purely analytic business will be as follows:

Thought, as infinite repeatability of A as A, is an abstraction, the first proposition expressed as activity. But now the second proposition is lacking, the non-thought. There must necessarily be a transition to it as the condition of the first; it, too, i.e., the matter, must be posited. Then the opposites will be complete; the transition from the first to the second is a certain kind of reciprocal connection between them, which is a very inadequate synthesis called an application of thought. But even this weak synthesis goes counter to the presupposition that thought is a positing of A as A *ad infinitum*. For in the *application*, A is at the same time posited as non-A; and thought, in its absolute standing as infinite repetition of A as A, is suspended.

What is opposite to thought is, through its connection with thought, determined as something thought $= A$. But such a thought, such a positing $= A$ is conditioned by an abstraction and is hence something opposite. Hence, that which is thought, besides the fact that it has been thought $= A$, has still other determinations $= B$, entirely independent of being merely determined [as something thought] by pure thought. These other determinations are brute data for thought. Hence for thought as the principle of the analytic way of philosophizing, there must be an absolute stuff. We shall discuss this further below. With this absolute opposition as foundation the formal programme, in which the famous discovery that philosophy must be reduced to logic consists, is allowed no immanent synthesis save that provided by the identity of the intellect, i.e., the repetition of A *ad infinitum*. But even for this repetition the identity needs some B, C, etc. in which the repeated A can be posited. In order for A to be repeatable, B, C, D, etc. have to be [literally 'are'] a manifold, in which each is opposed to the other. Each of them has particular determinations not posited by A. That is to say, there exists an absolutely manifold stuff. Its B, C, D, etc. must *fit in* with A, as best it can. This fitting in without rhyme or reason takes the place of an original identity. The basic fault can be presented as follows. There is no reflection, in respect to form, on the antinomy of the A = A and A = B. This whole analytic approach lacks the basic consciousness that the purely formal appearance of the Absolute is contradiction. Such consciousness can only come into being where speculation takes its point of departure in Reason and in the A = A as absolute identity of subject and object.

Transcendental Intuition

When speculation is viewed from the standpoint of mere reflection, the absolute identity appears in syntheses of opposites, i.e., in antinomies. The relative identities into which absolute identity differentiates itself are limited to be sure; they belong to the intellect and are not antinomic. At the same time, however, since they are identities, they are not pure concepts of the intellect. And they must be identities because nothing can stand as posited in a philosophy unless it is connected with the Absolute. But on the side of its connection with the Absolute, everything limited is a (relative) identity and hence something that is antinomic for reflection. – And this is the negative side of knowing, the formal aspect which, ruled by Reason, destroys itself. Besides this negative side knowing has a positive side, namely intuition. Pure knowing, which would be knowing without intuition, is the nullification of the opposites in contradiction. Intuition without this synthesis of opposites, [on the other hand,] is empirical, given, non-conscious. Transcendental knowledge unites both reflection and intuition. It is at once concept and being. Because intuition becomes transcendental, the identity of the subjective and objective, which are separated in empirical intuition, enters consciousness. Knowledge, in so far as it becomes transcendental, posits not merely the concept and its condition – or the antinomy of both, the subjective – but at the same time the objective, that is, being.

In philosophical knowledge, what is intuited is an activity of both intelligence and nature, of consciousness and the unconscious together. It belongs to both worlds at once, the ideal and the real. It belongs to the ideal world because it is posited in the intelligence and, hence, in freedom. It belongs to the real world because it gets its place in the objective totality, it is deduced as a link in the chain of necessity. If we take up the standpoint of reflection or freedom, the ideal is the first, and essence and being are only schematized intelligence. If we take up the standpoint of necessity or being, thought is only a schema of absolute being. In transcendental knowledge both being and intelligence are united. Likewise, transcendental knowledge and transcendental intuition are one and the same. The variation of expression merely indicates the prevalence of the ideal or real factor.

It is of the profoundest significance that it has been affirmed with so much seriousness that one cannot philosophize without transcendental intuition. For what would this be, philosophizing without intuition? One would disperse oneself endlessly in absolute finitudes. Whether these finitudes are subjective concepts or objective things and even though one may pass from one to the other, philosophizing without intuition moves along an endless chain of finitudes, and the transition from being to concept or from concept to being is an unjustified leap. Philosophizing of this sort is called formal. For thing as well as concept is, each taken by itself, just a form of the Absolute. Formal philosophizing presupposes destruction of the transcendental intuition, an absolute opposition of being and concept. If it talks of the unconditioned, it converts even that into something formal, say the form of an Idea that is opposed to Being for instance. The better the method, the more glaring the results. To speculation, [on the contrary,] the finitudes are radii of the infinite focus which irradiates them at the same time that it is formed by them. In the radii the focus is posited and in the focus the radii. In the transcendental intuition all opposition is suspended, all distinction between the universe as constructed by and for the intelligence, and the universe as an organization intuited as objective and appearing independent, is nullified. Speculation produces the consciousness of this identity, and because ideality and reality are one in it, it is intuition.

Postulates of Reason

As a work of reflection the synthesis of the two opposites posited by reflection required its completion; as antinomy that suspends itself, it needs its standing in intuition. Speculative knowledge has to be conceived as identity of reflection and intuition. So if one posits only the share of reflection, which, as rational, is antinomic, but stands in a necessary connection with intuition, one can in that case say of intuition that it is postulated by reflection. Postulating Ideas is out of the question; for Ideas are the products of Reason or rather, they are the rational, posited as a product by the intellect. The rational must be deduced in its determinate content, that is, it must be deduced starting from the contradiction of determinate opposites, the rational being their synthesis. The only thing that can be postulated is the intuition that fills and sustains this antinomic aspect. This sort of 'Idea' that used to get postulated, is the 'infinite progress', which is a mixture of empirical and rational elements: the intuition of time is empirical, while the suspension of all time, its expansion to infinity [*Verunendlichung*] is rational. But in the empirical progress, time is not purely infinitized, for in this progress time is supposed to have standing as something finite, as limited moments. It is an empirical infinitude. The true antinomy which posits both the limited and unlimited, not just side by side but together as identical, must *ipso facto* suspend the opposition. The antinomy postulates the determinate intuition of time, and this determinate intuition must be both the limited moment of the present and the unlimitedness of the moment's being self-externalized [*Aussersichgesetztsein*]. That is to say, it must be eternity. –

It is equally impossible to postulate intuition as something that is opposed to the Idea or rather, to the necessary antinomy. The intuition that is opposed to the Idea is a limited existent, precisely because it excludes the Idea. Intuition is indeed postulated by Reason, but not as something limited; it is postulated in order to complement the one-sidedness of the work of reflection in such a way that the intuitive complement does not remain opposed to reflection but is one with it. In general one can see that this whole manner of postulating has its sole ground in the fact that the one-sidedness of reflection is accepted as a starting point. This one-sidedness requires, as the complement of its deficiency, the postulation of the opposite that is excluded from it. But this point of view places the essence of Reason in distorted perspective, for it here appears as something that is not self-sufficient but needy. When Reason recognizes itself as absolute, however, philosophy begins where reflection and its style of thinking ends, that is, it begins with the identity of Idea and Being. Philosophy does not have to postulate one of the opposites, for in positing absoluteness it immediately posits both Idea and Being, and the absoluteness of Reason is nothing else but the identity of both.

Relation of Philosophizing to a Philosophical System

The need of philosophy can satisfy itself by simply penetrating to the principle of nullifying all fixed opposition and connecting the limited to the Absolute. This satisfaction found in the principle of absolute identity is characteristic of philosophy as such. [For a philosophizing that did no more than this] the known, as to its content, would be something contingent; the dichotomies, from whose nullification the known emerged, would have been given and would have vanished, but they would not themselves be reconstructed syntheses. The content of such philosophizing would have no internal coherence and would not constitute an objective totality of knowledge. But the philosophizing would not necessarily be abstract reasoning simply on account of the incoherence of its content. Abstract reasoning only disperses the posited into ever greater manifoldness; thrown into this stream the intellect drifts without an anchor, yet the whole extension of its manifold is supposed to stand fast unanchored. For true philosophizing on the other hand, even though it may be incoherent, the posited and its opposites disappear because it does not simply put them in context with other finite things, but connects them with the Absolute and so suspends them.

Since the finite things are a manifold, the connection of the finite to the Absolute is a manifold. Hence, philosophizing must aim to posit this manifold as internally connected, and there necessarily arises the need to produce a totality of knowing, a system of science. As a result, the manifold of these connections finally frees itself from contingency: they get their places in the context of the objective totality of knowledge and their objective completeness is accomplished. The philosophizing that does not construct itself into a system is a constant flight from limitations – it is Reason's struggle for freedom rather than the pure self-cognition of Reason that has become secure in itself and clear about itself. Free Reason and its action are one, and Reason's activity is a pure self-exposition.

In this self-production of Reason the Absolute shapes itself into an objective totality, which is a whole in itself held fast and complete, having no ground outside itself, but founded by itself in its beginning, middle and end. A whole of this sort appears as an organization of propositions and intuitions. Every synthesis of Reason is united in speculation with the intuition corresponding to it; as identity of the conscious and non-conscious it is for itself in the Absolute and infinite. But at the same time, the synthesis is finite and limited, in so far as it is posited within the objective totality and has other syntheses outside itself. The identity that is least dichotomous – at the objective pole, matter, at the subjective pole, feeling (self-consciousness) – is at the same time an infinitely opposed identity, a thoroughly relative identity. Reason, the faculty of totality (*qua* objective totality), complements this relative identity with its opposite, producing through their synthesis a new identity which is in turn a defective one in the face of Reason, and which completes itself anew in the same way. The method of the system should be called neither synthetic nor analytic. It shows itself at its purest, when it appears as a development of Reason itself. Reason does not recall its appearance, which emanates from it as a duplicate, back into itself – for then, it would only nullify it. Rather, Reason constructs itself in its emanation as an identity that is conditioned by this very duplicate; it opposes this relative identity to itself once more, and in this way the system advances until the objective totality is completed. Reason then unites this objective totality with the opposite subjective totality to form the infinite world-intuition, whose expansion has at the same time contracted into the richest and simplest identity.

It can happen that an authentic speculation does not express itself completely in its system, or that the philosophy of the system and the system itself do not coincide. A system may express the tendency to nullify all oppositions in the most definite way, and yet not pierce through to the most perfect identity on its own account. So in judging philosophical systems it is particularly important to distinguish the philosophy from the system. If the fundamental need has not achieved perfect embodiment in the system, if it has elevated to the Absolute something that is conditioned and that exists only as an opposite, then as a system it becomes dogmatism. Yet true speculation can be found in the most divergent philosophies, in philosophies that decry one another as sheer dogmatism or as mental aberration. The history of philosophy only has value and interest if it holds fast to this viewpoint. For otherwise, it will not give us the history of the one, eternal Reason, presenting itself in infinitely manifold forms; instead it will give us nothing but a tale of the accidental vicissitudes of the human spirit and of senseless opinions, which the teller imputes to Reason, though they should be laid only to his own charge, because he does not recognize what is rational in them, and so turns them inside out.

An authentic speculation, even when it does not succeed in constructing itself completely into a system, necessarily begins from the absolute identity. The dichotomy of the absolute identity into subjective and objective is a production by [or of] the Absolute. The basic principle, then, is completely transcendental, and from its standpoint there is no absolute opposition of the subjective and objective. But as a result the appearance of the Absolute is an opposition. The Absolute is not in its appearance, they are themselves opposites. The appearance is not identity. This opposition cannot be suspended transcendentally, that is to say, it cannot be suspended in such a fashion that there is no opposition in principle [*an sich*]. For then appearance would just be nullified, whereas it is supposed to have being just like [the Absolute does]. It is as if one were to claim that the Absolute, in its appearance, had stepped out of itself. So, the Absolute must posit itself in the appearance itself, i.e., it must not nullify appearance but must construct it into identity.

The causal relation between the Absolute and its appearance is a false identity; for absolute opposition is at the basis of this relation. In the causal relation both opposites have standing, but they are distinct in rank. The union is forcible. The one subjugates the other. The one rules, the other is subservient. The unity is forced, and forced into a mere relative identity. The identity which *ought* to be absolute, *is* incomplete. Contrary to its philosophy, the system has turned into a dogmatism, it has either turned into realism positing objectivity absolutely, or into idealism positing subjectivity absolutely. Yet both realism and idealism emerged from authentic speculation, though this is more doubtful with respect to realism than to idealism.

Pure dogmatism, if it is a dogmatism of philosophy, remains within the opposition even as a tendency. The basic governing principle in it is the relation of causality in its more complete form as reciprocal interaction: the intelligible realm has effects upon the sensible realm or the sensible upon the intelligible. In consistent realism and idealism the relation of causality plays only a subordinate role, even though it appears to govern – for in realism the subject is posited as produced by the object, and in idealism the object as produced by the subject. But the causal relation is essentially suspended, for the producing is an absolute producing, the product an absolute product; that is to say, the product has no standing apart from the producing; it is not posited as something self-sustaining, as something that has standing prior to and independent of the producing, as is the case with the pure causality relation, the formal principle of dogmatism. In dogmatism, the product is something posited by A and also, at the same time, not posited by A, so A is absolutely only subject, and A = A expresses merely an identity of the intellect. Even though philosophy in its transcendental business makes use of the causal relation yet B, which appears to be opposed to the subject, is in its oppositeness a mere possibility and it remains absolutely a possibility, i.e., it is only an accident. Thus the true relation of speculation, the substantiality relation [i.e., the relation of substance and accident] is the transcendental principle, though it appears under the guise of the causal relation. Or again, we might express this formally thus: genuine dogmatism acknowledges both principles A = A and A = B, but they remain in their antinomy side by side, unsynthesized. Dogmatism does not recognize that there is an antinomy in this and hence does not recognize the necessity of suspending the subsistence of the opposites. The transition from one to the other by way of the causality relation is the only synthesis possible to dogmatism, and this is an incomplete synthesis.

Notwithstanding this sharp difference between transcendental philosophy and dogmatism, the former is apt to pass over into the latter, when it constructs itself into a system. This is the case if transcendental philosophy while [rightly] refusing to allow any real causal relation on the ground that nothing exists but the absolute identity in which all difference and standing of opposites is suspended, yet introduces the causality relation, in so far as appearance is also supposed to have a standing so that the Absolute must have a relation to appearance other than that of nullification. Thus appearance is turned into something subservient, and likewise transcendental intuition is posited as something merely subjective and not objective, which is to say that the identity is not posited in the appearance. A = A and A = B remain both unconditioned whereas only A = A *ought* to be absolutely valid; that is, their identity is not set forth in their true synthesis which is no mere ought.

Thus in Fichte's system Ego = Ego in the Absolute. The totality sought by Reason leads to the second proposition which posits a non-Ego. Not only is this antinomy of the positing of both complete, but also their synthesis is postulated. But in this synthesis the opposition remains. It is not the case that both, Ego as well as non-Ego, are to be nullified, but one proposition is to survive, is to be higher in rank than the other. The speculation at the basis of the system demands the suspension of the opposites, but the system itself does not suspend them. The absolute synthesis which the system achieves is not Ego = Ego, but Ego *ought* to be equal to Ego. The Absolute is constructed for the transcendental viewpoint but not for the viewpoint of appearance. Both still contradict each other. The identity was not also placed in the appearance, or [in other words] the identity did not also pass completely into objectivity. Therefore transcendentality is itself something opposite, the subjective. One may also say that the appearance was not completely nullified.

In the following presentation of Fichte's system an attempt will be made to show that pure consciousness, the identity of subject and object, established as absolute in the system, is a *subjective* identity of subject and object. The presentation will proceed by showing that the Ego, the principle of the system, is a subjective Subject–Object. This will be shown directly, as well as by inspecting [not only] the deduction of nature, [but also] and particularly, the relations of identity in the special sciences of morality and natural law and the relation of the whole system to the aesthetic sphere.

It will be clear from what has been said that we are concerned in this presentation with Fichte's philosophy as a system and not as authentic philosophizing. As philosophy it is the most thorough and profound speculation, all the more remarkable because at the time when it appeared even the Kantian philosophy had proved unable to awaken Reason to the lost concept of genuine speculation.

Translated by H. S. Harris and Walter Cerf

Phenomenology of Spirit

INTRODUCTION

It is a natural assumption that in philosophy, before we start to deal with its proper subject-matter, viz. the actual cognition of what truly is, one must first of all come to an understanding about cognition, which is regarded either as the instrument to get hold of the Absolute, or as the medium through which one discovers it. A certain uneasiness seems justified, partly because there are different types of cognition, and one of them might be more appropriate than another for the attainment of this goal, so that we could make a bad choice of means; and partly because cognition is a faculty of a definite kind and scope, and thus, without a more precise definition of its nature and limits, we might grasp clouds of error instead of the heaven of truth. This feeling of uneasiness is surely bound to be transformed into the conviction that the whole project of securing for consciousness through cognition what exists in itself is absurd, and that there is a boundary between cognition and the Absolute that completely separates them. For, if cognition is the instrument for getting hold of absolute being, it is obvious that the use of an instrument on a thing certainly does not let it be what it is for itself, but rather sets out to reshape and alter it. If, on the other hand, cognition is not an instrument of our activity but a more or less passive medium through which the light of truth reaches us, then again we do not receive the truth as it is in itself, but only as it exists through and in this medium. Either way we employ a means which immediately brings about the opposite of its own end; or rather, what is really absurd is that we should make use of a means at all.

It would seem, to be sure, that this evil could be remedied through an acquaintance with the way in which the *instrument* works; for this would enable us to eliminate from the representation of the Absolute which we have gained through it whatever is due to the instrument, and thus get the truth in its purity. But this 'improvement' would in fact only bring us back to where we were before. If we remove from a reshaped thing what the instrument has done to it, then the thing – here the Absolute – becomes for us exactly what it was before this [accordingly] superfluous effort. On the other hand, if the Absolute is supposed merely to be brought nearer to us through this instrument, without anything in it being altered, like a bird caught by a lime-twig, it would surely laugh our little ruse to scorn, if it were not with us, in and for itself, all along, and of its own volition. For a ruse is just what cognition would be in such a case, since it would, with its manifold exertions, be giving itself the air of doing something quite different from creating a merely immediate and therefore effortless relationship. Or, if by testing cognition, which we conceive of as a *medium*, we get to know the law of its refraction, it is again useless to subtract this from the end result. For it is not the refraction of the ray, but the ray itself whereby truth reaches us, that is cognition; and if this were removed, all that would be indicated would be a pure direction or a blank space.

Meanwhile, if the fear of falling into error sets up a mistrust of Science, which in the absence of such scruples gets on with the work itself, and actually cognizes something, it is hard to see why we should not turn round and mistrust this very mistrust. Should we not be concerned as to whether this fear of error is not just the error itself? Indeed, this fear takes something – a great deal in fact – for granted as truth, supporting its scruples and inferences on what is itself in need of prior scrutiny to see if it is true. To be specific, it takes for granted certain ideas about cognition as an *instrument* and as a *medium*, and assumes that there is a *difference between ourselves and this cognition*. Above all, it presupposes that the Absolute stands on one side and cognition on the other, independent and separated from it, and yet is something real; or in other words, it presupposes that cognition which, since it is excluded from the Absolute, is surely outside of the truth as well, is nevertheless true, an assumption whereby what calls itself fear of error reveals itself rather as fear of the truth.

This conclusion stems from the fact that the Absolute alone is true, or the truth alone is absolute. One may set this aside on the grounds that there is a type of cognition which, though it does not cognize the Absolute as Science aims to, is still true, and that cognition in general, though it be incapable of grasping the Absolute, is still capable of grasping other kinds of truth. But we gradually come to see that this kind of talk which goes back and forth only leads to a hazy distinction between an absolute truth and some other kind of truth, and that words like 'absolute', 'cognition', etc. presuppose a meaning which has yet to be ascertained.

Instead of troubling ourselves with such useless ideas and locutions about cognition as 'an instrument for getting hold of the Absolute', or as 'a medium through which we view the truth' (relationships which surely, in the end, are what all these ideas of a cognition cut off from the Absolute, and an Absolute separated from cognition, amount to); instead of putting up with excuses which create the incapacity of Science by assuming relationships of this kind in order to be exempt from the hard work of Science, while at the same time giving the impression of working seriously and zealously; instead of bothering to refute all these ideas, we could reject them out of hand as adventitious and arbitrary, and the words associated with them like 'absolute', 'cognition', 'objective' and 'subjective', and countless others whose meaning is assumed to be generally familiar, could even be regarded as so much deception. For to give the impression that their meaning is generally well known, or that their Notion is comprehended, looks more like an attempt to avoid the main problem, which is precisely to provide this Notion. We could, with better justification, simply spare ourselves the trouble of paying any attention whatever to such ideas and locutions; for they are intended to ward off Science itself, and constitute merely an empty appearance of knowing, which vanishes immediately as soon as Science comes on the scene. But Science, just because it comes on the scene, is itself an appearance: in coming on the scene it is not yet Science in its developed and unfolded truth. In this connection it makes no difference whether we think of Science as the appearance because it comes on the scene alongside another mode of knowledge, or whether we call that other untrue knowledge its manifestation. In any case

Science must liberate itself from this semblance, and it can do so only by turning against it. For, when confronted with a knowledge that is without truth, Science can neither merely reject it as an ordinary way of looking at things, while assuring us that its Science is a quite different sort of cognition for which that ordinary knowledge is of no account whatever; nor can it appeal to the vulgar view for the intimations it gives us of something better to come. By the former *assurance*, Science would be declaring its power to lie simply in its *being*; but the untrue knowledge likewise appeals to the fact that *it is*, and *assures* us that for it Science is of no account. *One* bare assurance is worth just as much as another. Still less can Science appeal to whatever intimations of something better it may detect in the cognition that is without truth, to the signs which point in the direction of Science. For one thing, it would only be appealing again to what merely *is*; and for another, it would only be appealing to itself, and to itself in the mode in which it exists in the cognition that is without truth. In other words, it would be appealing to an inferior form of its being, to the way it appears, rather than to what it is in and for itself. It is for this reason that an exposition of how knowledge makes its appearance will here be undertaken.

Now, because it has only phenomenal knowledge for its object, this exposition seems not to be Science, free and self-moving in its own peculiar shape; yet from this standpoint it can be regarded as the path of the natural consciousness which presses forward to true knowledge; or as the way of the Soul which journeys through the series of its own configurations as though they were the stations appointed for it by its own nature, so that it may purify itself for the life of the Spirit, and achieve finally, through a completed experience of itself, the awareness of what it really is in itself.

Natural consciousness will show itself to be only the Notion of knowledge, or in other words, not to be real knowledge. But since it directly takes itself to be real knowledge, this path has a negative significance for it, and what is in fact the realization of the Notion, counts for it rather as the loss of its own self; for it does lose its truth on this path. The road can therefore be regarded as the pathway of *doubt*, or more precisely as the way of despair. For what happens on it is not what is ordinarily understood when the word 'doubt' is used: shilly-shallying about this or that presumed truth, followed by a return to that truth again, after the doubt has been appropriately dispelled – so that at the end of the process the matter is taken to be what it was in the first place. On the contrary, this path is the conscious insight into the untruth of phenomenal knowledge, for which the supreme reality is what is in truth only the unrealized Notion. Therefore this thoroughgoing scepticism is also not the scepticism with which an earnest zeal for truth and Science fancies it has prepared and equipped itself in their service: the *resolve*, in Science, not to give oneself over to the thoughts of others, upon mere authority, but to examine everything for oneself and follow only one's own conviction, or better still, to produce everything oneself, and accept only one's own deed as what is true.

The series of configurations which consciousness goes through along this road is, in reality, the detailed history of the *education* of consciousness itself to the standpoint of Science. That zealous resolve represents this education simplistically as something directly over and done with in the making of the resolution; but the way of the Soul is the actual fulfilment of the resolution, in contrast to the untruth of that view. Now, following one's own conviction is, of course, more than giving oneself over to authority; but changing an opinion accepted on authority into an opinion held out of personal conviction, does not necessarily alter the content of the opinion, or replace error with truth. The only difference between being caught up in a system of opinions and prejudices based on personal conviction, and being caught up in one based on the authority of others, lies in the added conceit that is innate in the latter position. The scepticism that is directed against the whole range of phenomenal consciousness, on the other hand, renders the Spirit for the first time competent to examine what truth is. For it brings about a state of despair about all the so-called natural ideas, thoughts, and opinions, regardless of whether they are called one's own or someone else's, ideas with which the consciousness that sets about the examination [of truth] *straight away* is still filled and hampered, so that it is, in fact, incapable of carrying out what it wants to undertake.

The necessary progression and interconnection of the forms of the unreal consciousness will by itself bring to pass the *completion* of the series. To make this more intelligible, it may be remarked, in a preliminary and general way, that the exposition of the untrue consciousness in its untruth is not a merely *negative* procedure. The natural consciousness itself normally takes this one-sided view of it; and a knowledge which makes this one-sidedness its very essence is itself one of the patterns of incomplete consciousness which occurs on the road itself, and will manifest itself in due course. This is just the scepticism which only ever sees pure nothingness in its result and abstracts from the fact that this nothingness is specifically the nothingness of that *from which it results*. For it is only when it is taken as the result of that from which it emerges, that it is, in fact, the true result; in that case it is itself a *determinate* nothingness, one which has a *content*. The scepticism that ends up with the bare abstraction of nothingness or emptiness cannot get any further from there, but must wait to see whether something new comes along and what it is, in order to throw it too into the same empty abyss. But when, on the other hand, the result is conceived as it is in truth, namely, as a *determinate* negation, a new form has thereby immediately arisen, and in the negation the transition is made through which the progress through the complete series of forms comes about of itself.

But the *goal* is as necessarily fixed for knowledge as the serial progression; it is the point where knowledge no longer needs to go beyond itself, where knowledge finds itself, where Notion corresponds to object and object to Notion. Hence the progress towards this goal is also unhalting, and short of it no satisfaction is to be found at any of the stations on the way. Whatever is confined within the limits of a natural life cannot by its own efforts go beyond its immediate existence; but it is driven beyond it by something else, and this uprooting entails its death. Consciousness, however, is explicitly the *Notion* of itself. Hence it is something that goes beyond limits, and since these limits are its own, it is something that goes beyond itself. With the positing of a single particular the beyond is also established for consciousness, even if it is only *alongside* the limited object as in the case of spatial intuition. Thus consciousness suffers this violence at its own hands: it spoils its own limited satisfaction. When consciousness feels this violence, its anxiety may well make it retreat from the truth, and strive to hold on to what it is in danger of losing. But it can find no peace. If it wishes to remain in a state of unthinking inertia, then thought troubles its thoughtlessness, and its own unrest disturbs its inertia. Or, if it entrenches itself in sentimentality, which assures us that it finds everything to be *good in its kind*, then this assurance likewise suffers violence at the hands of Reason, for, precisely in so far as something is merely a kind, Reason finds it *not* to be good. Or, again, its fear of the truth may lead consciousness to hide, from itself and others, behind the pretension that its burning zeal for truth makes it difficult or even impossible to find any other truth but the unique truth of vanity – that of being at any rate cleverer than any thoughts that one gets by oneself or from others. This conceit which understands how to belittle every truth, in order to turn back into itself and gloat over its own understanding, which knows how to dissolve every thought and always find the same barren Ego instead of any content – this is a satisfaction which we must leave to itself, for it flees from the universal, and seeks only to be for itself.

In addition to these preliminary general remarks about the manner and the necessity of the progression, it may be useful to say something about the *method of carrying out the inquiry*. If this exposition is viewed as a way of *relating Science* to *phenomenal* knowledge, and as an investigation and *examination of the reality of cognition*, it would seem that it cannot take place without some presupposition which can serve as its underlying *criterion*. For an examination consists in applying an accepted standard, and in determining whether something is right or wrong on the basis of the resulting agreement or disagreement of the thing examined; thus the standard as such (and Science likewise if it were the criterion) is accepted as the *essence* or as the *in-itself*. But here, where Science has just begun to come on the scene, neither Science nor anything else has yet justified itself as the essence or the in-itself; and without something of the sort it seems that no examination can take place.

This contradiction and its removal will become more definite if we call to mind the abstract determinations of truth and knowledge as they occur in consciousness. Consciousness simultaneously *distinguishes* itself from something, and at the same time *relates* itself to it, or, as it is said, this something exists *for* consciousness; and the determinate aspect of this *relating*, or of the *being* of something for a consciousness, is *knowing*. But we distinguish this being-for-another from *being-in-itself*; whatever is related to knowledge or knowing is also distinguished from it, and posited as existing outside of this relationship; this *being-in-itself* is called *truth*. Just what might be involved in these determinations is of no further concern to us here. Since our object is phenomenal knowledge, its determinations too will at first be taken directly as they present themselves; and they do present themselves very much as we have already apprehended them.

Now, if we inquire into the truth of knowledge, it seems that we are asking what knowledge is *in itself*. Yet in this inquiry knowledge is *our* object, something that exists *for us*; and the *in-itself* that would supposedly result from it would rather be the being of knowledge *for us*. What we asserted to be its essence would be not so much its truth but rather just our knowledge of it. The essence or criterion would lie within ourselves, and that which was to be compared with it and about which a decision would be reached through this comparison would not necessarily have to recognize the validity of such a standard.

But the dissociation, or this semblance of dissociation and presupposition, is overcome by the nature of the object we are investigating. Consciousness provides its own criterion from within itself, so that the investigation becomes a comparison of consciousness with itself; for the distinction made above falls within it. In consciousness one thing exists *for* another, i.e. consciousness regularly contains the determinateness of the moment of knowledge; at the same time, this other is to consciousness not merely *for it*, but is also outside of this relationship, or exists *in itself*: the moment of truth. Thus in what consciousness affirms from within itself as *being-in-itself* or the *True* we have the standard which consciousness itself sets up by which to measure what it knows. If we designate *knowledge* as the Notion, but the essence or the *True* as what exists, or the *object*, then the examination consists in seeing whether the Notion corresponds to the object. But if we call the *essence* or in-itself of the *object* the *Notion*, and on the other hand understand by the *object* the Notion itself as *object*, viz. as it exists *for an other*, then the examination consists in seeing whether the object corresponds to its Notion. It is evident, of course, that the two procedures are the same. But the essential point to bear in mind throughout the whole investigation is that these two moments, 'Notion' and 'object', 'being-for-another' and 'being-in-itself', both fall *within* that knowledge which we are investigating. Consequently, we do not need to import criteria, or to make use of our own bright ideas and thoughts during the course of the inquiry; it is precisely when we leave these aside that we succeed in contemplating the matter in hand as it is *in and for itself*.

But not only is a contribution by us superfluous, since Notion and object, the criterion and what is to be tested, are present in consciousness itself, but we are also spared the trouble of comparing the two and really *testing* them, so that, since what consciousness examines is its own self, all that is left for us to do is simply to look on. For consciousness is, on the one hand, consciousness of the object, and on the other, consciousness of itself; consciousness of what for it is the True, and consciousness of its knowledge of the truth. Since both are *for* the same consciousness, this consciousness is itself their comparison; it is for this same consciousness to know whether its knowledge of the object corresponds to the object or not. The object, it is true, seems only to be for consciousness in the way that consciousness knows it; it seems that consciousness cannot, as it were, get behind the object as it exists for consciousness so as to examine what the object is *in itself*, and hence, too, cannot test its own knowledge by that standard. But the distinction between the in-itself and knowledge is already present in the very fact that consciousness knows an object at all. Something is *for it* the *in-itself*; and knowledge, or the being of the object for consciousness, is, *for it*, another moment. Upon this distinction, which is present as a fact, the examination rests. If the comparison shows that these two moments do not correspond to one another, it would seem that consciousness must alter its knowledge to make it conform to the object. But, in fact, in the alteration of the knowledge, the object itself alters for it too, for the knowledge that was present was essentially a knowledge of the object: as the knowledge changes, so too does the object, for it essentially belonged to this knowledge. Hence it comes to pass for consciousness that what it previously took to be the *in-itself* is not an *in-itself*, or that it was only an in-itself *for consciousness*. Since consciousness thus finds that its knowledge does not correspond to its object, the object itself does not stand the test; in other words, the criterion for testing is altered when that for which it was to have been the criterion fails to pass the test; and the testing is not only a testing of what we know, but also a testing of the criterion of what knowing is.

In as much as the new true object issues from it, this *dialectical* movement which consciousness exercises on itself and which affects both its knowledge and its object, is precisely what is called *experience* [*Erfahrung*]. In this connection there is a moment in the process just mentioned which must be brought out more clearly, for through it a new light will be thrown on the exposition which follows. Consciousness knows *something*; this object is the essence or the *in-itself*; but it is also for consciousness the in-itself. This is where the ambiguity of this truth enters. We see that consciousness now has two objects: one is the first *in-itself*, the second is the *being-for-consciousness of this in-itself*. The latter appears at first sight to be merely the reflection of consciousness into itself, i.e. what consciousness has in mind is not an object, but only its knowledge of that first object. But, as was shown previously, the first object, in being known, is altered for consciousness; it ceases to be the in-itself, and becomes something that is the *in-itself* only *for consciousness*. And this then is the True: the being-for-consciousness of this in-itself. Or, in other words, this is the *essence*, or the *object* of consciousness. This new object contains the nothingness of the first, it is what experience has made of it.

This exposition of the course of experience contains a moment in virtue of which it does not seem to agree with what is ordinarily understood by experience. This is the moment of transition from the first object and the knowledge of it, to the other object, which experience is said to be about. Our account implied that our knowledge of the first object, or the being-*for*-consciousness of the first in-itself,

itself becomes the second object. It usually seems to be the case, on the contrary, that our experience of the untruth of our first notion comes by way of a second object which we come upon by chance and externally, so that our part in all this is simply the pure *apprehension* of what is in and for itself. From the present viewpoint, however, the new object shows itself to have come about through a *reversal of consciousness itself.* This way of looking at the matter is something contributed by *us*, by means of which the succession of experiences through which consciousness passes is raised into a scientific progression – but it is not known to the consciousness that we are observing. But, as a matter of fact, we have here the same situation as the one discussed in regard to the relation between our exposition and scepticism, viz. that in every case the result of an untrue mode of knowledge must not be allowed to run away into an empty nothing, but must necessarily be grasped as the nothing *of that from which it results* – a result which contains what was true in the preceding knowledge. It shows up here like this: since what first appeared as the object sinks for consciousness to the level of its way of knowing it, and since the in-itself becomes a *being-for-consciousness* of the in-itself, the latter is now the new object. Herewith a new pattern of consciousness comes on the scene as well, for which the essence is something different from what it was at the preceding stage. It is this fact that guides the entire series of the patterns of consciousness in their necessary sequence. But it is just this necessity itself, or the *origination* of the new object, that presents itself to consciousness without its understanding how this happens, which proceeds for us, as it were, behind the back of consciousness. Thus in the movement of consciousness there occurs a moment of *being-in-itself* or *being-for-us* which is not present to the consciousness comprehended in the experience itself. The *content*, however, of what presents itself to us does exist *for it*; we comprehend only the formal aspect of that content, or its pure origination. *For it,* what has thus arisen exists only as an object; *for us,* it appears at the same time as movement and a process of becoming.

Because of this necessity, the way to Science is itself already *Science,* and hence, in virtue of its content, is the Science of the *experience of consciousness.*

The experience of itself which consciousness goes through can, in accordance with its Notion, comprehend nothing less than the entire system of consciousness, or the entire realm of the truth of Spirit. For this reason, the moments of this truth are exhibited in their own proper determinateness, viz. as being not abstract moments, but as they are for consciousness, or as consciousness itself stands forth in its relation to them. Thus the moments of the whole are *patterns of consciousness*. In pressing forward to its true existence, consciousness will arrive at a point at which it gets rid of its semblance of being burdened with something alien, with what is only for it, and some sort of 'other', at a point where appearance becomes identical with essence, so that its exposition will coincide at just this point with the authentic Science of Spirit. And finally, when consciousness itself grasps this its own essence, it will signify the nature of absolute knowledge itself.

Translated by A. V. Miller

Elements of the Philosophy of Right

PREFACE

The immediate occasion for me to publish this outline is the need
to provide my audience with an introduction to the lectures on the
Philosophy of Right which I deliver in the course of my official duties.
This textbook is a more extensive, and in particular a more systematic, exposition of the same basic concepts which, in relation to this
part of philosophy, are already contained in a previous work designed
to accompany my lectures, namely my *Encyclopedia of the Philosophical
Sciences* (Heidelberg, 1817).

The fact that this outline was due to appear in print and thus
to come before a wider public gave me the opportunity to amplify
in it some of those *Remarks* whose primary purpose was to comment briefly on ideas [*Vorstellungen*] akin to or divergent from my
own, on further consequences of my argument, and on other such
matters as would be properly elucidated in the lectures themselves.
I have amplified them here so as to clarify on occasion the more
abstract contents of the text and to take fuller account of related
ideas [*Vorstellungen*] which are current at the present time. As a
result, some of these Remarks have become more extensive than
the aim and style of a compendium would normally lead one to
expect. A genuine compendium, however, has as its subject-matter
what is considered to be the entire compass of a science; and
what distinguishes it – apart, perhaps, from a minor addition here
or there – is above all the way in which it arranges and orders the
essential elements [*Momente*] of a content which has long been
familiar and accepted, just as the form in which it is presented
has its rules and conventions which have long been agreed. But
a philosophical outline is not expected to conform to this pattern,
if only because it is imagined that what philosophy puts forward is

as ephemeral a product as Penelope's weaving, which is begun afresh every day.

It is certainly true that the primary difference between the present outline and an ordinary compendium is the method which constitutes its guiding principle. But I am here presupposing that the philosophical manner of progressing from one topic to another and of conducting a scientific proof – this entire speculative mode of cognition – is essentially different from other modes of cognition. The realization that such a difference is a necessary one is the only thing which can save philosophy from the shameful decline into which it has fallen in our times. It has indeed been recognized that the forms and rules of the older logic – of definition, classification, and inference – which include the rules of the understanding's cognition [*Verstandeserkenntnis*], are inadequate for speculative science. Or rather, their inadequacy has not so much been recognized as merely felt, and then the rules in question have been cast aside, as if they were simply fetters, to make way for the arbitrary pronouncements of the heart, of fantasy, and of contingent intuition; and since, in spite of this, reflection and relations of thought inevitably also come into play, the despised method of commonplace deduction and ratiocination is unconsciously adopted. – Since I have fully developed the nature of speculative knowledge in my *Science of Logic*, I have only occasionally added an explanatory comment on procedure and method in the present outline. Given that the subject-matter is concrete and inherently of so varied a nature, I have of course omitted to demonstrate and bring out the logical progression in each and every detail. But on the one hand, it might have been considered superfluous to do so in view of the fact that I have presupposed a familiarity with scientific method; and on the other, it will readily be noticed that the work as a whole, like the construction [*Ausbildung*] of its parts, is based on the logical spirit. It is also chiefly from this point of view that I would wish this treatise to be understood and judged. For what it deals with is *science*, and in science, the content is essentially inseparable from the *form*.

It is true that we may hear it said by those who seem to adopt the most thorough approach that form is a purely external quality, indifferent to the matter [*Sache*] itself, which is alone of consequence; furthermore, the task of the writer, especially the philosophical writer, may be said to consist in the discovery of *truths*, the statement of *truths*, and the dissemination of *truths* and correct concepts. But if we consider how this task is actually performed, we see on the one hand how the same old brew is reheated again and again and served up to all and sundry – a task that may not be without its merits in educating and arousing the emotions, though it might sooner be regarded as the superfluous product of over-zealous activity – 'for they have Moses and the prophets; let them hear them.' Above all, we have ample opportunity to wonder at the tone and pretentiousness that can be detected in such writers, as if all that the world had hitherto lacked was these zealous disseminators of truths, and as if their reheated brew contained new and unheard-of truths which ought, as they always claim, to be taken particularly to heart, above all 'at the present time'. But on the other hand, we can see how whatever truths of this kind are handed out by one party are displaced and swept away by truths of precisely the same kind dispensed by other parties. And if, amidst this jumble of truths, there is something that is neither old nor new but enduring, how can it be extracted from these formlessly fluctuating reflections – how can it be distinguished and verified other than by *scientific* means?

The *truth* concerning *right, ethics, and the state* is at any rate *as old* as its *exposition and promulgation* in *public laws and in public morality and religion*. What more does this truth require, in as much as the thinking mind [*Geist*] is not content to possess it in this proximate manner? What it needs is to be *comprehended* as well, so that the content which is already rational in itself may also gain a rational form and thereby appear justified to free thinking. For such thinking does not stop at what is *given*, whether the latter is supported by the external positive authority of the state or of mutual agreement among human beings, or by the authority of inner feeling and the heart and by the testimony of the spirit which immediately concurs with this, but starts out from itself and thereby demands to know itself as united in its innermost being with the truth.

The simple reaction [*Verhalten*] of ingenuous emotion is to adhere with trusting conviction to the publicly recognized truth and to base one's conduct and fixed position in life on this firm foundation. But this simple reaction may well encounter the supposed difficulty of how to distinguish and discover, among the *infinite variety of opinions*, what is universally acknowledged and valid in them; and this perplexity may easily be taken for a just and genuine concern with the matter [*Sache*] itself. But in fact, those who pride themselves on this perplexity are in the position of not being able to see the wood for the trees, and the only perplexity and difficulty that is present is the one they have themselves created; indeed, this perplexity and difficulty is rather a proof that they want something other than what is universally acknowledged and valid, something other than the substance of the right and the ethical. For if they were genuinely concerned with the latter and not with the *vanity* and *particularity* of opinions and being, they would adhere to the substantial right, namely to the commandments of ethics and of the state, and regulate their lives accordingly. – A further difficulty arises, however, from the fact that human beings *think* and look for their freedom and the basis of ethics in [the realm of] thought. But however exalted, however divine this right may be, it is nevertheless transformed into wrong if the only criterion of thought and the only way in which thought can know itself to be free is the extent to which it *diverges from what is universally acknowledged and valid* and manages to invent something *particular* for itself.

The notion [*Vorstellung*] that freedom of thought, and of spirit in general, can be demonstrated only by divergence from, and even hostility towards, what is publicly acknowledged might seem to be most firmly rooted nowadays in *relation* [*Beziehung*] *to the state*; for this very reason, it might seem to be the essential task of a philosophy of the state to invent and propound *yet another theory*, and specifically a new and particular theory. If we examine this notion [*Vorstellung*] and the activity that is associated with it, we might well imagine that no state or constitution had ever previously existed or were in existence today, but that we had *now* (and this 'now' is of indefinite duration) to start right from the beginning, and that the ethical world had been waiting only for such intellectual constructions, discoveries, and proofs as are *now* available. As far as *nature* is concerned, it is readily admitted that philosophy must recognize it *as it is*, that the philosopher's stone lies hidden *somewhere*, but *within nature itself*, that nature is *rational within itself*, and that it is this *actual* reason present within it which knowledge must investigate and grasp conceptually – not the shapes and contingencies which are visible on the surface, but nature's eternal harmony, conceived, however, as the law and essence *immanent* within it. *The ethical world*, on the other hand, the state, or reason as it actualizes itself in the element of self-consciousness, is not supposed to be happy in the knowledge that it is reason itself which has in fact gained power and authority [*Gewalt*] within this element, and which asserts itself there and remains inherent within it.* The spiritual universe is supposed rather to be

---

* There are two kinds of laws, laws of nature and laws of right: the laws of nature are simply there and are valid as they stand: they suffer no diminution, although they may be infringed in individual cases. To know what the law of nature is, we must familiarize ourselves with nature, for these laws are correct and it is only our notions [*Vorstellungen*] concerning them which may be false. The measure of these laws is external to us, and our cognition adds nothing to them and does not advance them: it is only our cognition of them which can expand. Knowledge [*Kenntnis*] of right is in one respect similar to this and in another respect different. We get to know the laws of right in just the same way, simply as they are; the citizen knows them more or less in this way, and the positive jurist also stops short at what is given. But the difference is that, with the laws of right, the spirit of reflection comes into play and their very diversity draws attention to the fact that they are not absolute. The laws of right are something *laid down*, something *derived from* human beings. It necessarily follows that our inner voice may either come into collision with them or concur with them. The human being does not stop short at the existent [*dem Daseienden*], but claims to have within himself the measure of what is right; he may be subjected to the necessity and power of external authority, but never in the same way as to natural necessity, for his inner self always tells him how things ought to be, and he finds within himself the confirmation or repudiation of what is accepted as valid. In nature, the highest truth is that a law *exists at all*; in laws of right, however, the thing [*Sache*] is not valid because it exists; on the contrary, everyone demands that it should match his own criterion. Thus a conflict may arise between what is and what ought to be, between the right which has being in and for itself, which remains unaltered, and the arbitrary determination of what is supposed to be accepted as right. A disjunction and conflict of this kind is found only in the sphere [*Boden*] of the spirit, and since the prerogative of the spirit thus seems to lead to discord and unhappiness, we often turn away from the arbitrariness of life to the contemplation of nature and are inclined to take the latter as a model. But these very discrepancies [*Gegensätze*] between that

at the mercy of contingency and arbitrariness, to be *god-forsaken*, so that, according to this atheism of the ethical world, *truth* lies *outside* it, and at the same time, since reason is nevertheless *also* supposed to be present in it, truth is nothing but a problem. But, we are told, this very circumstance justifies, indeed obliges, every thinker to take his own initiative, though not *in search of* the philosopher's stone, for this search is made superfluous by the philosophizing of our times and everyone, whatever his condition, can be assured that he has this stone in his grasp. Now it does admittedly happen that those who live within the actuality of the state and are able to satisfy their knowledge and volition within it – and there are many of them, more in fact than think or know it, for *basically* this includes *everyone* – or at least those who *consciously* find satisfaction within the state, laugh at such initiatives and assurances and regard them as an empty game, now more amusing, now more serious, now pleasing, now dangerous. This restless activity of vain reflection, along with the reception and response it encounters, might be regarded as a separate issue [*Sache*], developing independently in its own distinct way, were it not that *philosophy* in general has incurred all kinds of contempt and

right which has being in and for itself and what arbitrariness proclaims as right make it imperative for us to learn to recognize precisely what right is. In right, the human being must encounter his own reason; he must therefore consider the rationality of right, and this is the business of our science, in contrast with positive jurisprudence, which is often concerned only with contradictions. Besides, the present-day world has a more urgent need of such an investigation, for in olden times there was still respect and veneration for the existing [*bestehenden*] law, whereas the culture [*Bildung*] of the present age has taken a new direction, and thought has adopted a leading role in the formation of values. Theories are put forward in opposition to what already exists [*dem Daseienden*], theories which seek to appear correct and necessary in and for themselves. From now on, there is a more special need to recognize and comprehend the thoughts of right. Since thought has set itself up as the essential form, we must attempt to grasp right, too, in terms of thought. If thought is to take precedence over right, this would seem to throw open the door to contingent opinions; but genuine thought is not an opinion about something [*die Sache*], but the concept of the thing [*Sache*] itself. The concept of the thing does not come to us by nature. Everyone has fingers and can take a brush and paint, but that does not make him a painter. It is precisely the same with thinking. The thought of right is not, for example, what everybody knows at first hand; on the contrary, correct thinking is knowing [*das Kennen*] and recognizing the thing, and our cognition should therefore be scientific.

discredit as a result of such behaviour. The worst kind of contempt it has met with is, as already mentioned, that everyone, whatever his condition, is convinced that he knows all about philosophy in general and can pass judgement upon it. No other art or science is treated with this ultimate degree of contempt, namely the assumption that one can take possession of it outright.

In fact, what we have seen the philosophy of recent times proclaiming with the utmost pretension in relation to the state has no doubt entitled anyone who wishes to have a say in such matters to the belief that he could just as well do the same thing on his own account, and thereby prove to himself that he was in possession of philosophy. In any case, this self-styled philosophy has expressly stated that *truth itself cannot be known* [*erkannt*], but that truth consists in what *wells up from each individual's heart, emotion, and enthusiasm* in relation to ethical subjects, particularly in relation to the state, government, and constitution. What has not been said in this connection to flatter the young in particular? And the young have certainly taken note of it. The saying 'for he giveth to his own in sleep' has been applied to science, so that all sleepers have counted themselves among the *chosen*; but the concepts they have acquired in their sleep have of course borne the marks of their origin. – A leader of this superficial brigade of so-called philosophers, Herr Fries,* had the temerity, at a solemn public occasion which has since become notorious, to put forward the following idea [*Vorstellung*] in an address on the subject of the state and constitution: 'In a people among whom a genuine communal spirit prevails, all business relating to public affairs would gain its *life from below, from the people itself; living* societies, steadfastly united *by the sacred bond of friendship*, would dedicate themselves to every single project of popular education and popular service'; and so on. – The chief tendency of this superficial philosophy is to base science not on the development of thought and the concept, but on immediate perception and contingent imagination; and likewise, to reduce the complex inner articulation of the ethical, i.e., the state, the

---

* I have testified elsewhere to the superficiality of his science; see my *Science of Logic* (Nürnberg, 1812), Introduction, p. xvii.

architectonics of its rationality – which, through determinate distinctions between the various spheres of public life and the rights [*Berechtigungen*] they are based on, and through the strict proportions in which every pillar, arch, and buttress is held together, produces the strength of the whole from the harmony of its parts – to reduce this refined [*gebildeten*] structure to a mush of 'heart, friendship, and enthusiasm'. According to this notion [*Vorstellung*], the ethical world, like the universe of Epicurus, should be given over to the subjective contingency of opinions and arbitrariness; but of course this *is* not the case. By the simple household remedy of attributing to *feeling* what reason and its understanding have laboured to produce over several thousand years, all the trouble involved in rational insight and cognition, guided by the thinking concept, can of course be avoided. Goethe's Mephistopheles – a good authority – says much the same thing in lines which I have also quoted elsewhere:

> Do but despise reason and science,
> The highest of all human gifts –
> Then you have surrendered to the devil
> And must surely perish.

The next step is for this view to assume the guise of *piety* as well; for what lengths has such behaviour not gone to in order to lend itself authority! By means of godliness and the Bible, however, it has presumed to gain the supreme justification for despising the ethical order and the objectivity of the laws. For it is surely also piety which envelops in the simpler intuition of feeling that truth which, in the world itself, is diversified into an organic realm. But if it is the right kind of piety, it abandons the form of this [emotional] region as soon as it emerges from [the condition of] inwardness into the daylight of the Idea's full development [*Entfaltung*] and manifest abundance, and it brings with it, from its inner worship of God, a reverence for the laws and for a truth which has being in and for itself and is exalted above the subjective form of feeling.

The particular form of bad conscience which betrays itself in the vainglorious eloquence of this superficial philosophy may be remarked on here; for in the first place, it is precisely where it is at its *most spiritless* that it has most to say about *spirit*, where its talk is driest and most lifeless that it is freest with the words 'life' and 'enliven', and where it shows the utmost selfishness of empty arrogance that it most often refers to the 'people'. But the distinctive mark which it carries on its brow is its hatred of law. That right and ethics, and the actual world of right and the ethical, are grasped by means of *thoughts* and give themselves the form of rationality – namely universality and determinacy – by means of thoughts, is what constitutes *the law*; and it is this which is justifiably regarded as the main enemy by that feeling which reserves the right to do as it pleases, by that conscience which identifies right with subjective conviction. The form of right as a *duty* and a *law* is felt by it to be a *dead, cold letter* and a *shackle*; for it does not recognize itself in the law and thereby recognize its own freedom in it, because the law is the reason of the thing [*Sache*] and reason does not allow feeling to warm itself in the glow of its own particularity [*Partikularität*]. The *law* is therefore, as I have remarked elsewhere in the course of this textbook, the chief shibboleth by which the false brethren and friends of the so-called 'people' give themselves away.

Since this arbitrary sophistry has usurped the name of *philosophy* and persuaded a wide public that such activities are philosophy, it has almost become dishonourable to continue to speak philosophically about the nature of the state; and right-minded [*rechtliche*] men cannot be blamed if they grow impatient as soon as they hear talk of a philosophical science of the state. There is even less cause for surprise that governments have at last directed their attention to such philosophizing, for philosophy with us is not in any case practised as a private art, as it was with the Greeks, for example, but has a public existence [*Existenz*], impinging upon the public, especially – or solely – in the service of the state. Governments have had enough confidence in those of their scholars who have devoted themselves to this subject to leave the development [*Ausbildung*] and import of philosophy entirely to them – granted that here and there, they may have done so not so much out of confidence in science as out of indifference towards it, retaining teaching posts in philosophy only for reasons of tradition (just as in France, to the best of my knowledge, chairs of metaphysics at least have been allowed to lapse). But their confidence has frequently been ill repaid, or alternatively, if they are thought to be motivated by indifference, the resultant decay of thorough knowledge [*Erkenntnis*] should be regarded as the penalty for this indifference. It may initially appear that this superficial philosophy is eminently compatible at least with outward peace and order, in that it never manages to touch the substance of things [*Sachen*], or even to suspect its existence; it would thus have no cause to fear police intervention, at least initially, if it were not that the state also contained the need for a deeper education and insight, and demanded that this need be satisfied by science. But superficial philosophy leads automatically, as far as the ethical [world] and right and duty in general are concerned, to those principles which constitute superficiality in this sphere, namely the principles of the *Sophists* as we find them so clearly described by Plato. These principles identify what is right with *subjective ends and opinions*, with *subjective feeling and particular* [*partikuläre*] *conviction*, and they lead to the destruction of inner ethics and the upright conscience, of love and right among private persons, as well as the destruction of public order and the laws of the state. The significance which such phenomena [*Erscheinungen*] must acquire for governments can scarcely be reduced, for example, by the claim that the very confidence shown by the state and the authority of an official position are enough to warrant the demand that the state should accept and give free rein to what corrupts the substantial source of all deeds, namely universal principles, and should even allow itself to be defied, as if such defiance were entirely proper. 'If God gives someone an office, he also gives him sense [*Verstand*]', is an old chestnut which will scarcely be taken seriously by anyone nowadays.

In the importance which circumstances have again led governments to attach to the way in which philosophers conduct their business, there is no mistaking the fact that the study of philosophy now seems in many other respects to require an element [*Moment*] of protection and encouragement. For in so many publications in the field of the positive sciences, as well as in works of religious edification and other indeterminate literature, the reader encounters not only that contempt for philosophy which I have already referred to, in that the very people who reveal that their intellectual development [*Gedankenbildung*] is extremely retarded and that philosophy is completely alien to them also treat it as something they have finished and done with; beyond this, we also find that such writers expressly impugn philosophy and declare its content, the *conceptual cognition of God* and of physical and spiritual nature, the *cognition of truth*, to be a foolish, indeed sinful presumption, and that *reason*, and again *reason*, and in endless repetition *reason* is arraigned, belittled, and condemned. Or at the very least, they let us see how, for a large proportion of those engaged in supposedly scientific study, the claims of the concept constitute an embarrassment from which they are nevertheless unable to escape. If, I say, one is confronted with such phenomena [*Erscheinungen*], one might almost begin to suspect that tradition is *from this point of view* no longer worthy of respect nor sufficient to guarantee *tolerance* and a continued public existence [*Existenz*] to the study of philosophy.* – The declamations and presumptuous outbursts against philosophy which are so common in our time afford the peculiar spectacle on the one hand of being in the right, by virtue of that superficiality to which philosophical science has been degraded, and on the other of themselves being rooted in the very element against which they so ungratefully turn. For by declaring the cognition of truth to be a futile endeavour, this self-styled philosophizing has reduced all thoughts and all topics *to the same level*, just as the despotism of the Roman emperors *removed all distinctions* between patricians and slaves, virtue and vice, honour and dishonour, and

---

* I was reminded of such views on reading a letter of Johannes von Müller (*Werke* [Tübingen, 1810–19], Part VIII, p. 56), where he says of the condition of *Rome* in 1803 when the city was under French rule: 'Asked how the public educational institutions were faring, a professor replied: "On les tolère comme les bordels." ["They are tolerated, like the brothels."]' One can still even hear people *recommending* so-called 'rational theory' [*Vernunftlehre*], i.e. *logic*, perhaps in the belief that no one in any case bothers about it any longer as a dry and unfruitful science, or that, if this does happen now and again, those who study it will find only vacuous formulae, neither beneficial nor detrimental, so that the recommendation cannot possibly do any harm, even if it does no good either.

knowledge [*Kenntnis*] and ignorance. As a result, the concepts of truth and the laws of ethics are reduced to mere opinions and subjective convictions, and the most criminal principles – since they, too, are *convictions* – are accorded the same status as those laws; and in the same way, all objects, however barren and particular [*partikular*], and all materials, however arid, are accorded the same status as what constitutes the interest of all thinking people and the bonds of the ethical world.

It should therefore be considered a stroke of *good fortune* for science – although in fact, as I have already mentioned, it is a *necessary consequence* of the *thing* [*Sache*] itself – that this philosophizing, which could well have continued to spin itself into its own web of *scholastic wisdom*, has come into closer contact with actuality, in which the principles of rights and duties are a serious matter, and which lives in the light of its consciousness of these principles, and that a *public* split has consequently resulted between the two. It is *this very relation of philosophy to actuality* which is the subject of misunderstandings, and I accordingly come back to my earlier observation that, since philosophy is *exploration of the rational*, it is for that very reason the *comprehension of the present and the actual*, not the setting up of a *world beyond* which exists God knows where – or rather, of which we can very well say that we know where it exists, namely in the errors of a one-sided and empty ratiocination. In the course of the following treatise, I have remarked that even Plato's *Republic*, a proverbial example of an *empty ideal*, is essentially the embodiment of nothing other than the nature of Greek ethics; and Plato, aware that the ethics of his time were being penetrated by a deeper principle which, within this context, could appear immediately only as an as yet unsatisfied longing and hence only as a destructive force, was obliged, in order to counteract it, to seek the help of that very longing itself. But the help he required had to come from above, and he could seek it at first only in a particular *external* form of Greek ethics. By this means, he imagined he could overcome the destructive force, and he thereby inflicted the gravest damage on the deeper drive behind it, namely free infinite personality. But he proved his greatness of spirit by the fact that the very principle on which the distinctive character of his Idea turns is the pivot on which the impending world revolution turned.

What is rational is actual;
and what is actual is rational.

This conviction is shared by every ingenuous consciousness as well as by philosophy, and the latter takes it as its point of departure in considering both the *spiritual* and the *natural* universe. If reflection, feeling, or whatever form the subjective consciousness may assume regards the *present* as *vain* and looks beyond it in a spirit of superior knowledge, it finds itself in a vain position; and since it has actuality only in the present, it is itself mere vanity. Conversely, if the *Idea* is seen as 'only an idea', a representation [*Vorstellung*] in the realm of opinion, philosophy affords the opposite insight that nothing is actual except the Idea. For what matters is to recognize in the semblance of the temporal and transient the substance which is immanent and the eternal which is present. For since the rational, which is synonymous with the Idea, becomes actual by entering into external existence [*Existenz*], it emerges in an infinite wealth of forms, appearances, and shapes and surrounds its core with a brightly coloured covering in which consciousness at first resides, but which only the concept can penetrate in order to find the inner pulse, and detect its continued beat even within the external shapes. But the infinitely varied circumstances which take shape within this externality as the essence manifests itself within it, this infinite material and its organization, are not the subject-matter of philosophy. To deal with them would be to interfere in things [*Dinge*] with which philosophy has no concern, and it can save itself the trouble of giving good advice on the subject. Plato could well have refrained from recommending nurses never to stand still with children but to keep rocking them in their arms; and Fichte likewise need not have perfected his *passport regulations* to the point of 'constructing', as the expression ran, the requirement that the passports of suspect persons should carry not only their personal description but also their painted likeness. In deliberations of this kind, no trace of philosophy remains, and it can the more readily abstain from such ultra-wisdom because it is precisely in relation to this infinite multitude of subjects that it should appear at its most liberal. In this way, philosophical science will also show itself furthest removed from the hatred which the vanity of superior wisdom displays towards a multitude of circumstances and institutions – a hatred in which pettiness takes the greatest of pleasure, because this is the only way in which it can attain self-esteem [*Selbstgefühl*].

This treatise, therefore, in so far as it deals with political science, shall be nothing other than an attempt *to comprehend and portray the state as an inherently rational entity*. As a philosophical composition, it must distance itself as far as possible from the obligation to construct a *state as it ought to be*; such instruction as it may contain cannot be aimed at instructing the state on how it ought to be, but rather at showing how the state, as the ethical universe, should be recognized.

> Ἰδοὺ ʻΡόδος, ἰδοὺ καὶ τὸ πήδημα.
> *Hic* Rhodus, *hic* saltus.

To comprehend *what is* is the task of philosophy, for *what is* is reason. As far as the individual is concerned, each individual is in any case a *child of his time*; thus philosophy, too, is *its own time comprehended in thoughts*. It is just as foolish to imagine that any philosophy can transcend its contemporary world as that an individual can overleap his own time or leap over Rhodes. If his theory does indeed transcend his own time, if it builds itself a world *as it ought to be*, then it certainly has an existence, but only within his opinions – a pliant medium in which the imagination can construct anything it pleases.

With little alteration, the saying just quoted would read:

> *Here* is the rose, dance *here*.

What lies between reason as self-conscious spirit and reason as present actuality, what separates the former from the latter and prevents it from finding satisfaction in it, is the fetter of some abstraction or other which has not been liberated into [the form of] the concept. To recognize reason as the rose in the cross of the present and thereby to delight in the present – this rational insight is the *reconciliation* with actuality which philosophy grants to those who have received the inner call *to comprehend*, to preserve their subjective freedom in the realm of the substantial, and at the same time to stand with their subjective freedom not in a particular and contingent situation, but in what has being in and for itself.

This is also what constitutes the more concrete sense of what was described above in more abstract terms as the *unity of form and content*. For *form* in its most concrete significance is reason as conceptual cognition, and *content* is reason as the substantial essence of both ethical and natural actuality; the conscious identity of the two is the philosophical Idea. – It is a great obstinacy, the kind of obstinacy which does honour to human beings, that they are unwilling to acknowledge in their attitudes [*Gesinnung*] anything which has not been justified by thought – and this obstinacy is the characteristic property of the modern age, as well as being the distinctive principle of Protestantism. What Luther inaugurated as faith in feeling and in the testimony of the spirit is the same thing that the spirit, at a more mature stage of its development, endeavours to grasp in the *concept* so as to free itself in the present and thus find itself therein. It has become a famous saying that 'a half-philosophy leads away from God' – and it is the same half-measure which defines cognition as an *approximation* to the truth – 'whereas true philosophy leads to God'; the same applies to philosophy and the state. Reason is not content with an approximation which, as something 'neither cold nor hot', it 'spews out of its mouth'; and it is as little content with that cold despair which confesses that, in this temporal world, things are bad or at best indifferent, but that nothing better can be expected here, so that for this reason alone we should live at peace with actuality. The peace which cognition establishes with the actual world has more warmth in it than this.

A further word on the subject of *issuing instructions* on how the world ought to be: philosophy, at any rate, always comes too late to perform this function. As the *thought* of the world, it appears only at a time when actuality has gone through its formative process and attained its completed state. This lesson of the concept is necessarily also apparent from history, namely that it is only when actuality has reached maturity that the ideal appears opposite the real and reconstructs this real world, which it has grasped in its substance, in the shape of an intellectual realm. When philosophy paints its grey in grey, a shape of life has grown old, and it cannot be rejuvenated, but only recognized, by the grey in grey of philosophy; the owl of Minerva begins its flight only with the onset of dusk.

But it is time to conclude this foreword; as a foreword, its function was in any case merely to make external and subjective comments on the point of view of the work to which it is prefaced. If a content is to be discussed philosophically, it will bear only scientific and objective treatment; in the same way, the author will regard any criticism expressed in a form other than that of scientific discussion of the matter [*Sache*] itself merely as a subjective postscript and random assertion, and will treat it with indifference.

Berlin, 25 June 1820
Translated by H. B. Nisbet

The Philosophical History of the World

SECOND DRAFT (1830)

[begun] 8. xi. 1830

Gentlemen,

The subject of these lectures is the philosophy of world history.

As to what is meant by history or world history, I need say nothing; the common conception of it is adequate, and we are more or less agreed on what it is. But what may strike you about the title of these lectures and call for a word of elucidation, or rather of justification, is that we are here concerned with a philosophy of world history, and are about to consider history from a philosophical point of view.

But the philosophy of history is nothing more than the application of thought to history; and thinking is something we cannot stop doing. For man is a thinking being, and it is this which distinguishes him from the animals. All that is truly human, as distinct from animal – feeling, knowledge, and cognition – contains an element of thought, and this applies to all historical studies. But to appeal in this way to the participation of thought in all human activities may seem inadequate, for it could be argued that thought is subordinate to being, to the data of reality, and is based upon and determined by the latter. Philosophy, on the other hand, is credited with independent thoughts produced by pure speculation, without reference to actuality; speculation, it might further be contended, approaches history as something to be manipulated, and does not leave it as it is, but forces it to conform to its preconceived notions and constructs a history a priori.

History, however, is concerned with what actually happened. Its methods would therefore seem completely at variance with the essentially self-determining activity of conceptual thought. It is, of course, possible to present events in such a way that we can imagine they

317

are taking place directly before our eyes. Even then, however, the links between the events must be taken into account; in other words, our procedure must be pragmatic, for we have to discover the causes and reasons behind the events. But as one can imagine, this will require the assistance of concepts, which does not, however, imply that the conceptual thought involved will be at odds with its own nature. Nevertheless, in a procedure of this kind, the events will always remain basic, and the activity of the concept will be limited to the formal and general aspects of the factual material, i.e., to rules, fundamentals, and principles. It is generally accepted that logical thinking is required for all such deductions from history; their justification, however, must come from the world of experience. But what philosophy understands by conceptual thinking is something quite different; in this case, comprehension is the activity of the concept itself, and not a conflict between a material and a form of separate origin. An alliance of disparates such as is found in pragmatic history is not sufficient for the purposes of conceptual thinking as practised in philosophy; for the latter derives its content and material essentially from within itself. In this respect, therefore, despite the alleged links between the two, the original dichotomy remains: the historical event stands opposed to the independent concept.

But [even if we disregard philosophy,] the same relationship emerges in the study of history itself as soon as we look at it from a higher vantage point. For on the one hand, we have in history ingredients and higher determinants which are remote from the conceptual world – i.e., all kinds of human arbitrariness and external necessity. On the other hand, we set up against this the idea of a higher necessity, an eternal justice and love, the absolute and ultimate end which is truth in and for itself. In contrast to natural being, this second, opposite pole is based on abstract elements, on the freedom and necessity of the concept. This opposition contains many interesting features; it comes to our notice once again in the Idea of world history. Our present aim is to show how it is resolved in and for itself in the world-historical process.

The sole end of history is to comprehend clearly what is and what has been, the events and deeds of the past. It gains in veracity the more strictly it confines itself to what is given, and – although this is not so immediately evident, but in fact requires many kinds of investigations in which thought also plays a part – the more exclusively it seeks to discover what actually happened. This aim seems to contradict the function of philosophy; and it is this contradiction, and the accusation that philosophy imports its own ideas into history and manipulates it accordingly, that I wish to discuss in the Introduction to these lectures. In other words, we must first obtain a general definition of the philosophy of world history and then consider its immediate implications. As a result, the relationship between thought and the events should automatically appear in the correct light. For this reason, and since I do not wish the Introduction to become too long-winded (for the material of world history itself is so abundant), there is no need for me to spend time refuting and correcting the endless individual misconceptions and mistaken reflections – some of which are current now, others of which are periodically resuscitated – regarding perspectives, principles, and opinions on the aim and interests of historical studies, and in particular on the relationship of conceptual thought and philosophy to historical fact. I can omit all this entirely, or merely touch on it in passing.

A [ITS GENERAL CONCEPT]

The first thing I wish to say concerning our provisional concept of world history is this. As already remarked, the main objection levelled at philosophy is that it imports its own thoughts into history and considers the latter in the light of the former. But the only thought which philosophy brings with it is the simple idea of reason – the idea that reason governs the world, and that world history is therefore a rational process. From the point of view of history as such, this conviction and insight is a presupposition. Within philosophy itself, however, it is not a presupposition; for it is proved in philosophy by speculative cognition that reason – and we can adopt this expression for the moment without a detailed discussion of its relationship to God – is substance and infinite power; it is itself the infinite material of all natural and spiritual life, and the infinite form which activates this material content. It is substance, i.e., that through which and in which all reality has its being and subsistence; it is infinite power, for reason is sufficiently powerful to be able to create something more than just an ideal, an obligation which supposedly exists in some unknown region beyond reality (or, as is more likely, only as a particular idea in the heads of a few individuals); and it is the infinite content, the essence and truth of everything, itself constituting the material on which it operates through its own activity. Unlike finite actions, it does not require an external material as a condition of its operation, or outside resources from which to derive its sustenance and the objects of its activity; it is self-supporting, and is itself the material of its own operations. On the one hand, it is its own sole precondition, and its end is the absolute and ultimate end of everything; and on the other, it is itself the agent which implements and realizes this end, translating it from potentiality into actuality both in the natural universe and in the spiritual world – that is, in world history. That this Idea is true, eternal, and omnipotent, that it reveals itself in the world, and that nothing is revealed except the Idea in all its honour and majesty – this, as I have said, is what philosophy has proved, and we can therefore posit it as demonstrated for our present purposes.

The sole aim of philosophical inquiry is to eliminate the contingent. Contingency is the same as external necessity, that is, a necessity which originates in causes which are themselves no more than external circumstances. In history, we must look for a general design, the ultimate end of the world, and not a particular end of the subjective spirit or mind; and we must comprehend it by means of reason, which cannot concern itself with particular and finite ends, but only with the absolute. This absolute end is a content which speaks for itself and in which everything of interest to man has its foundation. The rational is that which has being in and for itself, and from which everything else derives its value. It assumes varying shapes; but in none of them is it more obviously an end than in that whereby the spirit explicates and manifests itself in the endlessly varying forms which we call nations. We must bring to history the belief and conviction that the realm of the will is not at the mercy of contingency. That world history is governed by an ultimate design, that it is a rational process – whose rationality is not that of a particular subject, but a divine and absolute reason – this is a proposition whose truth we must assume; its proof lies in the study of world history itself, which is the image and enactment of reason. The real proof, however, comes from a knowledge of reason itself; for reason appears in world history only in a mediate form. World history is merely a manifestation of this one original reason; it is one of the particular forms in which reason reveals itself, a reflection of the archetype in a particular element, in the life of nations.

Reason is self-sufficient and contains its end within itself; it brings itself into existence and carries itself into effect. Thought must become conscious of this end of reason. The philosophical method may at first strike us as odd; bad habits of thinking may even lead us to imagine that it is itself contingent or no more than an arbitrary whim. But anyone who does not accept that thought is the sole truth and the highest factor in existence is not in a position to pass any judgement whatsoever on the philosophical method.

Some of you gentlemen, may not yet be acquainted with philosophy. I could easily appeal to all such persons to approach these lectures on world history with a faith in reason and a thirst for knowledge of it; – and we must surely assume that a desire for rational insight, for knowledge, and not just for a collection of assorted information, is the subjective motive which inspires those who seek to study the learned disciplines. But I need not, in fact, make any such claims upon your faith. These provisional remarks and the observations I shall subsequently add to them are not, even within our own discipline, to be regarded simply as prior assumptions, but as a preliminary survey of the whole, as the result of the ensuing inquiry; for the result is already known to me, as I have covered the whole field in advance. It has already been shown and will again emerge in the course of this inquiry that the history of the world is a rational process, therational and necessary evolution of the world spirit. This spirit [is] the substance of history; its nature is always one and the same; and it discloses this nature in the existence of the world. (The world spirit is the absolute spirit.) This, as I have said, must be the result of our study of history. But we must be sure to take history as it is; in other words, we must proceed historically and empirically. For example, we must not allow ourselves to be misled by the professional historians; for certain of them, at least in Germany (and they even include some leading authorities who pride themselves on what they call their study of the sources), are guilty of precisely what they accuse the philosophers of doing – of introducing a priori fictions into history. Thus it is a widely accepted fiction (to quote one example) that there was an original primeval people, directly instructed by God, living in perfect understanding and wisdom, and possessing a thorough knowledge of all natural laws and spiritual truth; or again, that various nations of priests at one time existed; or (to take a more specific example) that the Roman historians based their accounts of ancient history on a lost Roman epic, etc. Let us leave such a priori inventions to those ingenious professional historians, among whom (at any rate in Germany) they are not uncommon.

We can therefore lay it down as our first condition that history must be apprehended accurately. But general expressions such as apprehend and accurately are not without ambiguity. Even the ordinary, run-of-the-mill historian who believes and professes that his attitude is entirely receptive, that he is dedicated to the facts, is by no means passive in his thinking; he brings his categories with him, and they influence his vision of the data he has before him. The truth is not to be found on the superficial plane of the senses; for, especially in subjects which claim a scientific status, reason must always remain alert, and conscious deliberation is indispensable. Whoever looks at the world rationally will find that it in turn assumes a rational aspect; the two exist in a reciprocal relationship.

It is perfectly correct to say that the design of the world should be distinguishable by observation. But to recognize the universal and the rational, it is necessary to use reason too. The objects are stimuli to thought; otherwise, we find that the world takes on an aspect corresponding to the way in which we look at it. Anyone who views the world purely subjectively will see it in terms of his own nature; he will know everything better than everyone else, and see how things ought to have been done and what course events ought to have taken. But the overall content of world history is rational, and indeed has to be rational; a divine will rules supreme and is strong enough to determine the overall content. Our aim must be to discern this substance, and to do so, we must bring with us a rational consciousness. Physical perception and a finite understanding are not enough; we must see with the eye of the concept, the eye of reason, which penetrates the surface and finds its way through the complex and confusing turmoil of events. Yet people say that this approach to history is an a priori procedure, and intrinsically wrong. Whether they do so or not is a matter of indifference to philosophy. In order to perceive the substance, we must apply our own reason to it. This does not mean, however, that one-sided reflections are admissible; for they distort history and arise out of mistaken subjective opinions. But philosophy is not concerned with these. Sure in the knowledge that reason governs history, philosophy is convinced that the events will match the concept; it does not pervert the truth after the fashion which is now prevalent – especially among the philologists, who employ their so-called acumen to introduce wholly a priori ideas into history. Admittedly, philosophy does follow an a priori method in so far as it presupposes the Idea. But the Idea is undoubtedly there, and reason is fully convinced of its presence.

The perspective adopted by the philosophical history of the world is accordingly not just one among many general perspectives, an isolated abstraction singled out at the expense of the rest. Its spiritual principle is the sum total of all possible perspectives. It concentrates its attention on the concrete spiritual principle in the life of nations, and deals not with individual situations but with a universal thought which runs throughout the whole. This universal element is not to be found in the world of contingent phenomena; it is the unity behind the multitude of particulars. The object of history is the most concrete of all, for it comprehends every aspect of existence; the world spirit is its individuality. What philosophy is therefore concerned with in its treatment of history is the concrete object in its concrete form, and it traces the necessary development of this object. Thus the destinies, passions, and energies of nations are not its prime consideration, with the events following on in second place. On the contrary, its chief concern is the spirit of the events themselves, the moving spirit within them, for this is the true Mercury, the leader of nations. We must therefore not imagine that the universal object of the philosophical history of the world is only one aspect of history (no matter how important this aspect might be), with other alternative determinants existing independently of it. On the contrary, the universal object is infinitely concrete, all-comprehending and omnipresent, for the spirit is eternally present to itself; it has no past, and remains for ever the same in all its vigour and strength.

The understanding must always be brought to bear on history in order that we may comprehend the causes and effects at work in it. In this way, we try to discover what is essential in world history and to disregard what is inessential. The understanding brings out everything that is important and inherently significant. Its criteria of the essential and the inessential will vary according to the end it is pursuing in its examination of history, and the ends it sets itself can also vary enormously. Whenever a particular aim is chosen, further considerations at once present themselves, and we are compelled to distinguish between principal and secondary aims. Accordingly, when we are comparing the facts of history with the ends of the spirit, we will ignore everything which might otherwise be of interest and stick to essentials. Thus the historical content which presents itself to reason is not simply equivalent to the entire events of the past. Some ends are of essential interest to the intellect, and others to the emotions, so that we can be moved to sorrow, admiration, or joy when we read about them.

But it is not our business to discuss the various types of reflection, attitudes, and judgements, not even the ways of distinguishing the important from the unimportant (and these are the most obvious categories), or [of deciding what to emphasize most] in the unlimited material at our disposal.

[Nevertheless, we ought to give a brief account of the categories under which the historical process generally presents itself to thought.] The first category comes from our observation of the changing individuals, nations, and states which flourish for a while, capture our interest, and then disappear. This is the category of *change*.

We witness a vast spectacle of events and actions, of infinitely varied constellations of nations, states, and individuals, in restless succession. Everything that can occupy and interest the human mind, every sensation of the good, the beautiful and the great, comes into play; everywhere we see others pursuing aims which we ourselves affirm and whose fulfilment we desire, and we share their hopes and fears. In all these events and contingencies, our first concern is with the deeds and sufferings of men; we see elements of ourselves in everything, so that our sympathies constantly oscillate from one side to the other. Sometimes we are captivated by beauty, freedom, and riches, sometimes we are impressed by human energy, which can invest even vice with greatness. Sometimes we see the accumulated weight of a popular cause lose its impetus and finally disintegrate, to be sacrificed to an infinite complex of minor exigencies. Sometimes we see how a huge expenditure of effort can produce only a trifling result, or conversely, how an apparently insignificant thing can have momentous consequences. Everywhere we see a motley confusion which draws us into its interests, and when one thing disappears, another at once takes its place.

The negative aspect of the idea of change moves us to sadness. It oppresses us to think that the richest forms and the finest manifestations of life must perish in history, and that we walk amidst the ruins of excellence. History cuts us off from the finest and noblest of our interests: the passions have destroyed them, for they are transient. It seems that all must perish and that nothing endures. Every traveller has experienced this melancholy. Who has stood among the ruins of Carthage, Palmyra, Persepolis or Rome without being moved to reflect on the transience of empires and men, to mourn the loss of the rich and vigorous life of bygone ages? It is not a sorrow like that which we experience at the graves of those dear to us, when we lament our personal losses and the transience of our own aspirations; it is rather a disinterested sorrow at the downfall of the brilliant cultures of the past.

But the category of change has another, positive side to it. For out of death, new life arises. The Orientals have understood this idea; it is perhaps the greatest idea they have ever produced, and it is certainly the most sublime of their metaphysical doctrines. It is implicit, but with individual reference, in their notion of metempsychosis: but an even more celebrated example is the image of the Phoenix, of natural life, which for ever constructs its own funeral pyre and is for ever consumed upon it, only to rise again from the ashes as fresh and rejuvenated life. This, however, is only an image of the East; it applies to the body, but not to the spirit. Its Western counterpart is the realization that the spirit too rises up again, not only rejuvenated but also enhanced and transfigured. Admittedly, it becomes divided against itself and destroys the form it earlier occupied, but in so doing, it rises up to a new stage of development. But when it abandons the shell of its former existence, it does not merely migrate into a new shell; it emerges as a purified spirit from the ashes of its earlier form. This is the second category of the spirit, the category of *rejuvenation*. The rejuvenation of the spirit is not just a return to an earlier shape; it is a purification or further elaboration of itself. The solution of its problem creates new problems for it to solve, so that it multiplies the materials on which it operates. Thus we see how the spirit in history issues forth in innumerable directions, indulging and satisfying itself in them all. But the only result of its labour is that its activity is once more increased, and it is again consumed. Each of the creations in which it found temporary satisfaction presents itself in turn as a new material, challenging the spirit to develop it further still. The forms it produced become the material on which it labours to raise itself up to new forms. It manifests all its powers in every possible way. We learn what powers it possesses from the very wealth of forms it produces. In this sheer delight in activity, it is entirely absorbed in itself. Nature admittedly imposes internal and external limitations on it, and these not only resist it and place obstacles in its path but can even cause it to fail completely in its endeavours. But even when it is frustrated, it remains true to its character as a spiritual being, a being whose end is not the finished product but the activity of production, so that it still affords the spectacle of having exhibited its active nature.

But the immediate result of these intriguing speculations is that we grow weary of particulars and ask ourselves to what end they all contribute. We cannot accept that their significance is exhausted in their own particular ends; everything must be part of a single enterprise. Surely some ultimate end must be promoted by this enormous expenditure of spiritual resources. We are compelled to ask whether, beneath the superficial din and clamour of history, there is not perhaps a silent and mysterious inner process at work, whereby the energy of all phenomena is conserved. What may well perplex us, however, is the great variety and even inconsistency of the content of history. We see complete opposites venerated as equally sacred, capturing the attention of different ages and nations. We feel the need to find a justification in the realm of ideas for all this destruction. This reflection leads us to the third category, to the question of whether there is such a thing as an ultimate end in and for itself. This is the category of *reason* proper; it is present in our consciousness as a belief that the world is governed by reason. Its proof is to be found in the study of world history itself, which is the image and enactment of reason.

I only wish to mention two points concerning the general conviction that reason has ruled and continues to rule the world and hence also world history; for these should give us an opportunity to examine more closely the main difficulty which confronts us, and to touch provisionally on matters which will have to be discussed later.

The first point is as follows. As history tells us, the Greek Anaxagoras was the first to declare that the world is governed by a 'nous', i.e. by reason or understanding in general. This does not signify an intelligence in the sense of a self-conscious reason or a spirit as such, and the two must not be confused. The movement of the solar system is governed by unalterable laws; these laws are its inherent reason. But neither the sun nor the planets which revolve around it in accordance with these laws are conscious of them. It is man who abstracts the laws from empirical reality and acquires knowledge of them. An idea of this kind, that there is reason in nature or that it is governed by unalterable general laws, does not strike us as in any way strange, and Anaxagoras had as yet applied it only to nature. We are accustomed to such ideas, and do not find them at all extraordinary. One of the reasons why I mentioned this historical fact at all was to show how we can learn from history that what may now seem trivial was once unknown to the world, and that such ideas were in fact of epoch-making significance in the history of the human spirit. Aristotle says of Anaxagoras, as the originator of this idea, that he stood out like a sober man in a company of drunkards.

This idea was taken over from Anaxagoras by Socrates, and it then became the ruling principle in philosophy – except in the case of Epicurus, who attributed everything to chance. We shall see in due course what other religions and nations came to accept it. Plato (Phaedo, Stephanus edition pp. 97–8) makes Socrates say of this discovery that thought (not conscious thought but thought of a nature as yet undefined, equivalent to neither conscious nor unconscious reason) governs the world: 'I was delighted with it and hoped I had at last discovered a teacher who would explain nature to me rationally, who would reveal the particular end of each particular phenomenon and also the ultimate end, the good, in nature as a whole. It was a hope which I was not at all eager to relinquish. But how very disappointed I was', Socrates continues, 'when I turned, full of anticipation, to the writings of Anaxagoras himself! I discovered that, instead of reason, he dealt only with external causes such as air, ether, water, and the like.' It is evident from this that what Socrates took exception to was not Anaxagoras' principle as such, but his failure to apply it adequately to concrete nature, and to interpret nature in the light of the principle; for this principle was never anything more than an abstraction, or more precisely, nature was not presented as a development of the principle, as an organization produced by it, with reason as its cause.

I wish, from the outset, to emphasize this distinction between a definition, principle, or truth which remains abstract, and one whose specific determination and concrete development are also explained. This distinction is to be found throughout our subject, and one of the principal occasions on which we shall encounter it will be at the end of our survey of world history when we come to examine the political situation in recent times.

Another of the main reasons why I have cited this earliest instance of the idea that reason rules the world and discussed its inadequacy is because it has also been applied more fully to another subject with which we are all familiar and of whose truth we are personally convinced – I refer, of course, to the religious truth that the world is not a prey to chance and external, contingent causes, but is governed by providence. I declared earlier that I did not wish to make any demands on your faith in the above-mentioned principle. I might, however, have appealed to your faith in it in this religious form, if it were not that the peculiar nature of philosophy forbids us to attach authority to prior assumptions; or, to put it differently, I cannot do so, because the discipline we are studying must itself furnish the proof of the principle's correctness (if not of its actual truth), and display its concrete reality. The truth, then, that the world's events are controlled by a providence, indeed by divine providence, is consistent with the principle in question. For divine providence is wisdom, coupled with infinite power, which realizes its ends, i.e. the absolute and rational design of the world; and reason is freely self-determining thought, or what the Greeks called 'nous'.

But there is also a difference, indeed a contradiction, between this faith in providence and our original principle, a difference akin to that between the principle of Anaxagoras and the expectations with which Socrates approached it. For this general faith in providence is likewise indeterminate, and lacks a determinate application to the whole, to the entire course of world events. [Instead of giving it this] application [men are content] to explain history [by natural causes. They confine themselves to] human passions, the relative strengths of armies, the abilities and genius of this or that individual, or the lack of such an individual in a given state – in short, to so-called natural causes of a purely contingent nature, such as Socrates [criticized in the work of Anaxagoras. They conceive of providence as an] abstraction [and] make do with a general idea of it [without discussing its determinate application]. The determinate aspects of providence, the specific actions it performs, constitute the providential plan (i.e. the end and means of its destiny and aims). But this plan is supposed to be hidden from our view, and we are told that it is presumptuous to try to comprehend it. The ignorance of Anaxagoras as to how understanding manifests itself in reality was unfeigned; the development of thought, and man's awareness of its development, had not progressed beyond this point either in him or in Greece as a whole. He was as yet unable to apply his general principle to concrete reality, or to interpret reality in terms of the principle. It was Socrates who took the first step towards finding a means of combining the concrete with the universal, if only in a subjective and one-sided way; thus his polemics were not directed against concrete applications of the principle. But those who believe in providence are hostile to all attempts to apply the idea on a large scale, i.e. to any attempts to comprehend the providential plan. No one objects to it being applied in isolated cases, and pious souls discern in numerous particular occurrences, where others see only the agency of chance, not just dispensations of God himself, but of divine providence – i.e. the ends which providence pursues by means of such dispensations. But this usually happens only in isolated instances; and when, for example, an individual in great perplexity and distress receives unexpected help, we must not hold it against him if his gratitude at once leads him to see the hand of God at work. But the design of providence in such cases is of a limited nature; its content is merely the particular end of the individual in question. In world history, however, the individuals we are concerned with are nations, totalities, states. We cannot, therefore, be content with this (if the word be permitted) trivial faith in providence, nor indeed with a merely abstract and indeterminate faith which conceives in general terms of a ruling providence but refuses to apply it to determinate reality; on the contrary, we must tackle the problem seriously. The concrete events are the ways of providence, the means it uses, the phenomena in which it manifests itself in history; they are open to our inspection, and we only have to relate them to the general principle referred to above.

But in mentioning the possibility of comprehending the plan of divine providence, I have touched on a question which is of central importance today: I mean the question of whether it is possible to obtain knowledge of God – or rather, since it has ceased to be a question – the doctrine, now hardened into a prejudice, that it is impossible to know God, notwithstanding the teaching of the Scriptures that it is our highest duty not only to love God but also to know him. This prejudice goes against the Scriptural saying that the spirit leads into truth, searches all things, and penetrates even into the deep things of God.

Simple faith can well dispense with a fuller understanding of history and make do with the general notion of a divine world order; and we ought not to condemn those who take this course, so long as their faith does not become a polemical one. But it is also possible to defend such views in a spirit of prejudice, and the general proposition, by virtue of its very generality, can also be given a specifically negative application, so as to suggest that the divine being is remote from all human things and transcends human knowledge. Those who adopt this attitude reserve the right to dismiss the claims of truth and rationality, with the added advantage of being able to indulge their own fancies at will. Seen from this point of view, all ideas of God are reduced to empty talk. If God is placed beyond the reach of our rational consciousness, we are no longer obliged to trouble ourselves about his nature, or indeed to look for reason in world history; the way is then open for any arbitrary hypotheses. Pious humility knows very well what it stands to gain from its sacrifices.

I could have refrained from mentioning that our principle (i.e., that reason governs the world and always has done so) has a religious equivalent in the doctrine of a ruling providence; this would have allowed me to avoid the question of whether it is possible to obtain knowledge of God. But I did not wish to do so, partly in order to bring out some further implications of these questions, and partly also to allay any suspicions that philosophy has or should have any cause to fear discussing religious truths, or that it circumvents them because it does not, so to speak, have an easy conscience about them. On the contrary, we have recently reached the point where philosophy has had to defend the content of religion against certain kinds of theology.

As I have said, we are often told that it is presumptuous to try to fathom the plan of providence. This is a direct consequence of the

HEGEL

idea (which has now become an almost universally accepted axiom) that it is impossible to obtain knowledge of God. And when theology itself is in so desperate a position, we must take refuge in philosophy if we wish to learn anything about God. Certainly, reason is often accused of arrogance in presuming to attain such knowledge. But it would be more accurate to say that true humility consists precisely in recognizing and revering God in everything, especially in the theatre of world history. Furthermore, the traditional view that God's wisdom is manifest in nature has not yet been altogether abandoned. It was indeed fashionable at one time to admire the wisdom of God as manifested in animals and plants. But to marvel at human destinies or products of nature is already an indication that we have some knowledge of God. If we admit that providence reveals itself in such objects and materials, why should we not do the same in world history? Is it because history seems too vast a subject? It is certainly customary to conceive of providence as taking a hand only in minor matters, to picture it as a wealthy benefactor who distributes alms among men and furthers their ends. But it is a mistake to think that the material of world history is too vast for providence to cope with; for the divine wisdom is one and the same in great things and in small. It is the same in plants and insects as in the destinies of entire nations and empires, and we must not imagine that God is not powerful enough to apply his wisdom to things of great moment. To believe that God's wisdom is not active in everything is to show humility towards the material rather than towards the divine wisdom itself. Besides, nature is a theatre of secondary importance compared with that of world history. Nature is a field in which the divine Idea operates in a non-conceptual medium; the spiritual sphere is its proper province, and it is here above all that it ought to be visible. Armed with the concept of reason, we need not fear coming to grips with any subject whatsoever.

The contention that we should not attempt to know God in fact requires closer examination than is possible within the scope of these lectures. But since this matter has so close a bearing upon our present aim, it is essential that we should consider at least the general perspectives involved. Thus if knowledge of God is impossible, the only thing

332

left for the mind to occupy itself with is the non-divine, the limited, the finite. Of course it is necessary for man to occupy himself with finite things; but there is also a higher necessity which requires that there should be a sabbath in his existence, a time when he can rise above his daily labours to occupy his mind consciously with truth.

If the name of God is to be more than an empty word, we must consider God as benevolent, or at least as in some way communicative. In the earlier phases of Greek thought, God was seen as subject to envy, and there was much talk of the envy of the gods; it was said that the divinity is hostile to greatness, and that it is the mission of the gods to humble the great. Aristotle says, however, that poets are much given to lying, for envy cannot be an attribute of God. And if we were to maintain in turn that God does not reveal himself at all, this would amount to an allegation that he is envious. But God cannot lose anything by communication any more than a light can be diminished when a second one is lit from it.

It is often said that God does reveal himself, but only in nature on the one hand, and in the heart, in the feelings of men, on the other. We are usually told nowadays that this is the point at which we must draw a halt, for God is present only to our immediate consciousness or intuition. Intuition and emotion, however, are both unreflecting forms of consciousness, and we must insist in reply to such arguments that man is a thinking being, for it is thought which distinguishes him from the animals. He behaves as a thinking being even when he is himself unaware of it. When God reveals himself to man, he reveals himself essentially through man's rational faculties; if he revealed himself essentially through the emotions, this would imply that he regarded man as no better than the animals, who do not possess the power of reflection – yet we do not attribute religion to the animals. In fact, man only possesses religion because he is not an animal but a thinking being. It is a trivial commonplace that man is distinguished from the animals by his ability to think, yet this is something which is often forgotten.

God is the eternal being in and for himself; and the universal in and for itself is an object of thought, not of feeling. It is true that all spiritual things, all data of the consciousness, all products and objects of thought – and above all religion and morality – must also come to us through the medium of feeling, and indeed primarily through this medium. Feeling, however, is not the source from which they are derived, but only the form which they assume in man; and it is the basest form they can assume, a form which man shares in common with the animals. All substantial things must be able to assume the form of emotion, yet they can also assume a higher and worthier form. But to insist on translating all morality and truth and every spiritual substance into feeling, and to endeavour to preserve them in this form, is tantamount to saying that their proper form is the animal one – although the latter is in fact incapable of comprehending their spiritual content. Feeling is the lowest form which any such content can assume, for its presence in feeling can only be minimal. So long as it retains this form, it remains inchoate and completely indeterminate. The content of our feelings remains entirely subjective, and is only subjectively present to us. To say 'I feel such and such' is to shut oneself up within oneself. Everyone else is equally entitled to say 'But I feel differently', and then all common ground is lost. In purely particular matters, feelings are perfectly justified. But to maintain that a given content is present in the feelings of everyone is to contradict the emotional point of view one has adopted, the point of view of personal subjectivity. As soon as the emotions have a content, everyone is placed in a position of subjectivity. And if one person should choose to say unpleasant things about another who has acted only on his feelings, the second is entitled to say the same of the first, and both would be equally justified – from their own point of view – in taking offence. If one man says that he has religious emotions, and another says that he cannot feel God, they are both right. If the divine content – i.e., the revelation of God, the relationship between man and God, and the being of God for mankind – is reduced in this way to mere emotion, it is thereby confined to the level of individual subjectivity, of arbitrariness, of random inclinations. In fact, this has been a convenient way of getting round the problem of the truth which exists in and for itself. If I rely only on my emotions, which are indeterminate, and have no knowledge of God and his nature, I have nothing to guide me except random inclinations; the finite alone has validity and is the dominant power. And if I know nothing whatsoever of God, there can be no serious talk about the limits of such knowledge either.

The truth is inherently universal, essential, and substantial; and as such, it exists solely in thought and for thought. But that spiritual principle which we call God is none other than the truly substantial, inherently and essentially individual and subjective truth. It is the source of all thought, and its thought is inherently creative; we encounter it as such in world history. Whatever else we describe as true is merely a particular form of this eternal truth, which is its sole foundation; it is but a single ray of the universal light. If we know nothing of this truth, we must remain ignorant of all truth, rightness, and morality.

But what, we may ask, is the plan of providence in world history? Has the time come for us to understand it? [I shall confine myself for the present to] the following general remarks.

God has revealed himself through the Christian religion; that is, he has granted mankind the possibility of recognizing his nature, so that he is no longer an impenetrable mystery. The fact that knowledge of God is possible also makes it our duty to know him, and that development of the thinking spirit which the Christian revelation of God initiated must eventually produce a situation where all that was at first present only to the emotional and representational faculties can also be comprehended by thought. Whether the time has yet come for such knowledge will depend on whether the ultimate end of the world has yet been realized in a universally valid and conscious manner.

Now the distinctive feature of Christianity is that, with its advent, this time has indeed come. Its significance for the history of the world is therefore absolutely epoch-making, for the nature of God has at last been made manifest. If we say that we know nothing of God, Christianity becomes something superfluous, a belated arrival, or even a symptom of decay. But this is not the case, for Christianity does give us knowledge of God. Its content, admittedly, appeals to our emotions too. But since the feeling it evokes is a spiritual one, it at least brings into play the faculty of representation – and not just sensory representation either, but also representational thought, the true medium through which man perceives God. Christianity is the religion which has revealed the nature and being of God to man. Thus we know as Christians what God is; God is no longer an unknown quantity: and if we continue to say that he is, we are not Christians. Christianity demands that humility to which we have already referred, a humility which makes us seek to know God not through our own unaided efforts but with the help of divine knowledge and wisdom. Christians, then, are initiated into the mysteries of God, and this also supplies us with the key to world history. For we have here a definite knowledge of providence and its plan. It is one of the central doctrines of Christianity that providence has ruled and continues to rule the world, and that everything which happens in the world is determined by and commensurate with the divine government. This doctrine is opposed both to the idea of chance and to that of limited ends (such as the preservation of the Jewish people). Its end is the ultimate and absolutely universal end which exists in and for itself. Religion does not go beyond this general representation; it remains on the level of generality. But we must proceed from this general faith firstly to philosophy and then to the philosophy of world history – from the faith that world history is a product of eternal reason, and that it is reason which has determined all its great revolutions.

We can therefore conclude that, even in the absolute sense, the time has come in which this conviction and inner certainty need no longer remain a mere representation, but can also be thought, developed, and recognized as a definite piece of knowledge. The original faith makes no attempt to elaborate its content further or to gain any insight into historical necessity – for only knowledge can do that. The fact that the spirit never stands still guarantees that such a time must eventually come; the culminating phase of the spirit – thought or the concept – insists on its rights, and it alone, in its most general and essential being, constitutes the true nature of the spirit.

A distinction is often made between faith and knowledge, and the two have come to be commonly accepted as opposites. It is taken for granted that they are different, and that we therefore have no knowledge of God. People are affronted if we tell them that we seek to know and understand God, and to impart such knowledge to others. But if it is defined correctly, the distinction between faith and knowledge is in fact an empty one. For if I have faith in something, I also know it and am convinced of it. In religion, we have faith in God and in the doctrines which explain his nature more fully; but this is something we know and of which we are certain. To know means to have something as an object of one's consciousness and to be certain of it; and it is exactly the same with faith. Cognition, however, perceives that the content of knowledge – and indeed of faith – is necessary, and discerns the reasons behind it; it does so without reference to the authority of the Church or of feeling, which is something immediate, and goes on to analyse this content into its various determinate elements. These determinate elements must first become objects of thought before we can obtain a true cognition of them and perceive them in their concrete unity within the concept. And if there is any further suggestion that it is presumptuous to seek such cognition, we might then reply that all this fuss is unnecessary, since cognition merely takes note of necessity and watches the inner development of the content unfold before its eyes. As a further reason why such cognition cannot be branded as presumptuous, one might also maintain that it differs from faith only in its greater knowledge of particulars. But this argument would be misplaced, and indeed inherently false. For the spiritual is not by nature abstract, but a living thing, a universal individual, a subjective, self-determining, decision-making being. We cannot therefore truly know the nature of God unless we recognize its determinate elements. Christianity too speaks of God in this way, for it recognizes him as a spirit, and this spirit is not an abstraction, but the process in itself; and this is turn presupposes the existence of absolute distinctions – in fact, the very distinctions which Christianity has made known to mankind.

God does not wish to have narrow-minded and empty-headed children. On the contrary, he demands that we should know him; he wishes his children to be poor in spirit but rich in knowledge of him, and to set the highest value on acquiring knowledge of God. History is the unfolding of God's nature in a particular, determinate element, so that only a determinate form of knowledge is possible and appropriate to it.

The time has now surely come for us to comprehend even so rich a product of creative reason as world history. The aim of human cognition is to understand that the intentions of eternal wisdom are accomplished not only in the natural world, but also in the realm of the [spirit] which is actively present in the world. From this point of view, our investigation can be seen as a theodicy, a justification of the ways of God (such as Leibniz attempted in his own metaphysical manner, but using categories which were as yet abstract and indeterminate). It should enable us to comprehend all the ills of the world, including the existence of evil, so that the thinking spirit may be reconciled with the negative aspects of existence; and it is in world history that we encounter the sum total of concrete evil. (Indeed, there is no department of knowledge in which such a reconciliation is more urgently required than in world history, and we shall accordingly pause for a moment to consider this question further.)

A reconciliation of the kind just described can only be achieved through a knowledge of the affirmative side of history, in which the negative is reduced to a subordinate position and transcended altogether. In other words, we must first of all know what the ultimate design of the world really is, and secondly, we must see that this design has been realized and that evil has not been able to maintain a position of equality beside it.

In order to justify the course of history, we must try to understand the role of evil in the light of the absolute sovereignty of reason. We are dealing here with the category of the negative, as already mentioned, and we cannot fail to notice how all that is finest and noblest in the history of the world is immolated upon its altar. Reason cannot stop to consider the injuries sustained by single individuals, for particular ends are submerged in the universal end. In the rise and fall of all things it discerns an enterprise at which the entire human race has laboured, an enterprise which has a real existence in the world to which we belong. Phenomena have become real independently of our efforts, and all that we need to understand them is consciousness, or more precisely, a thinking consciousness. For the affirmative element is not to be found merely in emotional enjoyment or in the imagination, but is something which belongs to reality and to us, or to which we ourselves belong.

Reason, it has been said, rules the world. But 'reason' is just as indefinite a word as 'providence'. People continually speak of reason, without being able to define it correctly, to specify its content, or to supply a criterion by which we might judge whether something is rational or irrational. Reason in its determinate form is the true substance; and the rest – if we confine ourselves to reason in general – is mere words.

Translated by H. B. Nisbet

READ MORE IN PENGUIN

In every corner of the world, on every subject under the sun, Penguin represents quality and variety – the very best in publishing today.

For complete information about books available from Penguin – including Puffins, Penguin Classics and Arkana – and how to order them, write to us at the appropriate address below. Please note that for copyright reasons the selection of books varies from country to country.

In the United Kingdom: Please write to *Dept. EP, Penguin Books Ltd, Bath Road, Harmondsworth, West Drayton, Middlesex UB7 ODA*

In the United States: Please write to *Consumer Sales, Penguin Putnam Inc., P.O. Box 12289 Dept. B, Newark, New Jersey 07101-5289*. VISA and MasterCard holders call 1-800-788-6262 to order Penguin titles

In Canada: Please write to *Penguin Books Canada Ltd, 10 Alcorn Avenue, Suite 300, Toronto, Ontario M4V 3B2*

In Australia: Please write to *Penguin Books Australia Ltd, P.O. Box 257, Ringwood, Victoria 3134*

In New Zealand: Please write to *Penguin Books (NZ) Ltd, Private Bag 102902, North Shore Mail Centre, Auckland 10*

In India: Please write to *Penguin Books India Pvt Ltd, 11 Community Centre, Panchsheel Park, New Delhi 110017*

In the Netherlands: Please write to *Penguin Books Netherlands bv, Postbus 3507, NL-1001 AH Amsterdam*

In Germany: Please write to *Penguin Books Deutschland GmbH, Metzlerstrasse 26, 60594 Frankfurt am Main*

In Spain: Please write to *Penguin Books S. A., Bravo Murillo 19, 1° B, 28015 Madrid*

In Italy: Please write to *Penguin Italia s.r.l., Via Benedetto Croce 2, 20094 Corsico, Milano*

In France: Please write to *Penguin France, Le Carré Wilson, 62 rue Benjamin Baillaud, 31500 Toulouse*

In Japan: Please write to *Penguin Books Japan Ltd, Kaneko Building, 2-3-25 Koraku, Bunkyo-Ku, Tokyo 112*

In South Africa: Please write to *Penguin Books South Africa (Pty) Ltd, Private Bag X14, Parkview, 2122 Johannesburg*

READ MORE IN PENGUIN

A CHOICE OF CLASSICS

Aeschylus	The Oresteian Trilogy
	Prometheus Bound/The Suppliants/Seven against Thebes/The Persians
Aesop	Fables
Ammianus Marcellinus	The Later Roman Empire (AD 354–378)
Apollonius of Rhodes	The Voyage of Argo
Apuleius	The Golden Ass
Aristophanes	The Knights/Peace/The Birds/The Assemblywomen/Wealth
	Lysistrata/The Acharnians/The Clouds
	The Wasps/The Poet and the Women/The Frogs
Aristotle	The Art of Rhetoric
	The Athenian Constitution
	De Anima
	Ethics
	Poetics
Arrian	The Campaigns of Alexander
Marcus Aurelius	Meditations
Boethius	The Consolation of Philosophy
Caesar	The Civil War
	The Conquest of Gaul
Catullus	Poems
Cicero	Murder Trials
	The Nature of the Gods
	On the Good Life
	Selected Letters
	Selected Political Speeches
	Selected Works
Euripides	Alcestis/Iphigenia in Tauris/Hippolytus
	The Bacchae/Ion/The Women of Troy/Helen
	Medea/Hecabe/Electra/Heracles
	Orestes and Other Plays

READ MORE IN PENGUIN

A CHOICE OF CLASSICS

Hesiod/Theognis	**Theogony/Works and Days/Elegies**
Hippocrates	**Hippocratic Writings**
Homer	**The Iliad**
	The Odyssey
Horace	**Complete Odes and Epodes**
Horace/Persius	**Satires and Epistles**
Juvenal	**The Sixteen Satires**
Livy	**The Early History of Rome**
	Rome and Italy
	Rome and the Mediterranean
	The War with Hannibal
Lucretius	**On the Nature of the Universe**
Martial	**Epigrams**
Ovid	**The Erotic Poems**
	Heroides
	Metamorphoses
	The Poems of Exile
Pausanias	**Guide to Greece** (in two volumes)
Petronius/Seneca	**The Satyricon/The Apocolocyntosis**
Pindar	**The Odes**
Plato	**Early Socratic Dialogues**
	Gorgias
	The Last Days of Socrates (Euthyphro/ The Apology/Crito/Phaedo)
	The Laws
	Phaedrus and **Letters VII and VIII**
	Philebus
	Protagoras/Meno
	The Republic
	The Symposium
	Theaetetus
	Timaeus/Critias

A CHOICE OF CLASSICS

Plautus	**The Pot of Gold and Other Plays**
	The Rope and Other Plays
Pliny	**The Letters of the Younger Pliny**
Pliny the Elder	**Natural History**
Plotinus	**The Enneads**
Plutarch	**The Age of Alexander** (Nine Greek Lives)
	The Fall of the Roman Republic (Six Lives)
	The Makers of Rome (Nine Lives)
	Plutarch on Sparta
	The Rise and Fall of Athens (Nine Greek Lives)
Polybius	**The Rise of the Roman Empire**
Procopius	**The Secret History**
Propertius	**The Poems**
Quintus Curtius Rufus	**The History of Alexander**
Sallust	**The Jugurthine War/The Conspiracy of Cataline**
Seneca	**Four Tragedies/Octavia**
	Letters from a Stoic
Sophocles	**Electra/Women of Trachis/Philoctetes/Ajax**
	The Theban Plays
Suetonius	**The Twelve Caesars**
Tacitus	**The Agricola/The Germania**
	The Annals of Imperial Rome
	The Histories
Terence	**The Comedies (The Girl from Andros/The Self-Tormentor/The Eunuch/Phormio/ The Mother-in-Law/The Brothers)**
Thucydides	**History of the Peloponnesian War**
Virgil	**The Aeneid**
	The Eclogues
	The Georgics
Xenophon	**Conversations of Socrates**
	A History of My Times
	The Persian Expedition

READ MORE IN PENGUIN

A CHOICE OF CLASSICS

Francis Bacon	**The Essays**
Aphra Behn	**Love-Letters between a Nobleman and His Sister**
	Oroonoko, The Rover and Other Works
George Berkeley	**Principles of Human Knowledge/Three Dialogues between Hylas and Philonous**
James Boswell	**The Life of Samuel Johnson**
Sir Thomas Browne	**The Major Works**
John Bunyan	**The Pilgrim's Progress**
Edmund Burke	**Reflections on the Revolution in France**
Frances Burney	**Evelina**
Margaret Cavendish	**The Blazing World and Other Writings**
William Cobbett	**Rural Rides**
William Congreve	**Comedies**
Thomas de Quincey	**Confessions of an English Opium Eater**
	Recollections of the Lakes and the Lake Poets
Daniel Defoe	**A Journal of the Plague Year**
	Moll Flanders
	Robinson Crusoe
	Roxana
	A Tour Through the Whole Island of Great Britain
Henry Fielding	**Amelia**
	Jonathan Wild
	Joseph Andrews
	The Journal of a Voyage to Lisbon
	Tom Jones
John Gay	**The Beggar's Opera**
Oliver Goldsmith	**The Vicar of Wakefield**
Lady Gregory	**Selected Writings**

READ MORE IN PENGUIN

A CHOICE OF CLASSICS

William Hazlitt	**Selected Writings**
George Herbert	**The Complete English Poems**
Thomas Hobbes	**Leviathan**
Samuel Johnson/ James Boswell	**A Journey to the Western Islands of Scotland and The Journal of a Tour of the Hebrides**
Charles Lamb	**Selected Prose**
George Meredith	**The Egoist**
Thomas Middleton	**Five Plays**
John Milton	**Paradise Lost**
Samuel Richardson	**Clarissa**
	Pamela
Earl of Rochester	**Complete Works**
Richard Brinsley Sheridan	**The School for Scandal and Other Plays**
Sir Philip Sidney	**Selected Poems**
Christopher Smart	**Selected Poems**
Adam Smith	**The Wealth of Nations (Books I–III)**
Tobias Smollett	**The Adventures of Ferdinand Count Fathom**
	Humphrey Clinker
	Roderick Random
Laurence Sterne	**The Life and Opinions of Tristram Shandy**
	A Sentimental Journey Through France and Italy
Jonathan Swift	**Gulliver's Travels**
	Selected Poems
Thomas Traherne	**Selected Poems and Prose**
Henry Vaughan	**Complete Poems**

READ MORE IN PENGUIN

A CHOICE OF CLASSICS

Honoré de Balzac	**The Black Sheep**
	César Birotteau
	The Chouans
	Cousin Bette
	Cousin Pons
	Eugénie Grandet
	A Harlot High and Low
	Lost Illusions
	A Murky Business
	Old Goriot
	Selected Short Stories
	Ursule Mirouët
	The Wild Ass's Skin
J. A. Brillat-Savarin	**The Physiology of Taste**
Charles Baudelaire	**Selected Poems**
Pierre Corneille	**The Cid/Cinna/The Theatrical Illusion**
Alphonse Daudet	**Letters from My Windmill**
Denis Diderot	**Jacques the Fatalist**
	Selected Writings on Art and Literature
Alexandre Dumas	**The Count of Monte Cristo**
Gustave Flaubert	**Bouvard and Pécuchet**
	Flaubert in Egypt
	Madame Bovary
	Salammbo
	Sentimental Education
	The Temptation of St Antony
	Three Tales
Victor Hugo	**Les Misérables**
	Notre-Dame of Paris
Laclos	**Les Liaisons Dangereuses**
La Fontaine	**Selected Fables**
Madame de Lafayette	**The Princesse de Clèves**
Lautréamont	**Maldoror and Poems**

READ MORE IN PENGUIN

A CHOICE OF CLASSICS

Molière	**The Misanthrope/The Sicilian/Tartuffe/A Doctor in Spite of Himself/The Imaginary Invalid**
	The Miser/The Would-be Gentleman/That Scoundrel Scapin/Love's the Best Doctor/Don Juan
Michel de Montaigne	**An Apology for Raymond Sebond**
	Complete Essays
Marguerite de Navarre	**The Heptameron**
Blaise Pascal	**Pensées**
	The Provincial Letters
Abbé Prevost	**Manon Lescaut**
Rabelais	**The Histories of Gargantua and Pantagruel**
Racine	**Andromache/Britannicus/Berenice**
	Iphigenia/Phaedra/Athaliah
Arthur Rimbaud	**Collected Poems**
Jean-Jacques Rousseau	**The Confessions**
	A Discourse on Inequality
	Emile
Jacques Saint-Pierre	**Paul and Virginia**
Madame de Sevigné	**Selected Letters**
Stendhal	**The Life of Henry Brulard**
	Love
	Scarlet and Black
	The Charterhouse of Parma
Voltaire	**Candide**
	Letters on England
	Philosophical Dictionary
Emile Zola	**L'Assommoir**
	La Bête humaine
	The Debacle
	The Earth
	Germinal
	Nana
	Thérèse Raquin

READ MORE IN PENGUIN

A CHOICE OF CLASSICS

Jacob Burckhardt	**The Civilization of the Renaissance in Italy**
Carl von Clausewitz	**On War**
Meister Eckhart	**Selected Writings**
Friedrich Engels	**The Origins of the Family, Private Property and the State**
Wolfram von Eschenbach	**Parzival**
Goethe	**Elective Affinities**
	Faust Parts One and Two (in 2 volumes)
	Italian Journey
	The Sorrows of Young Werther
Jacob and Wilhelm Grimm	**Selected Tales**
E. T. A. Hoffmann	**Tales of Hoffmann**
Henrik Ibsen	**Brand**
	A Doll's House and Other Plays
	Ghosts and Other Plays
	Hedda Gabler and Other Plays
	The Master Builder and Other Plays
	Peer Gynt
Søren Kierkegaard	**Fear and Trembling**
	Papers and Journals
	The Sickness Unto Death
Georg Christoph Lichtenberg	**Aphorisms**
Karl Marx	**Capital** (in three volumes)
Friedrich Nietzsche	**The Birth of Tragedy**
	Beyond Good and Evil
	Ecce Homo
	Human, All Too Human
	Thus Spoke Zarathustra
Friedrich Schiller	**The Robbers/Wallenstein**
Arthur Schopenhauer	**Essays and Aphorisms**
Gottfried von Strassburg	**Tristan**
Adalbert Stifter	**Brigitta and Other Tales**
August Strindberg	**By the Open Sea**